Customary Law Ascertained

Volume 3

The Customary Law of the Nama, Ovaherero, Ovambanderu, and San Communities of Namibia

Customary Law Ascertained

Volume 3

The Customary Law of the Nama, Ovaherero, Ovambanderu, and San Communities of Namibia

Edited by Manfred O Hinz
assisted by Alexander Gairiseb

UNAM
PRESS

2016

UNIVERSITY OF NAMIBIA PRESS
Private Bag 13301
Windhoek
Namibia
www.unam.edu.na/unam-press
unampress@unam.na

First published: 2016

The research for this publication, the consultations with the communities whose customary law was ascertained, and the publication of the laws themselves were all generously funded by the Embassy of Finland in Namibia, with special financial assistance for this publication from the Centre of African and Migration Studies in the Faculty of Law of the University of Bremen.

EMBASSY OF FINLAND
WINDHOEK

CAMS
Centre of African & Migration Studies
University of Bremen

Freie
Hansestadt
Bremen

Editors of the English texts: Sandie Fitchat and Jill Kinahan
Editors of the texts of the Nama communities: Alexander Gairiseb, Levi Namaseb, Sandosca Jimmy-Naruses, Fredrika Motinga and Lochna Meeser (Afrikaans text)
Editors of the indigenous language texts of the Ovaherero and Ovambanderu communities: Jekura Kavari and Verinao Kamahene
Editors of the texts of the San communities: Andreas Haikera, Moses ǁKhumub and Charlie Nqeisji

Photographs of traditional leaders provided by the various Traditional Authorities
Cover photograph: Damian Maghambayi
Cover design: Gretta Gaspar
Printed by John Meinert Printing (Pty) Ltd, Windhoek

ISBN 978-99916-42-12-3

Distribution

(Namibia)	Namibia Book Market: www.namibiabooks.com email: info @namibiabooks.com
(International)	African Books Collective: www.africanbookscollective.com

TABLE OF CONTENTS

PART III THE LAWS OF THE OVAHERERO AND OVAMBANDERU COMMUNITIES

PART IV THE LAWS OF THE SAN COMMUNITIES

ANNEXURES

The Editors

Prof. Manfred O Hinz studied law and philosophy at the University of Mainz, Germany, where he graduated in law. He took his legal practitioner examination in 1964, the year in which he also obtained his PhD from the University of Mainz. After studying anthropology, sociology and African and Oriental languages at the same University, he became assistant lecturer, teaching anthropology and public law. In 1971, he was appointed full professor at the University of Bremen.

In 1989, he went to Namibia where, after its independence, he assisted the Ministry of Justice in its projects to restructure the traditional administration of justice and to make an inventory of customary law. He was later seconded to the office of the first Vice-Chancellor of the University of Namibia (UNAM) to help build the first institution for legal education on Namibian soil: UNAM'S Faculty of Law. He joined the Faculty upon its inception. He has served as Deputy Dean and Dean of the Faculty.

Prof. Hinz held the United Nations Educational, Scientific and Cultural Organisation (UNESCO) Chair: Human Rights and Democracy in the Law Faculty's Human Rights and Documentation Centre from 2000 to 2009. In 2009, Prof. Hinz retired from his full-time position at the University of Namibia. In 2010 he returned to Germany, but remains related to UNAM as research professor. Apart from holding the position of professor at the University of Bremen, he is Adjunct Professor of Law and African Studies at the Jacobs University in Bremen since 2014.

Prof. Hinz has published widely in his areas of specialisation, particularly in the fields of legal and political anthropology and constitutional and international (economic) law.

okavango@afol.com.na mhinz@uni-bremen.de

Alexander Gairiseb holds the degrees of BJuris and LLB from the University of Namibia. He is currently employed in the Ministry of Works and Transport (Directorate of Civil Aviation) as an Aviation Security Inspector: Regulations, and he is duly authorised to act as a Trademarks Agent in Namibia. For more than three years he has worked as an assistant to the Ascertainment of Customary Law Project which falls under the auspices of the Human Rights and Documentation Centre of the Faculty of Law at the University of Namibia.

agairiseb@gmail.com

Preface

The Namibian legal system is premised on the principle of legality. One of the essential elements of the principle of legality is that the law must be specific and clear. This presupposes that the law must be drafted clearly and in such a way that a person may ascertain the legality of a particular course of conduct. Implicit therein is also the requirement that the law should be accessible and foreseeable. These requirements, needless to say, equally apply to customary law given the pluralistic nature of our legal system.

The Customary Law Ascertainment Project, as mentioned elsewhere, is not aimed at codifying customary law in Namibia. That task is the preserve and prerogative of the Executive. The global objective of this Project seeks to assist in giving meaning and effect to the principle of specificity as it relates to the customary laws applicable in Namibia.

The principle of legality in all its facets is inextricably linked to human rights. The major international and regional human rights instruments all expressly and implicitly guarantee and protect this principle. For instance, the International Covenant on Civil and Political Rights (ICCPR), African Charter on Human and Peoples' Rights (ACHPR), and the European Convention for the Protection of Human Rights and Fundamental Freedoms all guarantee and protect this important legal principle.

During the workshops on good governance with Traditional Authorities in 2001 and 2002, sponsored by the Office of High Commission for Human Rights, Geneva, the traditional leaders strongly recommended that the Human Rights and Documentation Centre at the University of Namibia, assist in documenting their customary laws to enable current and future generations to become aware of their customary laws. It is against this backdrop that the Human Rights and Documentation Centre of the Law Faculty of the University of Namibia takes particular pride and joy in being associated with this epoch-making project. With this work we are not only seeking to contribute towards ascertaining and making customary law accessible to its users; through this project we are also trying to ensure that traditional and informal justice systems in our country evolve towards serving justice in full respect of international human rights standards.

In celebrating this work, a few names deserve special mention. In this regard, Professor Manfred Hinz, former Dean of the Faculty of Law (2000–2004) and a long-standing friend of the Faculty, the University itself and the Namibian nation, stands out. Prof. Hinz took the lead and started consultations with traditional leaders to verify the need. Prof. Hinz is a "Guru" of customary law in Namibia. His love, passion and commitment for Namibian customary law are beyond dispute. This project serves as a prime example. We therefore take this opportunity to acknowledge and give credit to his active involvement and guidance for the successful completion of this project.

Special thanks go to Professor Nico Horn, Professor Oliver Ruppel, Mr John Nakuta and Ivone Tjilale, all from the Human Rights and Documentation Centre, for their contribution to the success of this project.

Alexander Gairiseb was the senior student assistant for *Customary Law Ascertained volumes 2 and 3*. Mr Gairiseb had the difficult task of coordinating the work of the other student assistants, liaising with Prof. Hinz, and meeting and negotiating with the relevant traditional authorities. The sterling work done by Mr Gairiseb in performing these tasks is hereby acknowledged and sincerely appreciated.

All the student assistants and informants, especially Lotta Ambunda, Erastus Arnold, Andreas Haikera, Ritta Hengari, Susan Hinda, Sandosca Jimmy-Naruses, Verinao Kamahene, Moses ǀKhumub, Ilga Rheent and Willem Swartbooi are also acknowledged and appreciated. They have been the proverbial foot soldiers for this project and the successful completion thereof would not have been possible without their dedication and hard work.

Professor Jekura Kavari, Levi Namaseb, Andreas Haikera, Moses ǁKhumub, Charlie Nqeisji and Lochna Meeser gave invaluable support editing and checking indigenous language texts. Sandie Fitchat has to be thanked for editing some of the documents contained in this volume.

A special word of thanks is due to UNAM Press and its staff, Jane Katjavivi, Jill Kinahan and Fredrika Motinga. Jane and Jill did a wonderful job in ensuring the successful completion of this epoch-making project. Indeed, both were fully committed to the book and contributed to it in a way far beyond the borders of a publisher.

We are extremely indebted to the Finnish Embassy which generously funded this project and graciously extended the time-span for the usage of their funds to ensure the finalisation of the project and the publication of the book. Our thanks also go to the Department of Development Cooperation of the Free Hanseatic State of Bremen which generously supported our work on customary law over the years. We are particularly grateful for the special financial contribution they made in 2012.

Dr Chiku Mnubi-Mchombu
Acting Director: Human Rights and Documentation Centre (HRDC)
Faculty of Law
University of Namibia

Foreword

The societal entities that today we call traditional authorities were the more-or-less autonomous communities that governed the day-to-day life of their members for many years, before colonial powers came into our country and subjected them to their rule.

Many historical records contain evidence about the laws enacted by traditional rulers and their advisors in colonial times. These records also show that the law was not static, i.e. set for all time. It changed and was changed as need arose. In some cases it was also expected that a new ascendant to a chieftaincy could use the occasion of taking office to announce new laws.

There were many interventions into the laws and governing practices of the various traditional communities of Namibia during the colonial period, to transform them in the interests of the colonisers. The implementation of the policy of separate development and apartheid, under South African rule, is a good example of this. These interventions distorted customary laws and the rule of traditional leaders but did not destroy them. Indeed, the continued existence of customary law was recognised in the drafting of the Constitution of Namibia in 1989–90. Article 66 of the Constitution establishes customary law at the same level as the Roman–Dutch law introduced under colonial rule. This constitutional confirmation of customary law also included the confirmation of the custodians of this law – the traditional authorities.

The Presidential Commission of Inquiry into Matters Relating to Chiefs, Headmen and other Traditional or Tribal Leaders established in 1991,[1] under the able leadership of the late Advocate F. J. Kozonguizi, submitted its report (commonly referred to as the Kozonguizi Report) to government in the same year.[2] The report left no doubt that, despite many deformations resulting from colonial interventions, traditional authority and customary law were widely appreciated in Namibia and should be retained.

The Kozonguizi Report also submitted a draft bill for a Chieftainship Act,[3] which opened the debate about how to deal with chiefs and customary law in independent Namibia, and led to what became the Traditional Authorities Act of 1995,[4] later revised in 2000.[5] It is noteworthy that the revised version of the Traditional Authorities (2000) took note of the law-making capacity of traditional authorities. Section 3(3)(c) states that a traditional authority may 'in the performance of its duties and functions under this Act ... make customary law'.

1 See GN 32 of 1991.

2 Republic of Namibia (1991): Commission of Inquiry into Matters Relating to Chiefs, Headmen and other Traditional and Tribal Leaders. Windhoek: Republic of Namibia.

3 At 111ff.

4 Act 17 of 1995, amended by Act 8 of 1997.

5 Act 25 of 2000.

The Namibian Parliament – the National Assembly and the National Council – and the other organs of state, are well-advised to take note of what the traditional authorities do, in particular in terms of the above-mentioned capacity of making law.

Customary Law Ascertained Volume 3. The customary laws of the Nama, Ovaherero, Ovambanderu, and San communities of Namibia is the third volume from the Customary Law Ascertainment Project of the Human Rights and Documentation Centre of the University of Namibia. It completes the self-statement of laws of the recognised traditional authorities who participated in the project, all of which have been signed by the traditional leaders concerned. Although some traditional authorities did not participate, the customary laws of most recognised traditional authorities have now been stated by the communities themselves.

All three volumes are an invaluable collection of customary law in current practice. They give us an insight into what our traditional authorities have been doing in the years since Independence in making laws, streamlining the law, changing it, and applying it when deciding on cases brought before them.

A good example is that of widows who were deprived of their houses and the land they had worked on during many years of marriage, after the death of their husbands. This practice was much discussed in the country in the early 1990s, and also occupied the attention of Parliament. It was debated in meetings of the traditional authorities concerned and eventually resolved by changes in the customary law of all the Oshiwambo-speaking communities.[6] In this way, the custodians of customary law were able to offer new laws, even before the Namibian Parliament addressed the problem in the Communal Land Reform Act.[7]

What this shows is that, as much as traditional authorities need to learn about the work of Parliament, Parliament can also learn from the traditional authorities and customary law. When enacting laws that have a bearing on matters deemed to be in the realm of traditional authorities, consultations with those authorities could assist Parliament in finding rules that are in line with local perceptions and aspirations. This would enhance the general acceptance of new legislation, and compliance.

This collection of ascertained customary law reflects what the various traditional communities perceive to be their law, or rather, the parts of their law that are worthy of noting in written form. This is a resource we have not had before and that is also not found in most African countries where traditional authorities work and administer justice. It is a most commendable achievement. We are now in the position where we can listen in an informed manner when people say that such and such a provision is or is not 'our' law, and we have a benchmark against which to discuss such matters. Similarly, the

---

6 See Customary law workshop of Owambo traditional leaders – Ongwediva, 25 – 26 May 1993, in: Traditional Authority of Ondonga (1994): Ooveta (Oompango) dhOshilongo shOndonga – The laws of Ondonga. Oniipa: ELCIN: 85ff.

7 Act 5 of 2002, see Sec 26 of the Act.

self-statement of these laws allows us to see whether any of these provisions may need reconsideration in view of our constitutional principles or statutory law, and where to suggest specific amendments. It will now be up to the Namibian public in general and to the competent organs of state, i.e. the legislature, judiciary and executive, to effect any changes deemed necessary.

What we have in the three *Customary Law Ascertained* volumes is a collection with definite authority, but we must also understand that customary law ascertainment and law-making is a process that goes on, as does law making in any democratic society.

Professor Peter H. Katjavivi
Speaker, National Assembly of Namibia

Part I:
Introductory remarks

THE ASCERTAINMENT OF CUSTOMARY LAW: WHAT IS *ASCERTAINMENT OF CUSTOMARY LAW*, WHAT IS IT FOR AND WHAT IS THE WORK AHEAD?

Manfred O Hinz[1]

Background

Legal comparisons inform us that different legal orders have different ways of manifesting law. While some keep law orally, others opt for law in writing. While some limit the writing of law to writing law incidentally, i.e. in the application of cases, others choose for writing law in an abstract manner, by way of selective statutory enactment or even

---

1 The following is an amended version of my introductory remarks to the first and second volumes of *Customary law ascertained*. (Cf. MO Hinz, ed., assisted by NE Namwoonde (2010) *Customary law ascertained. Vol. 1. The customary law of the Owambo, Kavango and Caprivi communities*. Windhoek: Namibia Scientific Society, p 3ff. and MO Hinz, ed., assisted by A Gairiseb (2013) *Customary law ascertained. Vol. 2. The customary law of the Bakgalagari, Batswana ba Namibia and Damara communities of Namibia*. Windhoek: UNAM Press, p 13ff.) The amendments reflect, in particular, comments received after the publication of the second volume of *Customary law ascertained*. As a former member of the Faculty of Law of the University of Namibia, I was responsible for the *Customary Law Ascertainment Project* of the Human Rights and Documentation Centre of the Faculty. In this but also in my personal capacity, I wish to express my sincere gratitude to the Council of Traditional Leaders of Namibia and all the traditional leaders with whom I could work since the independence of Namibia for the years of trust and result-oriented cooperation. A word of special appreciation is due to *Elenga Enene* Ndilimani Herman Iipumbu, the supreme leader of the Uukwambi Traditional Authority and *Elenga Enene* Peter Kauluma from the Ondonga Traditional Authority, with whom I was able to work on matters of customary law for almost 20 years. With Peter Kauluma, I co-authored the introduction to the second edition of the *OoVeta dhOshilonga shOndonga – The laws of Ondonga* (Elelo lyOpashigwana lyOshilongo shOndonga – Traditional Authority of Ondonga, eds, 1994. Oniipa: Evangelican Luthern Church in Namibia, pp 27-57). I have published several articles on the ascertainment of customary law; cf. e.g. (1997) Law reform from within. Improving the legal status of women in Northern Namibia. *Journal of Legal Pluralism and Unofficial Law* (39): 69-79, (2009) Part 1 of the Namibian Ascertainment of Customary Law project to be completed soon. *Namibia Law Journal* (2): 109-119, and (2009) *"... to develop the customary law into the common law of the Sudan ..."* Customary law in Southern Sudan: A strategy to strengthen Southern Sudanese law as a source of law in an autonomous legal system, Juba/ Windhoek: United Nations Development Programme (UNDP) and Ministry of Legal Affairs and Constitutional Development (MoLACD). The following text uses parts of a paper contributed to the conference on Customary Justice and Legal Pluralism in Post-Conflict and Fragile Societies, organized by the United States Institute of Peace, the George Washington University and the World Bank in Washington from 17 to 18 November 2009. My publication titled *Developing customary law: Self-stated laws of Namibian communities and customary law consultative meetings with traditional leaders* (MO Hinz, assisted by S Joas (1995) Windhoek: Centre for Applied Social Sciences) is a predecessor of the three volumes of the customary law of the various Namibian traditional communities.

comprehensive codification. Common law systems (English, American, Roman-Dutch) prefer the appearance of law through its application in cases. Civil law countries show a practice of codification, going back to the 19th century.

It is important to recall these differences in order to underscore that it would not be appropriate to point at one way of manifesting legal rules as the only acceptable way of doing so. If one goes deeper into the history of given legal orders, one will detect that very concrete societal circumstances prompted the developments of the various legal orders.

Why then ascertaining African customary law? Who needs ascertained customary law and how should ascertainment be done? Do traditional leaders applying customary law need it to be ascertained? Before the many interventions by statutory law, and, more so, before the development of independent nation states, traditional leaders could state with good reasons: "Why ascertain customary law? We know our law. It is only you, the outsiders, who want to impose on us some kind of written version of the law, which will not be our law anyway!" This attitude to the ascertainment of customary law has changed. More and more traditional leaders understand the reasons for ascertaining customary law, accept ascertainment undertakings, even request to have the laws of their communities ascertained, and take the lead in ascertainment projects.

Traditional communities are not homogeneous communities as they used to be, when basically everybody knew what the law of the community was, and where traditional ways of communicating knowledge provided young people with the necessary education to grow within the value framework of the community. There is also a growing understanding that the legal complexity experienced in urban settlements where various customary laws apply forces attending to ascertaining and even to standardising customary law. There is a growing acceptance that the verdict of the chief is no longer necessarily the last word; dissatisfied parties may take the verdict of a chief to appeal. The judges sitting on appeals will not necessarily know the customary law applied by the court a quo and fail to get knowledge unless there is something in writing to inform them.

The *Customary Law Ascertainment Project* responds to this development. However, it does not respond by offering codified customary law. It responds by grounding an environment that opens space to traditional communities and their authorities for what we call the *self-stating* of customary law.[2] *Self-stating* customary law has a history in Namibia, going back to pre-independence developments in some of the traditional communities. The more or less independently undertaken efforts by some traditional communities eventually resulted in the nation-wide *Customary Law Ascertainment Project*. The Council of Traditional Leaders took it as its project and called on all traditional authorities to start their own projects to ascertain their customary law.

2 For the term *self-stating*, see below.

The very demanding challenge to the Human Rights and Documentation Centre of the Faculty of Law of the University of Namibia to direct and co-ordinate the project led to the decision to divide the project, first into two parts and, as the project developed, eventually into three parts: Part one encompasses the communities of the central and north-eastern area of the country, parts two and three cover the communities in north-western, central and southern Namibia.[3]

Based on the background of the project, the following will start by discussing the widely propagated call for the codification of customary law and, after this, attend to the meaning of ascertainment. Although these introductory remarks will not allow for a comprehensive reflection of the laws contained in the three volumes of *Customary law ascertained*, some arguments will be submitted to understand basic differences between the laws of volume 1 and the two subsequent volumes of *Customary law ascertained*. Suggestions on the way forward will conclude the introductory remarks.

African customary law and the call for codification

African customary law systems have, as African scholars hold, survived thousands of years as orally transmitted systems of law. They will not become 'more' law or law-like by being codified. Common law has survived history and remained a highly valued system of law without being codified. Why then argue, as lawyers do, that African customary law must be codified? This argument has accompanied the discourse in African jurisprudence since the days when many of the now independent African states achieved their independence!

Looking closer, it becomes obvious that many Western-educated lawyers from Europe and Africa never took it on themselves to enquire about the nature of African law. For them, African customary law was very different from the law learned in school and, therefore, had to be changed to become similar to the mainstream of law taught at school. Indeed, African customary laws show differences to Western law because both forms of law are based on different concepts of justice and maintain procedural rules geared towards achieving their concepts of justice. In view of this, and since there was no administration of justice in Africa comparable to the administration of common law that would produce reliable precedents, the call for codification appeared to be the easiest way to 'uplift' African customary laws to the so-called standard of real law. That African customary laws would lose their flexibility to be applied by the communities in the interest of restoration of peace and harmony among themselves was of no concern to the proponents of codification!

There are important lessons which legal anthropological research has developed over the years and which have also been acknowledged by courts of law. These lessons support the voices today that speak against the codification of customary law, because codification will destroy one of the most important qualities of customary law, namely its

---

3 See the reference to the two published volumes of the *Customary Law Ascertainment Project* in fn. 1.

openness to accommodate reconciliatory solutions to problems instead of allowing the law to win the parties over. It is worthwhile to mention that South African courts support the vote against codification.[4] South African courts were faced with the situation where the law, as lived in communities, had developed away from the law as it was offered in old records of customary law. It was found that the living law was the customary law to be accepted by courts and not the so-called official laws 'of the books'. This really challenging jurisprudential development accepts – as promoted by legal pluralism – that customary law as the local law of the people would lose its quality of being people's law if it were codified into a statutory type of document.

It is interesting to note that some self-stated customary laws refer to their respective laws as codification. In editing the laws, we were tempted to suggest the removal of the word *codification* to the community which used the term. We eventually left *codification* in the submitted text. We did this in line with the general policy of the *Customary Law Ascertainment Project* to leave the submitted text as it is wherever possible. The rules in the self-stated laws may be challenged in court when decisions of the community courts go on appeal to state courts. Customary law may also be challenged through public debates to which traditional authorities may respond. In other words, it is left to the respective traditional authority or to the interpretation of a competent court to decide whether the qualification of the self-stated law as codification is a mere folk qualification. Whatever the result, one needs to bear in mind that it is up to the discretion of the traditional community to change the contents of their self-stated law in exercising their authority in terms of section 3(3)(c) of the Traditional Authorities Act, according to which they have the power "to make customary law".[5]

Article 66 Sub-article (1) of the Constitution of Namibia recognises that the legal order of Namibia is pluralistic: there is, on the one hand, the system of general law (the Roman-Dutch common law and the statutory enactments) and, on the other, a plurality of customary laws. Both spheres do not only co-exist, they are interlinked. A number of rules have also been explicitly set by the state to regulate the relationship between the general law and the customary laws. This regulation starts with the constitutional rule just quoted, which subjects customary law to the constitution and other statutory law, and extends to such statutory enactments that deal with matters under customary law.[6] There are also many rules of common law that offer themselves for application to customary law.

---

4 Cf Mthembu v Letsela 1997 (2) SA 936 (T); *Hlohe v Mahlalela* 1998 (1) SA 449 (T); *Mabena v Letsoalo* 1998 (2) SA 1068 (T).

5 See here also *Hikumwah v Nelumbu*, unreported judgment of the High Court of Namibia of 13 May 2015, in which the question arose as to whether customary law of the Oukwanyama Traditional Community as contained in an unspecified publication of 2007 would mean that the customary law of the Oukwanyama Community was codified. For procedural reasons, the court opted for the view that the customary law of the Oukwanyama Community was not codified, but oral.

6 Such as the Traditional Authorities Act, 25 of 2000, and the Community Courts Act, 10 of 2003.

However, statutory law in place leaves us without answers to many questions.[7] Before we accept offers of common law for the application of customary law, we have to question the rationale behind those offers, and we have to consider whether or not the rationale behind is reasonable to justify the application to customary law.[8] Filling statutory gaps and applying rules of common law to customary law, however, require the jurisprudential understanding of legal pluralism. Accepting legal pluralism means accepting the differences in the operating and functioning of the plural legal strata. As much as the ascertainment of customary law by way of various traditional communities self-stating their laws may be welcomed as a contribution to legal certainty and the rule of law, the fact that customary law has been ascertained in the manner described does not automatically imply that the concepts and rules in operating the general law should similarly be applied to customary law – at least as long as the operation of customary law remains within the framework provided for by the general confirmation and recognition of customary law in Article 66 of the Constitution.

Conventionally-arguing legal minds may have difficulties with what is called the flexibility of customary law and may plead for one straightforward legal system without such flexibility, but legal anthropology has dismantled this centralist understanding of law as an illusion. What this leaves us with are the jurisprudential challenges of legal pluralism. *Customary law ascertained* can only open the debate on the said challenges, a debate to which all concerned must contribute. The coexistence of the various strata of law will only lead to a functioning legal system – a system that provides justice and, with this, the enjoyment of human rights as they are guaranteed in the Namibian Constitution and international instruments to which Namibia is a signatory – if research, legal education, the legal profession and the public at large take note of these challenges.[9]

What is the meaning of ascertaining customary law?

What do we refer to when talking about the ascertainment of customary law? What do we expect when suggesting the ascertainment of customary law?

The Community Courts Act[10] deals with the ascertainment of customary law in its Section 13. This section prescribes the procedures to be applied by courts in case of

---

7 The jurisdiction in murder or rape cases is one of those questions: The law of the state and some customary laws require jurisdiction. What is to happen when a person has spent time in prison after conviction of murder and is thereafter called by a community court to pay compensation? Horn ends his review of the first volume of *Customary law ascertained* by stating: "If one consults *Customary law ascertained* one thing is clear: the line between the jurisdictions of common law and customary law still needs to be drawn." N Horn (2011) *Customary law ascertained. Volume 1. The customary law of the Owambo, Kavango and Caprivi communities of Namibia*. In *Namibia Law Journal* 3(1): 133ff., 140.

8 The common law doctrine of *stare decisis* according to which certain statements of higher state courts have the quality of binding law is an example of this. Whether and if so to what extent *stare decisis* will apply in matters of customary law is, indeed, debatable.

9 Cf here MO Hinz (2011) African customary law – Its place in law and legal education. *Namibia Scientific Society Journal* 59: 83ff.

10 Act No. 10 of 2003.

doubt as to the existence or content of a rule of customary law. In such cases, courts have the power to ascertain customary law by consulting cases, text books and other sources or by calling for oral or written opinions. In other words, from a legal point of view, ascertainment of customary law means more than having customary law recorded in one way or another: The act of ascertainment also awards the ascertained version of customary law a legal qualification.

Mere academic records of customary law based on questionnaires, court observations, analyses of traditional courts' case books, collections of cases and cases-complementary information from parties to cases, cannot be considered as an ascertainment of customary law. As useful as records of this nature may be, and as much as they may potentially contribute to the ascertainment as evidence a court may or may not rely on, they remain aids to a possible subsequent ascertainment in the above-stated legal sense.

The Traditional Authorities Act[11] supports this view. According to the Act, *ascertainment* can be defined as any kind of authoritative transfer of orally transmitted customary law into a written form. According to section 3(1) of the Act, it is one of the tasks of traditional authorities:

> to ascertain the customary law applicable in that traditional authority after consultations with the members of that community, and assist in its codification; ...

From this language, it is clear that *ascertainment* is not synonymous with *codification*. *Codification* is just one form – and a very specific one at that – of consolidating customary law. Codification transforms customary law into an act of parliament. With this, customary law ceases to be owned by the communities in which it developed and can only be changed by an amending act of parliament. Although the call for codification is still being heard up to today, there is not much codification of customary law to which we could refer. To my knowledge and despite the calls for codification of customary law, as far as Africa goes, only the law of the Zulu in South Africa and the law of some groups in Southern Sudan have been codified to date.[12]

Apart from codification, we can also speak of the *ascertainment* of customary law when customary law is transferred into what has become known as the *restatement* of customary law. I refer here to the Restatement Project conducted by the School of Oriental and African Studies (SOAS) of the University of London under Antony Allott. Allott defines

11 Act No. 25 of 2000.

12 Cf. the Zulu code: TW Bennett (2004) *Customary law in South Africa*. Cape Town: Juta, p 46f; for the codification of customary law in Southern Sudan, see my above quoted report on customary law in Southern Sudan. A special case are the Laws of Lerotholi (the customary law of the Basotho in Lesotho), the first part of which was put into writing by the Basutoland Council in 1903. The legal status of the Laws of Lerotholi is still a matter of debate. See P Duncan (2006) *Sotho laws and customs*. Morija: Morija Museum and Archives (Reprint of the 1960 edition).

the restatement approach, borrowed, as he says, from the American Restatements, as follows: Restatements

> were authoritative, comprehensive, careful and systematic statements of common-law rules in such fields as torts, contracts and property. Necessarily cast in semi-codified form, they were still not codes, as they lacked the force of legislated law. Instead they were the most accurate and precise statements of what those producing them had concluded were the main principles and rules as evolved by the courts, and, as such, courts and practitioners alike could turn to them as guides.[13]

Customary law restatements were achieved in several African countries in the 1970s. However, the restatement approach fell into disuse for various reasons, one being that the restatement of customary law made today will not necessarily reflect the customary law of tomorrow.[14]

Finally, we can also speak of *ascertainment* of customary law when traditional communities produce their own versions of their customary law in writing – versions of customary law, for which, in the Namibian context, the term *self-statement* of customary law has been accepted. *Self-stating* customary law refers to a process of ascertaining customary law by the owners of the law to be ascertained: the people, the community, the traditional leaders as the custodians of customary law. The procedures of self-stating may differ from community to community. Nonetheless, the most important element in self-stating is that the end result will be a product created in the community which is to follow and apply the law. Instead of injecting into the communities what the law ought to be, it is left to the community to decide what part of their law is to be consolidated in writing, since the community and community stakeholders will know best what their law is, and where certainty through writing is needed.

The result of self-stating is binding on the community as part of their customary law. It is, however, important to note that the binding quality of the self-stated laws is neither an implicit repeal of the orally transmitted customary law or even only parts of it, nor does it imply a change in the nature of customary law as a set of flexible principles and

---

13 International development in customary law: The restatement of African law project and thereafter. In TW Bennett & M Rünger, eds (1996) *The ascertainment of customary law and the methodological aspects of research into customary law: Proceedings of workshop, February/ March 1995*. Windhoek: Law Reform and Development Commission, p 33.

14 Bennett (2004, fn 11: 48) notes what the Law Commission of South Africa said on the possible restatement of customary law in South Africa. According to Bennett the Commission held that "the facilities for such a project were not available in South Africa, and that, unless regularly updated, the restatement would fall behind social practice to become yet another 'official version' of customary law, i.e. a version that would not be in line with the law lived by the communities."

rules, nor will it prevent the community to amend their law as need arises.[15] It is part of the philosophy behind the approach to leave the ascertainment of customary law to the communities that the communities decide what part of customary law they want to have in writing and how they want the content of the self-statement to be worded. Therefore, what we find in the self-statements are only aspects of the respective customary law. The fact that certain rules of customary law have been ascertained in writing will keep untouched the application of the now ascertained rules practised so far. That is, the applying authorities will still handle the ascertained rules in the manner that appears appropriate to them in view of the interest in achieving the restoration of societal peace.[16]

Legislative drafting has developed to a very specialized art in many modern jurisdictions. However, the reader of the self-stated laws should not expect that these laws follow the sophisticated techniques of modern legislative drafting. In many instances, the self-stated customary laws give educative explanations or even state rather general societal aspirations – a fact which will be a challenge to interpretation!

Traditional authority and customary law: a complex reality[17]

When looking at the traditional landscape as it was inherited from the time before independence, the *Commission of Inquiry into Matters Relating to Chiefs, Headmen and Other Traditional and Tribal Leaders* established in 1991[18] found two different types of traditional authority: territorially-based traditional authorities, i.e. traditional authorities "settled in a particular area of jurisdiction" and traditional authorities the chief of which is a "Chief of the tribe and not of a particular area".[19] The Ovaherero and the Damara and their "paramount chiefs at large" were the obvious examples for the latter. The draft bill on traditional authority submitted by the Commission, therefore, recognised both: the position of chief and the position of paramount chief being the "principal Chief or an overall traditional leader of a Community".[20] The main point of reference for chieftaincy is the "recognized area of jurisdiction … for a Community". Whether a chief will be the chief of a community at large will depend on the wishes of the community.[21] An area or

15 FM d'Engelbronner-Kolff (1997) *Dispute resolution processes amongst the Sambyu of Northern Namibia*. Maastricht: Shaker Publications, p 149ff shows how traditional courts of the Shambyu community navigate between the self-stated version of their law and the legal principles behind the statement – thus allowing decisions appropriate to the cases to be decided.

16 Which is the main objective in adjudicating cases under customary law! Cf. MO Hinz, Justice for justice and justice for peace. In MO Hinz & C Mapaure, eds (2010) *In search of justice and peace. Traditional and informal justice systems in Africa*. Windhoek: Namibia Scientific Society, p 11ff).

17 The following paragraphs rely on MO Hinz (forthcoming, 2015) The Traditional Authorities Act and the "mushrooming" of traditional authorities. *Namibia Law Journal*.

18 Cf. GN 32 of 1991 by which the commission was appointed and also (1991) Report of the Commission of Inquiry into Matters Relating to Chiefs, Headmen and other Traditional or Tribal Leaders. Windhoek: Republic of Namibia. The commission was chaired by Adv. FJ Kozonguizi and is commonly referred to as the Kozonguizi Commission and the report as the Kozonguizi Report.

19 Ibid. 3.9.

20 See the definitions in Sec 1 of the draft bill, see: Report (1991): 111.

21 Sec 2(1) of the draft bill.

territory of jurisdiction is "such [an] area or territory set aside by the laws of the Republic for the settlement and occupation on a communal basis by a group or Community for the purpose and under the terms defined by the law governing the usage of land".[22] Each community in such a recognized area of jurisdiction "shall" have an office of the chief.[23]

What is a community? A community is "a group of people whose common interests are determined by origin and settlement and who may be linked but not exclusively through culture, tradition and language and recognized by law as such".[24] It is the right of any group of persons "who represents a substantial number of persons" to apply for recognition "on grounds of common culture, common origin, tradition or language".

As much as the general result of the Commission of Inquiry – the recommendation that the "traditional system" should be retained – was appreciated in the public debate and the subsequent enactment of law, the concept of "area or territory of jurisdiction" to be "set aside by the laws of the Republic" as the entry point for the establishment of an office of chief was not.[25] Instead, the legislative focus moved to the communities and their wishes to organize themselves as traditional community with a chief, or, in the language of the Traditional Authorities Act in force, a "chief" or "head" meaning the "supreme traditional leader of a traditional community".[26] The position of paramount chief was not confirmed in the subsequently enacted Traditional Authorities Act: the act knows only one supreme leader for each community and traditional councillors under the supreme leader.[27]

A sophisticated definition of "traditional community" came into the act, the act of 1995, the act of 2000, and was also repeated in another piece of legislation relevant for traditional authorities: the Community Courts Act[28]. According to this a "traditional community"

> means an indigenous homogeneous, endogamous social grouping of persons comprising families from exogamous clans which share a common ancestry, language, cultural heritage, customs and traditions, recognizes

22 Sec 1.

23 Sec 2(1).

24 Sec 1.

25 See the Technical Committee on Traditional Leaders Act which worked to advise the Ministry of Regional and Local Government and Housing while, at the same time, the Ministry of Justice was occupied preparing an act on the administration of justice by traditional courts (later named: community courts). See e.g. Minutes of 25 June 1993, on file with the author. See further the Traditional Authorities Bill, Republic of Namibia, National Assembly, B.33-94 and the minutes of the debates in the National Assembly and the National Council.

26 The Traditional Authorities Act, 25 of 2000, defines "chief" and "head" in two subsections identically. The definition of "head" was introduced to cater for traditional communities which do not have "royal families". The original act (Act 17 of 1995) defined "chief" as "chief" designed in accordance with the act. The amendment to this act (Act 8 of 1997), replaced "chief" in the definition with "supreme traditional leader".

27 See Sec 2 of Act 17 of 1995; 8 of 1997; and 25 of 2000.

28 No. 10 of 2003.

> a common traditional authority and inhabits a common communal area; and includes the members of that community residing outside the common communal area.

This is not the place to investigate to what extent this definition and the anthropological language used in it ever reflected the social reality of traditional communities. It is enough to state that the definition certainly does not correspond to the reality of today.[29] There is hardly a traditional community with people who have their own line of ancestors, who have joined the community for whatever reason years ago or recently, and by joining it have either accepted the prevailing tradition or created new traditions on the basis of the ones in place, adding new elements to them from their traditions.

Further, since Meyer Fortes and Evans-Pritchard,[30] we basically distinguish between three types of political systems in African anthropology: Firstly, there are "very small societies" the members of which are kinship-related and in which the political organisation and the organisation of kinship are, following Fortes and Evans-Pritchard, "completely fused".[31] Secondly, we find societies in which "the lineage structure is the framework of the political system". However, although the two structures are well-coordinated, "each remains distinct and autonomous in its own sphere".[32] In the third type of political system, "an administrative organization is the framework of the political structure".[33]

The typology of political organisation introduced by Fortes and Evans-Pritchard has remained influential in the analyses of political formations in Africa and other parts of the world until today although it does not reflect colonial interventions into the various forms of traditional government. The socio-political developments under colonialism and by the post-colonial orders resulted in structural changes of all the societies that represented political formations of the quoted typology. They were all made part of so-called modern political organisations, i.e. the states that claimed sovereignty over traditional governments, be they kingdoms or differently organised political formations. Colonial rule deprived the previously sovereign traditional political entities of their sovereignty. Indirect rule rendered or, at least had the intention to render, independent kingdoms and non-centralised political entities the task of administering their territories in the interest of the coloniser.

Although the degree of change following colonial interventions depended on the respective circumstances, it is fact that tradition is still very much part of the post-colonial reality, as proved by the above-quoted Kozonguizi report in the case of Namibia.[34] The traditional foundation of the various communities survived colonial transformations and

29 See E Shamena (1998) The concept of 'traditional community'. In: FM d' Engelbronner, MO Hinz & JL Sindano eds *Traditional authority and democracy in Southern Africa*. Windhoek: New Namibia Books, pp 323-327.

30 M Fortes & EE Evans-Pritchard (1940) Introduction. In: M Fortes & EE Evans-Pritchard eds. *African political systems*. London, New York, Toronto: Oxford University Press, p 1ff.

31 Ibid.: 8f.

32 Ibid: 9.

33 Ibid.

34 See fn 17.

subsequent inroads into the political, cultural and social set-up of the communities in many cases.

The reconstitutionalisations that followed colonialism did not lead to the abolition of the traditional political formations. Countries such as Namibia are democracies with political institutions that are expected to exist in democracies, but, nevertheless, accommodate traditional political formations. Looking at the Traditional Authorities Act, all these formations appear now to be formations with centralised authorities in so far as they all are to have a "supreme leader" in terms of the said act.[35] Nevertheless, the shape and format of authority differ depending on the political history of the respective community.

Most of the Oshiwambo communities and the communities of the Kavango and Zambezi Regions have a widely undisturbed history of succeeding members of their respective royal families.[36] They have a history of succeeding traditional leaders within a structure of leadership, either affiliated to royal families or, where such a family does not exist, consolidated on an ancestrally determined territory.

As far as the political structure of the Ovaherero is concerned, Malan suggests that these communities were historically *non-centralised* societies.[37] This is not the place to argue this. What is indeed true, is that the position of paramount chief emerged late and to some extent as response to colonial policy. It has, nevertheless, been maintained in the tradition of the Ovaherero, although it does not enjoy acceptance under the Traditional Authorities Act[38] and is also not appreciated by all Ovaherero. The attempts of the late Paramount Chief Kuaima Riruako to be recognised failed for many years.[39] Eventually, Riruako was accepted as chief of the Ovaherero Traditional Authority. Despite this name that could be read as meaning the traditional authority of all Ovaherero, the Ovaherero Traditional authority is just one community next to others recognised under the Traditional Authorities Act.

Budack holds that the political organisation of the Nama belongs to the centralised forms of government.[40] Various Nama communities developed permanent centres of authority with an organised structure of officials with special functions for governing the communities. However, there are differences if one compares the governments of the Nama communities, for example, with the governments of the Oshiwambo-speaking

---

35 Cf. Section 1 of the Act (No. 25 of 2000) defining "chief".

36 This paragraph and the following rely on MO Hinz, A Schmidt & C Mapaure (forthcoming, 2015) *The Constitution of Namibia: Part 1.*

37 J S Malan (1995): *Peoples of Namibia.* Pretoria: Rhino Publishers:78

38 The Traditional Authorities Act recognizes only the positions of chief and senior councillor. See Section 2 of the Act, No. 25 of 2000.

39 The application for recognition was subject to an unsuccessful court case, cf.: *Kuaima Riruako v Minister of Regional, Local Government and Housing*, Case No (P) 336/2001 (unreported case in the High Court of Namibia).

40 K F R H Budack (1972): Die traditionelle politische Struktur der Khoe-khoen in Südwestafrika. Stamm und Stammesregierung auf historischer Grundlage. Pretoria: PhD thesis of the University of Pretoria:13f.

groups. The Nama communities are smaller in size and were under much more pressure in colonial times which did not allow their traditional structures to function as was possible in the northern parts of the country. With respect to the law of the Nama community, one detail requires special attention. The self-stated laws of the Soromas community refer to a document titled *Ryksboek* which was written in 1847. The *Ryksboek* is the oldest statement of customary law in Namibia and so far has not been taken note of in the work on Namibian customary law.[41]

The traditional life of the San as hunters and gatherers did not support the establishment of centralised governmental structures. The San used to live in small groups without a centralised authority. There were people who led the group because they were respected as skilled hunters or because of other personal qualities from which the community profited. Under the Traditional Authorities Act several San groups received recognition. They all have now opted for having one "supreme traditional leader".

The legal texts and profiles submitted by the various communities reflect this difficult socio-political history: Quite a number of the communities of the central and southern part of the country offer very elaborated community profiles for the *Customary Law Ascertainment Project*. The complex history of communities, indeed, requires special efforts to set the framework of the respective group identity. Their laws have many sections on the constitutional structure of the communities, including provisions on succession to the position of their supreme leader.[42] Some of the laws are very detailed: the result of the need to establish the administration of law in a way which has not been practised so far. The socio-political history of most of the communities in central and southern Namibia is a history of territorial expropriation, forced removal and concentration in reserves and of political degradation in the interest of colonial expansion and settlement. All these inroads into the traditional structures of the communities resulted in substantial changes in their political organisation, their understanding of the law, and the administration of it. Mechanisms closer to indirect rule were implemented in central and southern Namibia by the South African government only with the introduction of the apartheid-based separate development that culminated in the establishment of second tier governments in 1980,[43] although the implementation of second tier governments applied country-wide. However, the different exposure to colonialism created special problems for the efforts

41 The full title of the *Ryksboek* is *Ryksboek bevattende alle wette en regten van het Kapiteinschap te Bethanië* and can be inspected in the archives of the Evangelical Lutheran Church in the Republic of Namibia, Windhoek, under elcrnx5-21. I thank the former head of the National Archives, Mr Werner Hillebrecht, for giving me access to the *Ryksboek*.

42 The many consultations conducted by the *Customary Law Ascertainment Project* with the communities of central and southern Namibia allow us to predict that the laws of these communities will be subject to many changes as time passes and the various community courts of these communities operate in full.

43 Cf. Representative Authority Proclamation, AG 8 of 1980 and the various subsequent proclamations establishing representative authorities for 11 population groups. AG 8 of 1980 and the subsequent proclamations were repealed by the Constitution of Namibia of 1990 (see Article 148 of the Constitution and its Schedule 8).

of the central and southern traditional communities to re-appropriate their traditional foundation and apply it to changed times.[44]

The work ahead

The publication of the laws of the Nama, the Ovaherero, Ovambanderu and the San communities marks the end of the *Customary Law Ascertainment Project.* The project has been completed in the sense that the three volumes with the customary laws of Namibian traditional communities contain what was received from the various communities in accordance with agreements decided upon in the various meetings the Human Rights and Documentation Centre was able to organise over the past years. Most of the communities honoured the agreements and delivered what was expected from them. Some, for different reasons, have not. Nevertheless, and despite the gaps, what has been assembled in the three volumes of *Customary law ascertained* is extraordinary. It is extraordinary as the three volumes assemble a portfolio of customary law that Namibia has never seen before, and which has no match yet in any other African country.

However, what is being presented by *Customary law ascertained* is certainly not the last word about customary law in Namibia. The communities will, of course, continue to develop their laws. Some communities meet regularly to decide on amendments to their laws. In particular, they meet to consult on changes to the value of the fines to be levied by the courts to remedy wrongs committed, or the so-called official price for one head of cattle, which is, to some extent, subject to changes in the market value of cattle.

The unification of customary law by some of the Kavango communities[45] may influence other clusters of communities to embark upon a similar process. Statutory changes by the Namibian parliament may provoke changes in customary law. Court decisions may have consequences for certain parts of customary law, as it was not the task of *Customary Law Ascertainment Project* to scrutinise the various pieces of customary law against existing statutes, including the Constitution of Namibia. Testing customary law against the Constitution and, in particular, the human rights in the Constitution to which customary law is subject is a very demanding undertaking which is left to the public discourse and, ultimately, to the competent courts.

The publication of the laws as they were submitted to the *Customary Law Ascertainment Project* will also generate revision processes by the communities themselves. The drafters and experts of customary law of the various communities will take note of the laws of other communities, compare them with their own laws, and most probably suggest amendments for improvement. They will also pay attention to the wording of their laws, the texts in their indigenous languages and the translations of which quite a number were done by the Project. We realised that there were some almost unsolvable language problems in certain instances. We hope that the English translations are as true

44 Cf. MO Hinz assisted by S. Joas (2003) *Customary law in Namibia: Development and perspective*. 8th edn Windhoek: Centre for Applied Social Sciences, pp 31ff.; 101ff.

45 See the first volume of *Customary law ascertained* (fn 1): 369ff.

as possible to the original texts, although it has to be noted that the indigenous language terms for certain legal concepts do not always express the same as the English concepts used.[46] Only further discussions, interpretations, applications and cases brought to the state courts will help to clarify any complexities. We were also very reluctant to make changes in the texts submitted to us. We changed, for example, the use of *tribal* into *traditional* and *tribe* into *traditional community* or just *community.* We did not alter references to headmen or senior headmen although these terms have not been kept in the language of the law-maker, i.e the language of the Traditional Authorities Act. Our reason for doing so was that both terms are very much still in use and reflect social reality, which is not necessarily identically reflected in the terms of the Act, which talks of *traditional* and *senior traditional councillors*. We also did not intervene when self-stated customary laws dealt with the question of ownership of communal land, and this not always in line with sections 17, 21 and 24 of the Communal Land Reform Act.[47]

It is, therefore, important that all who will make use of this publication understand it as a work in progress, progress in the service to improve and further develop the customary law of the various Namibian communities. Looking back to developments in self-stating customary laws in Namibia, one sees features which can be expected to influence further steps in this work in progress. Earlier versions of self-stated laws concentrated very much on fines for the usual catalogue of wrongs, which we find in any textbook on criminal law or the law of delict. Later versions have added wrongs from environmental law in particular. Later versions have also paid attention to constitutional matters relevant to traditional governance, meaning that there is a growing awareness to consider rule-of-law principles in the application of customary law and the administration under this law. Community participation has been noted in many of the more recently drafted self-statements. The community profiles which introduce the laws of the various communities illustrate a growing awareness of the foundation of the community, including the philosophical foundations on which their laws are built.

Some years ago, some of us working with traditional communities on their customary laws were criticised when we communicated the self-stated laws of some communities, which we had collected at the time, in meetings with other communities. We were said to have violated customary law by circulating documents which were seen to be secret of some kind. We objected to this and see now that many communities have obviously taken note of what others were doing and even integrated rules developed by other communities into their own laws. Today, in some drafts of self-stated documents, we even see references to scholarly work (such as work done by me or by the Legal Assistance Centre). This is very encouraging although we also note that some of the drafts show the authorship of knowledgeable local personalities, which might not always be in agreement with the aspirations of the members of the community.

46 *Ownership* is an example to illustrate this. Under common law, ownership of land means having all rights over the land, including the right to sell. Under customary law, there is no ownership of land in this sense; if the concept of *ownership* is referred to, it expresses the existence of a certain authority over the land, but bound to obligations towards the community.

47 Act No. 5 of 2003.

We will certainly observe as time goes on what happens to the self-stated laws when more and more references to them can be expected within the communities and from outside. These references may challenge communities to reconsider not only their approaches to their laws, but also to their profiles. What Advocate B Gawanas wrote in her foreword to the second volume of *Customary Law Ascertained* summarises this challenge in the following clear words:[48]

> Taking what we have now in front of us ... we will look more closely at the laws applied by our communities. We will be able to raise questions with community leaders; we will be able to have informed discussions with the members of the communities; and we will be able to suggest changes for the better – particularly as regards the lives of women and children – in terms of what we have in our Constitution and its fundamental rights and freedoms.

In one of the scholarly comments on the first volume of *Customary law ascertained*, it was held that the translation of orally transmitted customary law into writing may carry the danger of changing the attitude towards customary law by regarding the written version of it as inflexible – as is the case with acts of parliament.[49] It was argued that, although the *writing down* of customary law was not meant as its *codification,* it would gain this quality in practice and, thus, replace other, particularly oral, sources of customary law. State courts are also expected to contribute to this development, as they may take the self-stated versions of customary law as the last word on the respective law. Whether or not this will happen will become evident when the community courts become fully operational, and decisions will be taken on appeal to the state courts. What happens then will depend on how the traditional communities and their courts will apply their laws, but also on how they make use of the power "to make customary law" as spelled out in the Traditional Authorities Act. The legal outcomes will also depend on the general development of the jurisprudential reflections on the operation of customary law.

When compiling the documents received from the traditional authorities for the publication, the *Customary Law Ascertainment Project* was approached by some concerned members of certain communities who even requested to stop the publication. "I was not consulted," was the reason for that request. The reader will see when going through the self-stated customary laws of the various communities that, indeed, some of the communities have rules on how to make customary law. Responding to such requests, we explained that we did not see it to be our task to control whether or not the communities followed their rules when ascertaining their laws and making customary law. All that we expected was a certificate of consent to publish the documents to be submitted to us, duly signed and stamped by the respective traditional authorities. Incidents of this nature will certainly contribute to improvements in the process of traditional law-making.
Another point submitted to us was whether the self-stated laws were 'old' or 'new' customary law, that is, the law stated as the law of the olden days and, therefore, not

48 See volume 2 of *Customary law ascertained* (fn 1): XIII.
49 See Horn (2011), fn 6: 137ff.

of relevance today, or the law assembled in *Customary law ascertained*, i.e. the law as applied today. The reader will find that some documents in *Customary law ascertained* recall a time of the ancestors. However, this appears to be only a point of reference on which statements for today are built. The many consultations conducted during the Ascertainment of Customary Law Project left no doubt that *Customary law ascertained* was not meant to be a contribution to the history of customary law, but a reflection of the customary law as it is currently being applied. To what extent the communities met the expectation to self-state the presently applicable law must be left to the further process on the various customary laws.

Editors' general note

This note repeats some of the statements made in the introductory remarks to assist the user of the laws contained in this publication.

It was up to the communities to decide what aspect of customary law they wanted to have ascertained in writing. The self-statements do not intend to repeal orally transmitted customary law, nor parts of it: the orally transmitted customary law remains valid, and will assist in interpreting the stated rules. This means that the self-stated laws of the various communities are not codifications of customary law.

Legislative drafting has developed into a very specialised art in many modern jurisdictions. However, the reader of the self-stated laws should not expect that these laws follow the sophisticated techniques of modern legislative drafting. In many instances, the self-stated customary laws give educative explanations or even state rather general societal aspirations – a fact which will be a challenge to interpretation!

As the communities are the lawmakers, they also have the authority to amend their laws, subject to the applicable customary and statutory law, including the Namibian Constitution. The fact that the communities have accepted to write down parts of their customary law does not affect the generally employed flexibility of customary law, according to which the restoration of peace is the primary objective.

Many of the laws contained in this volume were originally written in indigenous languages and, thereafter, translated into English. This created many problems as the English legal terms are not necessarily always a proper reflection of what the source languages wanted to express. This means that, in cases of doubt, the text in the source language has to be consulted for clarification.

Although the editors and translators have made every attempt to ensure that the materials are accurate in their formal presentation, omissions, inadequacies or errors that remain as regards the content of such materials are the responsibility of the various Traditional Authorities that submitted them. The editors have deleted obvious repetitions and corrected language errors. When the editors had difficulty in understanding the meaning in a submitted text, they consulted the relevant Traditional Authority to receive clarification. It was not the task of the Customary Law Ascertainment Project to check the submitted laws with respect to their compatibility with the law of the state, including the constitutional law of Namibia. Checking this and, where necessary, working on amendments to customary law, must be left to the established procedures of the Namibian Parliament, the courts and the public debate at large.

In cases where the supreme leader of a Traditional Authority had passed away and no new leader had been gazetted, the picture of the deceased leader was kept in front of the respective community profile.

During the editorial process, the editor has received comments by members of some traditional communities who complained that they were "not consulted" in the drafting of the self-stated customary law of their community. The editors' response was that it was not the task of the Customary Law Ascertainment Project to intervene in the process of the self-stating by the communities. The Project conducted consultations with all the recognised traditional communities in Namibia, during which the communities were advised to do the self-stating in accordance with their respective rules. The Project recommended to the Traditional Authorities – in accordance with the gender policies of Namibia – to involve the voices of women, but again stated in clear terms that it would be up to the Traditional Authorities and communities to proceed with the drafting, as it was requested by their rules and customs. For the Project and the edition of the customary laws, it was eventually important to have the certificate of consent to publish the customary laws signed by the Traditional Authority. Whoever in a given traditional community is not satisfied with what has been submitted to the Project for publication is of course free to pursue his/her concern within the community and the public at large. Concerns of this nature will also remain qualified as arguments before Community Courts and a state court in the adjudication of cases.

Finally, the reader should be aware that the offical price for animals or the money to be paid as compensation for wrongs committed may have changed in accordance with the development of the respective market price sine the laws were submitted to the editors for publication.

Part II
The laws of the Nama communities[1]

1 Editor's note: The following Part does not contain the laws of the ǀHai-Khaua (Berseba) community. The recently gazetted community has just started compiling their customary law.

Afrikaner Traditional Authority
|Hôa|aran||aixa||aes !Haos

The supreme leader of the |Hôa|aran||aixa||aes (Afrikaner) Traditional Authority was *Gaos*[1] Hendrina Martha Afrikaner (above).
Date of designation: 7 March 2004
She passed away on 19 August 2011.
The Acting *Gaos* was Trooi Jantze.
She passed away on 16 November 2014.[2]

AFRIKANER TRADITIONAL AUTHORITY

/HOA/ARAN//AIXA//AES

P.O. Box 857, Mariental, Namibia
Tel.: (063) 242 542

1 Traditional title in terms of section 11, Traditional Authorities Act, 2000 (No. 25 of 2000).

2 Editor's note: There was no information on the appointment of an acting supreme leader or a successor to the late supreme leader of the community at the time of going to press.

PROFILE[3]

History

The history of the |Hôa|aran||aixa||aes (Orlam Afrikaner) began in the 17th century during the disintegration of the Khoekhoen. Through this process, a number of independent family groups came into existence. One of these, the Orlam Afrikaners, adapted to the changing circumstances. Thus, despite their relatively small numbers, they developed into a driving force in the history of Namaqua- and Namaland. The first two phases in this development were led by Klaas Afrikaner and his son, Jager Afrikaner.

At the time of Jager Afrikaner's death in 1822, his people were living at Blydeverwacht and Jerusalem in southern Namaland. On his deathbed, he handed over the leadership of the Orlam Afrikaner to his second son, Jonker Afrikaner. This gave rise to dissatisfaction, which eventually led to a split in the ranks. Jonker Afrikaner and his followers moved northwards as a result. Due to Jonker Afrikaner's military skills and the group's advantage in having access to firearms and ammunition, they established a reputation for effective warfare. In the 1830s, this in turn encouraged a Nama community, the Kai||kaun (Rooinasie/Red Nation) to ask for their help in preventing the Ovaherero from driving them from their traditional pastures. After compelling the Ovaherero to return north of the !Kuiseb River, Jonker Afrikaner and his followers settled in central Namaland, residing in places like Niais, Tsebis and, eventually, Windhoek.

Jonker persuaded British explorer James Edward Alexander, who visited him in 1837, to arrange a missionary for him. This set in motion a chain of events which clearly illustrated the interdependence between Namibia's indigenous peoples and the traders and missionaries that had begun to arrive and settle in the country.

Edward Cook and Joseph Tindall of the Wesleyan Methodist Missionary Society were the first missionaries to visit the Orlam Afrikaners. Their right to minister to Jonker, however, was not recognised by the Rhenish missionaries, Franz Heinrich Kleinschmidt, known to the Afrikaners as Heinrich "Kleinsch" Kleinschmidt, and Carl Hugo Hahn, who settled in Windhoek with Jonker's permission. It was there that a relationship developed between Jonker and Kleinschmidt. Jonker Afrikaner wished to reunite the Orlam Afrikaners in Windhoek with the groups in the south. However, the southern groups were being influenced by Wesleyan missionaries. Rivalry between the Wesleyan and Rhenish missionaries caused Kleinschmidt and Hahn to leave Windhoek, but the Rhenish Missionary Society was later to achieve pre-eminence.

Meanwhile traders had arrived in the country. They supplied firearms, ammunition, brandy and other commodities to Jonker Afrikaner and his people on credit. By 1846, the indigenous people were so indebted that they saw no option other than to raid the Ovaherero for their cattle in order to pay what they owed, intensifying clashes across cultural borders and even within communities. Tension between Jonker Afrikaner and one of his Ovaherero allies, Kahitjene, for example, led to Jonker's attack on Kahitjene

3 This profile was provided by the |Hôa|aran||aixa||aes (Afrikaner) Traditional Authority.

who was based in Okahandja, and the destruction of the mission station there in August 1850.

A further escalation in violence was temporarily prevented by the arrival of the English traveller, Francis Galton. He threatened Jonker Afrikaner with British reprisals. After Galton's departure, Kahitjene's growing resistance to Jonker erupted in an attack on Windhoek in May 1854.

Again, tension in the country was suppressed by external factors – this time by the arrival of copper miners. They promoted peace because the continuation of their work was impossible without it. Through their mediation, the Matchless Mine Peace was concluded in November 1855. At the same time, the way in which the miners played off the indigenous groups against each other forced the latter to form a collective forum against the mining community. This was done via the Treaty of Hoachanas, concluded in 1858.

In 1858, after various further relocations and temporary settlements at Grootwarmfontein and Okapuka, Jonker Afrikaner and his people moved to Okahandja. With Okahandja as his base, Jonker became involved in Oshiwambo politics. Two years later, when the outbreak of lungsickness made it impossible to obtain cattle in the interior, he directed raids on the Aawambo in the north. He returned to Okahandja an ill man and died there on 16 August 1861. He was succeeded by his eldest son, Christian Afrikaner.

After Jonker Afrikaner's death, it became clear that the Orlam Afrikaners owed their position of power to the latter's leadership. Through a combination of diplomacy, displays of strength, and by the way he manipulated people and group relations, he succeeded in establishing the Afrikaners' influence for 40 years across the expanse between the Orange and Kunene Rivers.

Jan Jonker Afrikaner became the new Afrikaner leader after the death of his brother Christian Afrikaner, who ruled for less than two years. Over the next seven years, the Afrikaner continually attacked the Ovaherero. The Ovaherero under their chief, Maharero, were stronger in battle and the Afrikaner took great losses. The Ovaherero were not always fortunate though, and in 1869, Maharero's troops were forced to eat scorpions to stay alive. This was a sad time in the history of the Afrikaners. They were scattered, starving and without a home.

In 1870, Jan Jonker Afrikaner asked the missionary Hahn to help with setting up a peace treaty with Maharero. In September that year, the Treaty of Okahandja was signed. The peace lasted 10 years.

In 1978, the |Hôa|aran||aixa||aes gathered in Baumgartsbrunn in the Windhoek District and nominated their leadership according to their customs and traditional laws.

Chief Neels Afrikaner and his Traditional Councillors were designated, and the leadership pattern was once again restored. The Namibian Government, after passing the Council of Traditional Leaders Act, 1997 (No. 13 of 1997) recognised the Afrikaner (ǀHôaǀaranǁaixaǁaes) Traditional Authority as one of the first such bodies to be registered in the new Republic.

However, during the reign of Chief Neels Afrikaner and after his death in 1996, during the reign of Acting Chief Jeremiah Wilfred Jagger, no traditional festivals were held.

In 2002, the ǀHôaǀaranǁaixaǁaes called for able-bodied leadership. The acting leadership did not heed the community's call, however. The ǀHôaǀaranǁaixaǁaes convened to resolve some of the problems with the Acting Chief, but without success. The unhappiness and dissatisfaction with the Acting Chief took a long time to resolve.

In the light of the above, the ǀHôaǀaranǁaixaǁaes community was confronted with the daunting task of restoring the community's pride, dignity, ownership of resources, and historical values and norms, without capable and committed leadership. Eventually, however, on 7 March 2004, all stakeholders witnessed the nomination and inauguration of Chief Hendrina Martha Afrikaner as their traditional leader. She became the second woman to lead the traditional community, the first having been the late Chief Anna ǂAos ("the Wind") in 1900.

Chronological order of the chieftaincies

Name of Chief	Tenure of rule	Number of years served
1. Klaas Afrikaner	From c. 1760	
2. Jager Afrikaner	1806–1822	16
3. Jonker Afrikaner	1823–1861	38
4. Christian Afrikaner	1861–1863	2
5. Jan Jonker Afrikaner	1863–1889	26
6. Christian Jonker Afrikaner	1889–1900	11
7. Anna ("The Great") ǂAos	1900–1915	15
8. Samuel Afrikaner[4]	1915–1978	35
9. Neels Afrikaner	1978–1996	18
10. Jeremiah Wilfred Jagger (Acting)	1996–2004	8
11. Hendrina Martha Afrikaner[5]	2004–2011	7

4 After Samuel Afrikaner's death, the Orlam Afrikaner decided not to appoint a Chief because they felt no one had the required leadership skills.

Geographical area of jurisdiction

The Khomas Hochland area is the ancestral home of the |Hôa|aran||aixa||aes; the graves of our forefathers in the area still bear silent witness to this. The colonial authorities forced the clan to uproot and relocate to the Gibeon District in 1986.

Through this action the traditional community lost everything – including their pride, their dignity and their cultural heritage. In the Gibeon District, six farms were taken from the Topnaar and Bondelswarts traditional communities and the |Hôa|aran||aixa||aes were resettled there. This is where the colonial occupiers gazetted them as residing.

Main seat

The |Hôa|aran||aixa||aes have no traditional office as yet, as the Traditional Authority is still in the process of negotiating with the Namibian Government.

The emblem

The lion is the symbol of the |Hôa|aran||aixa||aes. It represents the people's perseverance and strength.

Traditional colours

Mustard and light brown are the traditional colours of the |Hôa|aran||aixa||aes.

Traditional flag

The flag portrays a relaxed and peaceful lion's head on a light brown background.

Traditional song

The community's traditional song (*||Naetsânas*) is titled *Naimiab !A‡uisab*, meaning "Namibia the land of our heavenly cleanness".

Traditional festival

The first ever traditional festival was held at Kabias South in the Gibeon District from March to May 2005. The Community Trust Fund was also launched on this occasion by the Governor of the Hardap Region, Hon. Katrina M. Harmse Himarwa.

There is now a traditional festival each year in early March, as determined by the |Hôa|aran||aixa||aes Traditional Authority. All members of the |Hôa|aran||aixa||aes traditional community are invited to attend, along with several other guests and interested parties.

Population

The genocide carried out by the German colonial authorities during the 1904–1907 war drastically reduced the ǀHôaǀaranǁaixaǁaes traditional community. Since registration during the National Census of 1991 the community today numbers approximately 8 000–10 000 people. However, due to landlessness and looking for job opportunities in order to survive, members of the community are scattered all over Namibia.

Day-to-day activities

Daily activities are guided by the Laws of the ǀHôaǀaranǁaixaǁaes as well as the Namibian Constitution and statutory laws.

Holy fire

The holy fire is lit at a sacred communal area at the start of every day. The fire symbolises the beginning and ending of life, as well as everything in between.

The laws of the |Hoa|aran||aixa||aes (Afrikaner)[1]

1 The laws of the Afrikaner were submitted in English only.

1. The ǀHôaǀaranǁaixaǁaes Traditional Authority

1.1 There shall be a Traditional Authority for the ǀHôaǀaranǁaixaǁaes traditional community.

1.2 The establishment, powers and functions of the Traditional Authority are defined in the Traditional Authorities Act, 2000 (No. 25 of 2000).

1.3 The Traditional Authority is comprised of the Supreme Authority and the Royal House of the Chief.

2. Role and responsibilities of the Traditional Authority

2.1 The Traditional Authority shall:

(a) promote peace and welfare amongst community members, and shall supervise and ensure the observance of the Laws of the ǀHôaǀaranǁaixaǁaes.

(b) administer and execute the Laws of the ǀHôaǀaranǁaixaǁaes.

(c) preserve and maintain the cultural sites, works of art and literature, and oral history of the ǀHôaǀaranǁaixaǁaes.

(d) perform ǀHôaǀaranǁaixaǁaes traditional ceremonies and functions.

(e) perform any other function as may be conferred upon it by law or custom.

(f) ensure that the members of the traditional community use the natural resources at their disposal on a sustainable basis and in a manner that conserves the environment and maintains ecosystems for the benefit of all persons in Namibia.

(g) hear and settle disputes between the members of the traditional community in accordance with the Laws of the ǀHôaǀaranǁaixaǁaes.

3. Traditional Authority meetings

3.1 The ǀHôaǀaranǁaixaǁaes Traditional Authority shall meet 4 (four) times a year.

3.2 All Traditional Authority meetings shall be attended by the Chief, the Secretary and all 6 (six) Senior Councillors and 6 (six) Junior Councillors.

3.3 The meetings shall deliberate on issues concerning traditional matters, customary conduct and practices, and any other matter concerning the members of the ǀHôaǀaranǁaixaǁaes.

3.4 The Traditional Authority may invite anyone to their meetings.

3.5 The quorum for Traditional Authority meetings shall be a minimum of 7 (seven) members.

3.6 The Chief shall have the casting vote.

3.7 Every Traditional Authority member shall be obliged to attend these meetings.

3.8 Any Traditional Authority member who fails to attend 3 (three) consecutive meetings without a valid reason and without being excused by the Traditional Authority automatically discharges him-/herself from the Traditional Authority.

4. Community meetings

4.1 General meetings shall be held for the |Hôa|aran‖aixa‖aes community.
4.2 The meetings shall be open to every member of the community.
4.3 The meetings shall be convened by the Chief and his/her Councillors whenever necessary.
4.4 The purpose of such meetings may vary from disseminating information and consultation, to discussing serious traditional concerns, i.e. grazing, water related issues and crime.
4.5 Hearing and settlement of disputes between the members of the traditional community in accordance with the customary law will take place during community meetings.

5. The Royal House

5.1 The Royal House shall consist of the chief's family members, that is, the Chief's uncles, aunts, brothers, sisters, nieces, nephews and children.
5.2 The function of the members of the Royal Family shall be to recommend the heir to the throne in the event of the Chief's death, as well as to render moral support to the Chief in the performance of state matters and traditional rituals.

6. The Supreme Authority

6.1 There shall be a Supreme Authority for the |Hôa|aran‖aixa‖aes traditional community which shall consist of the Chief and his/her Council.
6.2 The Supreme Authority shall comprise all the members of the |Hôa|aran‖aixa‖aes Traditional Authority as well as 20 (twenty) members of the Elders' Council (*Kai-Khoen ǂNûs*).
6.3 The Supreme Authority shall inaugurate the Chief"s successor as recommended by the members of the Royal House.
6.4 The office of the Chief shall be deemed vacant only upon the Chief's death.
6.5 The Supreme Authority shall make funeral arrangements for the Chief.
6.6 The Supreme Authority shall designate the selected candidate as the Chief in terms of the Traditional Authorities Act after notifying the relevant Minister.

7. The Chief

7.1 The Chief shall be the Chairperson of all Traditional Authority and traditional community meetings, and shall have the right to delegate such authority to other persons.
7.2 The Chief shall be selected from the bloodline of the |Hôa|aran‖aixa‖aes Royal House or may be any other capable person from the community.
7.3 The Chief shall be at least 35 (thirty-five) years of age.

7.4 The Chief shall be the custodian of the laws of the ǀHôaǀaranǁaixaǁaes and shall exercise his/her powers and perform his/her duties and functions in accordance with such laws.

7.5 The inauguration of the Chief shall be conducted only by a person equal in position.

7.6 Any person to whom the Chief delegates his/her powers or functions shall deputise him/her.

8. Succession

8.1 Upon the death of the Chief, the members of the traditional community who are authorised by the laws of the ǀHôaǀaranǁaixaǁaes may designate his/her successor in accordance with traditional custom.

8.2 The successor may be selected from the bloodline of the ǀHôaǀaranǁaixaǁaes Royal House or may be any other capable person from the community.

9. Deputising

9.1 All 6 (six) Senior Councillors shall assist the Chief and shall deputise the Chief in his absence.

9.2 The Senior Councillor deputising the Chief for a specific period shall submit a written report to the Chief on his/her return.

9.3 If the Chief is on sick leave for 3 (three) months, a Senior Councillor will serve as Acting Chief for the entire period.

9.4 If the Chief is on sick leave for 6 (six) months, each of 3 (three) Senior Councillors will serve as Acting Chief for 2 (two) months.

9.5 If the Chief is abroad for a period of 2 (two) years, each of the 6 (six) Senior Councillors will serve as Acting Chief for 4 (four) months.

10. Removal of councillors

10.1 If there are sufficient reasons that warrant the removal of a Senior or Junior Councillor for having been disrespectful or disloyal towards the Traditional Authority or the traditional community, such person will be relieved of his/her traditional duties with immediate effect.

10.2 If a Senior or Junior Councillor has been absent without authorisation from his/her duties for three consecutive meetings without taking the necessary leave from such duties, such person will be released from his/her traditional duties with immediate effect.

11. Elders' Council

11.1 There shall be an Elders' Council (*Kai Khoen ǀHaos*) for the ǀHôaǀaranǁaixaǁaes community.

11.2 The Elders' Council shall consist of 20 (twenty) members of the elders of the |Hôa|aran||aixa||aes community.

11.3 The eligible age for membership of the Elders' Council shall be at least 55 (fifty-five) years.

11.4 The Elders' Council shall adopt its own rules for its activities within the limits of the Laws of the |Hôa|aran||aixa||aes.

11.5 The main function of the Elders' Council shall be to:

(a) advise the Chief about the culture and customs of the |Hôa|aran||aixa||aes community.

(b) ensure that |Hôa|aran||aixa||aes culture and customs are preserved.

(c) delegate not more than 20 (twenty) members to the |Hôa|aran||aixa||aes Supreme Authority when necessary.

12. |Hôa|aran||aixa||aes Youth and Adults' Cultural Groups

12.1 There shall be a Youth Cultural Group for community members aged between 6 (six) and 16 (sixteen) years.

12.2 There shall be an Adults' Cultural Group for community members aged between 17 (seventeen) and 70 (seventy) years.

12.3 These cultural groups shall adopt their own rules for activities, but are required to abide by the limits of the laws of the |Hôa|aran||aixa||aes.

13. |Hôa|aran||aixa||aes Traditional Trust Fund

13.1 According to Section 18 of the Traditional Authorities Act, the |Hôa|aran||aixa||aes Traditional Authority may, with the consent of the traditional community, establish a Community Trust Fund to be held in trust for the members of that community and towards which such members may contribute for the following purposes:

(a) financing projects in the community which promote and uplift the culture, preserve cultural sites, works of art, and literary works of the community.

(b) meeting the administrative costs of running the office of the Traditional Authority.

(c) meeting the costs of performing any of the functions and duties of the Traditional Authority, and

(d) meeting any other costs that the traditional community may agree on.

14. |Hôa|aran||aixa||aes Community Court

14.1 The Community Court shall comprise the Chief as Chairperson, a Secretary, 6 (six) Senior Councillors, 2 (two) senior members of the |Hôa|aran||aixa||aes community, and a judge and 12 (twelve) assessors.

15. Maintenance of law and public order

15.1 The prior consent of the ǀHôaǀaranǁaixaǁaes Traditional Authority shall be required for any person who wishes to conduct any of the following activities in the ǀHôaǀaranǁaixaǁaes area of jurisdiction:
(a) settle in or move into or move within such area.
(b) fence off any grazing or residential areas.
(c) hold meetings, festivals or any other gathering.
(d) collect firewood, water or any other natural resource.
(e) transport livestock or meat.
(f) sell livestock or meat.

16. Penalties

16.1 Theft

16.1.1 Theft is regarded as a very serious crime by the Community Court.
16.1.2 Cases of theft shall be dealt with directly by the Community Court.
16.1.3 For the theft of household items, personal articles, donkey carts and so forth, the fine shall be imposed according to the value of the goods stolen.
16.1.4 If one has stolen 1 (one) head of cattle, the fine is 3 (three) head of cattle for the first conviction, and 6 (six) head of cattle for the theft of 1 (one) head of cattle for the second conviction.
16.1.5 The fine is 5 (five) goats for the theft of 1 (one) goat by a first-time offender, and 10 (ten) goats if s/he repeats the crime.
16.1.6 The theft of horses and donkeys is treated in the same way as the theft of cattle.
16.1.7 In all cases, 1 (one) head of cattle or N$350 (three hundred and fifty Namibia Dollars) is contributed to the Community Trust Fund.

16.2 Smuggling

16.2.1 Cases of smuggling shall include illicit trade in alcohol, dagga, mandrax, heroin, diamonds, ammunition and semi-precious stones.
16.2.2 A case of smuggling shall first be heard by the magistrate and/or higher courts.
16.2.3 On conviction and having served a prison sentence or having paid a fine, the convicted smuggler shall also be tried by the Community Court.
16.2.4 A person found guilty of smuggling habit-forming drugs shall pay a maximum fine of 10 (ten) head of cattle to the Traditional Authority plus 1 (one) for the Community Trust Fund.
16.2.5 A person found guilty of smuggling semi-precious or fake gemstones, diamonds or liquor shall pay a maximum fine of 5 (five) head of cattle to the Community Trust Fund.
16.2.6 The number of head of cattle shall be reduced proportionally according to the nature and seriousness of the crime.

16.3 Poaching

16.3.1 Poaching entails the unlawful killing of game by shooting or any other method.
16.3.2 Cases of poaching shall be heard directly by the Community Court.
16.3.3 A fine shall be imposed according to the type of game poached.

16.4 Adultery and divorce

16.4.1 Extramarital relationships by either party in a marriage are usually a cause of grief because they end in divorce or claims for damages.
16.4.2 Divorce cases shall be heard directly by a Community Court.
16.4.3 At the first hearing of a first offence only a warning shall be given with emphasis given to both parties to try to save their marriage.
16.4.4 Minimum fines shall apply if the offence is repeated a second time.
16.4.5 The fine shall be 2 (two) head of cattle payable by the offending party to the party against whom the offence has been committed.
16.4.6 If an unmarried person is involved in adultery, the married person shall be fined and the money shall be deposited into the Community Trust Fund.
16.4.7 The maximum fine to be imposed in a case of divorce shall be 4 (four) head of cattle payable to the divorcee by the party who is the cause of the divorce.

16.5 Rape

16.5.1 The definition of rape shall include forced sexual contact with any married or unmarried female or male person of any age. It is rare for a male person to be raped by a female person.
16.5.2 A case of rape shall first be heard by a magistrate and/or a higher court.
16.5.3 On conviction and after having served any prison terms or having paid any fine, the guilty party shall also be tried by the Community Court.
16.5.4 The maximum fine of 10 (ten) head of cattle shall be imposed as compensation for the rape victim.
16.5.5 The number of cattle demanded as a fine shall be reduced proportionally to the number of years the guilty party spent in prison.
16.5.6 The rapist shall also pay 1 (one) head of cattle to the Community Trust Fund.

16.6 Vandalism

16.6.1 The definition of vandalism shall include wilful damage to water installations, fences and another person's property.
16.6.2 Cases of vandalism shall be dealt with directly by the Community Court.
16.6.3 In the case of extensive damage to water installations and fences, the maximum fine entails repairing the damage as well as paying 2 (two) head of cattle to the Community Trust Fund.

16.6.4 In the case of minor damage to another person's property, the fine entails repairing the damage as well as paying 1 (one) goat to the Community Trust Fund.

16.7 Deceased estates and inheritance

16.7.1 The definition of a deceased estate entails a deceased person's property of any kind, including his/her personal belongings, immovable property, livestock and cash.
16.7.2 All disputes in a deceased estate shall be heard directly by the Community Court.
16.7.3 When there is a dispute the Community Court determines the beneficiaries in an estate and apportions the estate accordingly.

16.8 Family disputes and gossip

16.8.1 Cases of family disputes and gossip, which shall include disputes between two parties in a relationship and interference by their family members, shall be heard by the Community Court.
16.8.2 The Community Court shall intervene to restore peace and harmony in the household.
16.8.3 At the first offence, the family members of each party in the relationship shall be warned not to interfere in the couple's household.
16.8.4 At the second offence, the family members shall be fined 2 (two) head of cattle.
16.8.5 At the first offence, gossipmongers shall be given a warning.
16.8.6 If gossipmongers persist, they shall be fined 2 (two) head of cattle.

16.9 Destruction of the environment

16.9.1 A definition of destruction of the environment shall include deforestation as well as any unnecessary cutting or knocking down of trees or shrubs, as well as the intentional lighting of veldfires.
16.9.2 Such cases shall be heard directly by the Community Court.
16.9.3 The maximum fine for the intentional destruction of the environment shall be 2 (two) head of cattle.

16.10 Assault

16.10.1 Assault shall include causing somebody malicious bodily harm or injury with the fist, sticks, knives, sharp objects, etc.
16.10.2 Cases of assault shall be heard directly by the Community Court.
16.10.3 The minimum fine for assault shall be 2 (two) goats and the maximum fine shall be 2 (two) head of cattle.
16.10.4 The fines imposed shall be payable in kind or by way of a cash equivalent.

17. Traditional festival

17.1 An annual traditional festival shall take place in early March on a date determined by the |Hôa|aran||aixa||aes Traditional Authority.

17.2 The traditional festival shall be attended by all the members of the |Hôa|aran||aixa||aes community, together with invited guests and interested parties.

18. Recommendations

18.1 Recommendations in connection with the Laws of the |Hôa|aran||aixa||aes may be sent to the Secretary of the |Hôa|aran||aixa||aes Traditional Authority.

19. Amendments

19.1 The laws of the |Hôa|aran||aixa||aes may be amended or repealed by a two-thirds majority of the community after proposals favoured by a two-thirds majority of the community.

CERTIFICATE OF CONSENT TO PUBLISH

Certificate of the consent to publish

UNIVERSITY OF NAMIBIA

FACULTY OF LAW

HUMAN RIGHTS AND DOCUMENTATION CENTRE

RE: CONSENT TO PUBLICATION

I, the undersigned, Chief of the /HOA /ARA //AIXA //AES Traditional Authority, hereby give consent to the Human Rights and Documentation Centre, to publish the following documents of the /HOA /ARA //AIXA //AES Traditional Authority:

1. The Customary Laws
2. The Community Profile
3. Picture of the Chief
4. Logo of the Traditional Authority

I acknowledge that the Human Rights and Documentation Centre will publish the laws in our indigenous language (DAMARA -NAMA), as well as the English language. I am familiar with the contents of the laws that will be published and further acknowledge that they were prepared by my traditional authority.

Signed on this 19 **day of** July **2012**

At WINDHOEK

Dantze

Chief (ACTING)

For HRDC: A. Gairiseb

AFRIKANER TRADITIONAL AUTHORITY
/HOA/ARAN //AIXA//AES
P.O. BOX 857
MARIENTAL
TEL: 063 - 242542

Blouwes Traditional Authority
ǁHaboben !Khara!oan !Haos

The supreme leader of the ǁHaboben (Veldskoendraer) and
!Khara-!Oan Traditional Authorities,
commonly known as the Blouwes Traditional Authority was
Acting *Gaob*[1] Moses Jacobs (above).[2]
Date of designation: 23 April 2009
He passed away on 6 May 2012.
Johannes Barman was accepted by the community in an acting capacity.

1 Traditional title in terms of section 11, Traditional Authorities Act, 2000 (No. 25 of 2000).
2 The Blouwes Traditional Authority did not submit a coat of arms.

PROFILE[3]

Governance

The Blouwes traditional community has an ancient history. It was gazetted by the Namibian Government after Independence in terms of the Traditional Authorities Act, and consists of a Chief, six Senior Councillors, six Junior Councillors and a Council Secretary.

The main activities of the governing body are to:

(a) ensure that government development programmes reach the intended beneficiaries.

(b) ensure, in cooperation with the relevant authorities and the police, that peace and stability are maintained, and

(c) help ensure that information on government policies reaches rural areas and is correctly understood and interpreted.

Main seat

The Blouwes Traditional Authority's main seat is located in the Berseba constituency of the Karas Region. One drives for 40 km down the B1 road from Keetmanshoop, and then 20 km north-east to reach the settlement, which measures about 341 262 ha in total.

Citizens

Children

The communal area inhabited by the Blouwes consists of a number of households scattered over a radius of 50 km. Children can only attend school if they leave their core family area and move to other relatives who live in the centre of Berseba village so that they can go to school there.

Because approximately 65% of the women are single mothers, they find it very difficult to provide adequate financial and material assistance to their children.

Women

Like all rural women elsewhere in Namibia, those in the Blouwes area live in social and economic backwaters. The majority of rural women have not benefited from formal education opportunities due to a gender bias which has persisted for decades. As a result, many women are hard-pressed to find gainful employment.

3 This profile was provided by the ||Haboben and !Khara-!Oan Traditional Authorities.

Men

Although slightly better off than women, the men endure economic hardship as well. Few find employment outside their traditional community. Their lack of skills is exploited, so they make extremely minimal contributions to the economic stability of households.

The elders

Prior to colonial times, kings or traditional leaders and their successors were from the royal houses. During these times, elders were consulted before final decisions were taken on appointing kings. There were different weights attached to opinions provided by elders based on the roles and responsibilities of their households in the community. For example, those households responsible for farming land, wildlife management and water management did not have major influence on appointment of the kings. Those households responsible for safety and security, spiritual leadership and sorcery had an influence on the appointment of the king, but also limited gain from their responsibilities. Elders of those households which were related to the kingship had the largest influence when appointing the king.

Elders were very much involved in transferring knowledge and skill since ancient times. Traditional ceremonies for weddings, funerals, rituals, for example, were continuously transferred to younger generations. Identification, monitoring and implementation of problem-solving was traditionally tasked to community elders. Even if an elder was not from a household with specific responsibilities, individual and collective wisdom of elders were employed in resolving challenges faced by the community.

Since the establishment of the Tses reserve in 1935, the !Khara-!Oa and ǁHaboben communities lived together with members from other Nama clans. The headman was needed by the Bantu Commissioner and as such the headman reported to the commissioner. The standard approach was that the commissioner would request the community to nominate someone for him so that he could appoint the person (headman) for services required. This is where the roles and responsibilities of the elders were slightly changed again to what we are experiencing in the current day. The elders were primarily tasked with identifying and nominating the candidate but did not take the final decision in appointing the headman.

With achievement of Namibia's independence, traditional authorities were registered and gazetted. The government to some extent restored old traditional methods as an approach for resource management. For example, water-point committees, conservancies, farmland management, etc. The roles and responsibilities of the elders were also restored to a large extent although household responsibilities are not in sections. For example, their roles in traditional ceremonies, knowledge and skills transfers, problem-solving, etc.

The roles, responsibilities and mandate of the elders can thus be summarized as follows:

(a) to provide consultative services to the community via the Chief, Blouwes Traditional Authority and also directly to the community members as part of knowledge and skills transfer.

(b) to make themselves available to engage and assist in resolving challenges faced by the community.

(c) as part of knowledge and skills transfer, to be involved in recording, sharing and instilling cultural values of the community.

(d) to recommend a candidate as traditional leader, the Chief, to the Traditional Authority. This means that they must deliberate on potential leaders for the community and finally recommend their selected candidate to the Traditional Authority. Their recommendation shall be endorsed by the Traditional Authority, followed by the normal appointment process, and

(e) to deliberate on and recommend candidates for traditional council to the Chief, but in this case the mandate lies with the Chief for appointment of the councillors.

Problems affecting the community:

(a) Drought and environmental degradation
(b) Insufficient water supply
(c) Unemployment
(d) Poverty
(e) Lack of awareness regarding hygiene
(f) HIV and AIDS
(g) School dropouts
(h) Early childhood pregnancy
(i) Alcohol and drug abuse

Physical and biological features

The northern area is dominated by the limestone plateau, while the eastern and southern parts are flat or undulating with panveld and some dolerite outcrops. Wildlife includes springbok, oryx and kudu. Jackals are common, and prey on farmers' livestock. Other animals include steenbok and hares. The vegetation of the area is dwarf shrub savanna.

Land use

The land is mainly used for livestock grazing. Some people are also engaged in home gardening.

Socio-economic features

The Blouwes area is divided into seven zones, as follows:
(a) Bloukuil
(b) Komnarib
(c) Kalk
(d) Tsawisis-Kameelrivier
(e) Blouwes
(f) !Nomexas
(g) Vergenoeg-Weltevrede

There are about 255 households inside the Blouwes area, with an average of six members per household. Most residents are Nama, but there are also some Damara, Ovaherero, Aawambo, and so-called Coloureds living in the area. Most residents are Christians. They attend the African Methodist Episcopal (AME) Church, the Evangelical Lutheran Church in the Republic of Namibia (ELCRN), the Roman Catholic Church and Pinkster Churches. The Blouwes area has one primary school, as well as a privately-run school hostel. There is no public transport available in the vicinity, so residents either hitchhike or use donkey- or horse-drawn carts.

Development

Development projects targeting Blouwes have included the following:
(a) Registration of communal land
(b) Installation of rural electrification
(c) Installation of a rural water supply
(d) Establishment of a community conservancy
(e) Setting up of a Conservancy Office
(f) Setting up of a campsite
(g) Setting up of a Traditional Activity Office
(h) Establishment of a private school hostel
(i) Establishment of a primary school
(j) Establishment of a farmers' association
(k) Building of an abattoir
(l) Establishment of a poultry farm
(m) Establishment of a hoodia farm
(n) Establishment of aquaculture, i.e. farming of freshwater fish
(o) Establishment of a community garden, and
(p) Various training programmes.

The laws of the Blouwes[1]

1 The laws of the Blouwes were submitted in English only.

1. Legal framework

1.1 The Traditional Authorities Act, 2000 (No. 25 of 2000) empowers every traditional community to establish a Traditional Authority consisting of:
(a) the supreme leader of that traditional community
(b) Senior Councillors, and/or
(c) Councillors.

2. Core concepts

2.1 The Laws of the Blouwes are based on generally accepted practices or habits and conventions, norms, rules of procedure, traditions and usages of the Blouwes traditional community insofar as they do not conflict with the Namibian Constitution or with any other written law applicable in Namibia.

2.2 The following core concepts are defined in order to strengthen the understanding of and enlighten the traditional community in respect of relevant processes in the community and in Namibia:

2.2.1 *Traditional community* shall mean a social grouping of persons:
(a) comprising families originating from the ǁHawo-ben and !Kharo-!oan clans.
(b) sharing a common language, cultural heritage, customs and traditions.
(c) recognising a common Traditional Authority.
(d) inhabiting a common communal area and shall include members that reside outside such communal area.

2.2.2 *Member* of a traditional community shall include:
(a) a person whose parent or parents belong to such traditional community.
(b) any person who is married to or adopted by an existing member, and
(c) any person who, through other circumstances, has adopted the culture and tradition of the traditional community and has been accepted by the majority of the traditional community as a member.

2.2.3 *Councillor* shall mean a member of the traditional community appointed to the Chief's Council, and

2.2.4 *Traditional leader* shall mean the Chief of the traditional community.

3. The core objectives of the Blouwes Traditional Authority

3.1 The Blouwes Traditional Authority was established by the Blouwes traditional community through elections and appointments to promote, maintain and instil:
(a) the provisions of the Traditional Authorities Act.
(b) peace and prosperity among community members.
(c) the language, cultural heritage, customs and traditions of the traditional community.

(d) a spirit of responsibility and accountability amongst community members, and

(e) customary practices into codified and enforceable customary law.

4. Applicability of the laws of the Blouwes

4.1 The laws of the Blouwes shall apply to all members of the Blouwes traditional community, and only to such members.

5. Geographic location

5.1 The Blouwes Traditional Authority shall have jurisdiction over the members of the traditional community inhabiting the current total area of 341 262 km^2.

5.2 Through historic, current and future endeavours, the established communal area may exceed 341 262 km^2, provided such changes follow duly regulated processes.

5.3 Provision for the potential expansion of the total communal area is anticipated because the traditional community consists of two Nama clans, namely the ǁHaboben and the !Khara !Oan which is unique to the Nama, as well as other Namibian traditional communities.

6. Population

6.1 The Blouwes pride themselves on their unique position of having combined two clans.

6.2 The Blouwes shall, thus, continuously conduct censuses to verify and maintain their basic population data to ensure the Blouwes Traditional Authority is empowered to execute their core responsibilities.

7. Symbolic values

7.1 Flag

7.1.1 The flag of the Blouwes traditional community consists of three colours: blue, white and red.

7.1.2 The red background colour is vertically divided into two equal parts by a blue line.

7.1.3 The left-hand side of the flag has white lines, while the right-hand side has white dots.

7.1.4 The blue colour represents perseverance and endurance; the white colour symbolises peace and tranquillity, and the red colour represents blood or heroism and emancipation or freedom.

7.2 Language

7.2.1 The official language of the Blouwes traditional community shall be Nama, although English shall be acknowledged as the official language of the Republic of Namibia, where the traditional community resides.

7.2.2 Customary or ordinary community activities and communication by the traditional community shall be in Nama.

7.2.3 A community member who is not sufficiently expert in Nama because he/she became a member through marriage, adoption or some other means shall be encouraged to learn and uphold the language.

7.2.4 Interaction and association with other Nama traditional communities shall also be in Nama.

7.2.5 Interaction with the Namibian Government shall be in English.

7.2.6 Interaction with other traditional communities shall be in English.

7.2.7 Interaction and relationship-building with foreign nations shall be in English.

7.3 Commemoration

7.3.1 The Blouwes traditional community shall honour and celebrate significant contributions and events in the life of the community.

7.3.2 Such commemorations include:
- (a) traditional festivals, prayers and thanksgiving
- (b) the remembrance of heroes of the traditional community, and
- (c) national and international commemorations.

8. Cultural values

8.1 The Blouwes traditional community accepts and upholds social and religious structures as well as intellectual and artistic manifestations at the core of our existence which shape and characterise our community, and shall accord due recognition to:
- (a) the protection and preservation of culture, language, tradition and related relevant traditional community values.
- (b) the familiarisation, presentation and promotion of traditional ceremonies.
- (c) safeguarding, maintaining and expanding the construction of cultural heritage sites which have immense historic, economic and spiritual value, and
- (d) encouraging the customary way of life in Nama traditional communities, including the concepts that:
  - (i) every human being is very important.
  - (ii) every human being shall be treated with the utmost respect in life and in death.
  - (iii) no human being shall ever be compared to an animal or any object.

(iv) the wisdom of one's elders shall be utilised.
(v) the strong shall look after the weak.
(vi) one shall not ignore an elder or child in need.
(vii) messages from the natural world, whether good or bad, shall be observed, communicated and appreciated, and
(viii) taboos on hunting, sharing meals, the use of sharp objects and the means of communication with a pregnant woman shall be observed.

8.2 Cultural activities for entertainment including traditional dances such as the well-known *Nama-*ǂab (*Namastap*) and *Langarm*, which are an essential part of community life, shall also be used to promote traditional community values.

9. Religious values

9.1 Nama traditional communities have always believed and praised a supreme being, resembling the Christian God.

9.2 The Nama in Namibia today accept and uphold Christianity as their main spiritual belief system and instrument of moral control.

9.3 In view of the fact that Namibia is a secular state, the Blouwes traditional community will respect any other religious practice(s) or any views held by those who do not practise religion, provided such practices and views have no harmful effects on the community's social fabric.

10. Ethical values

10.1 Every member of the Blouwes traditional community is obliged to conform to and uphold ethical behaviour and practices that have evolved over the years.

10.2 Community members must, therefore, regard themselves as leaders and custodians of their own ethical behaviour whilst upholding and adhering to the following core principles:
(a) Honesty and fulfilment
(b) Transparency and thoroughness
(c) Integrity and righteousness
(d) Responsibility and accountability
(e) Respect and tolerance
(f) Authority with consultation, and
(g) Appreciation and sharing.

11. Code of conduct

11.1 The spirit and foundation of the Blouwes traditional community comprises values that have evolved over time and are recorded in the laws of the Blouwes, which emphatically aspire to respecting, protecting and valuing human dignity and life.

11.2 Human dignity and life shall, thus, be jealously guarded in the fulfilment of the Word of the Creator, our God.

11.3 The property and other assets of members of the traditional community shall also be protected by the laws of the Blouwes in order to ensure the prosperity of the entire community.

11.4 The following intentional acts shall be prohibited within the Blouwes traditional community:

(a) Adultery
(b) Theft
(c) Physical or emotional assault
(d) Rape, including within marriage
(e) Murder
(f) Indecent behaviour
(g) Abuse of drugs and alcohol
(h) Spreading false information, e.g. spreading false accusations of witchcraft that would incriminate a victim; defamation of character
(i) Forceful dispossession of assets
(j) Depriving a widow or widower of his/her entitlements
(k) Depriving orphans of their entitlements
(l) Any form of denying children their legitimate rights, and
(m) Abuse of trust or authority.

11.5 Any community member who commits any of the above acts shall be subjected to but not limited to the following:

11.5.1 For less serious offences such as e.g. gossip or indecent behaviour, the member shall undergo counselling by a competent and qualified counsellor or member of the Chief's Council.

11.5.2 For more serious offences, such as e.g. rape or murder, the following procedures shall apply:

(a) All the parties involved shall be accorded equal opportunity to explain and/or justify their circumstances and actions.
(b) A judgment based on rational sense taking into account all the factors at play shall compel the guilty party to repent and compensate the victim or reconcile with the victim.
(c) After following and completing due process, the guilty party shall be presumed to have paid his/her fine or served his/her sentence, and shall thus be protected against any form of intimidation or further prosecution.

11.5.3 Criminal cases such as rape or murder shall be referred directly to the Community Court or to the Magistrate's Court in Keetmanshoop.

11.6 Court decisions shall be based on the processes described in section 11.5 of the laws of the Blouwes and any repentance, compensation or reconciliation claimed shall be in line with the prevailing laws in the Republic of Namibia.

11.7 The Traditional Authority shall be empowered to banish the guilty party from communal land if his/her behaviour has become intolerable.

11.8 For the intentional acts listed in section 11.4 of the laws of the Blouwes, the following will apply:

11.8.1 Adultery

(a) The parties involved shall be advised to undergo voluntary counselling, after which the relevant recommendations and decisions shall be implemented.
(b) If the Chief or members of the Traditional Authority are involved in acts of adultery, they shall be liable for suspension as soon as the act becomes a nuisance to the community and is reported to the Traditional Authority.

11.8.2 Theft

(a) The culprit shall first offer an apology, and shall then compensate the victim as agreed by all parties involved.
(b) The victim of theft shall be within his/her rights to approach the police directly, but he/she shall report the matter to the Traditional Authority as well for statistical and management purposes.

11.8.3 Physical or emotional assault

(a) The perpetrator shall offer the victim an apology and reconciliation, which shall include compensation for medical and other costs incurred.
(b) The victim of an assault shall be within his/her rights to approach the police directly, but he/she shall report the matter to the Traditional Authority as well.

11.8.4 Rape, including within marriage

(a) For rape by a spouse, the Traditional Authority shall ensure that the victim is informed of all available institutions for counselling and shall be encouraged to consult such institutions voluntarily.
(b) The onus shall be on the victim to take further steps against the spouse.
(c) In all other cases of rape, the police shall be approached directly and the Traditional Authority must be informed of the case as well.

11.8.5 Murder

(a) Murder is a police matter, which means it shall be referred directly to a Magistrate's Court.

11.8.6 Indecent behaviour

(a) The perpetrator shall offer an apology to the victim and shall pay an agreed compensation for any material damages.

11.8.7 Abuse of drugs and alcohol

(a) The perpetrator shall offer an apology to the victim and shall pay an agreed compensation for any material damages.
(b) The perpetrator shall also be strongly encouraged to undergo counselling at the available institutions within Namibia.

11.8.8 Spreading of false information

(a) The perpetrator shall apologise without losing dignity at public meetings for a stipulated period of time as agreed during counselling or at a hearing.

11.8.9 Forceful dispossession of assets

(a) The Traditional Authority shall ensure that all assets thus dispossessed are restored to their rightful owner and that due compensation is made.
(b) The perpetrator shall abide by the ruling of the Traditional Authority and/or shall be taken to a Magistrate's Court.

11.8.10 Depriving a widow or widower of his/her entitlements

(a) The Traditional Authority shall ensure that any deprivation of just entitlements to a surviving spouse is rectified and compensated.
(b) The perpetrator shall abide by the ruling of the Traditional Authority and/or shall be taken to a Magistrate's Court.

11.8.11 Depriving orphans of their entitlements

(a) The Traditional Authority shall ensure that any deprivation of just entitlements to a surviving child is rectified and compensated.
(b) The perpetrator shall abide by the ruling of the Traditional Authority and/or shall be taken to a Magistrate's Court.

11.8.12 Any form of denying children their legitimate rights

(a) The Traditional Authority shall ensure that all the necessary efforts are made to promote children's rights.
(b) Any person who violates the rights of a child shall abide by the ruling of the Traditional Authority and/or shall be taken to a Magistrate's Court.

11.8.13 Abuse of trust and authority

(a) The perpetrator shall remove him-/herself from such office or shall distance him-/herself from the victim of such abuse.
(b) The perpetrator shall be given time and opportunity to repent and prove him-/herself worthy of such trust or authority before being awarded any related office in future.

12. Community Court

12.1 The Blouwes Community Court shall be established and shall operate with defined powers and in line with the Namibian Constitution for the sole benefit of the Blouwes traditional community.

12.2 The Blouwes Community Court shall:
(a) be located within the Blouwes Settlement Area in order to:
  (i) conduct matters in a secure and fair manner, and
  (ii) deal with offences violating the community Code of Conduct;
(b) be manned by magistrates and clerks who are thoroughly knowledgeable about the customary values of the Blouwes traditional community, and
(c) refer all cases which are beyond its competence, especially capital offences such as rape and murder, to the relevant courts vested with more power and authority.

13. Resource management

13.1 The Blouwes traditional community is appreciative of all its available resources and strives to utilise such resources sustainably in order to ensure that:
(a) such resources are used optimally and to the benefit of present and future generations.
(b) the environment is preserved for current and future generations, and
(c) such resources remain available for the benefit of the entire Blouwes traditional community.

14. Natural resources

14.1 Non-renewable natural resources such as precious stones shall be explored and mined with the necessary competence and expertise and in a sustainable manner to ensure:
(a) no harm is done to the environment, and
(b) the best possible value is obtained.

14.2 Renewable natural resources shall be utilised with the necessary competence and expertise and in a sustainable manner to ensure:
(a) the economic sustainability of the community, and
(b) the entire community benefits in respect of their health and the creation of wealth.

15. Human resources

15.1 All community members are required to make themselves available to serve the community and allow the entire community to prosper.

15.2 Since its members are probably the community's most valuable resource, both the Traditional Authority and the traditional community are required to:

(a) treasure and develop members' skills through training and exposure.

(b) create and maintain an environment that is conducive to education.

(c) create and provide opportunities to community members to share their talents, and

(d) provide the necessary support to community members who need mentoring.

16. Other resources

16.1 All other resources acquired through any other means, including donations, access to funds and partnerships with other communities or governments must be handled with the utmost diligence and appreciation for such resources.

16.2 These resources in most cases require feedback to their providers/partners and thus good governance shall be exercised in order to ensure that:

(a) good relationships are maintained.

(b) all actions are transparent and benefit all members of the community, and

(c) the Blouwes traditional community is able to assist other communities if necessary.

17. Composition and core responsibilities of the Blouwes Traditional Authority

17.1 The Blouwes Traditional Authority established in terms of section 2(1) of the Traditional Authorities Act comprises:

(a) a Chief, the supreme leader

(b) Senior Councillors, and

(c) Councillors.

17.2 The core objectives of the Traditional Authority constitute but are not limited to those in section 3 of the laws of the Blouwes.

17.3 Customary law with limited powers is applicable to the Blouwes traditional community only.

17.4 Councillors

17.4.1 Any capable and committed community member shall make him-/herself available for traditional leadership.

17.4.2 Each Councillor shall comply with the following minimum requirements:

(a) either be married or be a widow or widower in order to ensure a sense of responsibility; an exception to this requirement may be made if a community member has a satisfactory track record, i.e. he/she leads an exemplary lifestyle and has no criminal record.
(b) have leadership potential and be worthy of being entrusted with the duty of serving as a Councillor in order to ensure reliable and valued contributions are made.
(c) not be involved in any activities contradicting the laws of the Blouwes in order to ensure the credibility of the Traditional Authority.
(d) have a clear understanding that the Chief is empowered to terminate his/her appointment if he/she fails to perform or performs poorly in his/her position, and
(e) be able to serve a term of 5 (five) years.

17.4.3 A Councillor shall be nominated, elected and/or appointed either by the traditional community or by the Chief.

17.4.4 The Chief shall be entitled to appoint 2 (two) Senior Councillors and 2 (two) Councillors without an election.

17.4.5 The remaining Councillors shall be appointed by way of elections.

17.5 Chief

17.5.1 The Blouwes traditional community shall designate a chief as their supreme leader.

17.5.2 Due to the fact that this traditional community embraces two Nama clans, the Chief cannot be appointed from the Royal Family.

17.5.3 The Chief's qualifications, term of office, removal from office, succession, and powers shall be as follows:

17.5.4 Qualifications

17.5.4.1 The Chief is the custodian of the customary law, the promoter of peace and tranquillity, the echo of fundamental values, the foundation of leadership, and the engineer of prosperity for the traditional community.

17.5.4.2 Thus, the Chief is required to be a Blouwes traditional community member who:

(a) has served the community through employment in the private or public sector, including by way of self-employment, to ensure he/she understands and appreciates that earning comes from serving.
(b) is either married or widowed, in order to ensure that he/she not only portrays an exemplary role to the community, but also has a sense of responsibility and accountability.
(c) has demonstrated his/her capability and holds a proven track record that shows he/she can lead, inspire and provide an environment of hope and prosperity to the traditional community in order to ensure its development.

(d) is a member of the community by birth into the ǁHaboben and !Khara!oan clans, in order to ensure the community's cultural heritage is valued at all times.
(e) has demonstrated and upheld the core ethical behaviour stipulated in these Laws under section 10, "Ethical values", in order to ensure such values are echoed by the leadership, and
(f) while accepting the position and provision of the Traditional Authority Act (No. 25 of 2000), the Chief is preferably available full-time, notwithstanding the provisions of the Traditional Authorities Act, which permits a part-time incumbent.

17.5.5 Term of office

17.5.5.1 The Chief shall hold office for a minimum of 7 (seven) years, after which he/she may be appointed through elections for another term.
17.5.5.2 The maximum number of terms that any one incumbent Chief shall be permitted to serve is 3 (three), which is the equivalent of 21 (twenty-one) years.
17.5.5.3 The term of 7 (seven) years will provide the Chief with ample time to execute his/her plans and duties.
17.5.5.4 The Chief shall be replaced through elections administered by the Traditional Authority within the provisions of the Traditional Authorities Act after his/her current term expires.

17.5.6 Removal from office and succession

17.5.6.1 The Chief may be removed and replaced by another before his/her term of office expires if the traditional community finds sufficient reason to do so and the qualification process prescribed in section 17.5.4, "Qualifications", is followed for such replacement.
17.5.6.2 The following reasons shall be deemed sufficient for the removal of a Chief from office:
(a) If the Chief dies or is rendered incapable of performing the functions of his/her office, provided that the Chief shall first be given the option to resign voluntarily for health reasons, which shall be followed by a referendum requesting the traditional community to decide the issue.
(b) If the Chief is found grossly negligent in failing to uphold and protect the customary law of which he/she is the custodian, provided that such failure has been proved and such removal recommended by an investigation committee appointed by the relevant Minister.
(c) If the Chief is involved in criminal activities and is found guilty in a court of law, he/she shall be requested to tender his/her resignation which shall be administered through the process stipulated in the Traditional Authorities Act.
(d) The Chief shall also not be involved in any activities that are aimed at exercising political influence on members of the traditional community.

17.5.7 Powers

17.5.7.1 The powers of the Chief shall be limited to the Traditional Authority and its traditional community in the service of upholding the laws of the Blouwes in accordance with the core objectives recorded in section 3 herein.

17.5.7.2 The Chief shall thus be empowered by the laws of the Blouwes to develop and maintain his/her administration in the most humane and efficient manner, which includes:

(a) designing administrative structures and profiles for Councillors
(b) scheduling meetings for Councillors and the community
(c) setting strategic goals and implementing such goals
(d) establishing a code of conduct specifically for traditional Councillors
(e) providing final decisions on issues in dispute during Traditional Authority management sessions, the prioritisation of projects and management matters, and
(f) appointing technical teams, tactical teams and/or consultants through the Traditional Authority as the need arises.

18. Special provisions

18.1 The Blouwes traditional community consists of two Nama clans which share a common language, culture and land, and which are governed by common customary laws.

18.2 Nonetheless each clan has its own memorable historic events that need to be recognised and celebrated.

18.3 Such commemorations shall be performed and celebrated without discrimination, with respect, in honour, and in peace.

18.4 The Chief and Traditional Authority shall be fully consulted for such commemorations because they are ultimately responsible for the peace and stability of the traditional community.

19. Amendments

19.1 The laws of the Blouwes are regarded as living law and, as such, are subject to amendments and deletions as determined from time to time by ever-unfolding demands for change.

19.2 The laws of the Blouwes, their customary practices or elements thereof shall be amended only with the explicit approval of a two thirds majority of the participating community members.

19.3 For any constitutional amendment to be considered valid, such amendment will be preceded by a referendum to decide on the amendment.

Certificate of consent to publish

Certificate of the consent to publish

UNIVERSITY OF NAMIBIA

FACULTY OF LAW

HUMAN RIGHTS AND DOCUMENTATION CENTRE

RE: CONSENT TO PUBLICATION

I, the undersigned, Chief of the BLOU- WES Traditional Authority, hereby give consent to the Human Rights and Documentation Centre, to publish the following documents of the BLOU-WES Traditional Authority:

1. The Customary Laws
2. The Community Profile
3. Picture of the Chief
4. Logo of the Traditional Authority

I acknowledge that the Human Rights and Documentation Centre will publish the laws in our indigenous language (AFRIKANS), as well as the English language. I am familiar with the contents of the laws that will be published and further acknowledge that they were prepared by my traditional authority.

Signed on this 30 **day of** SEPT **2012**

At KEETMANSHOOP

____

Chief CHAIRMAN J Botma

____

For HRDC: Mr. A. Gairiseb

Blouwes Traditional Authority
Box 2105, Keetmanshoop
Tel:
Blouwes / Namibia

Bondelswartz Traditional Authority
!Gami ǂnun !hao!nasi ǂGaeǂguis

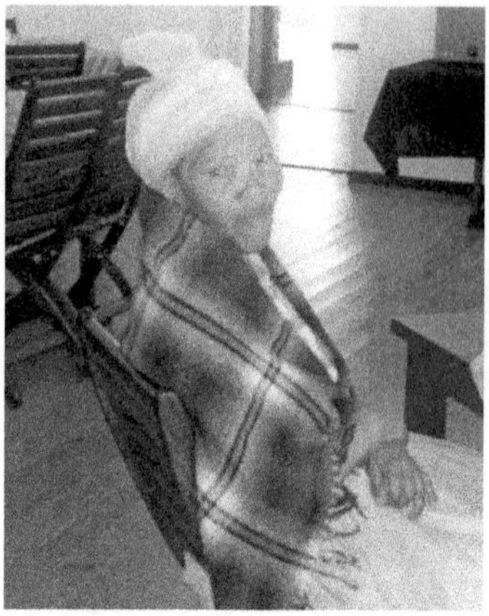 

The supreme leader of the !Gami ǂnun (Bondelswartz) Traditional Authority was *Gaos*[1] Anna Katrina Christiaan (left).
Date of designation 20 May 1974
She passed away on 7 September 2011.
The Acting *Gaob* was Joseph Christiaan (right).
He passed away on 19 June 2015[2].

God's work is wonderful

Bondelswarts Traditional Authority

!Gami ǂnûn /hao !nasi ǂgae ǂguis

!Khūb Sisengu ge a Buruxa

1 Traditional title in terms of section 11, Traditional Authorities Act, 2000 (No. 25 of 2000).

2 Joseph Christiaan had not been formally designated; there was no information on the appointment of an acting supreme leader or a successor to the supreme leader of the community at the time of going to press.

PROFILE[3]

The structural existence of the !Gami ǂnun (Bondelswartz) degenerated because of German colonial rule and as such they never regained self-determination during or after German interference. The subsequent South African illegal occupation further weakened tribal coherence, with the result that authority over subjects could not be exercised effectively – more so than with any other tribal group in Namibia. Consequently, the Bondelswartz' collective hold on the land they communally used and cared for was taken away by the very same foreigners and alienated by force. As their ownership was not individual, it was easy for the foreigners to draw up title deeds for themselves. Many members of the Bondelswartz community joined their brethren in towns as labourers while others tried to eke out a living on a diminished and thus overcrowded piece of reserved territory.

Just and fair compensation shall be paid for loss of land when determining boundaries. However, this does not preclude the return of legally acquired historical Bondelswartz land by non-Bondelswartz occupiers. Thus, acknowledgement should be given in the event of loss of land when determining boundaries and the subsequent consideration for compensatory purposes.

If, on the other hand, private utilisation is unavoidable, such users shall recognise that the Bondelswartz Traditional Authority, i.e. the *Gaos/Gaob* (Captain) and the Tribal Council have the right to negotiate levies on land use in conjunction with government of the day. After the rightful reallocation of land, subject to Article 16(2) of the Namibian Constitution, further rights on land shall be exercised and administered by the Bondelswartz Traditional Authority in its territory.

In acknowledgement of Section 1(1) of the Traditional Authorities Act, 2000 (No. 25 of 2000), any person alien to the Bondelswartz community shall be discouraged to acquire land within the said territory as such acquisition would impede the homogeneous application of customary law.

The Captain shall be regarded and recognised as the traditional head of the Traditional Authority over territory inclusive of land paid for by Bondelswartz or for the Bondelswartz in other territories such as the Gibeon District under the Odendaal Plan. Compensation shall be given for expropriation of said land, and the Traditional Authority shall aid with resettlement onto traditional Bondelswartz territory or declared privately owned farms of Bondelswartz individuals.

The Captain of the Bondelswartz binds him-/herself to bear authority over his/her subjects and territory.

3 This profile was provided by the !Gami ǂnun Traditional Authority.

THE LAWS OF THE !GAMI ǂNUN (BONDELSWARTZ)[1]

1 The laws of the Bondelswartz were submitted in English only.

Section 1: Definitions/interpretations

1.1 In this customary law, unless the context indicates otherwise:

(a) *Captain* means a Chief as per the Traditional Authorities Act, 2000 (No. 25 of 2000) and named Captain of the Bondelswartz community, who shall be its supreme traditional leader.

(b) C*ommunal land* means the communal area as per the Traditional Authority Act 2000 including any other land belonging to or occupied by the Bondelswartz for valid reasons, and any traditional land as per Section 2 of this Bondelswartz Constitution.

(c) C*ustomary law* refers to the Bondelswartz traditional community's customs, norms, rules of procedure, traditions, usages, and other aspects not mentioned here.

(d) *Traditional community* means the Bondelswartz community:
- (i) who are indigenous and homogeneous
- (ii) whose endogamous social grouping comprises families deriving from exogamous clans with a common ancestry, language, cultural heritage, and common customs and traditions
- (iii) who recognise the Bondelswartz Traditional Authority, and
- (iv) who inhabit the Bondelswartz communal area, including those who live outside the Bondelswartz communal area.

(e) *Traditional community member* means someone who:
- (i) has either one parent or both parents belonging to the Bondelswartz traditional community.
- (ii) is a member by way of marriage to or adoption by a member of the Bondelswartz, who has assimilated the culture and tradition of the Bondelswartz, and who has been accepted by the Bondelswartz as their member.

(f) *Traditional head* means the Captain.

(g) *Traditional leader* means any one of the Traditional Councillors elected by community members or appointed by the Captain.

(h) *Supreme Council* means the sole body of the Bondelswartz traditional community entrusted with the power to select and designate the Captain, and remove him/her from office.

(i) *Gao‖gâus* means the Royal House, which comprises 3 (three) chambers.

(j) *Gao-omams* means the Chamber of the Royal House where one finds the Captain and his/her sons, and which provides the directly eligible candidates to the royal throne.

(k) *Ai-omams* means the Chamber of the Royal House where one finds the Captain's brothers.

(l) *!Oa-omams* means the Chamber of the Royal House where one finds the Captain's sisters and extended family.

(m) *Vice-captain* means a Senior Traditional Councillor elected by the community.

Section 2: Traditional land

2.1 Bondelswartz traditional land includes any part of the land that has been allocated to the Bondelswartz Traditional Authority and/or that falls under its area of jurisdiction.[2]

2.2 No person has the right to sell such traditional land or to negotiate its sale.

2.3 No person is entitled to claim ownership over any part of such traditional land.

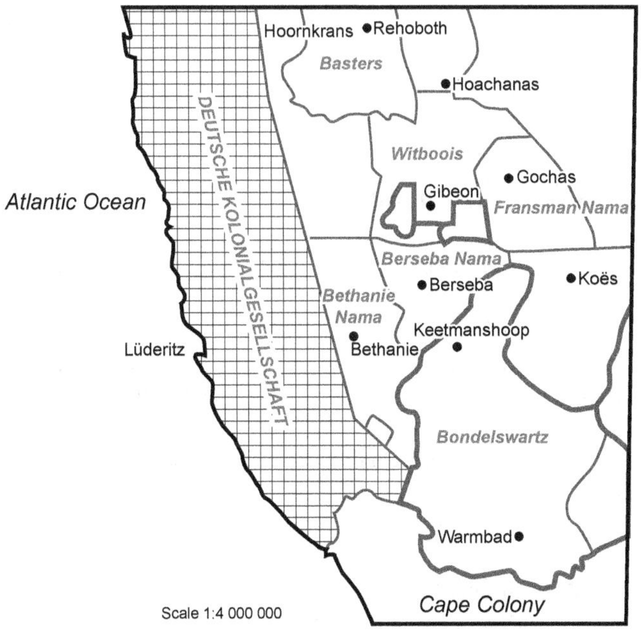

This map is based on the 1902 map of South West Africa by Dietrich Reimer, in Theodor Leutwein: *Elf Jahre Gouverneur in Deutsch-Südwestafrika.*

Section 3: Main seat

3.1 The main seat of the Bondelswartz is Warmbad, where the discovery of a spring led to the unforgotten and unforgiving history of the Bondelswartz.

Section 4: Traditional emblem

4.1 The following traditional emblems are part and parcel of the history of the Bondelswartz:

(a) The Warmbad Spring

---

2 Editor's note: The area in respect of which the Bondelswartz Community Court exercises jurisdiction is described in Part 1 of the Schedule to GG 86 of 2009 on the Establishment of Bondelswartz Community Court and appointment of assessors and justices: Community Courts Act, 2003.

(b) The mountain which contained the spring that was discovered with buck and a lion hiding in the grass, and men on top of the mountain
(c) A dog on his way back from the spring, and
(d) The wet footprints of the dog that were later followed by the men.

Section 5: Traditional colours

5.1 The traditional colours are white, blue and black.

5.2 White and black were the original colours of the Bondelswartz, while dark blue was introduced during the German colonial period, when the Germans held what were known as the *Blue Peace* talks with the Bondels even while planning and preparing for war on the sly.

Section 6: Traditional anthem[3]

6.1 The following traditional anthem will be sung at meetings and festivals:

ǁAes Tsanas
Aiǂoasa xu (!Gami-ǂnû ǁnaetsanas)

(2x)	Aiǂoasa xu huriǂoas !oa doe, Karooba xu ǁHui!gaeb ǀkhāb !oa, Gaogu !Hūb ǀNanub, ǀAeb, ǂOab ǂgaeǂgui.	Trekking from East to West, From the Karoo in the direction of the Cape Land of the Kings, Rain, Fire, Wind lead.
(2x)	ǀAexa-aibes, Aogu-ābes, Arigu ǂguro ge hō, ǀgû gere ǀaus Soǀôa axūn, !Gamiǂnû.	'ǀAexa-aibes', place where men drink water, Dogs first found the boiling fountain, Medicine for the Bondelswartz.
	Xoaǁnae-aob: !Nagamab: Josef Rooi 2004/ ǂNūǁnâiseb.	Composer: Josef Rooi, Junior 2004
	!Khō!gâ-aob: !Nae !khaedidib Josef Rooi Gamemâ ǂAriseb: ǂGâbesa xu.	Proposer and seconder of the history: Josef Rooi, Senior Gamemâ ǂAriseb, from Gobis

3 Editor's note: This anthem, by Josef Rooi, Junior, is based on the original 4-stanza poem written in 2004 by Josef Rooi, Senior (see below at 6.2).

6.2 ǁAesi ǁnae tsanas[4]

I
Ai ǂoasa xu Huriǂoas !oa doe -
Karooba xu ǁHu!gaeb ǀkhab !oa
Gaogu !Hūb, ǀNanub, ǀAeb, ǂOab ǂgae-ǂgui
ǁîgu ǂgâ!gâgu tsî gaoga suri
ǂHā !gâgukha Elo-!oabas !Gamiǂnû !nae.

II
!Khub Elob sîsengu buruxa
Xamari ǀgoreǀî ǁae ra !nae kai
Tsēs ai Kai ǁKhaus !Gamiǂnûs !hui
Tsîgu gaoga ǂgai!ā he
!Gariba !gâuxa tsî ǀAwas !oa.

III
Buruxa Elob Khoeb ǁÎb ǂâis !oa kuru
Khoe !hū!khē tsî ǀaude, !û-aide ho
Tsēs ǀAexa-aibes, ǀgû ra ǀaus ho
ǀHau gere ǀau, solôa tsî axun !hūsi ǁui
ǁNaba xu ǀAexa-aibes - Bas t'mi ǂgai.

IV
Sida suri ǁnâuro da, !Khūba gangan
ǂÂis !nâ ǁnâu!nāba ôa tsî sîsen
Sida ǁNaokain, ǁnaoǂkhamn în ǁkhore
Mâpa u da ǀAudi !oa gere !gû
!Khūb sîsengu buruxa Tsēkorobe.

Section 7: Natural resources

7.1 The Bondelswartz are entitled to ancestral rights of use of the land in their communal area.

7.2 The Bondelswartz are entitled to ancestral rights of use of the hot springs in their communal area at Warmbad and Ai-Ais.

7.3 The Bondelswartz are entitled to ancestral rights of use of the minerals, fish and other natural resources in their communal area.

Section 8: Sacred places

8.1 The following are sacred places of the Bondelswartz traditional community:

(a) Grave sites of the Bondelswartz captains where marked
(b) The !Ke-!homs Mountain in Warmbad
(c) Grave sites along the Hom River near Sandfontein, and
(d) The ǀGuruxas and Sandfontein battlefields.

4 It is almost impossible to translate the poetic language into English. The editor accepted the wish of the Bondelswartz traditional community to publish the poem in Khoekhoegowab only.

Section 9: The Royal House (*Gao‖gaus*)

9.1 Composition

9.1.1 Gao-omams

9.1.1.1 The *Gao-omams* is the House (Chamber) of the *Gaob* (Chief) and his sons/family.

9.1.1.2 The *Gao-omams* provides candidates for Captaincy.

9.1.1.3 The *Gao-omams* is responsible for supervising and monitoring customary practices such as the rules of succession and governance.

9.1.2 Ai-omams

9.1.2.1 The *Ai-omams* is the House (Chamber) of the brothers of the Chief (*Gaob*).

9.1.2.2 The Chief's brothers also advise him on matters relating to the Royal House *(Gao‖gaus)*.

9.1.3 !Oa-omams

9.1.3.1 The *!Oa-omams* is the House (Chamber) of other relatives of the *Gaob* (Chief).

9.1.3.2 The members of the *!Oa-omams* Chamber are responsible for any task assigned to them by the *Gao-omams* Chamber.

9.2 Selection of, designation as and succession to the Captain

9.2.1 The Captain is selected and designated from the Christiaan Royal House by the Supreme Council in conjunction with the *Gao‖gâus*.

9.2.2 Only the direct patrilineal descendants of the earliest Bondelswartz leaders, namely the late Captain Willem Christiaan and the late Captain AKA ǂNaoxab, who died in 1901, are entitled to the throne, provided that such descendants are competent to assume the throne and at least 25 years of age.

9.2.3 The Captaincy is a hereditary title in the Bondelswartz traditional community, since title shall be passed from father to son.

9.2.4 It is standing customary practice in the Bondelswartz that:

(a) The Captain shall be succeeded by his eldest son subject to his competency to the throne.

(b) If the eldest son is absent or incompetent to rule, the next eldest son shall succeed.

(c) If the son of the Captain is younger than 25 years, the Supreme Council, in conjunction with the *Gao‖gâus*, shall designate a Vice-captain as Acting Captain.

(d) Such Acting Captain shall return the Captaincy once the eligible successor has reached the age of 25.

(e) In the total absence of a son of the Captain, the Supreme Council, in conjunction with *Gao‖gâus*, shall select a competent brother of the Captain from the *Ai-omams* (Chamber of the Captain's brothers) to succeed.

9.2.5 A Chieftainess or the Regent's own sons may not succeed their parent for they are true descendants of their father's direct family bloodline, which is not the royal bloodline, and consequently are not entitled to the royal bloodline throne.

9.3 Removal of the Captain

9.3.1 The Captain can be removed and succeeded if he:

(a) has been involved in committing or has committed a murder.

(b) has been involved in or has committed theft.

(c) has been involved in or has committed fraud or related crimes.

(d) is in gross violation of Bondelswartz customary law and customary practices.

(e) suffers from ill-health or mental incapacity, which shall be certified by at least 2 (two) medical doctors or clinical psychologists, as the case may be, or

(f) resigns of his own free will.

9.3.2 The grounds for the removal of a Captain must be laid as a formal charge with the Supreme Council for discussion and the launching of a formal investigation.

9.3.3 The outcome of such investigation will be discussed by the Supreme Council in order for them to take a resolution.

9.3.4 The Supreme Council may resolve to discuss the issue with the relevant Captain for possible rectification measures or, if this is not possible, the Council may resolve to remove the Captain.

9.3.5 The resolution of the Supreme Council to remove the Captain will be cause for further discussion among all the members of the Chief's Council in order for this Council to take a resolution on removal.

9.3.6 The resolution of the Chief's Council to remove the Captain will be cause for further discussion among the Chamber of Elders and the Chamber of Women to take a resolution on removal.

9.3.7 The resolution of the Chamber of Elders and the Chamber of Women to remove the Captain will cause the Chief's Council to call a special meeting with the members of the Bondelswartz regarding the removal of the Captain, at which meeting a minimum of 300 members will constitute a mandate.

9.3.8 If the community supports the removal, then the powers and duties of the Captain will cease with immediate effect and the Chief's Council, chaired by the Vice-captain, will take office for the interim period of a maximum of 90 (ninety) days.

9.3.9 The relevant minister will be informed in person if possible of the Captain's removal with full documentation.

9.3.10 At an arranged meeting, the Supreme Council will then select 2 (two) competent candidates as Acting Captain, with motivation.

9.3.11 At the meeting referred to in clause 9.3.10, the Captain's Council, the Chamber of Elders, the Chamber of Women and the Youth Chamber will vote for an Acting Captain.

9.3.12 Within 30 days of election, the Acting Captain will take office under the supervision of the Supreme Council for a period of 3 (three) years, during which period a successor to the Captain will be selected from the Royal House.

9.3.13 The relevant minister will be informed of the identity of the new Acting Captain with full documentation.

9.3.14 If there is a dispute in respect of the removal of the Gaob and the election of the new Acting Gaob, the matter should be directed to a ministerial arbiter with documentary proof and related information.

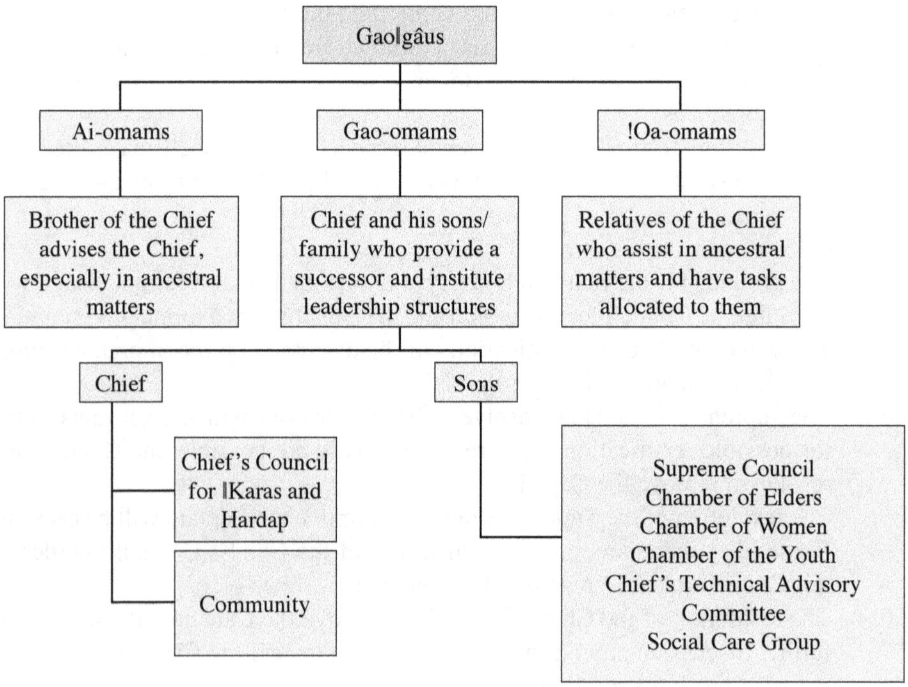

Figure 1: Governing structure

9.4 The Acting Captain

9.4.1 A competent Acting Captain will be selected and designated as such by the Supreme Council in conjunction with the *Gao‖gâus* to hold office for a maximum period of 3 (three) years under the supervision of the Supreme Council and the *Gao‖gâus*:

(a) if the Captain is removed as stated in subsection 9.3.

(b) in the complete absence of a successor from the Christiaan royal bloodline, or

(c) if the descendant from the royal bloodline is younger than 25 years at the time the office of Captain becomes vacant.

Section 10: The Traditional Authority

10.1 The Traditional Authority or leadership of the Bondelswartz will be bound by and restricted to the boundaries of the Bondelswartz traditional territory (communal land) and/or the persons living on such territory.

10.2 The Traditional Authority will also have jurisdiction over persons living on Bondelswartz communal land or land occupied by the Bondelswartz for valid reasons.

10.2 The Traditional Authority will comprise the Captain, the Vice-captain and Traditional Councillors, of which 6 (six) are Senior Traditional Councillors and 6 (six) Traditional Councillors.

Section 11: The Captain (*Gaob*)

11.1 Powers and functions of the Captain

11.1.1 The powers and the functions of the Captain are to:

(a) draft, amend, repeal, uphold and protect the customary law and traditional practices of the Bondelswartz.

(b) motivate, mobilise and organise the Bondelswartz community to the next level of development in respect of traditional, educational and socio-economic spheres.

(c) institute and manage the Customary Courts and the Traditional Fund.

(d) be entitled to appoint members to all levels of traditional leadership.

(e) ensure that all levels of leadership comply with their duties, and uphold and protect the customary law of the Bondelswartz.

(f) appoint and groom a successor if deemed necessary, and notify the Royal House and the leadership accordingly.

(g) be entitled to dismiss a member from the leadership in keeping with the spirit of the Bondelswartz customary law after proper investigation by him or by an investigative body appointed by him.

(h) in crucial matters, have the discretionary right to terminate a member's leadership with immediate effect during an investigation into his/her actions, and shall have the discretionary right to reinstate such a member if deemed necessary.

(i) ensure discerning use of grazing and natural resources.

(j) protect all forms of the ancestral legacy of the Bondelswartz.

(k) represent the Bondelswartz at any level the community requires.

(l) be the official voice of the Royal House and the Bondelswartz traditional community.

(m) be entitled to appoint a spokesperson if needed.

(n) offer advice in tribal conflicts and troubled marriages.
(o) be entitled to call and conduct meetings at all levels of leadership, including annual general meetings with the Bondelswartz traditional community, at which he normally would deliver an address on the state of the Bondelswartz community and provide direction for the road ahead.
(p) have the ancestral right to institute legal action to evict any person who occupies Bondelswartz communal land without the valid approval of the leadership and mandate by the Captain.
(q) be entitled to impose conditions on grazing rights related to the use of commonage in order to serve the traditional community's best interests and to protect such land against misuse, and
(r) be entitled to institute an action for an interdict to remove illegal fences in the Bondelswartz territory.

11.2 Inauguration of the Captain

11.2.1 Only someone who is equal to a Captain or who has been selected by the Supreme Council and the *Gao‖gâus* shall be empowered to inaugurate another Captain.
11.2.2 All inaugurations shall be conducted in the Nama language.

11.2.3 Inauguration procedure

[The inaugurator requests the incoming Captain to rise and face the audience. He then reads the following to him:]

.... [full name], do you believe that the Almighty God is the creator of heaven and earth and also mankind? (Yes, I do.)
Do you believe that God is the King of kings in heaven and on earth? (Yes, I do.)
Do you believe that everything and every soul on earth belongs to the Lord Jesus, the creator, redeemer and the saviour? (Yes, I do.)
Do you believe that God, through the hands of Moses, gave his Ten Commandments to guide mankind through his life on earth? (Yes, I do.)
Do you believe that God is the Lord of all nations, tribes and languages on earth? (Yes, I do.)

.... [full name], do you intend, as the incoming Captain, in keeping with this Christian belief and truth, to advise, mobilise, motivate and lead by example the Bondelswartz community here present, and those in absentia, by their customary law and traditional practices to the next level of human development to become a community living by God's grace and righteousness, and to be a meaningful citizen of the broader Namibian Nation?

Gaob di mâiǂgās do Sao!gûgub

[‖Nauǂgā-aob ǂgâxa ra Gaoba ais ǀkhāb !oa ra ǂgai, îb ga ‖aes !oa ǂnan timî. ‖Îb ge sao ra !âsa ra khomai!â bi:]

.... [ǀoasa ǀons] ǂgom its ta Hoaǀgaixa Elob ǀHommi tsî !Hūbaib tsî ‖khāti khoeb di kuru-ao !khaisa? (Aa, ‖nāti ta ge ra ǂgom.)

ǂGom its ta Elob ǀguib a Gao-aogu di Gao !khaisa, ǀhomi !nâ tsî !hūbaib ai? (Aa, ǁnāti ta ge ra ǂgom.)
ǂGom its ta hoaraga !hūbaib tsî ǀoms hoas a Jexub Xristub, kuru-aob tsî hui-aob di !khaisa? (Aa, ǁnāti ta ge ra ǂgom.)
ǂGom its ta Elob ǁîb di Disi Mmāde Moseb !nâ-ū Khoeba ge māsa, daoǁgau tsî ra ǂgae ǂgui gagab ase, !hūbaib ai? (Aa, ǁnāti ta ge ra ǂgom.)
ǂGom its ta !Hūb a ǁaedi, !haodi tsî gowagu di Elo !khaisa? (Aa, ǁnāti ta ge ra ǂgom.)
.... (ǀoasa ǀons) hāǂgâxa ra Gaots ǂâibasen tsî mîmâi-e khā hâ nē Xristesi ǂgoms tsî (ǀoasa ǀons) Amab di !gao!gaob ai nē ǂnôa tsî ǀkhai a !Gamiǂnûǁaesa, ǀawemā, ǀhaoǀhao, ǁapoǁapo tsî aiǁgaus ǀkha ǂgaeǂguisa !Gamiǂnûǁaes ǂûs di ǂhunuma !Hao!nâsi ǁaesi ǂhanub tsî ǁnaetigu !nâ-ū? Îs ga !Gamiǂnûǁaes ǀgawi !haridi, khoesi omkhâisens dide sī!nâ timî. Tsî ǁkhāti ǁaes Elob di ǀkhommi tsî ǂhanu-aisib ase, !gâi ǂâibasens ǀkha nē !hūb Namibiab !nâ ǁanǂgāsa.

Oath

I, ... [full name], intend as the incoming Captain of the Bondelswartz, to uphold and protect the customary law and ancestral inheritance of the Bondelswartz.
I intend to advise, mobilise and lead by example the Bondelswartz community by their customary law and practices to become God abiding and future driven citizens of the broader Namibian Nation. So help me, Lord, to lead by Thy wisdom as Solomon, the son of David, did.

Mîǁguis

Tita ....ǀoasa ǀons] nîra !Gamiǂnûǁaes di !hao!nâsi ǂhanub tsî Aiǁgûsi ǀomide ǂnoaba tsî !khōǀgarasa !goaxa surib !aroma. Tita ra ǁkhāti ti aiǁgaus ǀkha, !Gamiǂnûǁaesa nîra ǀawemā, ǀhaoǀhao tsî ǁaesi !hao!nâsi ǂhanub tsî ǁnaetigu ǀkha ǂgaeǂgui. ǁKhāti ta ge !Gamiǂnûǁaesa nîra ǂgaeǂgui Elo!ao!gâxa tsî !goaxa ǁaeb xa ra ǂâi!gâ ǁaes ase Namibiab !nâ.
Nēs !nâ hui te re, ti !Khūtse, î ta !Gamiǂnûǁaesa Elosi ga-aisib ǀkha ǂgaeǂgui, Gao-aob Salomob, Davib di ôab ge dī khami.

Declaration

All of you present here today witnessed the oath taken by the incoming Captain, ... [full name]. [The inaugurator puts the robe/token on the Captain.]
I, in my capacity as the .... [capacity], with the power vested in me, officially declare .... [full name] as the Captain of the Bondelswartz community in Namibia. [The inaugurator gives him a Bible and the customary law with a handshake.].

Mîǁawoǁawos

!Gôahesa ba te ǁaes tsî ǂai tani -aon tsî ǀhûǁare – aodu hoado sadu ge ǀnauǂgãhe ra Gaob di mîǁguira nûsa go ǀnâu. [Nauǂgã-aob ge Gaoba ra ana tsî ra mî].
Tita, ..., ta ge nēsi ti ǂaibǀ!hros !nâ hâ ǁkaisib ǀkha !gâsab .... [ǂaib] ba !Gamiǂnû ǁaes, Namibiab dis, di Gaob ase go ǁNauǂgâ tsî ǀawoǀawo. [ǁîb ge Gaoba ǀGuǀgarus tsîra ra mâ tsî tawede.]

Symbolic handover

[Thereafter, the most senior member of the Supreme Council gives the Captain a hat as a token of leadership and shakes his hand.
Then, a member of the *Gaoǁgâus* gives him the rod as a token of direction and shakes his hand.
A spiritual leader then gives him a ring as a token of loyalty to the *Gaoǁgâus* and the Bondelswartz community. He then prays and gives the blessings.
All standing deliver the Bondelswartz Anthem, while the traditional flag is hoisted.]

Mûhesa ǁgauǁgaudi

[ǁNâs khao !gâ ib ge hoan xa a kai kairab (ǀgawi ǀawema!nans/Supreme Council) dība ǀGawasa Gaoba ra mâ,ǁgauǁgaus ǂgaeǂguis dis ase, tawede rase.
Sara se Ige gaoǁgâus di ǁani-e ǂgaeǂguis di haiba ra mâ, ǁnaeǁgaura ǂgaeǂguis do saos ase, tawede rase.
Gagase ǂgaeǂgui-aob ge ǀkhunuǂnuidasa Gaoba ra mâ, ǂgomǂgomsasīb, gaoǁgâus stî !Gamiǂnû ǁaes !oagu hâb, di saos ase. Tsîb ge ǀgore tsî Elosi ǀkhaeba ra gowaǂui.
ǁAes tsî ǀhûǁae aon ge ǂgōse mâ stî !Gamiǂnû ǁaes di tsanasa ra ǁnae, ǁNa ǁaeb aib ge !Gamiǂnû ǁaes di !Khauba ra ǂgaekhâhe.]

Section 12: The Vice-Captain

12.1 The Supreme Council, in conjunction with the *Gaoǁgâus*, selects a competent candidate as Vice-Captain, and he/she is elected democratically by the community by majority vote.

12.2 The Vice-Captain must be:
(a) at least 35 years of age or married
(b) living and/or farming in the communal area
(c) acquainted with the Bondelswartz traditions, and
(d) loyal to the Captain, Royal House, all levels of leadership, and the community.

12.3 The additional duties, powers and functions of the Vice-Captain are as follows:
(a) Chairperson of the Captain's Council without voting powers.

(b) To be in charge in the absence of the Captain.
(c) On request, act on behalf of the Captain.

12.4 The functions, duties and powers of the Captain's/Chief's Council also apply to the Vice-Captain. See 12.5 below.

12.5 Limited powers

12.5.1 The Vice-Captain of the Bondelswartz Traditional Authority:
(a) is the custodian of the customary law of the Bondelswartz traditional community.
(b) exercises his/her powers and perform his or her duties and functions in accordance with that customary law.
(c) performs such other powers and exercises such other duties or functions as may be conferred upon him by statutory law or the applicable customary law.
(e) assigns one or two Senior Traditional Councillors to assist him/her in the administering of the affairs of the Captain's (*Gaob*'s) Council.

Applicable: Traditional Authorities Act,[5] section 7.

12.6 Removal and succession

12.6.1 If there is sufficient reason to warrant the removal of the Vice-Captain from office, such Vice-Captain may be removed from office in accordance with the customary law of the Bondelswartz Traditional community.

12.6.2 The Vice-Captain to be removed and succeeded if he/she:
(a) has been involved in committing or has committed a murder.
(b) has been involved in or has committed theft.
(c) has been involved in or has committed fraud or related crimes.
(d) is in gross violation of Bondelswartz customary law and customary standing practices.
(e) suffers from ill-health and or mental incapacity, which state shall be certified by at least 2 (two) medical doctors or clinical psychologists, as the case may be, or
(f) resigns of his/her own free will.

12.6.3 The procedure laid down in section 9.3 shall be followed for the removal of the Vice-Captain.[6]

Section 13: The Captain's (*Gaob*'s) Council

13.1.1 The Captain's Council, as referred to in this Constitution and in the interpretation thereof, shall be in charge at ground level, appointed by the Captain.

13.1.2 A minimum of 5 members of the Captain's Council shall form a quorum of the proceedings of the meetings.

---

5 Unless otherwise indicated, this is Act No. 25 of 2000.

6 The provisions of section 8 of the Traditional Authorities Act, (Act No. 25 of 2000) apply where appropriate.

13.2 Functions, duties and powers

13.2.1 Applicable: Section 9, Traditional Authorities Act, 2000 (No. 25 of 2000). [Traditional Authorities Act 1995 (Act no. 17 Sect. 10) in original]

13.2.1.1 There is hereby established for the Bondelswartz traditional community the Captain's (*Gaob*'s) Council.

13.2.1.2 The Captain (*Gaob/s*) shall be the chairperson of the Captain's Council.

13.2.1.3 The Captain's Council shall be responsible for the day-to-day administration of the affairs of the Bondelswartz Traditional Authority of the traditional community.

13.2.1.4 The chairperson of the Captain's Council shall cause a written record to be kept of the proceedings of meetings.

13.2.2 The Captain's Council shall:

(a) advise the Captain and report to him/her as regards monthly events of importance.
(b) monitor the movement of persons and the optimal use of grazing.
(c) see to the health of community members as well as animals.
(d) conserve fauna and flora.
(e) see to the standard of farming.
(f) manage the Traditional Fund and report on it to the Captain, and
(g) organise entertainment and other projects.

13.3 Management of the Traditional Fund

13.3.1 The Captain and the Captain's Council are to see to the institution of a Traditional fund, administered by a trained person or persons and or a selected member or members of the Traditional community.

13.3.2 The Captain shall be the head of the Fund.

13.3.3 The Fund shall be fed by the following sources of income:

(a) grazing fees
(b) disposal of property
(c) gifts
(d) building projects
(e) levies on land use etc, and/or
(f) any other source of income.

13.3.4 The Fund shall be used for any purpose determined by the traditional community at a general meeting or at a Captain's Council meeting with proper representation and a quorum, and with the consent of the Captain.

13.4 Suspension of Traditional Councillors and Senior Traditional Councillors

13.4.1 In terms of section 10(2) of the Traditional Authorities Act, the removal from office of a Senior Traditional Councillor or Traditional Councillor shall be regulated by the customary law of the traditional community in respect of which such Councillors are appointed or elected.

13.4.2 In respect of Bondelswartz customary law, a Traditional Councillor or Senior Traditional Councillor shall be suspended from duty if he/she:

(a) fails to fulfil or perform his/her duties.
(b) fails to attend 3 (three) consecutive meetings without proper arrangements and reasonable grounds.
(c) fails to comply with lawful orders given by the Captain.
(d) fails to keep secrets or is disloyal to the Chief.
(e) without permission sells or is involved in any negotiations to sell or lease any part of communal land.
(f) keeps or gives free or paid grazing to commercial farmers or any other person not permitted to be in the communal area.
(g) is an embarrassment to the community in any way or at any place.
(h) is involved in or is found guilty of any stock or other theft, murder, or any crime proving him/her to be untrustworthy, or
(i) is involved in any form of corruption, including bribery, as a leader or in his/her private life.

Section 14: Supreme Council

14.1 The Supreme Council comprises 6 (six) Senior Traditional Councillors elected by Traditional Councillors among themselves, plus 5 (five) members from the Chamber of Elders and 5 (five) from the Chamber of Women.

14.2 The Supreme Council selects and designates a Captain from the Christiaan royal bloodline after consultation with the Royal House and after notification to the Minister.

14.3 One of the 5 (five) Councillors will be voted onto the Supreme Council by colleagues to serve as Secretary of the Council in order to chair the body without voting powers.

14.4 The Secretary shall be assisted by the Vice-secretary, who shall have voting powers.

Section 15: Chamber of Elders

15.1 There shall be a Chamber of Elders for the Bondelswartz.

15.2 Members of the Bondelswartz community who are 60 years and older shall be eligible for membership of the Chamber of Elders.

15.3 The Chamber shall adopt its own rules for activities provided they are within the framework of the Bondelswartz customary law, and have the consent of the Captain.

15.4 The body will be chaired by its Secretary, assisted by the Vice-secretary.

15.5 The person who chairs the Chamber of Elders shall have no voting power.

15.6 The main functions of the Chamber of Elders shall be to:

(a) advise the Captain on the customs and culture of the Bondelswartz.

(b) see to it that the Bondelswartz flame does not diminish in that Bondelswartz culture shall always be taught to younger generations.

(c) delegate 5 (five) members to the Supreme Council, when necessary.

(d) teach boys and young men how to behave in public.

(e) teach customary values and traditions to the Captain's son(s).

(f) instil customary values and traditions in the Captain's sons.

(g) teach life skills, and

(h) teach respect for the Traditional Authority.

Section 16: Chamber of Women

16.1 Any Bondelswartz woman who is interested in developing and practising the Bondelswartz culture shall be eligible for membership of the Chamber of Women.

16.2 The Chamber shall adopt its own rules for activities provided they are within the framework of the Bondelswartz customary law, and have the consent of the Captain.

16.3 The Chamber will be chaired by its Secretary, assisted by the Vice-secretary.

16.4 The person who chairs the Chamber of Women shall have no voting power.

16.5 The main functions of the Chamber of Women shall be to:

(a) develop cultural projects for the community.

(b) organise cultural activities and teach Bondelswartz culture to all the women and children.

(c) teach girls and young women about Bondelswartz culture and traditions as well as life skills, and

(d) mobilise women to respect their husbands and the Traditional Authority.

Section 17: Youth Chamber

17.1 Any member of the Bondelswartz community who is 35 years or younger and who is interested in becoming a member of the Youth Chamber shall be eligible to do so.

17.2 The Youth Chamber shall adopt its own rules for its activities provided they are within the framework of the Bondelswartz customary law, and have the consent of the Captain.

17.3 The Chamber will be chaired by its Secretary, assisted by the Vice-secretary.

17.4 The person who chairs the Youth Chamber has no voting power.

17.5 The main functions of the Chamber shall be to:
- (a) organise the cultural dances of the Bondelswartz.
- (b) organise income-generating projects within the community.
- (c) organise sport and other youth activities within the community, and
- (d) keep contact with other cultural youth groups.

Section 18: Social Care Group

18.1 Since it is by custom illegal to sell drugs or alcohol to any member of the community in the Bondelswartz territory, such activities should be reported, with supporting evidence, to the Captain for prosecution.

18.2 History has proved beyond doubt that drugs and alcohol break down marriages, households and socio-economic structures, and contradict Biblical morals. Because shebeens, clubs and gambling houses add to immorality, they have no right to operate in Bondelswartz territory, and any attempt made to establish them in such territory should be investigated and prosecuted.

18.3 Because children are the future of the nation, their parents and other adults should raise children as Christians who follow good social practices.

18.4 Children should be brought up to respect all adults.

18.5 Children should be brought up to love work so that they can provide for themselves one day as adults.

18.6 Parents and guardians shall ensure that their children are educated and qualified to enter the work force.

18.7 Any adult may join the Social Care Group of their own free will in order to take care of our vulnerable elders, since they are the custodians of our history and traditions. Members of the Social Care Group should be assets in relevant situations where elders might need help (e.g. when receiving pensions, at ATMs or when they pay debts, etc).

Section 19: The Captain's Technical Advisory Committee

19.1 A Captain's Technical Advisory Committee shall be established by the Captain personally in order to advise him.

19.2 Such Committee will have no restriction as to the number of members, their whereabouts, their origin, their nationality, etc.

19.3 The members of the Advisory Committee will have no executive powers.

Section 20: Traditional or Customary Court

20.1 The Captain and the Senior Traditional Councillors shall appoint judges for the Customary Court.

20.2 The Captain may invite some expertise from the state judiciary and the Namibian Police to be his advisors when the need arises.

20.3 The Captain will appoint a Clerk of the Court and a Court Messenger from the community, each for a term of one year.

20.4 A complainant shall meet the Court Messenger or Traditional Councillor who shall file the complaint with his/her Senior Traditional Councillor for a hearing.

20.5 Any person suspected of a crime or an injustice, including corruption, should be duly accused and charged.

20.6 The Court Messenger, the Traditional Councillors or any person duly assigned by the Captain shall conduct the required investigations.

20.7 Evidence shall be given by witnesses.

20.8 If the evidence shown validates the case against the accused, he/she shall be issued with a summons giving the date of the charge and venue for the hearing.

20.9 In the absence of the Captain, one of the appointed Senior Traditional Councillors shall act as the judge/chairperson of the proceedings.

20.10 Other Traditional Councillors and invited expertise, if any, shall advise the judge/chairperson on the final judgement.

20.11 The Court Messenger shall show the accused where to sit during the court session.

20.12 The accused shall be entitled to be protected and his/her views respected.

20.13 The rights of the victims and witnesses shall be valued and respected.

20.14 The general public may be granted permission to attend the court proceedings.

Section 21: Meetings

21.1 General Assembly, *Stamvergadering*

21.1.1 A General Assembly is convened by the Captain whenever he/she deems it necessary or at the request of community members if an issue necessitates such meetings.

21.1.2 The General Assembly discusses matters concerning the Bondelswartz.

21.1.3 Such Assembly is open to all Bondelswartz community members as well as to persons of expertise and specialists invited by the Captain for their advisory input.

21.1.4 The Assembly prepares, participates in, and presents arguments for a decision to be taken by the Captain.

21.1.5 General Assemblies should be advertised at least 30 (thirty) days prior to the date of such meetings.

21.1.6 As in any democratic society, the rule of the majority applies, provided that, if there is a dispute, the matter is referred to the Captain who may, in consultation with the Supreme Council, refer the issue to a state court.

21.1.7 The quorum for a General Assembly constitutes the Captain; 3 (three) members of the Chamber of Elders; 3 (three) members of the Chamber of Women; 3 (three) members of the Youth Chamber; 1 (one) member of the Social Care Group, and a minimum of 300 (three hundred) members of the community.

21.1.8 In extraordinary circumstances, due to urgency or an emergency, the Captain and 2 (two) of the Captain's Councillors, and 300 community members at such a meeting may proceed with the meeting.

21.2 Meetings of the Captain's Council

21.2.1 Meetings of the Captain's Council are convened by the Captain or Vice-captain, or at the request of community members.

21.2.2 Such meetings may be chaired by one of the Senior Traditional Councillors.

21.2.3 Such meetings discuss traditional concerns, customary conduct, customary laws and any other matter affecting the traditional community.

21.2.4 Such meetings are open only to the Vice-captain, the Senior Traditional Councillor and the Captain.

21.2.5 The Captain only takes part in such meetings if invited to do so or if he/she wishes to take part.

21.2.6 The quorum for such meetings shall be a minimum of 5 (five) members of the Captain's Council.

21.2.7 All resolutions taken by such meetings shall be referred to the Captain for his/her approval with the minutes of the relevant discussion, if necessary.

21.3 Other meetings

21.3.1 The Captain may convene any other meetings with the Supreme Council, the Chamber of Elders, the Chamber of Women, the Youth Chamber, the Social Care Group or his/her Technical Advisory Committee when necessary.

Section 22: Conflict of interest

22.1 Public accountability and liability

22.1.1 The responsibilities of the Traditional and Senior Traditional Councillors and other community stakeholders includes:

(a) acting in good faith, in the best interest of the organisational structure.

(b) avoiding conflicts of interest.

(c) being diligent with regard to the duties, functions and the confidentiality of information.

(d) obtaining a degree of confidence in fellow colleagues and leaders, and

(e) ensuring financial accountability and prudence.

22.2 Organisational culture

22.2.1 Because the culture of the office of the Captain and the Captain's Council are intertwined, the one usually affects the other and, together, they can have an impact on the effectiveness of both the office of the Captain and the leadership, and the quality of governance.

22.2.2 Organisations should place a high value on:
(a) Open communication.
(b) Commitment to the organisation.
(c) Accountability for actions and results.
(d) Respect for individual rights and privacy, etc which are especially supportive of good governance.
(e) An environment where members do not feel inhabited in openly asking questions, and
(f) Confronting issues and saying "no" when necessary in a constructive manner.

22.2.3 The test of this environment comes in times of stress, when things go wrong: is the culture one where the priority is to fix the problem or attribute blame?

22.2.4 The leadership sets the tone as regards norms of behaviour for the community, which entails them being open, up front, honest and accountable in all their dealings with each other, the community, their staff, and the public at large. They should stress the importance of the organisation's value and live up to its codes of conduct in their behaviour and actions.

Section 23: Regulations

23.1 The Bondelswartz Traditional Authority may make regulations relating to:
(a) the inheritance of land, livestock or any other property
(b) the grazing of livestock on communal land
(c) Bondelswartz traditional festivals
(d) rules of succession to the Christiaan throne, and
(e) any other matter required to achieve the aims of this customary law.

Section 24: Short title, commencement and amendment

24.1 This Constitution shall also be called the *Bondelswartz Customary Law* and shall come into force immediately after it has been signed by the Captain.

24.2 The Captain may amend or repeal any part of this customary law, provided such amendment or repeal has been discussed and approved by the Captain's Council, whereafter such amendment or repeal may be signed by the Captain to come into effect.

24.3 If deemed necessary, the Captain's Council may refer such amendment or repeal for further discussion to all levels of leadership, upon whose recommendation the Council will approve such amendment or repeal or motivate its disapproval thereof.

24.4 The Captain shall have no right to sign any amendment or repeal of a customary law without the approval of the Captain's Council.

24.5 The Traditional Authorities Act and or any law over traditional matters shall be complied with, provided that any statutory or other non-customary law which, in our opinion or according to our beliefs, is not satisfactory, shall be settled in a statutory court or otherwise.

Certificate of consent to publish

Certificate of the consent to publish

UNIVERSITY OF NAMIBIA

FACULTY OF LAW

HUMAN RIGHTS AND DOCUMENTATION CENTRE

RE: CONSENT TO PUBLICATION

I, the undersigned, Chief of the BONDELSWARTZ Traditional Authority, hereby give consent to the Human Rights and Documentation Centre, to publish the following documents of the BONDELSWARTZ Traditional Authority:

1. The Customary Laws
2. The Community Profile
3. Picture of the Chief
4. Logo of the Traditional Authority

I acknowledge that the Human Rights and Documentation Centre will publish the laws in our indigenous language (NAMA/ENGLISH), as well as the English language. I am familiar with the contents of the laws that will be published and further acknowledge that they were prepared by my traditional authority.

Signed on this 23 **day of** JULY **2012**

At UNAM (HRDC)

WINDHOEK

Chief

For HRDC: Mr. A. Gairiseb

Kai‖khaun Traditional Authority
Kai‖khaun !Hao!nasi ǂGaeǂguis

The supreme leader of the Kai‖khaun Traditional Authority is
Gaob[1] Petrus Simon Moses Kooper.
Date of designation: 3 December 1988

KAI//KHAUN FOLK

1 Traditional title in terms of section 11, Traditional Authorities Act, 2000 (No. 25 of 2000).

PROFILE[2]

Hoachanas is one of the oldest settlements in southern Namibia. According to the legends of our time, Hoachanas was settled in 1695 when the hunting dogs of the Kai‖khaun discovered a spring there, which came to be known as *Arigu-|aus* (Fountain of Dogs). The leaders of the clan decided to settle around the spring because of the sufficient availability of water and the fertility of the vicinity of the spring for crop production.

As the years went by, the Kai‖khaun clan multiplied. Today, there are reportedly over 5,000 inhabitants at Hoachanas.

Most of the inhabitants of Hoachanas are very religious. For this reason there are six churches in the small settlement.

Two schools cater for Primary and Junior Secondary phases, respectively. For Senior Secondary grades, learners are sent to Gibeon, Mariental or Rehoboth.

As regards health services, one clinic caters for the sick and vulnerable in the community. For serious and emergency cases, patients are sent to the Mariental State Hospital by ambulance, which first has to come from Mariental.

The overwhelming majority of the inhabitants of Hoachanas are jobless. The only people that have income from a monthly salary are teachers, clinic staff, hostel staff and police officers, who are all employed by the government. Pensioners also receive a monthly income. The rest of the inhabitants make a living from seasonal jobs.

Hoachanas was declared a settlement and, as such, is currently administered by the Hardap Regional Council. Before that, the community of Hoachanas was run solely by the Kai‖khaun Traditional Authority. They maintained law and order, and had no need for police assistance.

Salutation by Chief PSM Kooper

It is with a sense of mixed feelings that I salute you with deep fatherly affection and concern, the descendants of the Kai‖khaun, over which, by the Grace of God and by the patience, prayer and support of the individual Kai‖khaun and community members, we, as the Traditional Authority, are privileged to serve.

We salute you at a time of unusual political, social, economic and moral strain, at a time when the entire world structure seems to be breaking at the seams; and when, once more, we face the 'hour of Babel', the hour of judgement for Babylon, the confusion of tongues and egoism of different mindsets. The Kai‖khaun people have crossed many rivers of adversity. The Kai‖khaun have for many centuries challenged and fought the enemies of

2 This profile was provided by the Kai‖khaun Traditional Authority.

justice, freedom and goodwill. It is altogether fitting that this clan should be at the very centre of action for peace and equality, with justice for all. We challenge you to work for its glorious fulfilment.

We will fail dismally in our duty if we do not pay homage to our fallen heroes and heroes that laboured so hard and sacrificed their lives for the future generations of this tribe. This includes our late *Gaon* (*Gaogu*) or Kings, Senior Traditional and Traditional Councillors, religious leaders, teachers and ordinary members alike. Unity amongst themselves and love for one another ensured their victory. We would urge loyalty, devotion and compliance on the part of male elders and women alike in reaching out for full service in youth development, both in the collective life of the clan and the deeper personal experience of every member of our society. We commend these statements as our distinctive mission and duty to all in faithfulness towards the Almighty Lord the Creator and to promote the Kai‖khaun legacy.

We suggest the following guidelines to make this customary law workable after we have digested and accepted it, approved it and finally, it has been signed by the *Gaob*.

1. That our task is to uplift and honour customary law.
2. That we study, understand and know our customary law.
3. That we respect the constituted body that will regulate the observance of customary law.
4. That we work collectively to protect and safeguard the image of our clan.
5. That, in the same way as we protect our own rights, we also respect the rights of others, and
6. That the *Gaob* is the representative of both order and servant life.

The guidelines above are the foundation of our exploration, both general and historical, of the ancestral values, norms and customs as part of the role of the Kai‖khaun Traditional Authority in the continuing search for the meaning of customary law in the traditional community.

Historical background

After the Second World War, one of the leaders of the Hoachanas community, Rev. Markus Kooper, was with Hosea Kutako and Samuel Hendrik Witbooi, one of the first Namibian leaders to petition the United Nations to grant independence to Namibia. In 1959, Rev. Kooper rejected South African apartheid plans to evict the Red Nation (also known as *Rooinasie*, referring to the term used against the Kai‖khaun during the apartheid years by the South African Administration) from Hoachanas and to resettle them at Aminuis and Tses. Consequently, the South African Administration forcefully led Rev. Kooper at gunpoint to |Tsawisis near Tses Reserve.

Only upon national independence did the wheel of Namibia's 200 years of resistance come full circle. The legacy of Manase !Noreseb Gamab for a free, united and peaceful Namibia was continued by successive *Gaon (Gaogu)* of the Kai‖khaun of Hoachanas, a people who were dispersed and impoverished – firstly by the Germans and later by the South Africans – and have to be restored to their former glory. Namibia should take note of the Kai‖khaun contribution to the independence of this country.

Chronological order of the *Gaon (Gaogu)* of the Kai‖khaun

Name	Tenure of rule	Number of years served
ǂHāb	1695–1710	15
‖Khomab ǂHāmab	1710–1725	15
‖Khaub Gaib ‖Khomab	1725–1740	15
ǂŌ‖nâib ‖Khaumab	1740–1755	15
ǀHanab ǂŌ‖nâimab	1755–1770	15
!Gaob ǀHanamab	1770–1800	30
Gameb !Gaomab	1800–1814	14
Tsawub Gaomab	1814–1824	10
ǀNakhom Gomab	1824–1840	16
Cornelius ‖Oaseb !Nakhomab	1841–1867	26
Barnabas ǂGoraxab ‖Oasmab	1867–1877	10
Petrus ǀGâbeb ǂGoraxmab	1877–1880	3
Manase !Noreseb	1881–1905	24
Fritz ‖Oaseb	1907–1936	29
Noach Tsaitsaib	1937–1948	11
Matteus Kooper	1949–1986	37
Petrus Simon Moses Kooper	1988 to date	23

THE LAWS OF THE KAI||KHAUN[1]

1 The laws were submitted in English only.

Preamble

The structural existence of the Kai‖khaun degenerated because of German and South African colonial rule. As a result, traditional authority could not be effectively exercised over the Kai‖khaun. Thus, their collective possession of the land they communally used and cared for was taken away by colonisers and alienated by force. The extent of white settler dominance in the area was eventually so great that Hoachanas was regarded and treated as a black spot in the white area.

The traditional land of the Kai‖khaun was later confiscated and given to the surrounding land-hungry white settlers that arrived from Germany and South Africa.

The South African apartheid machinery tried to relocate the Kai‖khaun community to the south – especially the |Tsawisis area – by force, but they refused to move. Thus, they were under extreme pressure to accept third-class treatment from the respective colonial administrations.

Only after independence was achieved, the Namibian Constitution was in place and the new government had taken over, could the Kai‖khaun breathe the fresh air of freedom with relief – albeit still without land and completely immersed in poverty.

Now therefore the Kai‖khaun traditional community thank:
(a) God the Almighty Father for the independence of this country.
(b) the Founding Fathers of our Republic for the Supreme Law that brought back the dignity of our people, and
(c) the Head of State and his Government for the wise and timely decision to recognise the traditional communities and their leaders.

God bless our Government and our beautiful Republic.

Section 1: Definitions

1.1 In this customary law, unless the context indicates otherwise:

(a) *Additional member* means any member co-opted from the Kai‖khaun community by the Kai‖khaun Traditional Authority to assist the leadership, or who is entrusted to represent the Kai‖khaun Traditional Authority anywhere in Namibia or elsewhere.

(b) *Gaob* means a Chief as defined in the Traditional Authorities Act, 2000 (No. 25 of 2000) and named *Gaob* by the Kai‖khaun traditional community.

(c) *Communal land* means the communal area as defined in the Traditional Authority Act, including any other land belonging to the Kai‖khaun community.

(d) *Customary law* means the customary law as defined in the Traditional Authorities Act.

(e) *Supreme Council* means the sole organ of the Kai||khaun traditional community entrusted with the power to select, remove or designate the *Gaob.*

(f) *Traditional community* means the traditional community as defined in the Traditional Authorities Act.

(g) *Traditional leader* means and includes traditional leaders as defined in the Traditional Authorities Act.

(h) *Traditional land of the Kai||khaun* means the geographical area habitually inhabited by our ancestors, that is, Hoachanas and all its surrounding farms – for example, Bitterwasser, Brooklyne, Gemini, Jena, Panama, Sekretarispan and Wolfputs), and

(i) *Deputy-Gaob* means one of the Senior Traditional Councillors appointed by the *Gaob* to deputise or act as the *Gaob* in his absence.

Section 2: Traditional land

2.1 The traditional land of the Kai||khaun community shall be the geographic area habitually inhabited by our ancestors, being Hoachanas with all its surrounding farms that were forcefully taken away from us by the colonisers and later declared by the apartheid regime as white commercial farms.

Section 3: Main seat

3.1 The main seat of the Kai||khaun is to be Hoachanas, where the discovery of the spring led to the unforgotten history of the Kai||khaun community.

Section 4: Emblems

4.1 The Kai||khaun emblems, as represented on its coat of arms, shall be the Bible with tufts of grass, supporting a shield emblazoned with a bow and a quiver with arrows, a club and spear, at the head of which stands a dog in profile, and at whose flanks to the left and right are rampant horses.

Section 5: Colours

5.1 The traditional colours of the Kai||khaun are to be red and white.

5.2 Red symbolises the blood that was shed during the protracted battles fought by our forefathers.

5.3 White symbolises the peace that has always existed amongst the various people making up the Kai||khaun community, and between the Kai||khaun and other communities.

Section 6: Traditional flag

6.1 The main colour of the traditional flag is red with a band of white that crosses from the top left to the bottom right.

Section 7: Traditional anthem

7.1 There shall be a traditional anthem (*!Haos-ams*) for the Kai‖khaun community.
7.2 The Kai‖khaun Traditional Authority shall decide on the traditional anthem.

Section 8: Organs of the Kai‖khaun

8.1 The Kai‖khaun Traditional Authority

8.1.1 There shall be a Traditional Authority for the Kai‖khaun traditional community.
8.1.2 The establishment, powers, duties and function of such Traditional Authority are defined in the Traditional Authorities Act.

8.2 The Supreme Council

8.2.1 There shall be a Supreme Council for the Kai‖khaun traditional community.
8.2.2 The Supreme Council shall be composed of at least 10 (ten) members of the Kai‖khaun Traditional Authority and 20 (twenty) members of the Council of Elders (*Stam Oudstes*).
8.2.3 The main function of the Supreme Council shall be to:
(a) select, after consultation with members of the Kai‖khaun Royal House and the community, the successor to the *Gaob* in accordance with the rules of succession. (The rules of succession to be included in the Regulations).
(b) remove the *Gaob* from office, provided there is sufficient reason to warrant such removal, and provided further that such removal be in accordance with section 8 of the Traditional Authorities Act.
(c) designate the selected candidate as *Gaob* in terms of the Traditional Authorities Act, after notifying the relevant Minister.

8.3 The *Gaob*

8.3.1 The *Gaob* shall be the supreme traditional leader of the Kai‖khaun traditional community.
8.3.2 The *Gaob* shall be selected from the royal bloodline, in this case the Kai‖khaun bloodline.
8.3.3 The *Gaob* shall be at least 35 (thirty-five) years of age.
8.3.4 The *Gaob* shall be the custodian of this customary law and shall exercise his powers and perform his duties and functions in accordance with it.

8.3.5 The inauguration of the *Gaob* shall be done only by a person equal to him.

8.3.6 The inauguration of the *Gaob* shall be done in the Nama language.

8.3.7 The inauguration procedure shall be included in the Regulations of this customary law.

8.3.8 The *Gaob* shall chair all traditional meetings.

8.3.9 The *Gaob* shall be entitled to delegate his chairmanship to another.

8.3.10 A *Gaob*'s term of office shall terminate only after his death. The *Gaob* shall not be replaced while he is alive and shall not be removed from office unless there are sufficient grounds to warrant such replacement or removal.

8.3.11 The *Goab* shall be replaced and/or removed from office under the following circumstances:

(a) if he commits a serious offence such as murder, theft, fraud and he is found guilty of that offence.

(b) if he fails to uphold the customary law and customary practices of the Kai||khaun traditional community, or

(c) if he suffers from ill-health and/or mental incapacity.

8.4 The Deputy *Gaob*

8.4.1 In the absence of the *Gaob*, the Deputy *Gaob* shall act as the *Gaob*.

8.4.2 In all other circumstances when necessary the Deputy *Gaob* shall deputise the *Gaob*.

8.5 The Council of Elders *(Stam Oudstes)*

8.5.1 There shall be a Council of Elders for the Kai||khaun traditional community.

8.5.2 Membership of the Council of Elders shall be a minimum of 60 (sixty) years.

8.5.3 The Council of Elders shall adopt its own rules for its activities, subject to customary law.

8.5.4 The main functions of the Council of Elders shall be to:

(a) advise the *Gaob* on the custom and culture of the Kai||khaun.

(b) ensure that the Kai||khaun 'flame' does not diminish in that the Kai||khaun culture shall always be taught to the younger generation.

(c) delegate 20 (twenty) members to the Supreme Council when need be.

8.6 The Youth Cultural Group

8.6.1 There shall be a Youth Cultural Group for the Kai||khaun traditional community.

8.6.2 Membership shall be 35 (thirty-five) years or younger.

8.6.3 The Youth Cultural Group shall adopt its own rules for its activities, subject to customary law.

8.6.4 The main function of the Youth Cultural Group shall be to:

(a) organise cultural dances for the community.

(b) maintain contact with youth and cultural groups in other traditional communities.
(c) organise income-generating projects within the community.
(d) organise sporting and other activities among the youth.

8.7 The Women's Cultural Group

8.7.1 There shall be a Women's Cultural Group for the Kai‖khaun traditional community.
8.7.2 Membership shall be open to all Kai‖khaun women who are interested in developing and practising the Kai‖khaun culture.
8.7.3 The Women's Cultural Group shall adopt its own rules for its activities, subject to customary law.
8.7.4 The main function of the Women's Cultural Group shall be to:
(a) develop cultural projects within the community.
(b) organise and teach the culture of the Kai‖khaun to all women and children.
(c) maintain contact with other women's and cultural groups.

Section 9: Meetings

9.1 Traditional Assembly

9.1.1 There shall be a Traditional Assembly for the Kai‖khaun community.
9.1.2 The Traditional Assembly shall be held annually with the Kai‖khaun traditional festival.
9.1.3 The date of the Traditional Assembly shall be included in the Regulations.
9.1.4 The Traditional Assembly shall be open to all members of the Kai‖khaun community throughout Namibia.
9.1.5 The Traditional Assembly shall be advertised at least 30 (thirty) days prior to the meeting.
9.1.6 The Traditional Assembly shall have the power to amend or repeal this customary law subject to a two-thirds majority of members present.
9.1.7 The Traditional Assembly shall consist of the *Gaob*, at least 10 (ten) members of the Kai‖khaun Traditional Authority, and at least 50 (fifty) members of the Kai‖khaun community.

9.2 Traditional Authority meetings

9.2.1 The Traditional Authority shall meet once every quarter, that is, four times a year.
9.2.2 Such meetings shall be attended by the *Gaob*, the Deputy *Gaob*, Senior Traditional and Traditional Councillors only.

9.2.3 The meetings will discuss traditional concerns, customary conduct or laws, and any other matter related to the traditional community.
9.2.4 The Traditional Authority may invite anyone to their meetings.
9.2.5 The quorum for Traditional Authority meetings shall be 7 (seven) members.
9.2.6 Every Traditional Authority member shall be obliged to attend meetings.
9.2.7 Any member of the Traditional Authority who fails to attend 3 (three) consecutive meetings without a valid reason and without being excused by the Authority automatically discharges himself or herself from the Traditional Authority.

9.3 General community meetings

9.3.1 There shall be General Community Meetings for the Kai||khaun community.
9.3.2 Such meetings shall be open to every member of the community.
9.3.3 Such meetings shall be convened by the *Gaob* and the Senior Traditional and Traditional Councillors whenever necessary.
9.3.4 The purpose of such meetings will be either to consult with or to give general information to the community.

Section 10: Maintaining law and order

10.1 No person shall be entitled to take communal land for him-/herself without the written permission of the *Gaob*.
10.2 No person shall be entitled to settle or move into the jurisdiction area of the Kai||khaun Traditional Authority without the written permission of the *Gaob*.
10.3 No person shall be entitled to move from one communal farm to another without the written permission of the *Gaob*.
10.4 No person shall be entitled to fence off communal land without the written permission of the *Gaob*.
10.5 No person shall be entitled to hold meetings, festivals or any other activities at Kai||khaun cultural sites such as gravesites or the Arigu-|aus spring, or at any other place so declared by the Kai||khaun Traditional Authority, without the written permission of the *Gaob*.
10.6 No person shall be entitled to collect firewood or any natural resource for any purpose other than household use without the written permission of the *Gaob*.
10.7 No person shall be entitled to transport meat or livestock without a letter from the headman or Councillor of the area where he/she usually resides.
10.8 No person shall be entitled to sell meat or livestock without the written permission of the Kai||khaun Traditional Authority.
10.9 If someone is found guilty of having stolen another person's livestock, such as their cattle, goats, sheep, donkeys or horses, the thief shall compensate the victim on a two-for-one basis or shall pay an amount equal thereto in addition to a fine determined by the Community Court.

10.10 If someone is found guilty of having stolen another person's property other than livestock, the thief shall return the victim's property in the same state as it was when it was stolen and shall be fined by the Community Court.

10.11 If an unmarried man commits adultery with another man's wife and impregnates her, he shall pay 6 (six) head of cattle or their equivalent value in cash; 2 (two) head of cattle shall go to the Traditional Authority and the remaining 4 (four) shall be paid to the wronged spouse.

10.12 In instances where a married man has a sexual relationship with an unmarried woman and impregnates her, he shall be guilty of adultery and he shall pay 6 (six) head of cattle or equivalent value in cash, 2 (two) head of cattle to the Traditional Authority and the remainder to the wronged spouse.

10.13 In instances where a married man impregnates any woman outside his marriage, he shall pay 3 (three) head of cattle or equivalent value in cash, one head of cattle to the Traditional Authority and the remainder to the unmarried woman for impregnating her.

10.14 Even if the adulterous man does not impregnate the women referred to in sub-clauses 10.11 – 10.12, he shall pay 3 (three) head of cattle or their equivalent value in cash, one head of cattle to the Traditional Authority and the remainder to the wronged spouse.

10.15 If a woman is raped, she shall be paid 4 (four) head of cattle or their equivalent value in cash, one head of cattle to the Traditional Authority and the remainder to the victim while the rapist will be fined by a Community Court or another competent court.

10.16 If a spouse has sexual intercourse with another spouse in his/her communal house or any other place and gets caught, he/she shall pay 3 (three) head of cattle or their equivalent value in cash, one head of cattle to the Traditional Authority and the remainder to the wronged spouse.

10.17 If a man impregnates a schoolgirl, he shall pay 3 (three) head of cattle, or their equivalent value in cash, one head to the Traditional Authority and the remainder to the girl or her parents.

10.18 If an unmarried man impregnates an unmarried woman, he shall pay 3 (three) head of cattle or its equivalent value in cash for impregnating her.

10.19 No person shall be entitled to swear or fight in any public place.

10.20 Any person who is found guilty of having murdered another shall pay 10 (ten) head of cattle or their equivalent value in cash, in addition to being tried in a state court.

Section 11: Regulations

11.1 The Kai||khaun Traditional Authority may make regulations relating to:

(a) customary marriages
(b) the inheritance of land, livestock or any other property
(c) the grazing of livestock on communal land
(d) traditional festivals of the Kai||khaun community
(e) the rules of succession to the Kai||khaun throne

(f) the traditional anthem (*!Haos-ams*), and
(g) any other matter required in order to achieve the purpose of this customary law.

Section 12: Short title, commencement and amendment

12.1 The Constitution shall be called the Kai‖khaun Customary Law and shall come into force immediately after the *Gaob* has signed it.
12.2 This customary law or any clause therein may be amended or repealed by a two-thirds majority of the members present at a Traditional Assembly.
12.3 Recommendations in connection with this customary law must be sent to the Secretary of the Kai‖khaun Traditional Authority at least 30 (thirty) days prior to the commencement of the Traditional Assembly.

Certificate of consent to publish

Certificate of the consent to publish

UNIVERSITY OF NAMIBIA

FACULTY OF LAW

HUMAN RIGHTS AND DOCUMENTATION CENTRE

RE: CONSENT TO PUBLICATION

I, the undersigned, Chief of the KAI-IIKHAUN Traditional Authority, hereby give consent to the Human Rights and Documentation Centre, to publish the following documents of the KAI-IIKHAUN Traditional Authority:

1. The Customary Laws
2. The Community Profile
3. Picture of the Chief
4. Logo of the Traditional Authority

I acknowledge that the Human Rights and Documentation Centre will publish the laws in our indigenous language (NAMA), as well as the English language. I am familiar with the contents of the laws that will be published and further acknowledge that they were prepared by my traditional authority.

Signed on this 30th **day of** JULY **2012**

At HOACHANAS

Chief

For HRDC: Mr. A. Gairiseb

KAI-IIKHAUN TRADITIONAL AUTHORITY
Signed:
Date:
HOACHANAS
GAOBI PSM KOOPER

Simon Kooper Traditional Authority
!Khara-khoen ǁAes

The supreme leader of the !Khara-Khoen ǁAes (Simon Kooper) Traditional Authority was *Gaob*[1] Fredrik Hanse (above).
Date of designation: 4 April 2008
He passed away on 26 January 2011.
The Acting *Goab* is David Hanse.[2]

1 Traditional title in terms of section 11, Traditional Authorities Act, 2000 (No. 25 of 2000).

2 Editor's note: Samuel Goliath was Acting Gaob from February 2011 to 29 September 2014, succeeded by David Hanse who had not yet been gazetted at the time of going to press.

PROFILE[3]

The structural existence of the !Khara-Khoen Traditional Authority degenerated because of German and South African colonial rule. As a result, authority over !Khara-Khoe subjects could not be effectively exercised. Consequently, their collective hold on the land they communally used and cared for was taken away by the colonisers and alienated by force. The traditional land of the !Khara-Khoen was later declared commercial farming land for the colonisers and the main !Khara-Khoe settlement, Gochas, declared a town and business area for Whites.

During the genocide of the Ovaherero and Nama people between 1904 and 1908 by Germany, the late Captain Simon Kooper (!Gomxab) and some traditional community members fled to Botswana and their descendants are currently based at a village called Lekwabe in Botswana; of those left behind who survived the genocide, some were forcefully removed to the Gibeon area by the former South African Government. Some refused to move and still reside in Gochas and its environs.

After Namibia achieved national independence, a constitution was put in place which made provision for a Traditional Authorities Act. The !Khara-Khoen (or !Khap Khoe) traditional community is now determined to exercise its rights as a traditional community and pledges to uphold and respect the laws of the Namibian Government and to act as a responsible community to uplift the standard of living of its people.

1. Traditional land

The !Khara-Khoen Traditional Authority has been gazetted and registered on the Amper-bo communal land and execute or perform their duties from this land.

2. Main seat

The main seat of the !Khara-Khoe/!Khap Khoe traditional community is at Amper-bo which comprises 11 (eleven) farms or villages. These villages are headed by the Chief.

3. Traditional title

The traditional title is *Gaob* – “chief” as defined in the Traditional Authorities Act, 2000 (No. 25 of 2000).

3 This profile was provided by the !Khara-Khoe ǁAes Traditional Authority.

4. The Leadership of the !Khara-Khoe ǁAes (Simon Kooper clan)

The leadership structure comprises the following:
(a) The Chief
(b) Deputy Chief
(c) Senior Councillors
(d) Traditional Councillors

The Chief is the father and also the head of the traditional community. The Chief is appointed from the Royal Family. If there are two or more contenders from the Royal House, the Supreme Council has the right to choose one person, male or female, to take over the leadership. If there is no agreement on the successor, an election shall be held in which all the community members may vote. The Supreme Council shall automatically facilitate the election process as the Election Committee to the Chief. All the councillors shall be responsible for duties and activities in the community and also to solve disputes and conflicts. All the councillors shall also advise the Chief in the allocation of grazing land, land for crop production and land for business erven.

The Supreme Council shall have the right to stop the duties of the Chief and also to remove him/her from office if he/she is unable to run the office due to mental illness or if the chief is engaged in criminal activities or misconduct.

The Chief is also the chairperson of all traditional community or Council meetings and may delegate such authority to other members if needed. It is also the task of the Chief to act as custodian of the !Khara-Khoe customs and heritage. The inauguration of the Chief shall be done only by a person equal to him, through the medium of the Nama language, and this may be translated into any other languages.

5. Office duties

The !Khara-Khoen Traditional Authority shall have a Secretary to administer the office. The Secretary is appointed by the Chief. He must be knowledgeable and hardworking. His duties are as follows:
(a) to record all council and community meetings.
(b) to do filing.
(c) to administer correspondence.
(d) to carry out office duties.
(e) to record finances.
(f) to compile agendas and take minutes.
(g) to receive visitors.
(h) to make appointments, and
(i) to take messages.

6. Traditional Assembly

There shall be a Traditional Assembly for the !Khara-Khoe traditional community. The !Khara-Khoen Traditional Assembly shall meet annually during the traditional festival and shall be open to all community members throughout Namibia. The Traditional Assembly shall have the right to amend or repeal this customary Law with a 2/3 (two thirds) majority of members present. The Assembly shall comprise the Chief, and at least 10 (ten) members of the Authority and at least 50 (fifty) members of the community.

Councillors shall be required to be open-minded, knowledgeable and eager to learn something new. They shall also be hardworking, friendly, polite, patient and honest. They shall also show love and respect to their followers.

Land within the boundaries of the !Khara-Khoen Authority is owned and governed by the Traditional Authority. People residing within the !Khara-Khoe boundaries are livestock farmers of animals such as goats, sheep and cattle. Donkeys and horses are normally used for transport. Some households cultivate vegetables and fruit on a small scale just for household use and not for sale. All types of grass and trees growing in the area belong to the Traditional Authority, whether or not they bear fruit, and are owned by the Traditional Authority.

7. Culture

The culture, customs and language of the !Khara-Khoe traditional community shall be respected. The language of the !Khara-Khoen is Nama. It is expected of all parents to raise youngsters in the customs and norms of the !Khara-Khoen. Cultural values and norms shall be promoted amongst the community. Manufacturing and wearing of traditional costumes shall be promoted too. Traditional dances, songs, food and beliefs should also be fostered and encouraged.

8. Community health

People who use traditional methods of healing are welcome, e.g. using herbs and roots from plants and also products from animals to heal diseases such as diarrhoea, is acceptable.

THE LAWS OF THE !KHARA-KHOEN ǁAES (SIMON KOOPER)[1]

1 The laws were submitted in English only.

Preamble

The !Khara-Khoe community is determined to exercise its rights as a traditional community and pledges to uphold and respect the laws of the Namibian Government and to act as a responsible community to uplift the living standards of its members.

Therefore, the !Khara-Khoe traditional community thank:

(a) God the Almighty for the independence of this country.
(a) the Founding Father, Dr Sam Nujoma, of our Republic of Namibia, for the Supreme Law that brought back the dignity of our people.
(a) the Government for the decision to recognise the traditional communities and their leaders.

God bless our Government and our beautiful Namibia.

Section 1: Definitions

1.1 In this Customary Law unless the content indicates otherwise:

(a) *Additional member* means any member co-opted from the !Khara-Khoe traditional community by the Traditional Authority to assist the leadership or who is entrusted to represent the !Khara-Khoe community anywhere in Namibia or elsewhere.

(b) *Captain* means the chief as defined in the Traditional Authorities Act, 2000 (No. 25 of 2000) and named Captain of the !Khara-Khoen Traditional Authority and community.

(c) *Customary law* means traditional laws which will govern the traditional community to enhance the unity, peace and stability to support the current Government in its efforts to improve the living standards of our community and Namibian people in general (Traditional Authorities Act, 2000).

(d) *Traditional community* means the traditional community as defined in the Traditional Authorities Act, 2000 (No. 25 of 2000).

(e) *Traditional land* of the !Khara-Khoe traditional community means the geographic area habitually inhabited by our ancestors, that is, Gochas and all surrounding farms which were declared by the former South African Government as commercial farming land and given to the Whites, and are now governed by the local and regional authorities of our Government.

(e) *Traditional leader* means and includes the traditional leaders as defined in the Traditional Authorities Act, 2000.

(f) *Supreme Council* means the sole organ of the !Khara-Khoe traditional community entrusted with the power to select, remove or designate the Captain.

Section 2: Traditional land

2.1 The !Khara-Khoe traditional community has been forcefully removed by the colonisers, the former South African regime, and find themselves now in an area around the Amper-bo communal land which had been put aside by the said regime according to the Odendaal Plan.

2.2 The Traditional Authority has been gazetted and registered on this communal land and executes or performs its duties from this land.

Section 3: Main seat

3.1 The main seat of the !Khara-Khoe traditional community is to be at Amper-bo which is also the main centre of the !Khara-Khoen.

Section 4: Emblems

4.1 The emblems are tokens of a leopard and a horse shoe.

4.2 The leopard symbolises the aggressive approach, from its determined method of attacking its prey, the way it outmanoeuvres its enemies and the way leopards collectively protect their territory for their own benefit. Leopards also give love to followers, live in solidarity and depict the spirit of freedom and courage that the Traditional Authority of the !Khara-Khoe community seeks to evoke. Mother leopard is also willing to share her territory and meals with a full-grown youngster who has recently left her care; so too is the !Khara-Khoe traditional community concerned to care for its young people.

4.3 The horse shoe symbolises unity and strengthened natural ability.

Section 5: Colours

5.1 Plain yellow or yellow with fine white spots.

5.2 Yellow symbolises how the community fought for what belongs to them with jealousy and eagerness for what they thought was correct.

5.3 The white spots represent peace and stability after the hardships experienced during the struggle for independence of the Republic of Namibia.

Section 6: Traditional flag

6.1 The main colour of the flag is yellow which symbolises how the community fought for what belongs to them with jealousy and eagerness for what they thought was correct.

6.2 The white stripes on the edge of the yellow colour symbolise peace, tranquillity and stability.

6.3 The token of the tiger head in the middle of the flag symbolises the description as outlined in section 4.

Section 7: Traditional anthem

7.1 The pride of every nation is their national anthem. The !Khara-Khoe traditional community have their own traditional anthem which will be sung at traditional occasions.

7.2 The anthem will be treated with honour and dignity as follows:

7.2.1 All present at any occasion will rise except those who cannot stand due to circumstances beyond their control;

7.2.2 All males present will take off their hats, and

7.2.3 Silence will be required from all present at that specific function or occasion.

7.3 The Anthem[2]

Torodī tsî toa hâ !haos ge
!Khar' Khoe ǁaesa
Kai !hoadi hoadi xa a ǀguis
Xawe nētsē a ǂkhari

Torodī tsî torob xa
Ge toa !haos ge a ǁî
Taradi tsî ǀgôan ǀaob ge ǁgoe
Xawes ǁōǂoa tide

Omdi ge nētsē ǀkhai!nâse mâ
Xawes ge ǁōǂoa tide
ǀAob âs ge ǁgam-i khami gere dâu
Sa ôan ge ra āba si

Tā !ao ûi hâ sa !Khūb ge
Sa sores tsîn ge nî ǁhai
Mâ ǀgai Î !khamdan

!Khara-Khoen waged war and were diminished,
Used to be one of the greatest nations
But are insignificant today.

They waged war and because of war were finished.
The blood of women and children flowed
But this nation will never become extinct.
The houses are deserted and stand empty today
But your nation will not die out.
Your blood flowed like water,
Your children cry for you.

Your God lives, do not be afraid.
Your sun will rise.
Stand firm, you will conquer.

Section 8: Organs of the !Khara-Khoe traditional community

8.1 The Supreme Council

8.1.1 There shall be a Supreme Council for the !Khara-Khoe traditional community.

8.1.2 The composition of the Supreme Council shall be at least 4 members of the !Khara-Khoen Traditional Authority and 6 members of the Elders' Council (*Stam Oudstes*).

---

2 Translated by Levi Namaseb, Department of African Languages, Language and Literature Studies, University of Namibia

8.1.3. The main functions of the Supreme Council shall be to:
- (a) select or identify after consultations with the community the successor to the Captain in accordance with the rules of succession (the latter to be included in the Regulations), as subject to section 4 of the Traditional Authorities Act 25 of 2000, out of the Royal House. If there is no royal successor, the Supreme Council will do the appointment subject to the provisions in section 8.2 below.
- (b) remove the Captain from office, only if there is sufficient reason to warrant the removal, and in accordance with section 8 of the Traditional Authorities Act, 2000.
- (c) designate the selected or identified candidate as the Captain in terms of the Traditional Authorities Act, 2000 after notifying the Minister of Regional and Local Government, Housing and Rural Development.

8.2 The Captain

8.2.1 Designation of the Chief or head of traditional community.

8.2.1.1 One person, male or female, from the Royal House shall assume leadership. If there are two or more people from the Royal House/Family, the Supreme Council has the right to choose one person, male or female, out of the two, or they can give the community the right to elect one.

8.2.1.2 If there is still no successor from the Royal House/Family, the Supreme Council gives the opportunity to the community to elect one person, male or female, as the leader.

8.2.1.3 The Supreme Council will automatically facilitate the election process as the election committee.

8.2.1.4 The candidate will be scrutinised by the Supreme Council to confirm his/her loyalty towards the !Khara-Khoen Traditional Authority.

8.2.2 Scrutiny of the candidate for the position of Chief shall include:
- (a) whether he/she truly is a !Khara-Khoe community member.
- (b) whether he/she is a Namibian citizen in that particular communal area, e.g. Amper-bo.
- (c) whether he/she is loyal to the customary law of the !Khara-Khoen, customs and culture, and
- (d) whether he/she is a fully paid-up member contributing to the !Khara-Khoe traditional community.

8.3.1 The Captain shall be the supreme traditional leader of the !Khara-Khoe traditional community.

8.3.2 The Captain shall be the chairperson of all traditional meetings and may delegate such authority to other people.

8.3.3 The Captain shall be 35 years or above.

8.3.4 He/she shall be democratically elected by the community but the Supreme Council will have the right to oppose the elected person if his/her personality, attitude and other requirements are not favourable for the position he/she has been elected for.

8.3.5 The Captain shall be the custodian of the Customary Law and exercise his/her powers and perform his/her duties and functions in accordance with it.

8.3.6 The inauguration of the Captain shall be done only by a person equal to the Captain or by a designated senior Government official in the presence of other senior traditional heads.

8.3.7 The inauguration of the Captain shall be done in Nama and be translated to any other language needed to accommodate all present during the occasion.

8.3.8 The inauguration procedures shall be included in the regulations of the Customary Law.

8.3.9 The traditional attire of the Captain shall only be assigned to the Captain.

8.4 The Vice Captain

8.4.1 In the absence of the Captain, the Vice Captain shall act as the Captain.

8.4.2 In all other circumstances when necessary, the Vice Captain shall deputise the Captain.

8.5 Elders' Council *(Stam Oudstes)*

8.5.1 There shall be an Elders' Council for the !Khara-Khoe traditional community.

8.5.2 The members shall be 60 years or above.

8.5.3 The Elders' Council shall adopt its own rules for its activities within the limits of customary Law.

8.5.4 The term of office for councillors is 3 (three) years.

8.5.5 The main functions of the Elders' Council shall be to:

(a) advise the Captain and his Council about the customs and culture of the !Khara-Khoen.

(b) see that the !Khara-Khoe customs and culture do not diminish.

(c) delegate members to the Supreme Council when need be.

8.6 !Khara-Khoe Youth Cultural Group

8.6.1 There shall be a Youth Cultural Group for the !Khara-Khoe traditional community.

8.6.2 Members shall be 30 years and younger.

8.6.3 The Youth Cultural Group shall adopt its own rules within the limits of this Customary Law.

8.6.4 The main functions of the Youth Group shall be to:

(a) organise the cultural dances of the community.

(b) keep contact with the cultural groups of other traditional communities.

(c) organise income generating activities and projects within the community for employment creation.

(d) organise sport and other activities among the youth.

8.7 The !Khara-Khoe Women's Cultural Group

8.7.1 There shall be a Women's Cultural Group for the traditional community.
8.7.2 Membership shall be open to all !Khara-Khoe women who are interested in developing and practising the !Khara-Khoe culture.
8.7.3 The cultural group shall adopt its own rules for activities within the limits of this Customary Law.
8.7.4 The main functions of the Women's Cultural Group shall be to:
(a) develop cultural projects within the community.
(b) organise and teach the !Khara-Khoe culture to all women and children.
(c) keep contact with other women and cultural groups.

Section 9: Meetings

9.1 Traditional Assembly

9.1.1 There shall be a Traditional Assembly for the !Khara-Khoe traditional community.
9.1.2 The !Khara-Khoe Traditional Assembly shall be held annually with the Traditional Festival of the !Khara-Khoen.
9.1.3 The date of meetings of the Traditional Assembly shall be included in the Regulations.
9.1.4 The !Khara-Khoe Traditional Assembly shall be open to all members of the !Khara-Khoen throughout Namibia.
9.1.5 Meetings shall be advertised 60 (sixty) days prior to the meeting.
9.1.6 The Traditional Assembly shall have the power to amend or repeal this Customary Law with a 2/3 (two-thirds) majority of members present.
9.1.7 The Assembly shall consist of the Captain, at least 10 members of the !Khara-Khoen Traditional Authority and at least 50 members of the community.

9.2 Traditional Authority meetings

9.2.1 There shall be Traditional Authority meetings once every quarter (i.e. 4 times each year).
9.2.2 Emergency meetings will be held depending on the matter arising and the seriousness of such circumstances.
9.2.3 The meeting shall be attended by the Captain, Vice Captain and Traditional Councillors only to discuss traditional concerns, customary conduct/laws and/or other matters concerning the traditional community.
9.2.4 The Traditional Authority may invite anyone to their meetings.
9.2.5 The quorum for the Traditional Authority meetings shall be seven members.
9.2.6 Every Traditional Authority member shall be obliged to attend the meetings.
9.2.7 Any Traditional Authority member who fails to attend 3 (three) consecutive meetings without a valid reason and without being excused by the Authority automatically discharges him/herself from the Traditional Authority.

9.3 Community meetings

9.3.1 There shall be community meetings for the !Khara'Khoe community.
9.3.2 The meetings shall be open to every member of the community.
9.3.3 The meetings shall be convened by the Captain and his Councillors whenever it is necessary.
9.3.4 The purpose of the meetings shall be either to consult or to give general information to the community.

Section 10: Maintaining law and order

10.1 The laws shall be compiled by the Traditional Council and Elders' Council and shall be accepted by the traditional community after consultations with them.

Section 11: Regulations

11.1 The !Khara-Khoen Traditional Authority may make regulations relating to:

(a) customary marriages
(b) traditional festivals
(c) rules of succession
(d) the traditional anthem
(e) illegal hunting
(f) stock theft
(g) smuggling
(h) vandalism
(i) disputes
(j) rape
(k) environment
(l) assault, and any other matters required in order to achieve the purpose of this customary law.

Section 12: Handling of offences

All fines shall be payable in goats, sheep or cattle, or their monetary equivalent.

12.1 Illegal hunting

12.1.1 Illegal hunting is the killing of game with firearms or any other method without permission.
12.1.2 Sentence and fine: The case shall be referred to the criminal court by the community court.

12.2 Stock theft

12.2.1 If one unit of small stock is stolen, 2 units of small stock are payable.

12.2.2 In the case of one unit of large stock, one head of cattle is payable, or 6 (female) goats and one goat to the Community Trust which brings the total number of animals fined to 7 (seven).

12.3 Smuggling

12.3.1 Smuggling is the bringing in of addictive drugs such as alcohol, cannabis, mandrax, etc.

12.3.2 Cases involving heroin, ammunition and precious stones are referred to the criminal court.

12.4 Vandalism

12.4.1 Damage to buildings, water pipes, fences, etc. shall be dealt with directly and heard by the Community Court.

12.4.2 Sentence and fine: In case of damages to water installations and fences, the maximum fine will be imposed.

12.4.3 In cases of minor damage to other property, the sentence will be community duty as instructed by the traditional court.

12.5 Disputes

12.5.1 Disputes between a couple:
Procedure: The Traditional Court shall restore peace and harmony in the household or between couples.

12.5.2 Interference from family members:
Procedure: Family members on both sides of the couple shall be warned not to interfere.

12.5.3 Gossip:
Procedure: Gossip makers shall be warned not to break peace.

12.6 Rape

12.6.1 Rape shall be directly dealt with by the community court and then referred to the criminal court.

12.7 Damage to the environment

12.7.1 This includes the cutting down of trees and veld fires.

12.7.2 Sentence and fine: These cases shall be dealt with directly by the Traditional Court.

12.7.3 Maximum fine: one head of cattle or 2 units of small stock payable.

12.8 Assault

12.8.1 Assault includes malicious bodily harm and injuries to others.
12.8.2 The maximum sentence shall be 2 (two) units of small stock to be paid to the Community Trust.

Section 13: Community Trust Fund

13.1 The Community Trust Fund shall consist of all fines, donations, contributions or any other sources of income.

13.2 In accordance with section 1 of the Traditional Authorities Act, 2000 (No. 25 of 2000) the !Khara-Khoen Traditional Authority with the consent of its members shall establish a community trust fund for the following purposes:
(a) meetings/administration
(b) travelling/projects.

Section 14: Short title, commencement and amendments

14.1 This Constitution shall be called the !Khara-Khoe Customary Law and shall come into effect immediately after the elected captain has signed it.

14.2 This customary law or any section thereof may be amended or replaced by a 2/3 (two-thirds) majority of the members present at the Traditional Assembly.

14.3 Recommendations in connection with the customary law must be sent at least (30) days before the commencement of the Traditional Assembly to the Secretary of the !Khara-Khoen Traditional Authority.

This document was approved by the Traditional Community.
[Signed by the Chief]

Certificate of consent to publish

UNIVERSITY OF NAMIBIA

FACULTY OF LAW

HUMAN RIGHTS AND DOCUMENTATION CENTRE

20 Nov 2014

RE: CONSENT TO PUBLICATION

I, the undersigned, Chief of the !Khara Khoen Traditional Authority, hereby give consent to the Human Rights and Documentation Centre, to publish the following documents of the !Khara khoen Traditional Authority:

1. The Customary Laws
2. The Community Profile
3. Picture of the Chief
4. Logo of the Traditional Authority

I acknowledge that the Human Rights and Documentation Centre will publish the laws in our indigenous language (__________), as well as the English language. I am familiar with the contents of the laws that will be published and further acknowledge that they were prepared by my traditional authority.

Signed on this 20 day of Nov. 2014 at Amper-bo

Acting Chief

for HRDC: E N Namwoonde

!KHARA-KHOEN ǁAES (FRANSMAN)
20 NOV 2014
SIMON KOOPER TRADITIONAL AUTHORITY

Soromas Traditional Authority
!Aman[1] !Hao!nasi ǂGaeǂGuis

1 Used to be known as ǀUi-ǂGandes !haos (people of Bethanie) but the name was changed in 2012 to !Aman ǁAes.

The supreme leader of the !Aman Traditional Authority is
Gaob[2] David Frederick.
Date of Designation: 1 June 1984

2 Traditional title in terms of section 11, Traditional Authorities Act, 2000 (No. 25 of 2000).

PROFILE[3]

Chief

Chief David Frederick was born in Bethanie district in Groot-Swartkop (ǂNu-!Hom) on 14 September 1932. A son of David Frederick and Anna Maria Sophia Karolis Frederick, he grew up as a farmer in Berseba Community. In 1962 he married Anna Mayer, and had ten children, five boys, one of whom passed away, and five girls.

From 1972 to 1984 he was an Advisor and Councillor to Jan Samuel Herero. In 1984 he was designated as the Chief of !Aman traditional community.

Area of jurisdiction

The area of jurisdiction of the !Aman Traditional Authority is marked in the north by Landshut (Almpomp); in the south by Kosis; in the west by Groot-Swartkop and in the east by Garies.

What is the meaning of the community name?

The community name means to check thoroughly with curiosity for a good place to settle.

Population

The population of the community numbers between 4 000 and 5 000.

Language

The language spoken by the traditional community is Nama.

What is the traditional title of the Chief or the head of the traditional community?

It is *Gaob* which means supreme leader of a tribe.

Origins of the traditional community

The !Aman people came from South Africa in 1750 and 1775, under the leadership of Jacobus Fredrick, also known as Oukobeb, and they settled in Bethanie. They were also

3 This profile was provided by the !Aman Traditional Authority

called *Soromas* which means people who stand in the sun queueing for a long time to fetch water for their cattle.

The customary law of succession

The Chief is chosen from the blood line (patrimonial side) but only a man; if there is no candidate in the bloodline, the elders gather and nominate a suitable candidate from the community.

Chronological order of succession of the chieftainship

Name of the Chief/Head or Traditional Community	Year of chieftainship	
	From	Until
1. Kaptein: Kobus (Jakobus) Fredrick		1818
2.		1825
3. Kaptein: Josef Fredrick I	1825	1842
4. Petrus Frederick	1842	1846
5. David Christian Frederick	01.01.1847	12.12.1880
6. Josef Frederick II	20.11.1880	1893
7. Paul Frederick	12.21.1893	1905
8. Samuel Frederick	21.04.1897	02.1916
9. Eduard Frederick	26.03.1916	1922
10. Josef Frederick III	1922	1938 (+1957)
11. Simon Boo (Hanamub)	1938	1977
12. Jan Samuel Herero (ǀHoa-ǀarab)	1974	1984
13. David Frederick	1984	

Agriculture

The modes of agricultural production are livestock farming and gardening. Goats were the first animals adapted to the situation, and then later cattle and sheep.

Tobacco, pumpkins and water melons are cultivated, while hoodia and sweet potatoes (ǁ*haban*) are collected from the veld.

Water

Traditional wells were the source of water in the Soromas traditional community e.g. Xamis, ǀKhar-khoes, ǀGaris, ǁHatsiames and ǀUigandes. People dig wells (6 to 10 feet deep) in the two rivers, !Gawa-ǁgam and Gurib, and water remains there for a long time.

Traditional sport and culture

The traditional sport in our traditional community is *|Khaus,* played by men, horse-riding and playing the boardgame *‖Hus.*

Nama stap is the cultural dance of our Traditional Authority community, performed by both men and women, especially during festivals, weddings, and girls' first menstruation ceremony.

Art includes making traditional axes, wooden snuff-holders and smoking pipes.

The man is the head of the household.

Cultural festivals always take place in May, normally starting on a Friday and ending on a Sunday with Holy Communion. The aim is to bring the people together to practise their cultural traditions. It reminds the tribe of their old festival in Lüderitz, Shark Island, after every two years to commemorate their forefathers who were killed by the Germans. During this festival, they dress in blue (to refer to the sea and heaven) and pink (to refer to the importance of tenderness).

The !Aman traditional community has no holy fire.

Industrial activities

Manufacturing activities include the making of Nama dresses and shoes from animal skin.

Traditional medicine

Traditional medicine is practised using herbs that grow in the veld.

Mode of transport

Donkey carts, horses and cows provide transport.

Source of information

This information comes from a questionnaire devised by the Ministry of Regional and Local Government, Housing and Rural Development, Subdivision: Secretariat to the Council of Traditional Leaders, and was completed on 17 January 2011 by the following members of the Traditional Community:

Chief David Frederick; Senior Councillors Salomon Swartbooi, Hendrik Frederick, Petrus Isak Frederick, Magdarena Uth; Councillors Elizabeth Keiser, Fredericka Nassauw; community members Anna Frederick, Werner |Haeirob, Rachel Fredrick, Isak Boois-Kusab, Magrietha van Kent, Isak Boois, Salmon Motinga, Willem Boois, Christiaan Kooper, Salomon Motiga, Cornelius Cloete, Lea Boois, Christa Zacharias, Eric Anderson, Lukas Conrad, Paul Frederick.

Die Gewoontereg van die !Aman ǁAes (Soromas)

Inleiding

Hierdie Tradisionele Wet (Gewoontereg) word beskou as die basis waarop die tradisie van die !Aman stam berus.

Leuse: "Gee dus aan u kneg 'n opmerksame hart om reg te spreek oor u Volk" (1 Konings 3: 9)

Artikel 1

Die Kaptein

1. Die Kaptein is die oorhoofse, gesaghebbende leier wat aangewys en/of verkies word, deur die volk, uit die volk, vir die volk.
2. Indien 'n opvolger vanuit die kapteinskraal nie beskikbaar is nie, sal hy uit die volk uit aangewys word of genomineer en verkies word (s. Tradisionele Owerheidswet Nr. 25, 2000, Afdeling 4) (T.O.W).
3. Die aanwysing van die Kaptein uit die kapteinskraal, of uit die volk, geskied opgrond van die reëls van die demokrasie nadat die geskikte kandidaat gevind is. Al die kandidate vir die kapteinsamp moet egter afkomstig wees uit die !Aman-stam en moet bewese aansien in die gemeenskap hê (s. Art. 4, T.O.W. Nr. 25 van 2000.
4. Die Kaptein in sy hoedanigheid as die leier van die !Aman-stam is verantwoordelik vir die beleidsaankondigings en vir die uitvoering van sodanige sake wat die volk raak.
5. Nuwe raadslede en amptenare sal deur die Kaptein in rade benoem en aan die volk voorgestel word. Op 'n vergadering wat by die Kaptein se plek gehou word, moet hulle deur die volk aanvaar word. Addisionele raadslede of amptenare is nie lede van die Kapteinsraad nie.
6. Indien die Kaptein bedank voordat hy die aftreeouderdom van tussen 70 en 75 jaar bereik, of vroeër te sterwe kom, dan alleen mag die volk sy opvolger aanwys of kies en hom/haar inhuldig, tensy die volk weens onvermydelike redes anders besluit.

Artikel 2

Senior Raadslede en Raadslede se jurisdiksies

2.1 Anders as in die geval van die Kaptein wat jurisdiksie het oor die !Aman-stam as geheel, is die magte van die senior raadslede beperk tot die wyke waarin aan hulle verantwoordelikhede toevertrou word en hulle werksaam is.

2.2 Alle raadslede (senior en junior) sal van tyd tot tyd aan die Kaptein verslag doen aangaande die uitvoering van die pligte wat aan hulle opgedra is.

2.3 Senior raadslede en raadslede wat behoorlik benoem en deur die volk aanvaar is, sal dien as skakelbeamptes tussen die Kaptein en die stam.

2.4 Om te verhoed dat die Kaptein sowel die raadslede opsetlik informasie weerhou, is dit verpligtend dat elke ampsdraer aan die volle sitting van die Tradisionele Owerheid verslag sal doen van alle onderhandelings en konsultasies met ander instansies.

2.5 Verslae ten opsigte van goedgekeurde onderhandelings en samesprekings met sodanige instansies sal deur die Tradisionele Owerheid by wyse van omsendbriewe en/of Tradisionele Gemeenskapvergaderings bekend gemaak word.

Artikel 3

Tradisionele Raad (Kapteinsraad) (s. Afdeling 9(1), vgl. T.O.W. Nr. 25 van 2000)

3.1 Die Tradisionele Owerheid bestaan uit 14 lede, die Kaptein, 6 (ses) senior raadslede, 6 (ses) raadslede en die sekretaris (sekretaresse) wat 'n maandelikse toelaag van die regering ontvang (s. Art 10; Art 17, T.O.W. Nr. 25 van 2000).

3.2 Addisionele raadslede genoem die Volksraad van mintens 8 (agt) lede word deur die Kapteinsraad benoem en aan die volk vir aanvaarding voorgestel en aanbeveel (s. Art 9.2 a en b T.O.W. Nr. 25 van 2000).

3.3 Die Volksraad vorm 'n eenheid in samewerking met die Kapteinsraad en verrig 'n vrywillige diens aan die volk.

3.4 Alle raadslede word in die wyke van die Bethaniën-distrik ingedeel om hul volksgenote te bedien en halfjaarliks verslag te doen aan die volle Raadsitting.

3.5 Die Kapteinsraad vergader kwartaalliks.

3.5.1 Volksraadslede mag die Kapteinsraad-vergaderings bywoon. Hulle mag aan besprekings deelneem, maar het nie stemreg nie.

3.5.2 Die Kapteinsraad en die Volksraad hou twee keer per jaar gesamentlik vergaderings.

3.5.3 Buitengewone vergaderings mag na gelang van omstandighede deur albei Huise gehou word.

3.5.4 Die Kaptein is die voorsitter van die Kapteinsraad, sowel as van die Volksraad.

Artikel 4

Dagbestuur

4.1 Die Dagbestuur is verantwoordelik vir die daaglikse diens van die Raad en bestaan uit lede van die Kapteinsraad wat plaaslik woonagtig is en nie aan ander permanente werksaamhede gebonde is nie, en die sekretaris (sekretaresse) van die Raad.

4.2 Die voorsitterskap van die Dagbestuur sal op 'n maandelikse basis tussen die genoemde senior raadslede roteer (s. Afdeling 9(5), T.O.W. Nr. 25 van 2000).

4.3 Die voorsitter van die Dagbestuur ondersteun die sekretaris van die Raad in die uitvoering van sake en besluite van die Kapteinsraad.

4.4 Besluite van die Dagbestuurvergaderings moet genotuleer en vir bekragtiging aan die Kapteinsraad voorgelê word.

4.5 Die Kaptein is ampshalwe (*ex officio*) lid van die Dagbestuur. Hy mag te eniger tyd die vergaderings van die Dagbestuur bywoon en aan besprekings deelneem, maar sonder stemreg.

Artikel 5

Die Oudstes Raadgewende Raad

5.1 Die Oudstes Raadgewende Raad bestaan uit sewe lede van die !Ama-volk.

5.2 Die Oudstes Raadgewende Raad word deur die !Ama-volk aangewys en aangestel vir 'n tydperk van 5 (vyf) jaar. Hulle mag herbenoem word.

5.3 Die Oudstes Raadgewende Raad is nie 'n lid van die Kapteinsraad nie en neem ook nie deel in die vergaderings van die !Ama Tradisionele Owerheid nie, tensy hulle amptelik daarheen uitgenooi word.

5.4 Wettiglik is die Oudstes Raadgewende Raad ondergeskik aan die Tradisionele Owerheid, maar onafhanklik in sy werksaamhede (s. T.O.W. Nr. 25 van 2000).

5.5 Die opdrag en pligte van die Oudstes Raadgewende Raad is om die Kaptein en sy/haar Raad van advies ten opsigte van die sake rakende die !Ama-volk te voorsien en te dien.

5.6 Die Oudstes Raadgewende Raad sal die Kaptein te alle tye ondersteun om in samewerking met sy Raad 'n vreedsame bestaan binne die !Ama-volk en alle inwoners op ǀUi-ǂgandes/Bethaniën en in die omgewing te verseker.

5.7 Interne dispute

5.7.1 'n Onderlinge dispuut binne die Kapteinsraad wat die Kaptein nie self kan besleg nie, sal na die Oudstes Raadgewende Raad verwys word.

5.7.2 Indien die Kaptein en sy/haar raad versuim om die Oudstes Raadgewende Raad van 'n onopgeloste stryd en/of sake binne hul geledere te verwittig, mag die Raad ingryp met die doel om die orde te herstel.

5.8 Voorsitter

5.8.1 Die Oudstes Raadgewende Raad benoem en verkies by hulle eerste sitting 'n voorsitter uit hulle geledere wat die vergadering sal lei.

5.8.2 Daarna sal die voorsitterskap jaarliks roteer en wel volgens die alfabetiese volgorde van die name van die raadslede.

5.9 Skriba

5.9.1 Die skriba of die notuleskrywer sal 'n lid van die Oudstes Raadgewende Raad wees, en sal deur die Raad aangewys word.

5.9.2 Hy/sy sal in samewerking met die voorsitter die agenda vir die vergaderings opstel en dit tien dae voor die datum van die vergadering aan die lede stuur.

5.9.3 Hy/sy sal die notule binne 'n week ná die sitting van die Raad aan elke lid oorhandig of per pos aanstuur.

5.9.4 Die notule sal as **streng vertroulik** beskou en gehandhaaf word.

5.10 Vergaderings

5.10.1 Die Oudstes Raadgewende Raad mag 2 (twee) of meer vergaderings per jaar hou.

5.10.2 Die Kaptein of sy/haar verteenwoordiger mag die vergadering slegs op uitnodiging van die Raad bywoon.

5.10.3 Buitengewone vergaderings mag gehou word, indien nodig.

5.10.4 Alle vergaderings van die Oudstes Raadgewende Raad vind plaas in die kantoor van die !Aman Tradisionele Owerheid te ǀUi-ǂGandes/Bethaniën.

Artikel 6

Amptelike korrespondensie

6.1 Alle amptelike korrespondensie moet op 'n briefhoof van die !Aman-volk gedoen word, die stempel van die stam dra en slegs deur die Kaptein onderteken word.

6.2 Indien korrespondensie in die afwesigheid van die Kaptein dringend uitgevoer moet word, mag 'n senior raadslid wat 'n voorsitter van die Dagbestuur is, dit namens die Kaptein onderteken.

6.3 Indien die voorsitter van die Dagbestuur ook afwesig sou wees, moet die sekretaris (sekretaresse) dit onderteken.

6.4 Geen private korrespondensie sal op die amptelike briefhoof uitgevoer word sonder die stempel van die volk nie. Dit sal beskou word as 'n ernstige oortreding. As dit gebeur, sal straf soos voorgeskryf deur die wet toegepas word.

Artikel 7

Die setel

7.1 Die setel van die !Aman Tradisionele Owerheid is op ǀUi-ǂGandes /Bethaniën, Quellenstraat 10 & 11, van waar dienste onder die !Aman-volk plaaslik en in die buitewyke gedoen en besluite van die Kapteinsraad uitgevoer word.

Artikel 8

8.1 Spesifieke dienste aan die gemeenskap

8.1.1 Die kinders en jeug van vandag is die ouers en leiers op verskeie gebiede van die lewe in die toekoms. Om hierdie verantwoordelikhede (ouerskap en leierskap) op die regte manier te kan handhaaf, is akademiese kwalifikasies onontbeerlik.

8.1.2 Daarom moet die !Aman Tradisionele Owerheid alle ouers aanmoedig en ondersteun, om hul kinders vir opleiding na die kindergartens en skole te stuur.

8.1.3 Om 'n sukses van die opleiding van alle kinders op ǀUi-ǂGandes/Bethaniën, Kosis, ens. te verseker, is gesonde samewerking met die onderwysers en onderwyseresse van plaaslike opleidingsinrigtings nodig.

8.1.4 Daarom sal die !Aman Tradisionele Owerheid te alle tye poog om samewerking tussen die ouers, leerkragte en leerlinge te bevorder.

8.1.5 Om hierdie strewe te bewerkstellig en te bereik moet die Kaptein saam met die lede van die Dagbestuur van tyd tot tyd met die plaaslike skoolhoofde samebesprekings voer ten opsigte van verhoudings tussen ouers, onderwysers en leerlinge, asook oor die wedersydse verpligtinge van die betrokkenes.

8.1.6 In geval van onopgeloste vraagstukke, probleme en konflikte op die gebied van onderwys moet die Tradisionele Owerheid die streekkantoor van Karas-streek of selfs die betrokke ministeries kontak en 'n vreedsame oplossing daarvoor soek.

8.2 Gesondheid

8.2.1 Liggaamlike gesondheid is baie belangrik vir elke mens. Dit is net 'n gesonde liggaam wat 'n gesonde gees en verstand kan akkommodeer.

8.2.2 Daarom, met die doel om 'n gesonde volk te hê, poog die !Aman Tradisionele Owerheid om jonk en oud onder hulle volksgenote aan te moedig om die mediese dienste wat plaaslik beskikbaar is en aangebied word, ten volle te gebruik.

8.2.3 Ter bestryding van MIV/Vigs wat verwoesting onder die jeug saai en ontydige sterftes veroorsaak, het die Tradisionele Owerheid oorlog teen die epidemie verklaar en sal altyd hul uiterste bes doen om dit in samewerking met plaaslike mediese kundiges te beveg.

8.2.4 Die jeug sowel ander belangstellende volwassenes sal aangemoedig en ernstig versoek word om gereeld van die programme en kursusse wat vir die voorkoming daarvan (MIV/Vigs) aangebied word, gebruik te maak.

8.2.5 Die !Aman Tradisionele Owerheid sal altyd poog om met die mediese personeel van die regering te ǀUi-ǂGandes/Bethaniën saam te werk en hulle aanmoedig om goeie menseverhoudings met hulle pasiënte te handhaaf en ook andersom (pasiënte met personeel).

8.2.6 Waar nodig sal die Tradisionele Owerheid albei bogenoemdes met raad en daad bystaan.

8.3 Ontwikkelingsprojekte

8.3.1 Met die doel om die las van werkloosheid te verlig en die lewenstandaard van die !Aman Tradisionele Gemeenskap te |Ui-ǂGandes Bethaniën en omgewing, veral in die kommunale gebied te verbeter en positief te verander, het die !Aman Tradisionele Owerheid besluit om verskillende ontwikkelingsprojekte te inisieer.

8.3.2 Hierdie projekte sluit in tuinbou, vee-, hoender-, volstruis- en varkboerdery, broodbak, naaldwerk, toesig oor en beskerming van die grond en diere van die veld (*xamanin*), en andere (*conservancy*).

Artikel 9

Bestryding van alkohol- en dwelmmisbruik

9.1 Misbruik van alkoholiese drank en dwelms veroorsaak die afbreek van goeie sedes in die gemeenskap vir mense wat hulleself daaraan skuldig maak.
Dit tas die hart sowel as die gesondheid van die hele liggaam aan en bring aanhoudende armoede oor die alkoholis en sy/haar familie. Kortom, misbruik van alkohol en dwelms veroorsaak verwaarlosing van die liggaam en die gees van die mens (innerlik en uiterlik). Die slegte gevolge van die misbruik van alkoholiese drank en dwelms is verreikend, nie slegs vir die alkoholis nie maar vir die hele !Aman-volk.

9.2 Daarom het die Kaptein en die !Aman-volk as geheel besluit om so ver hulle in staat is en met die samewerking met plaaslike leiers van verskillende instansies en ampdraers (hospitaal/kliniek, gesondheidsentrum, skole, onderwysers, maatskaplike werkers, polisie, geestelike leiers, ens.) die misbruik van alkohol en dwelms te bestry.

9.3 Die gebruik van alkoholiese drank, so ook van verskillende soorte tuisgemaakte sterk drank en dwelms, is totaal verbode vir kinders en jeugdiges.

Artikel 10

Finansies

10.1 Die algemene fondse van die !Aman-stam sal verkry word uit die volgende bronne: stamfonds, opbrengste van funksies, vrywillige skenkings, heffings, telefoonoproepe, donasies, bemarkings, die verkoop van stamleesstof en stamprojekte.

10.2 Alle nasionale fondse sal in die bankrekening gedeponeer word en aansoeke om geld te onttrek, moet geteken wees deur die gemagtigdes, te wete die Kaptein en tesourier of Kaptein en sekretaris.

10.3 Die finansiële jaar van die !Aman-stam begin op die eerste dag van Januarie en eindig op die laaste dag van Februarie van die daaropvolgende jaar.

10.4 Die finansiële state van die !Aman-stam moet deur goegekeurde ouditeurs geoudit word.

10.5 Fondse wat vir 'n spesifieke doel deur lede van die volk en ander bygedra word, sal nie vir 'n ander doel gebruik word nie, tensy die Stamraad anders besluit.

10.6 'n Gemeenskap-trustfond is verpligtend vir die !Aman-volk en moet gehandhaaf word soos dit voorgeskryf is in Afdeling 18 van die Tradisionele Owerheidswet, Nr. 25 van 2000.

Artikel 11

Regsbevoegdheid

11.1 Die Kaptein in rade sal namens die Stamraad en die !Ama-stam as geheel, regsbevoegdheid hê.

Artikel 12

Ontbinding of wysigings van die tradisionele wet

12.1 Hierdie Tradisionele Gewoontereg (Wet) of enige deel daarvan mag herroep, gewysig, verander of aan toegevoeg word deur 'n tweederdemeerderheid van lede teenwoordig by 'n !Aman stam-vergadering.

12.2 Aanbevelings in verband met enige verandering aan die Tradisionele Wet moet gestuur word aan die Stamsekretaris, minstens dertig dae voor die Volksvergadering. Veranderings aan die Tradisionele Wet sal vooraf in al die wyke gesirkuleer word vir bestudering voor die Volksvergadering.

Saamgestel en onderteken deur beide die !Ama Tradisionele Owerheid en lede van die !Ama Geskiedenis Ondersoekkomitee

Kaptein David Frederick, Salomon Swartbooi, Petrus Isak Frederik, Hendrik Frederik (Hotageb), Elisabeth Keiser, Fredrika Nassauw, Christor Boois, Salmon Blaauw, Willem Boois (!Oasib), Christiaan Uth (Boetietjie), Izak Fredericks (Pastoor), Hendrik Frederik (Biskop).

[Geteken by die Kaptein]

Bylaag A

Aanwysing van die !Aman-ǁAes tradisionele leiers

Inleiding

In die verlede is die Kaptein van !Ama-ǁAes nie gekies nie, maar aangewys. Maar aangesien bestaande tradisionele wette en gewoontes met verloop van tyd verander, sal die verkiesing van 'n Kaptein in die toekoms as volg gereël word. Vir die aanwysing van 'n Kaptein moet 'n komitee uit die senior en jongmense van die stam benoem word. Daardie benoeming moet deur die gemeenskap tydens 'n Volksvergadering gedoen word.

A1. Volgens die RYKSBOEK van 1847 [1] is die aanwysing van die Kaptein as volg voorgeskryf:
"Volgens voorgeskrewe reëls moet die kapteinskap slegs onder die mans wees. Daarom sal die oudste seun van die Kaptein hom as kaptein opvolg. Maar indien daardie oudste seun, voordat hy aangewys word, sterwe, maar self geen kinders nagelaat het nie, sal die kapteinskap op die seun van die Kaptein wat die oudste een opvolg, val. Indien die Kaptein geen ander seuns sou hê nie, sal die kapteinskap na die ouer broer van die Kaptein gaan. Ander jonger seuns van die Kaptein het geen aanspraak op die kapteinskap nie. Die kapteinskap mag ook nie tussen twee (2) of meer seuns (van die Kaptein) verdeel word om so die volksleiding oor te neem en oor die stam te heers nie".

A2. Sedert Kaptein Josef Frederick (3de) deur die destydse regering in die jaar 1938 aan die !Ama-volk teruggegee is en die twee pond wat hy maandeliks van die regering ontvang het, nietig verklaar is, is die voorskrif vir die aanwysing van 'n kaptein vir die !Ama-ǁAes, nie meer gevolg nie. Die Tradisionele Leiers wat hom opgevolg het, is deur die owerheid wat Namibië onder toesig van die Suid-Afrikaanse regering bestuur het, volgens sy reëls aangewys.

A3. Die Namibiese regering het nou aan alle tradisionele gemeenskappe en stamme die reg toegestaan om hulle tradisionele leiers volgens hulle tradisionele wette en gewoontes aan te wys of te verkies. (s. Tradisionele Owerheidswet, Nr. 25, 2000, Afdeling 4.)

A4. Met die doel om kapteins in die toekoms meer regverdig aan te wys of te verkies het die !Ama-ǁAes besluit om –

(a) navorsing te doen ten opsigte van die oorspronklike !Aman kapteinsfamilie/bloedlyn, en in besonder vir kennisname en geskiedenis doeleindes, en

(b) 'n komitee te benoem wat ondersoek sal instel of daar nog mans van die oorspronklike kaptein-stamboom is wat in die toekoms as kaptein-kandidaat benoem kan word.

---

1 Redakteur se nota: Die *Ryksboek bevattende alle wetten en rechten van het Kapiteinschap te Bethanië* is die oudste weergawe van gewoontereg in Namibië. Dit is beskikbaar in die argief van die Evangeliese Lutherse Kerk in die Republiek van Namibië (ELCRN) onder elcrnx 15–21.

A4.1 Aanwysing van die Kaptein

A4.1.1 Drie manskandidate vir die kapteinskap van !Ama-ǁAes sal deur die genoemde komitee benoem word.
A4.1.2 Daarna moet hulle aan die hele stam voorgestel word, sodat die volk hulle benoeming kan aanvaar.
A4.1.3 Indien die stam hulle nie aanvaar nie, moet die komitee ander kandidate soek, totdat mans gevind word wat deur die hele stam as kandidate aanvaar sal word.

A4.2 Die stemprosedure is soos volg:

A4.2.1 Uit die drie (3) kandidate sal die verkiesing oor twee rondtes gaan.
A4.2.2 Die kandidaat wat in die eerste verkiesingsrondte die minste stemme trek, sal onttrek en nie verder aan die verkiesing deelneem nie.
A4.2.3 Net die oorblywende twee kandidate sal aan die tweede rondte deelneem.
A4.2.4 Die kandidaat wat in die tweede verkiesingsrondte met die gewone meerderheid van stemme verkies word, sal die gekose kaptein wees.
A4.3 Die komitee sal ná die instelling van die Kaptein ontbind.
A4.4 Elke keer wanneer die !Ama-ǁAes 'n kaptein benodig, moet 'n komitee wat kandidate nomineer, opnuut benoem word.
A4.5 Die mans (kandidate) wat vir die kapteinskap benoem word, moet 40 jaar of ouer wees.
A4.6 Die Kaptein moet aftree as hy die ouderdom van 70 jaar bereik. Maar indien sy gesondheid en sy liggaamskragte dit toelaat en die hele stam ten gunste is daarvan, mag hy dien totdat hy die ouderdom van 75 jaar bereik.
A4.7 Die eienskappe en dienste wat van die !Ama-ǁAes kaptein verwag word, word in sy diensregulasies voorgeskryf.

A4.8 As die stam nie met die gedrag en dienste van die Kaptein tevrede is nie –

A4.8.1 moet die lede van die Stamraad vertroulik met hom gesprek voer.
A4.8.2 Indien verdere gesprekvoering met die Kaptein noodsaaklik word, moet senior lede uit die volk ingeroep word om die Stamraad te ondersteun.
A4.8.3 As die geprekke met die Kaptein ten opsigte van sy gedrag en diens suksesvol is, hoef dit nie aan die volk gerapporteer te word nie.
A4.8.4 Slegs indien die bonoemde gesprekke nie vrugte afwerp nie, moet dit aan die volk gerapporteer word sodat hulle 'n finale besluit kan neem.

A5. Senior en Junior Tradisionele Raadslede

A5.1 Senior en Junior Tradisionele Raadslede word deur die Kapteinsraad benoem en aan die volk voorgestel vir aanvaarding. Die volk mag die benoeming wysig en na die Kapteinsraad terugverwys (s. Afdeling 10 van die Tradisionele Owerheidswet, Wet Nr. 25, 2000.).

A5.2 Addisionele raadslede kan in hul hoedanigheid as raadgewers benoem en/of aangewys word, op grond van hulle akademiese kwalifikasies, bekwaamheid en ondervinding.

A5.3 'n Persoon wat as Senior of Junior Raadslid benoem en aangestel word, moet 18 jaar of ouer wees.

A5.4 Hulle dienstermyne sal aanhou tot hulle die ouderdom van 70 jaar bereik.

A5.5 Hulle tree uit die amp as Raadslid ná bedanking, ontslag of afsterwe.

A5.6 As die volk nie tevrede is met die gedrag en die uitvoering van die pligte van Senior en Junior Tradisionele leiers nie:

A5.6.1 In geval van wangedrag of diensverwaarlosing, sal die Kaptein met hom/haar gesprek voer en aan die hele Raad verslag doen.

A5.6.2 Indien die gesprekke met die Kaptein nie suksesvol is nie, moet die Stamraadslede ingeroep word.

A5.6.3 As die geprekke met die hele Stamraad nie enige vrugte afwerp nie, moet die betrokke Raadslid uit die aktiewe diens ontslaan en die volk dienooreenkomstig verwittig word.

Bylaag B

Strafregtelike sake

Inleiding

Die !Ama Volk Tradisionele Gemeenskapshof *(Traditional Community Court)* sal die ondergenoemde misdade en dispute verhoor en beoordeel. Die strafreëls van die genoemde misdade verskyn in afsonderlike statutêre voorskrifte en wetboeke wat deur die Ministerie van Justisie vir alle Tradisionele Owerhede in Namibië voorgeskryf word.

B1 Diefstal is 'n strafbare misdaad wat selfs deur die Bybel streng verbied word. JY MAG NIE STEEL NIE! In werklikheid is diefstal van eiendom van mense wat deur middel van harde werk en besparing oor 'n tydperk van baie jare vir hulleself en hul nageslagte besittings versamel en opgebou het, 'n ernstige oortreding. Kortom: dit is 'n ernstige siviele oortreding en word nie as 'n ligte misstap beskou nie.

Oortreders wat deur middel van diefstal hul landgenote groot skade berokken en sodoende verarm, sal swaar boetes opgelê word, sodat hulle dit nie sal herhaal nie. Die strafoplegging van skuldiges sal vir seker volgens die voorgeskrewe strafreëls geskied.

B2 Smokkel

Die *Handwoordeboek van die Afrikaans Taal (HAT)* beskrywe smokkel as volg: Dit is om verbode goedere of belasbare goedere sonder betaling van belasting in die geheim in en uit te voer. Smokkelhandel is om goud, diamante of dagga die land in te bring of na die buiteland te smokkel.

Smokkelhandel is 'n onwettige praktyk. Daarom verbied die !Aman Tradisionele Owerheid smokkelhandel geheel en al onder sy volgelinge, ten einde die voorsetting van verarming van die volk wat daardeur veroorsaak word, te verhoed.

B3 Wilddiefstal, stroop, inbreek en steel

Bogenoemde negatiewe optredes gaan gepaard met diefstal, maar verskil in dié sin dat daardie handelinge op groot skaal met geweld gepaard gaan. Mense wat wild sonder toestemming van die regering jag, maak hulleself skuldig aan wilddiefstal en stropery, wetende dat hulle 'n hoë boete opgelê sal word as hulle sonder die nodige permitte betrap en gearresteer word.

Inbrekers betree soms huise terwyl die eienaars nie daar is nie, maar in die meeste gevalle in die nagtelike ure. Deesdae is inbrekers gewapen en verkeer die eienaars van huise in gevaar as hulle waag om teenstand te bied. Die gevolg kan wees dat jy in jou eie huis vermoor kan word.

Met die doel om genoemde misdade te bekamp sal die !Aman Tradisionele Owerheid poog om dit in noue samewerking met die polisie te beveg. Mense wat hulle daaraan skuldig maak sal volgens die voorgeskrewe wette gestraf word.

B4 Owerspel en egskeiding

Om die betekenis van owerspel te verstaan moet dit saamgelees word met egbreuk. Onder die Israeliete (die volk van God) was owerspel verbied en diegene wat owerspel gepleeg het, is ter dood veroordeel. "En as iemand owerspel pleeg met 'n man se vrou, of owerspel pleeg met sy naaste se vrou, moet hy en sy wat owerspel pleeg, sekerlik gedood word" (Levitikus 20:10).

Die Christelike leer laat ook nie owerspel toe nie, alhoewel die oortreders nie die doodstraf opgelê word nie. Elke Christelike sowel tradisionele gemeenskap het sy eie metodes oor hoe owerspel hanteer moet word.

Ten opsigte van egskeiding die volgende:

Oorspronklik is egskeiding nie aan die huwelik verbind nie; dit was slegs ter wille van die hardheid van hulle harte dat Moses egskeiding onder sy volksgenote toegelaat het (Matteus 19:8).

Die !Aman Tradisionele Owerheid doen 'n beroep op sy volksgenote om te alle tye te poog en hulle te weerhou van owerspel en egskeiding. Voorts gee die Tradisionele Owerheid sy ondersteuning en samewerking aan die plaaslike geestelike leiers en hulle rade, sodat die voorkoms van owerspel en egskeiding onder die !Aman volk beperk kan word.

B5 Verkragting

Verkragting gaan ook gepaard met geweldpleging, omdat verkragting sonder toestemming van die persoon wat verkrag word, plaasvind. In die meeste gevalle is dit die vroulike geslag wat die prooi daarvan is. Verkragting is nie net 'n kriminele oortreding nie, maar 'n vernedering van 'n mens wat lewenslank onthou word. Daarom moet iemand met wie dit gebeur, geestelik, sielkundig en medies versorg word.

Die !Aman Tradisionele Owerheid sal alles in sy vermoë doen om iemand wat so iets oorgekom het, te help om die trauma (letsel) daarvan te verwerk. Hierdie Owerheid sal die klaer ondersteun en aanmoedig om die klag nie terug te trek nie, selfs teen vergoeding. Die verkragter wat 'n oortreder is, moet volgens die voorgeskrewe wette beboet word.

B6 Vandalisme

Iemand wat die eiendom van 'n ander person moedswillig en opsetlik vernietig, pleeg vandalisme. So 'n persoon verniel nie slegs iemand anders se waardevolle besittings nie, maar breek die eienaar/es sielkundig af deur middel van sy barbaarse vernielsug. Iemand wat betrap word terwyl hy/sy met vandalisme besig is, sal onmiddellik gearresteer word, maar die eienaar moet hom/haar offisieel aankla sodat die vandalis wettig deur die Stamowerheid of die polisie vervolg kan word na gelang van die mate van vandalisme wat gepleeg is.

B7 Erfenis – oneerlikheid en bedrog in erfenis

Sommige ouers en naasbestaandes versuim om 'n geskrewe testament vir hul nageslag op te stel. Dit veroorsaak dat oneerlikheid en bedrog in die verdeling van erfgoed ondervind word. Sommige erfgename kry nie die erfporsie wat hulle toekom nie.

Die !Aman Tradisionele Owerheid het besluit om sy volgelinge aan te moedig om betyds 'n testament op te stel waarin elkeen moet verklaar hoe hulle hulle roerende en onroerende eiendomme en besittings onder hulle erfgename wil laat verdeel.

Verder het die Owerheid besluit om die familielid wat vir die verdeling van erfgoed verantwoordelik sal wees te help met die aanstelling van 'n kundige wat hom met die opstel van die testament en die uitvoer daarvan, sal assisteer.

B8 Familietwis en skinder

Dit word dikwels deur verskeie redes veroorsaak. In sommige gevalle word familietwis en skinder ondervind ná die afsterwe van ouers en/of naasbestaandes sonder dat hulle in 'n testament hul laaste wil vasgelê het oor hoe hulle besittings onder die wettige erfname verdeel moet word.

B9 Vernietiging van die omgewing

Elke burger van 'n land, insluitend Namibië, moet die wette van die land waarin hulle leef respekteer as gevolg van die feit dat elke klein stukkie grond waardevol is vir enige land. Dit is die werklike rede waarom die vernietiging van die omgewing nie toegelaat word nie. Mense wat skuldig bevind word aan die vernietiging van die land sal gestraf word volgens die wet.

Met die doel om bewustheid onder sy mense oor die vernietiging van die omgewing te skep sal die Tradisionele Owerheid die onderrig van toepaslike inligting aan sy mense aanmoedig. Oortreders sal gestraf word.

B10 Aanranding

Aanranding gaan hand aan hand met geweld. Aanranding is wanneer 'n persoon deur een of meer mense aangeval en beseer word. In die meeste gevalle het aanranding te doen met wapens. Goeie mense met goeie name word aangerand om hul beeld te vernietig. Om sy ondersteuners teen aanranding te beskerm, het die Tradisionele Owerheid besluit om saam met die polisie alle soorte aanrandings stop te sit.

B11 Verskillende soorte dwelms

Dwelmmisbruik veroorsaak verslawing net soos alkoholiste verslaaf raak aan alkohol. Oormatige gebruik van dwelms het al baie jong mense in die wêreld mislei, waar studente skool toe gaan en in 'n netwerk van dwelmgebruikers asook die misbruik van alkohol vasgevang word. Dit is waarom die Tradisionele Owerheid met alles tot sy beskikking teen die gebruik van enige vorm van dwelms en teen die misbruik van alle vorme van die dinge wat beskadig of die gesondheid van sy mense vernietig sal veg. Die gebruik van dwelms word heeltemal deur die wet verbied en diegene wat betrap word met die gebruik van dwelms sal voor die reg gebring word en dienooreenkomstig aangekla word.

The laws of the !Aman (Soromas)

Introduction

This Traditional Customary Law is regarded as the basis on which the tradition of the !Ama clan has been grounded.

Motto: "Give your servant therefore an understanding heart to govern your people, that I may discern between good and evil" (1 Kings 3: 9).

Article 1

The Captain

The Captain is the ultimate authority, a leader who has been appointed or elected by the people from the clan for themselves.

However, if no successor is available from the original !Ama clan Captain's bloodline, his successor will be appointed or elected from the members of the !Ama clan (cf. Traditional Authorities Act, 2000 (No. 25 of 2000, Section 4).

Appointment or election of the Captain by the !Ama Clan, whether or not from the original Captain's bloodline, is based on the rules of democracy, provided that a qualified candidate has been found. All candidates for captainship must be descendants of the !Ama Clan and hold a respected position in the community as well, cf. Section 4, Traditional Authorities Act, 2000 (No. 25 of 2000).

The Captain in his capacity as traditional leader of the !Ama Clan is responsible for making policy statements and for the implementation of matters that concern his people.

Newly appointed traditional councillors must be introduced to the people. At a meeting at the Captain's palace or residence, they must be accepted by the clan. Additional traditional councillors and officials shall not be voting members of the Captain's Council.

Only if the Captain resigns or dies before reaching his retirement age of from 70 to 75 years, may the people of his clan designate and elect a successor, unless they decide differently because of unavoidable reasons due to his behaviour.

Article 2

Powers of Senior Traditional Councillors and Traditional Councillors

2.1 Powers of the Senior and Traditional Councillors shall be limited to the districts in which they operate according to the responsibilities entrusted to them. The powers of the Captain are unlimited and cover the whole area of jurisdiction of the !Ama Clan.

2.2 All Traditional Councillors (Senior and Junior) shall be obliged to submit reports to the Captain regularly). These reports should address the execution of their duties, including activities, improvements and challenges in their districts.

2.3 The Senior and Traditional Councillors who have been appointed by the Captain's Council according to the Customary Law and accepted by the clan shall operate as linkage between the Captain and the people.

2.4 The Captain and Councillors shall have no right to withhold information that has been received from meetings with other bodies/institutions. They all shall be compelled to report it to an official meeting of the Traditional Authority.

2.5 Reports on negotiations of certain issues with different institutions that were approved must be circulated to the community in writing or made known through traditional community meetings.

Article 3

Traditional Council (Captain's Council) (cf. Traditional Authorities Act, 2000 (No. 25 of 2000, Section 9(1))

3.1 The Traditional Authority shall consist of 14 members. They are the captain, 6 (six) Senior Traditional Councillors, 6 (six) Traditional Councillors and the Secretary who receive monthly allowances from the government (cf. Traditional Authorities Act, 2000 (No. 25 of 2000, Sections 10 and 17).

3.2 Members without voting rights additional to the Council called the *Volksraad*, which consists of 8 (eight) members shall be appointed by the Captain's Council and recommended to the people for acceptance (cf. Traditional Authorities Act, 2000 (No. 25 of 2000, Section 9.2 a & b).

3.3 The *Volksraad* shall co-operate closely with the Captain's Council and perform their voluntary service to the people.

3.4 Each Traditional Councillor shall be responsible for a ward in the area of jurisdiction of the !Ama Clan. They shall be obliged to submit reports about their operations to the Council meetings every 6 (six) months.

3.5 The Captain's Council shall meet quarterly (every 3 (three) months).

3.5.1 Members of the *Volksraad* may attend the Captain's Council meetings. They may participate in discussions of matters, but without voting rights.

3.5.2 The Captain's Council and *Volksraad* shall hold meetings twice (2 times) a year.

3.5.3 Extraordinary meetings may be called by both houses, the Captain's Council and *Volksraad* as required by circumstances.

3.5.4 The Captain is the Chairperson of the above mentioned 2 (two) Houses, i.e. both the Captain's Council and the *Volksraad*.

Article 4

The management

4.1 The Management shall consist of members of the Captain's Council, including the Secretary of the Council. They are responsible for the day to day activities of the !Ama Traditional Authority. In order to be available at anytime, they should not have permanent employment and should be resident locally.

4.2 Chairmanship of the Management will rotate monthly among the Senior Traditional Councillors who are members of the Management (cf. Traditional Authorities Act, 2000 (No. 25 of 2000, Section 9(5)).

4.3 The Chairperson of the Management will assist the Secretary of the Captain in implementing matters and resolutions of the Captain's Council.

4.4 Decisions of the Management shall be noted and submitted to the Captain's Council for confirmation.

4.5 The Captain is an ex-officio member of the Management. He may attend meetings of the Management at any time. He may participate in discussions of agenda items, but has no voting rights.

Article 5

The Elders' Advisory Council

5.1 The Elders' Advisory Council shall consist of 7 (seven) members from the !Ama Clan.

5.2 The Elders' Advisory Council shall be appointed by the !Ama Clan for a period of 5 (five) years. They may be re-elected.

5.3 The members of the Elders' Advisory Council shall not be members of the Captain's Council. They shall also not attend meetings of the Captain's Council, unless they are invited officially.

5.4 Legally the Elders' Advisory Council is subordinate to the !Ama Traditional Authority; however, it shall be independent in its operation (cf.Traditional Authorities Act, 2000 (No. 25 of 2000).

5.5 The directives and duties of the Elders' Advisory Council shall be to advise and serve the Captain and his/her Council on all matters concerning the !Ama people.

5.6 The Elders' Advisory Council shall at all times assist and support the Captain and in co-operation with his Councillors strive to secure peace among the !Ama people and all inhabitants of the environs of ǀUi-ǂgandes/Bethanie.

5.7 Internal disputes

5.7.1 Cases of internal disputes within the Captain's Council which the Captain himself cannot settle, shall be directed to the Elders' Advisory Council.

5.7.2 If the Captain and his Council fail to inform the Elders' Advisory Council about unresolved matters among themselves, the Elders' Advisory Council may intervene in order to restore peace and order.

5.8 Chairperson

5.8.1 The Elders' Advisory Council members nominate and elect a Chairperson from among their members at their first meeting.
5.8.2 Thereafter, the chairmanship will rotate annually, in alphabetical order.

5.9 Secretary

5.9.1 The Secretary will be a member of the Elders' Advisory Council who will be designated by the said council.
5.9.2 The Secretary shall draft the Agenda for the meetings in co-operation with the Chairperson. He/she shall provide it to the members 10 (ten) days before commencement of the meetings.
5.9.3 The Secretary will deliver the minutes within one week after meetings to each member of the Elders' Advisory Council.
5.9.4 The minutes shall be regarded as strictly private.

5.10 Meetings

5.10.1 The Elders' Advisory Council may call 2 (two) or more meetings per annum.
5.10.2 The Captain or his representative may attend meetings of the Elders' Advisory Council only on official invitation.
5.10.3 Extraordinary meetings may be held, if necessary.
5.10.4 All meetings of the Elders' Advisory Council shall take place at the office of the !Ama Traditional Authority in Bethanie.

Article 6

Official correspondence

6.1 All official correspondence must be done on the official letterhead of the !Ama Clan must carry the stamp of the clan, and be signed by the chief only.
6.2 If any correspondence must be carried out urgently in the absence of the Captain, a Senior Councillor who is the chairperson of the Management Committee, may sign on behalf of the Captain.
6.3 If the Chairperson of the Management Committee is also absent, the Secretary must sign it.
6.4 No private correspondence shall be carried out on the official letterhead without the stamp of the clan. It will be regarded as a very serious violation, punished as prescribed by law.

Article 7

The headquarters

7.1 The headquarters of the !Ama Traditional Authority are at 10 & 11 Quellen Street, Bethanie. From these offices, the !Ama Traditional Authority performs its services and carries out decisions among the !Ama people both locally and in the wider communal area.

Article 8

8.1 Particular community services

8.1.1 The children and the youth of today are the parents and leaders in different spheres of life in the future. In order to maintain the above mentioned responsibilities of parenthood and leadership properly, academic qualifications are indispensable.

8.1.2 For this reason, the !Ama Traditional Authority shall encourage and support all parents in sending their children to kindergarden or pre-primary institutions and schools.

8.1.3 In order to make a success of education for all children in Bethanie, Kosis and the Soromas community, a positive and healthy relationship is needed between the Traditional Authority, and local teachers.

8.1.4 Therefore the !Ama Traditional Authority will strive at all times to promote co-operation among the parents, teachers and learners.

8.1.5 With the aim of putting this into practice, the Captain and his Councillors and members of the Management Committee shall hold meetings with the principals of local schools from time to time to discuss issues such as the relationships among parents, teachers and learners, including mutual obligations of those concerned.

8.1.6 In the case of unresolved matters, problems or conflicts in the area of education, the Traditional Authority should contact the Karas Regional Office or the Ministry of Education in order to find a peaceful solution for all concerned at home.

8.2 Health

8.2.1 Physical health is very important for everybody. A healthy body is necessary for spiritual and intellectual well-being, and common sense.

8.2.2 Therefore, with the aim to have healthy people, the !Ama Traditional Authority advises and encourages both the youth and adults to make full use of the medical services that are provided at the local Medical Centre.

8.2.3 In combating HIV/AIDS which undermines the health of the youth and causes untimely death, the !Ama Traditional Authority will do its utmost to fight it, in co-operation with the medical staff at Bethanie.

8.2.4 The youth, and all interested adults, are encouraged and earnestly requested to participate in programmes and courses which are offered and conducted for the prevention of HIV/AIDS.

8.2.5 The !Ama Traditional Authority shall try continuously to co-operate with the medical staff at Bethanie and encourage them to practise a positive relationship with their patients and vice versa (patients with the medical staff).

8.2.6 Where necessary, the !Ama Traditional Authority will advise and support both medical staff and patients.

8.3 Development projects

8.3.1 In order to lighten the burden of unemployment and improve the quality of life of the !Ama people at Bethanie and surroundings, in particular to improve the way of life in the communal area, the !Ama Traditional Authority has decided to initiate development projects, such as:

8.3.2 Gardening; farming with cattle, chickens and ostriches; bread baking; sewing and needlework. The !Ama Traditional Authority shall also oversee and protect the land and animals, as well as conservancies.

Article 9

Combating of alcohol and drug abuse

9.1 Abuse of alcoholic drinks and drugs causes destruction of good moral values in the communities. The people themselves are guilty of abusing alcohol and drugs. Abuse affects the heart (emotions) as well as the health of the body and brings constant poverty for the alcoholic and his/her family. In short, abuse of alcoholic drinks and drugs causes destruction of the body and spirit of human beings (their inner and external life). The negative or bad consequences of alcohol and drug abuse is far-reaching, not for alcoholics only, but for the entire !Ama Clan.

9.2 For this reason, the Captain and his people of the !Ama Clan have decided that as far as possible they shall fight against abuse of alcohol and drugs in co-operation with leaders and officials of institutions such as: Bethanie Hospital/ Clinic; health centres; schools, and police stations, and also with spiritual leaders and social workers.

9.3 The use of alcoholic drinks, including different kinds of home-brewed strong drink is totally prohibited for children and youth.

Article 10

Finance

10.1 Finances for the General Fund (see 10.6 below) of the !Ama will be obtained from the following sources: !Ama Clan General Fund, gifts, levies, phone calls, donations, marketing, selling of reading material and projects of the !Ama Clan.

10.2 All national funds will be deposited into the bank account of the !Ama Clan and application to withdraw money must be signed by 2 (two) signatories in law: the captain and treasurer, or captain and secretary.

10.3 The !Ama Clan financial year begins on the first (1st) January and closes on the last day of February, the next year.

10.4 The financial statements of the !Ama Clan must be audited by an officially approved auditor, every year.

10.5 Funds that have been donated for a specific purpose by members of the Clan should not be spent for another purpose unless the Traditional Authority decides to the contrary.

10.6 A Community Trust Fund is compulsory for the !Ama Clan and must be maintained according to the prescription in Section 18 of the Traditional Authorities Act, 2000 (No. 25 of 2000).

Article 11

Jurisdiction

11.1 The Captain-in-Council will have juristic capacity on behalf of the Council and the entire !Ama Clan.

Article 12

Dissolving or amendment of the customary law

12.1 This Traditional Customary Law or any part thereof may be repealed, amended or changed, or added to by a two-thirds majority of the members present at an !Ama Clan meeting.

12.2 Recommendations regarding any amendment of the Customary Law or any part thereof must be sent or directed to the Secretary of the Traditional Authority at least thirty (30) days before the commencement of a meeting. Amendment to this Customary Law will be circulated to all districts for perusal before the date of the abovementioned meeting.

Compiled and signed by both the !Ama Traditional Authority and members of !Ama History Investigating Committee

Chief David Frederick, Salomon Swartbooi, Petrus Isak Frederik, Hendrik Frederik (Hotageb), Elisabeth Keiser, Fredrika Nassauw, Christor Boois, Salmon Blaauw, Willem Boois (!Oasib), Christiaan Uth (Boetietjie), Izak Fredericks (Pastor), Hendrik Frederik (Bishop).

[Signed by the Captian].

APPENDIX A

Appointment of !Ama clan traditional leaders, senior and junior traditional leaders

Introduction

In the past, the Captain of the !Ama Clan was not elected, but appointed. However, seeing as existing laws and customs change with the course of time, the election of a captain shall be arranged in future. To nominate candidates, a committee will be appointed from the senior and young members of the clan. Such nominations shall be done by the community during an official meeting.

A1 According to the "*RYKSBOEK*" of 1847[1] the appointment of a Captain was as follows:
"According to the prescribed rules of the !Ama Clan, Captainship had to be carried by men only. For that reason, the eldest son of the Captain succeeded his father, but if the eldest son died before he was appointed and also had no children, the Captain's position was to be entrusted to the son who followed the eldest one. If the Captain had no other son, the Captain's position had to be taken by an elder brother of the Captain. If the Captain had younger sons than the first and second born, they did not qualify to be his successor in that office. The Captain's position may not be shared by 2 (two) or more sons (of the Captain)." A woman was prohibited from becoming a Captain and from practising leadership of the !Ama Clan

A2 Ever since Captain Josef Frederick (III) was sent home to the !Ama people by the government officials at Bethanie in the year 1938 and his monthly allowance of 2 (two) English pounds was withdrawn, the appointment of a Captain according to the rules of bloodline of the !Ama Clan could not be followed until today. The traditional leaders who succeeded him were appointed under the control and administration of the South African government.

A3 Currently the Namibian government has given all the traditional communities the right to appoint or elect their traditional leaders according to their traditional laws and customs (cf. Traditional Authorities Act, 2000 (No. 25 of 2000, Section 4).

A4 In order to appoint their Captain rightfully in the future, the !Ama Clan has decided as follows:
(a) to investigate the original !Ama Captain's family bloodline, in particular for information and historical purposes.

1 Editor's note: The *Ryksboek bevattende alle wetten en rechten van het Kapiteinschap te Bethanië* is the oldest statement of customary law in Namibia. It can be inspected in the archives of the ELCRN under elcrnx 15–21.

(b) to nominate a committee that will conduct research into whether any men from the original Captain's family are still alive and may be designated candidates for captaincy of the !Ama Clan in the future.

4.1 Designation of the Captain

A4.1.1 The above-mentioned Committee shall nominate 3 (three) male candidates for captainship of the !Ama Clan.

A4.1.2 These 3 (three) nominated candidates shall then be introduced to the whole clan for acceptance.

A4.1.3 If the clan refuses to accept the candidates who have been nominated, the said Committee has to look for other candidates, until men are found who will be accepted by the Clan as qualified candidates.

A4.2 The voting procedure will be as follows:

A4.2.1 Voting will done in two (2) consecutive rounds.

A4.2.2 The candidate who receives fewer votes in the first (1st) round will be left out of the second (2nd) round.

A4.2.3 Only the two (2) remaining candidates will participate in the second round.

A4.2.4 The candidate who receives the bare majority votes shall be the elected Captain of the !Ama Clan.

A4.3 After the inauguration of the chief, the nomination committee shall be dissolved.

A4.4 Each time the !Ama Clan appoints a successor for traditional leadership (the position of Chief), a new nomination committee shall be appointed to nominate candidates.

A4.5 The male candidates appointed for captainship must be 40 years or older.

A4.6 The Captain must retire when he reaches the age of 70 years. However, if his health and physical condition are good and the whole clan is in favour, he may remain in office until the age of 75 years.

A4.7 The character and duties of the Captain shall be prescribed in his service regulations.

A4.8 If the clan is not satisfied with the behaviour and the execution of duties of the Captain:

A4.8.1 The members of the Traditional Authority shall have a confidential discussion with him.

A4.8.2 If further discussion with the Captain is needed, the Elders' Advisory Council must be called in to assist the Traditional Council.

A4.8.3 If the discussion with the Captain about his behaviour and duties is successful, the process should be regarded as completed; consequently, no reporting to the !Ama community about the discussion will be necessary.

A4.8.4 Only in the case that the above-mentioned discussion is not fruitful, must it be reported to the community so that the latter may takes the final decision.

A5 Senior and junior traditional leaders

A5.1 Senior and Junior traditional leaders are appointed by the Captain's Council and introduced to the clan for acceptance. The clan may amend the decision on those appointed and refer it back to the Captain's Council, cf. Section 10 of the Traditional Authority Act, 2000 (No. 25 of 2000).

A5.2 Additional council members may be nominated and/or appointed as advisors on the basis of their academic qualification, competence and experience (Article 5 of the !Aman Customary Law).

A5.3 A person who is nominated and appointed for the Senior or Junior Council must be 18 years or older.

A5.4 Their term of office may be till the age of 70 years.

A5.5 They retire from their position as councillors when they resign or are discharged or die.

A5.6 If the clan is not satisfied with the behaviour and the execution of duties of the senior and junior traditional leaders

A5.6.1 In the case of misbehaviour, ignorance or neglect of duties, the Captain shall discuss the issue with him/her and report the results of the discussion to the whole Council.

A5.6.2 If the discussion between the Captain and the Councillor is not successful, the Traditional Councillors will be called in.

A5.6.3 If the discussion with the entire Traditional Council is not fruitful, the Councillor involved shall be suspended and the people as well as the clan be informed accordingly.

Appendix B

Punishable cases

Introduction

The !Ama Traditional Community Court will give a hearing and conviction for the crimes mentioned below. The rules of punishment for these crimes appear in separate statutory regulations and law books which the Ministry of Justice has prescribed to all Traditional Authorities in Namibia.

B1 Theft is a punishable crime which even through the words of the Bible is strongly forbidden. YOU MUST NOT STEAL. In fact theft of property that people have acquired through hard work and saving over a period of many years for themselves and their offspring is a serious offence and is not considered a light misstep.

Stiff penalties will be meted out to offenders who through theft cause great loss, damage and consequent impoverishment to citizens, so that the offenders do not repeat the same crime again. Certainly, the guilty person will receive the prescribed punishment.

B2 Smuggling

The Afrikaans dictionary, *Handwoordeboek van die Afrikaans Taal (HAT)* describes smuggling as follows: It is to prohibit the import and export of goods or taxable goods without paying tax; "contraband trade"; to bring illegally, gold, diamonds, dagga (marijuana), into or out of the country. Smuggling is an illegal business practice. That is why the !Ama Traditional Authority completely forbids all its followers to smuggle in order to reduce impoverishment of the clan.

B3 Poaching, burglary and stealing

The above-mentioned negative actions are allied to theft, but differ due to the fact that force goes with the above mentioned crimes. People who hunt game without permission from the government are guilty of the offence of poaching and if they are caught hunting without a valid licence will be arrested and shall be liable on conviction to a stiff sentence.

Burglars usually break into houses while the owners are not present and in most cases during evening hours. Nowadays housebreakers are also heavily armed and houseowners resisting them run the risk of being murdered in their own house. With the aim of countering the above-mentioned crimes, the Traditional

Authority will make sure to work in close partnership with the police. People who make themselves guilty of the above-mentioned crimes will be punished according to the law.

B4 Adultery and divorce

Understanding the meaning of adultery should be thought of as breaking one's marriage vows. Among the Israelites (People of God), adultery was forbidden and anyone found guilty of committing adultery was put to death. "And the man that commits adultery with another man's wife, even he that commits adultery with his neighbour's wife, the adulterer and the adulteress shall surely be put to death." (Leviticus 20:10).

The Christian theory does not allow adultery, although the transgressors are not put to death. Every Christian as well as the traditional community has its own methods on how to deal with adultery.

In respect of divorce the following:

Originally, divorce was not connected to marriage. It was only because of the hardness of their hearts that Moses permitted divorce to his followers (Matthew 19:8).

The !Ama Traditional Authority calls on its people to restrain themselves at all times from adultery and divorce; furthermore, the Traditional Authority assures its local spiritual leaders and councillors of its support and co-operation, so that the spreading of adultery and divorce is reduced or limited within the !Ama Clan.

B5 Rape

Rape is also paired with violence, because rape is committed without the consent of the person being raped. In most cases, women are the victims of rape. Rape is not only a criminal offence but it also destroys and humiliates the person who was raped who will remember it for the rest of his/her life. This is why victims of rape should be treated spiritually, medically and psychologically. The !Ama Traditional Authority will do everything in its power to help those who become victims of rape, so that they do not suffer from trauma. This Traditional Authority will support as well as encourage the complainant or victim not to withdraw the case against the rapist/accused. The rapist should be punished according to law.

B6 Vandalism

Any person who deliberately destroys another's property commits vandalism. Such a person does not only destroy people's valuable assets, but also destroys the owners spiritually with her/his barbaric vandalism. Any person caught committing vandalism shall be arrested immediately. The owners of the property are encouraged to open a case officially against the culprit, so that the culprit may be brought before the Traditional Authority and police to determine the seriousness of the vandalism that was committed.

B7 Inheritance, dishonesty and fraud in inheritance

Some parents and next of kin neglect to draw up their last Will for their heirs. This may lead to fraud and dishonesty when property is divided, and some heirs do not inherit the portion they are entitled to.

The !Ama Traditional Authority has decided to encourage their followers to draw up a legal Will timeously where they make it clear how their moveable and immovable properties and assets should be divided between their heirs. Furthermore, the Traditional Authority has decided to help with the appointment of a qualified person to assist the family member who is responsible for the distribution of the inheritance to draw up and execute a last Will and Testament.

B8 Family feuds and gossip

Feuding and gossip are caused by different reasons. In many cases, family feud and gossip are experienced after the parents or next of kin die without drawing up a Will specifying how their assets should be divided amongst the lawful heirs. With the aim of settling such cases, the !Ama Traditional Authority will use all the resources at its disposal.

B9 Environmental destruction

Every citizen of a country, including Namibia, should respect the laws of the country they live in, due to the fact the every little piece of land is valuable to any country. That is basically the reason why environmental destruction is not allowed. People found guilty of destroying land will be charged according to law.

With the aim of bringing awareness to its people about environmental destruction, the Traditional Authority will encourage the teaching of appropriate information to the people. The environment is damaged, for example, by starting veld fires, or the mass uprooting of trees. The Traditional Authority currently has no specific law punishing environmental destruction. The matter is dealt with in accordance with State laws. The role of the TA is to educate members of the community on protecting the environment, but perpetrators will be charged.

B10 Assault

Assault goes hand in hand with violence. Assault is when a person is attacked and hurt by one or more people. In most cases, assault is committed with weapons. Good people with good names are also assaulted to destroy their image. Aiming to protect its supporters from assault, the Traditional Authority has decided together with the police to stop assaults of all kinds.

B11 Different kinds of drugs

Drug abuse causes addiction, just as alcoholics are addicted to alcohol. Overuse of drugs has roped off many young people in the world from their youth, where students going to school have landed in a network of drugusers as well as misuse of alcohol. That is why the Traditional Authority will fight with all it has at its disposal against the use of any kind of drugs and against the misuse of all things that damage or destroy the health of its people. The use of drugs is totally prohibited by law and those caught using drugs will be brought before law and charged accordingly.

Certificate of consent to publish

Certificate of the consent to publish

UNIVERSITY OF NAMIBIA

FACULTY OF LAW

HUMAN RIGHTS AND DOCUMENTATION CENTRE

RE: CONSENT TO PUBLICATION

I, the undersigned, Chief of the !Aman Traditional Authority, hereby give consent to the Human Rights and Documentation Centre, to publish the following documents of the !Aman Traditional Authority:

1. The Customary Laws
2. The Community Profile
3. Picture of the Chief
4. Logo of the Traditional Authority

I acknowledge that the Human Rights and Documentation Centre will publish the laws in our indigenous language (Nama), as well as the English language. I am familiar with the contents of the laws that will be published and further acknowledge that they were prepared by my traditional authority.

Signed on this 18 **day of** March **2015**

At Windhoek

Chief David Frederick

For HRDC: Mr. A. Gairiseb

!AMAN TRADITIONAL AUTHORITY
P.O. Box ..., Bethanie
Tel: ...
REPUBLIC OF NAMIBIA

Swartbooi Traditional Authority
ǁKhau-ǀgôan !Haos ǂGaeǂguis

The supreme leader of the ǁKhau-ǀgôan Traditional Authority is
Gaob[1] Daniel Sardine Luipert.
Date of designation: 15 November 1986

1 Traditional title in terms of section 11 of the Traditional Authorities Act, 2000 (No. 25 of 2000).

PROFILE[2]

In order to understand the Swartbooi Community Profile fully, one must first understand the colonial oppression the Swartbooi community has undergone under German and South African colonial rule (see the Preamble to the Laws of the ǁKhau-ǀgôan (Swartbooi) on page 11).

Chief Daniel Sardine Luipert, born on 7 February 1937, was appointed *Gaob* (traditional chief, or captain) of the Swartbooi (ǁKhau-ǀGôan) community in 1986. The Swartbooi community numbers approximately 2 000–3 000 people. The people speak the Nama language but have a high degree of proficiency in Afrikaans.

Area of jurisdiction of the Swartbooi Traditional Authority

South– border with ǂAodaman (Ward 7)
North– border with ǀGaiodaman (Ward 10)
West – border with Riemvasmaker (Ward 11)
East – border with commercial farming area

The first chief of the Swartbooi Traditional Authority (ǁKhau-ǀGōan), Chief Kananab, who formed the Swartbooi community was born dark in complexion in contrast to his four siblings who were light in complexion. Consequently, the community named him Swartbooi, the name deriving from the *Nederlands* meaning "black boy". When Chief (*Gaob*) Kananab became the chief of the community, being called Swartbooi, the name was also given to the community.

The Swartbooi community diverged from the main Nama community called ǁKhaun in the northern Cape Republic in South Africa in 1725. Five brothers could not agree with each other on leadership disputes, and consequently, Swartbooi moved into southern Namibia with the group that supported him. They lived around Bethanie River, and Uis River. In 1845 they moved to ǀAnes (Rehoboth) in order to get a missionary, who was Heinrich Riechman from Germany. They were told by the Germans that if they wanted a missionary, they had to move away from traditional control.

Chief Jan Jonker Afrikaner approached Swartbooi to help him fight Kamaharero to capture cattle but Swartbooi refused. Then Jan Jonker turned against Swartbooi, and Swartbooi joined to rescue the Herero. Swartbooi and Kamaharero pushed Jan Jonker and his people out, back to their original area.

The Swartbooi clan moved from Rehoboth (ǀAnes) in the year 1867 under the leadership of Captain !Huiseb Haobemab – Willem Swartbooi – in a westerly direction because of the never-ending attacks of the neighbouring tribes. They later moved north up to the

2 This profile was provided by the ǁKhau-ǀGôan Traditional Authority

Kunene River and reached the place today called Swartboois Drift. Later, they moved through Otjikaoko in a southerly direction and settled at a place called Otjitambi. Because of the saltiness of the water at Otjitambi, Captain ǀHoa-ǀArab – Cornelius Swartbooi – who was leading the Swartbooi clan, then wished to move to a place where the water was not salty. Frans Frederick, the chief hunter for Captain Cornelius, discovered the spring today known as ǀKhomi-ǀAus and the village of Fransfontein was established. The discovery of the spring is unforgotten in the history of the Swartbooi.

The Swartbooi community settled after the fountain was expanded with the help of the British geologist Mr Blaauw from Walvis Bay. The discovery of water at the fountain and the expansion of the fountain encouraged the Captain to mobilise all his followers to come to what is today called Fransfontein. The name Fransfontein is derived from the hunter called Frans from the Swartbooi Community. Frans found the fountain when he saw the bird and horse wet.

The Swartbooi community practises crop farming such as wheat, pumpkin, oranges, watermelon, sweet melon, beans, beetroots, carrots, onion and paprika. They also farm livestock such as cattle, sheep, goats, donkeys, horses, pigs and poultry.

The staple foods in the community are mealie-meal, meat and milk.

Our ancestors established gardens at Fransfontein to produce food for the community from the very beginning. They have been self-sufficient all along in terms of food production because of the Fransfontein community gardens. The community garden is irrigated with water from the ǀKhomi-ǀAus spring.

Other traditional sources of water in the Swartbooi area of jurisdiction are wells, earth dams and, most recently, boreholes.

The people in the Swartbooi community conduct light industrial activities such as textiles, production of charcoal and firewood for sale and wood carving.

The common modes of transport in the Swartbooi communal area are ox-wagons, donkey carts or carts drawn by horses.

Games are important to the Swartbooi traditional community and include *ǀHus*, a board game similar to chess, usually played with pebbles representing cattle and depressions in the sand, where the opponents must outwit each other to acquire most of the tokens.

The cultural dance called *!Hudans* is performed when younger girls get their first menstruation (period). This is also known as *Nama-stap* (meaning Nama step). People wear traditional attire and perform this dance. This is a gentle, slow dance of the Nama People. The *Nama-stap* is danced at any celebration, but the most important one is the final stage of a young Nama girl's initiation into womanhood.

According to the customary law of the Swartbooi traditional community, a man is only head of the house because he is the more responsible one who customarily used to go and hunt (or look) for food and bring it to the house, while the women remain at home, waiting for the men to come home with food.

Festivals used to celebrate the harvesting of agricultural produce that different people grew during the rainy season. The festivals are no longer held regularly. Currently the people are planning to hold a festival to commemorate the founding chief of Fransfontein, their Captain Cornelius Swartbooi, on the date of his death. They will erect a monument (or tombstone) for him.

According to the customary law of the Swartbooi traditional community, they have never kept a holy fire, not even at any given time as far back as they can recall. They depend on the Holy Spirit only.

The Fransfontein community graveyard is seen as "**holy land**" and must be respected as such by any individual who enters the graveyard.

Our forefathers and the current community members used to contact our ancestors in times of sorrow and difficulties from our graveyard.

The customary law of the Swartbooi traditional community as recognised by the Government of the Republic of Namibia states in Section 10(5) "nobody shall be allowed to hold meetings, festivals or any other activities at the Swartbooi Cultural sites like gravesites, the spring or any other place so declared by the Swartbooi Traditional Authority without the written permission by the captain".

The information in this profile comes from answers to a questionnaire drawn up by the Ministry of Regional and Local Government, Housing and Rural Development and was completed by the following members of the Traditional Community:
Captain (*Gaob*) Daniel Sardine Luipert, Vice-Captain Essegiel M. ǀUirab, Senior Councillors Anna ǀHuhua, Lucia ǀGuidao-oas, Titus Bamm, Councillors Charles ǀUirab, Johannes Luipert, Ester Swartbooi and Eddie Sabatha.

Chronological order of the Swartbooi captaincy succession

Name of the Chief	Year of Chieftainship	
	From	Until
ǀKanabeb		(The very first captain of the Swartbooi)
Tsamkau		
Tsaugab		
Tsauxab		
Haob Tsauxamab (Manasse Swartbooi)		(He became old)
!Huiseb Haobemab (Willem Swartbooi)	1830	1864 (old age)
!Abeb !Naxama !Huisemab (Abraham Swartbooi)	1864	1880 (old age)
ǀHoa-ǀArab !Abemab (Cornelius Swartbooi)	1880	1894 (died of illness)
!Hanamub !Abemab (Dawid Swartbooi)	1894	1897 (captured and returned again)
!Hanamub !Abemab (Lazarus Swartbooi)	1897	1904 (tortured by Germans and died)
!Hanamub !Abemab (Dawid Swartbooi)	1923	1925 (he became old)
!Harageib !Hanamumab (Petrus Swartbooi)	1925	1965 (removed by the South African colonial administration)
Emil Pienaar	1965	1972 (removed by Commissioner Jan Piek of the South African colonial administration)
Daniel Sardine Luipert	1986	Till today

According to Swartbooi customary law a new chief shall be designated from the royal bloodline exclusively by the Swartbooi traditional community at a community gathering convened to look for a suitable candidate within the within the royal bloodline from the Royal House. After the completion of the selection, the chairperson of the selection committee of the Swartbooi Royal House shall inform the Swartbooi Traditional Authority about their readiness to meet the Supreme Council. The purpose of the meeting shall be for the Swartbooi Royal House to consult the Supreme Council about the selected candidate to discuss, *inter alia*, his/her competency, character, popularity and personal behaviour in public, before finalizing the appointment of the candidate. After the meeting, the Supreme Council shall then convene a public meeting with the community members to introduce the selected candidate to them.

The successor of the Chief is allowed to come from the matrilineal or patrilineal side. The child succeeding the Chief would be drawn from within wedlock or out of wedlock. The senior traditional leaders of the Swartbooi community are appointed from other families, not from the royal blood family; only the Captain should come from the royal bloodline.

Community Court

The Fransfontein Community Court was recognised in terms of the Community Courts Act (Act no. 10 of 2003).

1. Areas in respect of which the Fransfontein Community Court exercises jurisdiction are:
   (a) Fransfontein Reserve
   (b) Former Ward 9
   (c) Eastern Block farms of Gainetzeb
   (d) Tsumamas
   (e) Kranspoort
   (f) Eastwood
   (g) ǀNaracha-ams
   (h) Duurwater

Community Court assessors at the time of going to press

Lucia ǀGuidao-aos
Charlse ǀUirab,
Sara Jod
Francois Dawids
Alexia Ortner
Emma Jood
Titus Bamm
Esegiel Pienaar
Lydia ǀUiras
Anna IHuhua

Community Court justices at the time of going to press

Chief Daniel Luipert
Vice-Captain Essegiel Max ǀUirab
Cornelius Bowe
Ernst Amporo
Nahor Haraeb and
Josef Seibeb.

Swartbooi Traditional Authority

The Swartbooi Traditional Authority was established and recognised in terms of Traditional Authorities Act, 2000 (Act 25 of 2000). The following office-holders were incumbent at the time of going to press:

- Honourable Chief Daniel Luipert
- Vice-Captain Essegiel Max ǀUirab
- Senior Councillors: Cornelius Bowe, Anna ǀHuhua, Ernst Amporo (who replaced Ewald Murorua after he had passed away[3]), Lucia ǀGuidao-Oas and Titus Bamm, Councillors Murorua Helmuth John[4] (who replaced Ernst Amporo when he became a Senior Councillor), Nahor Haraeb, Charlses ǀUirab, Johanna Luipert, Esegiel Pienaar and Ester Swartbooi.

[Signed by the Vice Captain: E.M ǀUirab, Swartbooi Traditional Authority]

3 Government Gazette No. 4783 of 23 August 2011.
4 Government Gazette No. 4783 of 23 August 2011.

THE LAWS OF THE ǁKHAU-ǀGOAN (SWAARTBOOI)[1]

1 The laws were submitted in English only.

PREAMBLE

This is the customary law of the Swartbooi traditional community, which is the basis of their traditions, norms, usages and rules. In order to understand the Swartbooi community fully, one must first understand the colonial oppression the Swartbooi community has undergone under German and South African colonial rule.

The structural existence of the Swartbooi community degenerated because of German and South African colonial rule. As a result, traditional authority over subjects could not be effectively exercised.

Consequently, their collective hold over the land they communally used and cared for was taken away by the colonisers and alienated by force.

The traditional land of the Swartbooi was later declared part of the homeland for the Damara-speaking Namibians under the Odendaal Commission.

The South African apartheid machinery tried to relocate the Swartbooi community to southern Namibia (especially the Gibeon area) by force, but they refused to move, with the result that they were under extreme pressure to accept second class treatment from the authorities.

Only after independence was achieved, the new constitution was in place and new government took over, could the Swartbooi community breathe the fresh air of freedom with relief.

Therefore:

> The Swartbooi traditional community thank the Almighty God for the independence of this country.
>
> The Swartbooi traditional community thank the founding Fathers and Mothers of our Republic for the Supreme Law that brought back the dignity of our people.
>
> The Swartbooi traditional community thank the Head of State and his government for the wise and timely decision to recognise the Traditional Communities and their Leaders.

God bless our Government and our beautiful Republic.

Section 1: Definitions

1.1 In this customary law, unless the context indicates otherwise:

(a) *Additional member* means any member co-opted from the Swartbooi traditional community by the Swartbooi Traditional Authority to assist the leadership, or who is entrusted to represent the Swarbooi Traditional Authority in Namibia or elsewhere.

(b) *Captain* means a chief as defined in the Traditional Authorities Act, 2000 and named Captain of the Swartbooi traditional community.

(c) *Communal land* means the communal area as defined in the Traditional Authorities Act, 2000, including any other land belonging to the Swartbooi traditional community.

(d) *Customary law* means the customary law as defined in the Traditional Authorities Act, 2000.

(d) *Supreme Council* means the sole organ of the Swartbooi traditional community, entrusted with the power to select, remove or designate the captain.

(e) *Traditional community* means the traditional community as defined in the Traditional Authorities Act, 2000 (No. 25 of 2000).

(f) *Traditional leader* means and includes the traditional leaders as defined in the Traditional Authorities Act, 2000.

(g) *Traditional land of the Swartbooi* means the geographic area habitually inhabited by our ancestors, that is Fransfontein and all its surrounding farms that were forcefully taken away by the colonizers and later declared as part of the Damara homeland by apartheid South Africa.

(h) *Vice Captain* means one of the Senior Councillors appointed by the Captain to deputize him/her or act as Captain in his/her absence.

Section 2: Traditional land

2.1 The traditional land of the Swartbooi community shall be the geographical area habitually inhabited by our ancestors, being Fransfontein with all its surrounding farms that were forcefully taken away by the colonisers and later declared by the then Odendaal Commission as part of the Damara homeland.

Section 3: Main seat

3.1 The main seat shall be Fransfontein, where the discovery of the spring led to the unforgotten history of the Swartbooi community.

Section 4: Emblems

4.1 The emblems are the spring, the mountain behind the spring and the oxen drinking water from the spring.

Section 5: Colours

5.1 The colours shall be red and white.
5.2 Red symbolises the blood that was shed during the long protracted battles fought by our forefathers.
5.3 White symbolises peace that has always existed amongst the various peoples making up the Swartbooi community, and between the Swartbooi community and other communities.

Section 6: Traditional flag

6.1 The traditional flag is red with white spots similar to those of a guinea fowl (*ǀwawa-ǀkhina*), with an open Bible and a white dove in the upper left corner.

Section 7: Traditional anthem

7.1 There shall be a traditional anthem (*!hoas-ams*) for the Swartbooi community.
7.2 The Swartbooi Traditional Authority shall decide upon the anthem.

Section 8: Organs of the Swartbooi traditional community

8.1 The Swartbooi Traditional Authority

8.1.1 There shall be a Traditional Authority for the Swartbooi traditional community.
8.1.2 The establishment, powers, duties and function of such Traditional Authority shall be as defined in the Traditional Authorities Act, 2000.

8.2 The Supreme Council

8.2.1 There shall be a Supreme Council for the Swartbooi traditional community.
8.2.2 The composition of the Supreme Council shall be at least 10 (ten) members of the Swartbooi Traditional Authority and 20 (twenty) members of the Elders' Council (*Stam Oudstes*).
8.2.3 The main functions of the Supreme Council shall be to:

(a) select, after consultations with the members of the Swartbooi Royal House and the community, the successor of the captain in accordance with the rules of succession. The Rules of Succession shall be included in the Regulations.

(b) remove the captain from office, only if there is sufficient reason to warrant the removal. The removal shall be in accordance with Section 8 of the Traditional Authorities Act, 2000.

(c) designate the selected candidate as the captain in accordance with the Traditional Authorities Act, 2000 after notifying the Minister of Regional and Local Government and Housing.

8.3 The Captain

8.3.1 The Captain shall be the supreme traditional leader of the Swartbooi Traditional Community.

8.3.2 The Captain shall be the chairperson of all traditional meetings and may delegate such authority to other people.

8.3.3 S/he shall be selected from the royal bloodline, in this case the Swartbooi bloodline.

8.3.4 The Captain shall be thirty five (35) years or above.

8.3.5 The Captain shall be the custodian of this customary law, and exercise his/her powers and perform his/her duties and functions in accordance with it.

8.3.6 Only a person equal to the Captain shall do the inauguration of the Captain.

8.3.7 The inauguration of the Captain shall be done in the Nama language.

8.3.8 The inauguration procedures shall be included in the regulations of this customary law.

8.4 Vice Captain

8.4.1 In the absence of the Captain, the Vice Captain shall act as the Captain.

8.4.2 In all other circumstances when necessary the Vice Captain shall deputise the Captain.

8.5 Elders' Council *(Stam Oudstes)*

8.5.1 There shall be an Elders' Council for the Swartbooi traditional community.

8.5.2 The membership of the Elders' Council shall be sixty (60) years old or above.

8.5.3 The Elders' Council shall adopt its own rules for its activities within the limits of customary law.

8.5.4 The main functions shall be to:

(a) advise the Captain about the customs and culture of the Swartbooi.

(b) see to it that the Swartbooi "flame" does not diminish. The Swartbooi culture must always be taught to the younger generations.

(c) delegate 20 (twenty) members to the Supreme Council when need be.

8.6 Swartbooi Cultural Youth Group

8.6.1 There shall be a Youth Cultural Group for the Swartbooi traditional community.

8.6.2 The membership of the Youth Cultural Group shall be thirty five (35) years old and younger.

8.6.3 The Youth Cultural Group shall adopt its own rules for its activities within the limits of customary law.

8.6.4 The main functions of the Youth Cultural Group shall be to:

(a) organise cultural dances of the community.

(b) keep contact with the youth and cultural groups of other Traditional Authorities.

(c) organise income-generating projects within the community.

(d) organise sports and other activities with the youth.

8.7 Swartbooi Cultural Women's Group

8.7.1 There shall be a Cultural Women's Group for the Swartbooi traditional community.

8.7.2 The membership shall be open to all Swartbooi women who are interested in developing and practising the Swartbooi culture.

8.7.3 The Cultural Women's Group shall adopt its own rules for its activities within the limits of customary law.

8.7.4 The main functions of the Women's Cultural Group shall be to:

(a) develop cultural projects within the community.

(b) organise and teach the Swartbooi culture to all women and children.

(c) keep contact with other women's and cultural groups.

Section 9: Meetings

9.1 Traditional Assembly

9.1.1 There shall be a Traditional Assembly for the Swartbooi traditional community.

9.1.2 The Swartbooi Traditional Assembly shall be held annually with the traditional festival of the Swartbooi.

9.1.3 The date of the Traditional Assembly shall be included in the Regulations. The date shall be as determined by the Traditional Assembly.

9.1.4 The Swartbooi Traditional Assembly shall be open to all members of the Swartbooi community throughout Namibia.

9.1.5 Meetings shall be advertised at least 30 (thirty) days prior to the meeting.

9.1.6 The Traditional Assembly shall have the power to amend or repeal this customary law with a two-thirds majority of the members present.

9.1.7 The Traditional Assembly shall consist of the Captain, at least 10 (ten) members of the Swartbooi Traditional Authority and at least 50 (fifty) members of the community, duly delegated by the various structures of the Swartbooi traditional community.

9.2 Traditional Authority meetings

9.2.1 There shall be Traditional Authority meetings once every quarter, i.e. 4 (four) times per year.
9.2.2 The Captain, Vice Captain, and Traditional Council shall attend the meetings only.
9.2.3 The meetings will discuss traditional concerns, customary conduct and matters concerning the Swartbooi traditional community.
9.2.4 The Traditional Authority may invite anyone to the meetings.
9.2.5 The quorum shall be seven members of the Traditional Authority, and the Captain shall have the casting vote.
9.2.6 Any Traditional Authority member who fails to attend 3 (three) consecutive meetings without a valid reason, and without being excused by the Traditional Authority automatically discharges him/herself from the Traditional Authority.

9.3 Community meetings

9.3.1 There shall be general community meetings for the Swartbooi traditional community.
9.3.2 The meetings shall be open to every member of the community.
9.3.3 The Captain and his/her Councillors shall convene the meetings whenever it is necessary.
9.3.4 The purpose of the meetings shall be either to consult the community or to give general information to the community.

Section 10: Maintaining law and order

10.1 No person shall take land for him/herself without the written permission of the Captain.
10.2 No person shall settle or move into the jurisdiction area of the Swartbooi Traditional Authority without the written permission of the Captain.
10.3 No person shall move from one communal farm to another without the written permission of the Captain.
10.4 No person shall be entitled to fence off communal land without the written permission of the Captain.
10.5 No person shall be entitled to hold meetings, festivals or any other activities at the Swartbooi cultural sites such as gravesites, the spring or any other place so declared by the Swartbooi Traditional Authority, without the written permission of the Captain.

10.6 No person shall be entitled to collect firewood or any other natural resource for any purposes other than for household use, without the written permission of the Swartbooi Traditional Authority.

10.7 No person shall be entitled to transport livestock or meat without a letter from the Headman or Councillor of the area where s/he usually resides.

10.8 If a person is found guilty of having stolen another person's livestock, the thief shall compensate the victim on a two-for-one basis or shall pay an equivalent value in cash, in addition to a fine to be determined by the Traditional Court.

10.9 If a person is found guilty of having stolen another person's property other than livestock, s/he shall return the person's property in the same condition it was when it was stolen, and shall be fined by the Traditional Court.

10.10 If a man commits adultery with another man's wife and impregnates her, he shall pay 6 (six) head of cattle or an equivalent value in cash to the husband; two will go to the Traditional Court.

10.11 If he does not impregnate her, he shall pay 3 (three) head of cattle or the equivalent value in cash to the husband, and one will go to the Traditional Court.

10.12 If a woman is raped, she shall be paid 4 (four) head of cattle or an equivalent value in cash and the rapist shall be fined by a traditional or another competent court.

10.13 If a spouse has sexual intercourse with another person and is caught, s/he shall pay 3 (three) head of cattle or an equivalent value in cash to the other spouse; one will go to the Traditional Court.

10.14 If a man impregnates a schoolgirl, he shall pay 2 (two) head of cattle or an equivalent value in cash to the schoolgirl or her parents, and one will go to the Traditional Court.

10.15 If a man impregnates a woman out of marriage, he shall pay 1 (one) head of cattle or an equivalent value in cash to the woman.

10.16 No person shall be entitled to swear or fight in any public or other place.

10.17 Any person who is found guilty of having murdered another shall pay 10 (ten) head of cattle or an equivalent value in cash in addition to being sentenced in a state court.

Section 11: Regulations

11.1 The Swartbooi Traditional Authority may make regulations relating to:

(a) customary marriages
(b) inheritance of land, livestock or any other property
(c) grazing of livestock on communal land
(d) traditional festivals of the Swartbooi community
(e) rules of succession to the Swartbooi throne
(f) the traditional anthem (*!hoas-ams*), and
(g) any other matter required in order to achieve the purpose of this customary law.

Section 12: Short title, commencement and amendment

12.1 This Constitution shall be called the Swartbooi Customary Law and shall come into force immediately after the Captain has signed it.

12.2 This customary law or any section thereof may be amended or repealed by a two-thirds majority of the members present at the Traditional Assembly.

12.3. Recommendations in connection with this customary law must be sent at least 30 (thirty) days before the commencement of the Traditional Assembly to the Secretary of the Swartbooi Traditional Authority.

[Signed by the Captain]

Annexure 1

Regulations

REGULATIONS made in terms of the customary law of the Swartbooi traditional community – ǁKhau-ǀGôan of Fransfontein.

The Captain of the Swartbooi traditional community has under Section 11 (eleven) of the customary law, made the Regulations set out in the schedule.

[Signed by the Captain]

Code of Conduct and disciplinary procedure

1. Objective

1.1 The objective of this disciplinary code and procedure is to ensure the maintenance of good order in the Swartbooi Traditional Authority and in the community.

1.2 All Senior Traditional Councillors, Traditional Councillors, the Secretary, or any other worker of the Swartbooi Traditional Authority must accept that it is the responsibility of the Captain to maintain discipline in the Authority, and that the code of conduct is intended to be corrective and not punitive.

2. Principles of the Code of Conduct

2.1 Disciplinary action must always be applied in a prompt, fair and consistent manner.

2.2 All members, and any other worker of the Swartbooi Traditional Authority, must at all times:

2.2.1 comply with the customary law, and the Regulations in terms of the customary law;

2.2.2 carry out reasonable and lawful instructions given to them;

2.2.3 behave in an orderly and lawful manner, and

2.2.4 treat other people with respect.

3. Suspensions/removal from office

A member shall be suspended or removed from office by the Captain if s/he:

3.1 fails to attend 3 (three) consecutive meetings of the Authority.

3.2 fails to carry out lawful instructions given to him/her by his/her superiors.

3.3 fails to execute or maintain his/her duties.
3.4 fails to keep secrets.
3.5 is involved in or found guilty of any stock theft, fraud, corruption, murder or any crime, proving him-/herself not to be trustworthy.
3.6 becomes an embarrassment to the Traditional Authority and the community in any way or at any place.
3.7 without permission, sells, leases or is involved in any negotiations to sell/lease any part of the traditional land, or
3.8 is involved in clique formation, furthering of racial or tribal hatred, conspiracy or holding illegal meetings to do harm to the Swartbooi Traditional Authority, the Captain or to any other member of the Authority.

4. Removal from office

4.1 If misconduct is not of a serious nature the Captain may instruct a disciplinary hearing, after a verbal warning and a written reprimand/warning has failed.
4.2 If a member or any other worker of this Traditional Authority fails or refuses to attend a formal hearing or any meeting called by the Captain to discuss his/her misconduct, the hearing and or meeting shall continue in his/her absence.
4.3 After a formal hearing, it is in the Captain's power to remove or dismiss summarily or with notice, depending on circumstances and the severity of the case.
4.4 If misconduct is of a serious nature, the Captain may in terms of the regulations of the Swartbooi Customary Law summarily remove a member or any other worker of this Traditional Authority from office.
4.5 On removal from office, a formal letter will be drafted to the member, which will state the transgression(s) as well as the reasons on which the dismissal is based.

5. Suspension

5.1 In the case of a member allegedly having committed a serious or major offence, the member may be suspended from office with full allowance pending the hearing.
5.2 A suspension may at any time be withdrawn.

6. Appeal

6.1 Every member has a right to appeal to the Captain against any decision which involves an entry on his/her disciplinary record, and which may thus affect his/her future employment.

[Signed by the Captain]

Annexure 2

Rules of Succession and the Inauguration Procedures to the Swartbooi Throne

1. Objective

1.1 The objective of the *Rules of Succession and the Inauguration Procedures* is to ensure that the correct and consistent procedures are followed at all times.

2. Swartbooi Royal Bloodline

In order to understand the Rules of Succession of the Swartbooi Royal Throne, one must first know the order in which the Swartbooi chiefs succeeded one another.

2.1 Swartbooi captaincy succession

Captain ǀKanabeb – the very first captain of the Swartbooi Clan.
Captain Tsamkau
Captain Tsaugab
Captain Tsauxab
Captain Haob Tsauzamab (Mannasse Swartbooi)
Captain !Huiseb Haobemab (Willem Swartbooi)
Captain !Abeb !Naxama !Huisemab (Abraham Swartbooi)
Captain ǀHoa-ǀArab !Abemab (Cornelius Swartbooi)
Captain !Hanamub !Abemab (Dawid Swartbooi)
Captain ǀKhurisa !Abemab (Lazarus Swartbooi)
Captain !Hanamub !Abemab (Dawid Swartbooi)
Captain !Harageib !Hanamumab (Petrus Swartbooi)
Captain Emil Pienaar
Captain Daniel Sardine Luipert (current Captain of the Swartbooi)

3. Selection of the successor to the Swartbooi captaincy/throne

3.1 The Selection Committee of the Swartbooi Royal House shall convene a Royal House meeting to look for a suitable candidate within the royal bloodline.

3.2 After the completion of the above-mentioned process, the Chairperson of the Selection Committee of the Swartbooi Royal House shall inform the Swartbooi Traditional Authority about their readiness to meet the Supreme Council.

3.3 The Swartbooi Traditional Authority shall, after consultations with the Supreme Council and the Swartbooi Royal House, decide on a date for the meeting between the two.

3.4 The purpose of the meeting shall be for the Swartbooi Royal House to consult the Supreme Council about the selected candidate to discuss inter-alia his/her competency, character, popularity and personal behaviour in public, before finalizing the appointment of the candidate.

3.5 After the meeting with the Swartbooi Royal House, the Supreme Council shall convene a public meeting with the community members to introduce the selected candidate to them.

4. Designation of the Swartbooi captain

4.1 The designation of the Swartbooi Captain shall be done in terms of the Traditional Authorities Act, 2000 (Act No. 25 of 2000), Sections 4, 5 and 6 and the Regulations made in terms of the Swartbooi Customary Law.

4.2 Inauguration procedures

4.2.1 Shall be done only by a person equal to the Captain; the Head of State; Ministers, or a person selected by the Swartbooi Traditional Community.

4.2.2 Shall be done in Damara/Nama.

4.3 ǀNau-ǂGas (Inauguration)

1 Samuel 16:7
Tita ge gao-ao-e go mû-ǂûibasen. Ta isib âba go î, khoe-i ra mû khemi – i tama !kheis ge. Khoe-i ge mûti ei - !â hâna ra go xui – ao, xawe !khúb ta ǂgaoba go - ǀî.

4.3.1 Mâsen-xats kha a ǂgaob âts !nâ ne ǂgei-ǂamsa !kho-!oasa?
...!KHUB HUIB ǀKHA !!

4.3.2 Xare Eloba !ao-!gâts nî ne !oabasats ta sisen -ǂûi ǁaeb ai?
...HUB HUIB ǀKHA !!

4.3.3 Xare hoa-ǁae ǂhâanub tsî ǂhanu-aisib tsîkha ǀgui-khats nî sao-!gon?
...KHUB HUIB ǀKHA !!

4.3.4 Xare ǂhansendi ne ǁaes dide ǂgurose mâits nî, sa ǂhansendi ose?
...!KHUB HUIB ǀKHA !!

4.3.5 Né !ereamsa !kho-!oats ta, marib tsî ai-ǂhanugu omaris digu !aroma tama-i tsî, xawe ai-ǂhanugu tsî ei-!gûs !hao tsî hoaraga ǁaes dis !aroma?
...!KHUB HUIB ǀKHA !!

4.3.6 Mâsen-xats kha a né ǁaes tsî né !hub !aroma ǀhawi-ǂga-amhe tsî ǂnao-ǂnaohesa, xawe !ao-o !nâse amab ǀguiba gowase tsî kai-ǁgûgu âts khêmi !huba ǁobasa?
...!KHUB HUIB ǀKHA !!

4.3.7 O ǁnêi nesi ǁnati ǁnâu-!â tsîts nî u-!oas ga-o, né ǁnâu-mâra ǀaes tsî !hū-ǁîn ai-!â, neti !eream re.

"AB ELOBA ǁNAS !OA HUI TSÎ ǂGAE-ǂGUITE"

[Signed by the Captain]

[Translation]

1 Samuel 16:7
But the Lord said to Samuel, "Do not look on his appearance or on the height of his stature, because I have rejected him. For the Lord sees not as man sees: man looks on the outward appearance, but the Lord looks on the heart."

4.3.1 Are you willing in your heart to accept this title?... Yes, with the help of God!
4.3.2 Will you be respectful to God during the execution of this duty?... Yes, with the help of God!
4.3.3 Will you at all times follow righteousness and lawfulness?... Yes, with the help of God!
4.3.4 Will you place the concerns of this nation first and not those that are personal to you?... Yes, with the help of God!
4.3.5 Do you accept this responsibility, not for your domestic financial benefits and privileges but for the progress of the nation as a whole? …Yes, with the help of God!
4.3.6 Are you in agreement to be accused and stigmatised for the sake of this nation and this land but to remain fearless and to speak only the truth and to die for this land just like your ancestors did?…Yes, with the help of God!
4.3.7 Now, if you so understand and accept, before this attending nation and the citizens, answer this way:
"Let God help me towards it and lead me!"

[Signed by the Captain]

Annexure 3

Swartbooi law of inheritance "ǀ*UMIS*"

1. The Swartbooi traditional community are deeply religious and all their laws are deeply rooted in the word of God, namely the Bible and teachings of the church.

2. Therefore the marriage ceremony is always in the church and the priest officiates.

3. This law contains the rules and the procedures that the Swartbooi traditional community of Fransfontein and its surrounding villages follow when a mother or father dies. It will also cover who inherits what and from whom.

4. If the deceased left a will, the surviving spouse shall ensure that he/she administers the estate as the will states.

5. To ensure that the word of the will is followed, the headman/traditional leader is also involved in the process of administering the estate of the deceased. Although the traditional leader is part of the administration, he does not get anything from the estate. His work is to oversee the whole process and make sure that the correct procedures are followed.

6. In the case where the other spouse is predeceased, the estate is administered by the firstborn of the family.

7. An oral will may also exist and is acceptable in the Swartbooi tradition. A dying person can express her/his wish about the disposal of the property. What happens is that the dying person can tell an elder member of the family or the headman who gets what out of his/her estate.

8. If the deceased was not married, elders normally administer the estate.

9. Administration of estate after death

9.1 Deceased man's estate

In the Swartbooi traditional community, in a situation where a husband or father dies, and he leaves behind his wife and his children, the widow will then normally inherit everything, meaning she will be in charge of her deceased husband's estate or she will in legal terms administer it. The husband's relatives do not remove any property after he has died.

9.2 Deceased woman's estate

In the Swartbooi traditional community, when the wife dies, her widower husband is then left in charge of her estate and of their children.

A Swartbooi husband and wife usually marry in community of property; this results in the fact that in the case of either spouse dying, the surviving spouse becomes the ultimate heir. The wife's relatives do not remove any property after she dies.

9.3 Both husband and wife die

In the case where both the father and the mother have died, the property is shared among all the surviving children. However, children born out of wedlock do not have any right to the property. Inheritance is gender neutral, meaning that it is not according to sex. Children can only succeed to their own father's estate. They are rightful heirs to their own father and cannot lay claims to their uncle's estate.

9.4 Testament or Will "XOA-ǁGUIB"

In the past most of the Swartbooi traditional community members could not read or write, with the result that they could not draft a written will.

They usually did it orally, by telling an elder or higher person in their community who will inherit what and how they wanted their property to be distributed among their children.

Today, the majority of the Swartbooi community can read and write. Therefore they prepare *Xoa-ǁguib,* meaning a written will.

[Signed by the Captain]

Annexure 4

Removal from Office of the Swartbooi Captain

1. Objective

1.1 The objective of the Rules of Removal of the Swartbooi Captain is to ensure that the correct and consistent procedures are followed in accordance with the traditions and norms of the Swartbooi traditional community at all times.

2. Removal from office of the captain of the Swartbooi Traditional Authority

1.2 In terms of the Traditional Authorities Act, 2000 (Act No. 25 of 2000) Section 8 subsection (1) a chief of a traditional community may be removed from office by the members of his/her traditional community in *accordance with the customary law of that traditional community,* if there is sufficient reason to warrant the removal.

3. Reasons for removing the Swartbooi captain

The Swartbooi Captain may be removed if he/she is:

3.1 involved in or found guilty of murder.
3.2 involved in or found guilty of corruption.
3.3 involved in or found guilty of fraud.
3.4 involved in or found guilty of theft.
3.5 involved in or is furthering racial or tribal hatred.
3.6 involved in any crime proving him/her not to be trustworthy.
3.7 Out of own free will.

4. Procedures to be followed on removal from office of the Swartbooi captain

4.1 A formal charge must be laid with the Supreme Council by the Swartbooi Traditional Authority for discussion.
4.2 If there is any proof or sufficient reason to warrant the removal, the Supreme Council shall inform the Swartbooi Traditional Authority in writing.
4.3 The Swartbooi Traditional Authority shall within thirty (30) days after receiving the said letter, convene a community meeting to inform members about the removal.

4.4 The Supreme Council shall within twenty one (21) days after the information meeting with the community, notify the Minister of Regional and Local Government & Housing about the removal.

[Signed by the Captain]

Annexure 5

Regulations of the Fransfontein Community Court

Regulation 1: Objective

1.1 To provide for the rules, proceedings, procedure and for connected and incidental matters in the Fransfontein Community Court.

> *"Crime is everyone's problem. It reflects an inability of people to be just and fair in their dealings with one another. It meanders to the shadow side of human nature where greed, violence and injustice lurk in each of us. Crime is a complex issue involving family background, employment opportunities, education levels, economic and social positions, as well as individual and personal choice...... the solutions are complex".*
>
> *Archbishop Desmond Tutu*

1.2 Therefore:

1.2.1 It is important that the Community Court is competent, impartial and independent. The rules, procedures and proceedings of the Community Court should enable the Court to make fair decisions without fear of intimidation.

1.2.2 It is also important that the Court have the power to be in charge.

1.2.3 In any proceedings before it the Community Court shall apply the Customary Law of the Swartbooi traditional community residing in the area of the Court's jurisdiction, but shall be in accordance with the principles of fairness and natural justice.

Regulation 2: Composition of the Fransfontein Community Court

2.1 The Fransfontein Community Court shall be presided over by a Justice appointed by the Minister of Justice.

2.2 The Justice may be assisted by one or more Assessors to advise the Court on any matter being dealt with by the Court.

2.3 A Justice or Assessor may not sit in a case in which they have a personal or monetary interest.

2.4 The Court must also have a Clerk and a Messenger of Court to exercise the functions imposed by the Community Court's Act.

Regulation 3: Appointment of the Justice for the Fransfontein Community Court

3.1 The Minister of Justice shall appoint Justices from names supplied by the Swartbooi Traditional Authority.

3.2 The Justice must:

3.2.1 know the customary law of the Swartbooi traditional community.

3.2.2 be a fit and proper person for the office because of his/her integrity.

3.2.3 not be involved in or found guilty of any stock theft, fraud, corruption, murder or any crime, proving him/her not to be trustworthy.

3.2.4 not be involved in furthering racial or tribal hatred or conspiracy to do harm to the good name of the Swartbooi Traditional Authority and its community.

3.2.5 not be a Member of Parliament, or of a Regional or Local Authority Council, or a leader of a political party.

Regulation 4: Appointment of Assessors of the Fransfontein Community Court

4.1 The Minister shall appoint assessors from names supplied by the Swartbooi Traditional Authority.

4.2 The Minister shall approve by notice in the Government Gazette a minimum of 5 and a maximum of 10 Assessors for the Court.

4.2 The Court must give due consideration to, but is not bound by the advice of an Assessor.

Regulation 5: Jurisdiction of the Fransfontein Community Court

5.1 The area of jurisdiction (geographic area) of the Fransfontein Community Court shall be the whole of Ward 9 and the Eastern Block (Gainatseb farms), which is also the jurisdiction area of the Swartbooi Traditional Authority.

5.2 Fransfontein Community Court may decide any claim for the compensation (paying for loss or damage), restitution (giving back what has been lost or stolen or the value thereof) or other claim recognized by customary law.

Regulation 6: Language to be used in the Fransfontein Community Court

6.1 The Community Court may decide upon any language for a particular case before it may be used.

6.2 In cases where all parties do not understand the chosen language, the court must call a competent interpreter.

Regulation 7: Representation in the Fransfontein Community Court

7.1 A person may represent him/herself in court.
7.2 A person may also be represented by any person of his/her choice.

Regulation 8: How are documents of the Fransfontein Community Court served upon a person?

8.1 A Messenger of Court or a Police Officer may serve all orders, notices, summons or other writings issued by the Court. This process of the Court is in force throughout Namibia.

Regulation 9: Court records and attendance of the Fransfontein Community Court

9.1 A Clerk of the Court must write up all proceedings of the Community Court.
9.2 Copies of all Court records must be given to the Magistrate's Court of the District, and to the Permanent Secretary of the Ministry of Justice.
9.3 The Clerk of the Court shall also keep a record of all sittings attended by an Assessor or Justice for the purpose of payment.

Regulation 10: Proceedings of the Fransfontein Community Court

10.1 The practice and procedure used by the Community Court, and the manner in which an order of the Court is carried out must be in accordance with the Swartbooi Customary Law. However, all proceedings must be in accordance with the principles of fairness and natural justice.
10.2 Before giving evidence, a person must either take an oath or make an affirmation.

Regulation 11: How are persons summoned to attend the Fransfontein Community Court?

11.1 The Community Court will issue a summons requiring a person to attend the Court at the time and place stated in the summons, and to testify before the court.
11.2 If a person fails to obey a summons delivered to him/her personally, or fails to stay at the court while so required, the court may order the person to be arrested.
11.3 The Messenger of the Court or a Police Officer may arrest the person and bring him/her to the Court.

11.4 The Community Court may give a maximum fine of N$100.00 or payment in kind, valued at N$100.00 for failure to obey a summons.

Regulation 12: When can cases be transferred?

12.1 If the Community Court considers that it does not have jurisdiction in a case before it, or if there is a good reason to think so, it may, when a party so applies, or upon its own initiative, refer the case to the Magistrate's Court for directions on the transfer thereof.

Regulation 13: What orders can the Fransfontein Community Court make?

13.1 An order for compensation: compensation is the making of amends to a person for his/her loss of property, and an act of counterbalancing the loss of property by giving money as a form of restoration.

13.2 An order of restitution: restitution is an act of restoring a thing to its proper or original owner. It also means the reparation (in money form) for an injury where a thing can no longer be replaced.

13.3 An order of specific performance: specific performance is an order issued in a case where there is a contract. The claimant alleges that s/he has complied with his/her obligations, but that the defendant has failed or refused to carry out his/her reciprocal obligations under the contract, and that the court should order specific performance, i.e. the defendant should carry out his/her obligations under the contract.

13.4 An order for damages: damages are a quantifiable amount payable as a consequence of:

13.4.1 A breach of contract: the Claimant wants to be placed in the position he/she would have been in, had the contract been properly performed, so far as this can be done by payment of money without undue hardships to the defaulting party.

13.4.2 An injurious accident: the claimant claims an intentional impairment of the person, dignity or reputation.

13.4.3 Damages to property: Claim of damages as a result of damage to property.

13.4.4 Damages as a result of bodily injury.

13.5 Order for costs, fees and other charges: the Court may make an order for:

13.5.1 Costs to a successful litigant.

13.5.2 Fees for services rendered by the Community Court.

13.5.3 Charges for services rendered by the Community Court.

13.6 The costs, fees and charges may be paid in cash or an equivalent amount in kind.

Regulation 14: What fines can the Fransfontein Community Court impose?

14.1 The Community Court may impose fines, but only in those cases provided for by the Community Courts Act:

14.1.1 Section 20, Subsection (5): Not exceeding N$100.00 for failure to obey a Community Court summons;

14.1.2 Section 30: Not exceeding N$1 000.00 for contempt of court;

14.1.3 Section 31: Not exceeding N$4 000 for unlawfully acting as a member of the Community Court (Justice).

Regulation 15: Imprisonment

15.1 The Community Court may imprison a person but only as provided by the Community Courts Act:

15.1.1 Section 31: Not exceeding 12 months for unlawfully acting as a member of a Community Court (Justice).

Regulation 16: How may a person appeal against an order or decision of the Fransfontein Community Court?

16.1 A person in a case may appeal an order of the Community Court to the Magistrate's Court.

16.2 However, a person must first appeal to the Body of Appeal of the Fransfontein Community Court.

16.3 The Body of Appeal of the Fransfontein Community Court shall be the Captain of the Swartbooi Traditional Authority, who is also the Chief Justice, and any two of the remaining Justices.

16.4 If still not satisfied, the person may then appeal to the Magistrate's Court.

16.5 The appeal to the Magistrate's Court must be made within 30 days (or such further period allowed by the Magistrate concerned) after the Community Court's decision.

16.6 An order of the Community Court may not be carried out until the appeal is decided or withdrawn.

Regulation 17: Offences - Sections 30 & 31

17.1 Obstructing, interfering or preventing the serving of a summons.

17.2 Dissuading, hindering or preventing a person summoned from going to court.

17.3 A penalty of a maximum fine of N$1 000.00 or equivalent payment in kind will be given for Sections 17.1 and 17.2 above.

17.4 Insulting any member of the Community Court while the court is in session.

17.5 Interrupting the proceedings of the Court.

17.6 Disturbing the peace and order of proceedings of the Court.

17.7 A penalty of removal and detention until the Community Court has finished its business and/or a maximum fine of N$1 000.00 or equivalent payment in kind, is applicable for Sections 17.4, 17.5 and 17.6 above.

17.8 Acting as Justice without being appointed.

17.9 A penalty of a maximum fine of N$4 000.00 or imprisonment of 12 months, or both the fine and imprisonment will be applicable for Section 17.8 above.

17.10 Any decision made by such a person is invalid.

[Signed by the Captain]

Annexure 6

Appointment, promotion, demotion, tenure and the power to remove from office

Regulations made in terms of the Customary Law of the Swartbooi Traditional Community–ǁKhau-ǀGoan of Fransfontein.

The Captain of the Swartbooi Traditional Community has under Section 11 (eleven) of the Customary Law, made the Regulations set out in the schedule.

[Signed by the Captain]

A. QUALIFICATIONS FOR

Appointment, Promotion, demotion and the tenure of the office of the Senior Traditional Councillors, Traditional Councillors, the Secretary and any other person so appointed by the Captain of the Swartbooi Traditional Community.

B. THE POWER TO REMOVE FROM OFFICE

1. Objective

To provide for the appointment, removal from office, promotion, demotion and the tenure of office of the Senior Traditional Councillors, Traditional Councillors, the Secretary or any other person so appointed by the Captain to serve the Swartbooi traditional community and to provide for matters incidental thereto.

(a) In terms of the Swartbooi Customary Law and the Traditional Authorities Act, 2000 (Act no. 25 of 2000) section 10, any appointment of any member or any officer to any position in the Swartbooi Traditional Authority and community is at the sole discretion of the Captain.

(b) In terms of these Regulations the Captain shall also have the sole power to promote, demote or remove from office any member, officer or the Secretary of the Swartbooi Traditional Authority.

(c) In terms of these Regulations, these powers of the Captain cannot be delegated to any member or any organ of the Swartbooi Traditional Authority or community.

2. Qualifications for Appointment

To qualify for appointment to any position in the Swartbooi Tradistionl Authority, a member must:

(a) be 18 years or above.

(b) accept, respect and comply with the Customary Law, and the Regulations as the guiding tool of all traditional activities, customs, norms, usages and rules of procedure of the Swartbooi traditional community.

(c) protect and defend the supreme law, (the Constitution) and the laws of the Republic of Namibia.

(d) not be a member of the National Assembly.

(e) not be a member of the National Council.

(f) not be a member of a Regional Council or Local Authority Council.

(g) not be a Leader of a Political Party.

(h) not be involved in or found guilty of fraud, corruption, murder, stock theft or any crime proving him/her not to be trustworthy.

(i) not be involved in or instigate racial or tribal hatred or discriminatory practices.

(j) treat other people with respect.

(k) always be ready to serve the Swartbooi community with dedication, and report all activities to the headquarters in Fransfontein.

3. Tenure of office of the Senior Traditional Councillors and Traditional Councillors

(a) The senior Traditional Councillors and Traditional Councillors shall be appointed for 5 (five) years; however, a member may be reappointed if the Captain is of the opinion they served the community with excellence.

4. Tenure of office of the Secretary/Clerk/Messenger or any other officer

(a) The secretary and all other officers shall from time to time be appointed from amongst the Swartbooi community members by the Captain and shall perform such duties and functions as may be assigned to him or her by the Captain of the Swartbooi traditional community.

5. Demotions/promotions

If the Captain is of the opinion that the performance of any Senior Traditional Councillor or Traditional Councillor in exercising his or her duties and functions is not satisfactory, the Captain may demote such a councillor.

If the Captain is of the opinion that a Traditional Councillor or any other officer has performed his or her duties and functions with excellence the Captain may promote such councillor or officer.

[Signed by the Captain]

Annexure 7

Declaration of Cultural Sites as "Holy Land"

Regulations made in terms of the Customary Law of the Swartbooi Traditional Community–ǁKhau-ǀGoan of Fransfontein.

The Captain of the Swartbooi Traditional Community has under Section 11 (eleven) of the customary Law, made the Regulations set out in the schedule.

[Signed by the Captain]

To provide for the protection and preservation of places, (cultural sites) and objects of cultural significance to the Swartbooi Traditional Community and to future generations, and to provide for incidental matters.

Cultural sites as "Holy Land"

The Traditional Authorities Act, 2000 (Act no. 25, 2000) states clearly under section 3(1) *Powers, duties and functions of Traditional Authorities*, that one of those powers, functions and duties is to "Preserve and maintain the cultural sites, works of art and literary works of that Traditional Community" (Section 3 (1) d).

Therefore, in conformity with the abovementioned section, I hereby declare the undermentioned areas in Fransfontein Reserve Farm No 6, as Cultural Sites:

(a) PERENNIAL SPRING – "ǀKHOMI-ǀAUS"

(i) The history of Fransfontein starts with the discovery of the spring by Frans Frederick, the chief hunter of Captain Cornelius Swartbooi. Captain Cornelius Swartbooi was the founder and the first Swartbooi captain in Fransfontein.

(ii) The discovery of the spring led to the unforgotten history of the Swartbooi community.

(iii) "ǀKhomi-ǀAus" spring served as a life-vein of our ancestors.

(iv) It is a firm wish of our ancestors, therefore a command to each and every generation, to protect and preserve the spring for the future.

(b) <u>FRANSFONTEIN COMMUNITY GARDENS</u>

(i) Our ancestors established Fransfontein gardens to produce food for the community. From the very beginning, they have been self-sufficient all along in terms of food production, because of the Fransfontein Community Gardens.

(ii) The community gardens are irrigated with the water from the ǀKhomi-ǀAus spring.

(iii) It is therefore a wish and a command of our ancestors to protect and preserve the community gardens for future generations to come.

(c) <u>FRANSFONTEIN COMMUNITY GRAVEYARD</u>

(i) Fransfontein Community Graveyard is seen by the Swartbooi community as holy land and must be respected as such by any individual who enters the graveyard.

(ii) Our forefathers and the current community members used to contact our ancestors in times of sorrow and difficulties from our graveyard.

(iii) The customary law of the Swartbooi traditional community, as recognized by the Government of the Republic of Namibia, states in Section 10 (5) "Nobody shall be allowed to hold meetings, festivals or any other activities at the Swartbooi cultural sites like Gravesites, the Spring or any other place so declared by the Swartbooi Traditional Authority, without the written permission of the Captain."

THEREFORE:
It is the wish and belief of the Swartbooi Traditional Authority that anybody who wants to hold any activity at the so declared areas, must first seek the consent of the Swartbooi Captain and that those areas remain under the supervision and control of this Traditional Authority.

[Signed by the Captain]

Certificate of consent to publish

Certificate of the consent to publish

UNIVERSITY OF NAMIBIA

FACULTY OF LAW

HUMAN RIGHTS AND DOCUMENTATION CENTRE

RE: CONSENT TO PUBLICATION

I, the undersigned, Chief of the Swartbooi Traditional Authority, hereby give consent to the Human Rights and Documentation Centre, to publish the following documents of the Swartbooi Traditional Authority:

1. The Customary Laws
2. The Community Profile
3. Picture of the Chief
4. Logo of the Traditional Authority

I acknowledge that the Human Rights and Documentation Centre will publish the laws in our indigenous language (Nama), as well as the English language. I am familiar with the contents of the laws that will be published and further acknowledge that they were prepared by my traditional authority.

Signed on this 23 **day of** July **2012**

At Windhoek

Daniel Luipert

Chief [illegible]

[illegible]

For HRDC: Mr. A. Gairiseb

CAPTAIN D. LUIPERT
P. O. Box 416 Khorixas
Tel: 067-331194
23 JUL 2012
Tel/Fax: 061-233598 Windhoek
Swartboois Traditional Authority

Topnaar Traditional Authority
ǂAonin !Haos

The supreme leader of the Topnaar Traditional Community is *Gaob*[1] Seth Matawa Kooitjie.
Date of designation: 28 June 1980

1 Traditional title in terms of section 11 of the Traditional Authorities Act, 2000 (No. 25 of 2000).

PROFILE[2]

The ǂAonin (Topnaar) are one of the oldest communities in the south-western part of Namibia, living in the oldest desert of the world, in the area called Namib Naukluft Park, and the more recently-proclaimed Dorob National Park which runs along the coast south-west from Walvis Bay (!Gomen ǁams), between the dunes and gravel plains of the Namib Desert. This area was originally known as ǂAoni traditional land from 1420–1900, until the proclamation of Namib Naukluft park.

The ǂAoni traditional community resides along the !Kuiseb river from Rooibank (ǀAwa !haos) up to Homeb which is the jurisdiction area of the ǂAonin/Topnaar Traditional Authority. The ǂAoni community is unique in that they developed a desert livelihood and culture based on harvesting the endemic *!nara* melon, hunting wildlife, herding mixed livestock and arable farming. Each settlement, especially near the !Khuiseb river, consists of a family group that can trace ownership of that land historically.

In general, the Topnaar community is called nomadic and known for the uniqueness of their culture and history. Most of the ǂAoni men are hunters. In the past their weapons were spears, traps, and bows and arrows which they crafted themselves by hand. Those of the Topnaar community living along the coast were fishermen in their own right, subsisting from marine resources as their staple food, the historical heritage of the ǂAoni people. The ǂAoni/Topnaar people are a peace-loving community, but if provoked, they will defend themselves.

The ǂAonin build houses from branches of trees, especially the *ana* tree as well as other trees in the !Kuiseb river. The palm tree was used as an example of Christianity by all members of the community. These practices and beliefs are still maintained by the ǂAoni people.

The !Kuiseb river is the most important source of water and food for the ǂAoni/Topnaar community. The river provides the only means of subsistence in the south-western coastal desert area for wildlife, people and their livestock, where large camelthorn and ana trees provide the security of shelter, building material and browse for the community, livestock and animal life.

The *!nara* plant

The *!nara* is generally known as a source of food for people and animals in the desert. It is also the basis of ǂAoni/Topnaar culture and history, and a guarantee of the uniqueness of the ǂAoni people.The *!nara* plant today is at the centre of most of the community members' economic life through the sale of *!nara* pulp, *!nara* seeds, *!nara* sap and *!nara* fruit.

2 This profile was provided by the Topnaar Traditional Authority.

The royal family

The ǂAonin originally had royal families up to 1910, by when most of the royal families had died because of wars and other inhumane situations. Since the death of the last *Gaob* (Chief) in 1910, the Royal House of the ǂAonin has never been restored and the community also failed to restore the inheritance of the ǂAoni Kingdom and *Gaob-Oms* (Palace or Royal House). According to ǂAoni customary beliefs, the Palace or Royal House is where the holy fire is kept as a token of respect and power to the *Gaob* so that he might exercise strong control over the community and general matters.

The *Gaob* has always exercised strong control over the allocation of land, and whether cattle and trade should be taxed. The Chief gives judgment on conflict. The Chief is responsible for all agricultural activities in all seasons. The Chief determines when the hunting season is to start and when to end. Hunting is called *|hamis -!au ǁaeb*. The *Gaob* is not allowed to lead military expeditions personally if these go beyond his own territory or land.

The laws of the ǂAonin (Topnaar)[1]

1 The laws of the Topnaar were submitted in English only.

Preamble

The structural existence of the Topnaar community degenerated because of German and South African colonial rule. As a result Topnaar authority over subjects could not be effectively exercised.

Consequently, their collective ownership of the land that they communally used and cared for was taken away by the colonisers and declared a National Park.

South African apartheid machinery tried to relocate the Topnaar community to the south (especially the Gibeon area) by force but the community refused to move – with the result that they were under extreme pressure to accept second class treatment from the colonial regime.

Therefore

(a) The Topnaar traditional community thank God for the independence of this country (Namibia).

(b) The Topnaar traditional community thank the Founding Father of our Republic.

(c) The Topnaar traditional community thank the Head of State and his Government for the wise and timely decisions to recognise the traditional communities and their leaders.

God bless our Government and our beautiful Republic.

Section 1: Definitions

1.1 In this Customary Law, unless the context indicates otherwise:

(a) *Additional member* shall mean any member co-opted from the Topnaar traditional community by the Topnaar Traditional Authority to assist the leadership, or who is entrusted to represent the Traditional Authority anywhere in Namibia and abroad.

(b) *Captain* shall mean the chief as defined in the Traditional Authorities Act, 2000 (No. 25 of 2000) and named Captain of the Topnaar Traditional Authority.

(c) *Communal land* shall mean the communal area as defined in the Traditional Authorities Act, 2000 (No. 25 of 2000) including the Topnaar community.

(d) *Customary law* shall mean the customary law as defined in the Traditional Authorities Act, 2000 (No. 25 of 2000).

(e) *Supreme law* shall mean the sole organ of the Topnaar Traditional Authority, entrusted with the power to select, remove or designate the captain/councillors.

(f) *Traditional community* shall mean the traditional community as defined in the Traditional Authorities Act, 2000 (No. 25 of 2000).

(g) *Traditional leader* shall mean and include the traditional leader as defined in the Traditional Authorities Act, 2000 (No. 25 of 2000).
(h) *Traditional land of the Topnaar* shall mean the geographical area habitually inhabited by our ancestors, that is Walvis Bay and all its surrounding farms that have been declared as the Namib Naukluft Park in the !Khuiseb river.
(i) *Vice Captain* shall mean a senior councillor appointed by the Captain to deputise him or act as a captain in his absence.

Section 2: Traditional land

2.1 The traditional land of the Topnaar community shall be the geographical area habitually inhabited by our ancestors, being Walvis Bay with all its surrounding farms that stretch up to Homeb in the !Khuiseb River. Much of this area was later declared by the then Odendaal Commission as a National Park.

Section 3: Main seat

3.1 The main seat of the Topnaar shall be at Utuseb.

Section 4: Traditional anthem

4.1 There shall be a traditional anthem for the Topnaar community.
4.2 The anthem shall be decided upon by the Topnaar traditional community.

Section 5: Organs of the Topnaar Traditional Authority

5.1 Topnaar Traditional Authority

5.1.1 There shall be a Traditional Authority for the Topnaar traditional community.
5.1.2 The establishment, powers, duties and functions are defined in the Traditional Authorities Act, 2000 (No. 25 of 2000) as amended according to this customary law.

5.2 The Supreme Council

5.2.1 There shall be a Supreme Council for the Topnaar traditional community.
5.2.2 The composition of the Supreme Council shall be at least ten (10) members of the Topnaar Traditional Authority and 14 members of the Elders' Council (*Stam Oudstes*).
5.2.3 The main functions of the Supreme Council shall be:
(a) To select, after consultation with the members of the Topnaar Community, the successor for the Captain in accordance with the rules of succession (the rules of succession to be included in the regulations) and according to customary law.

(b) To remove the Captain from office upon proof of sufficient reason to warrant the removal. The removal shall be in accordance with Section 8 of the Traditional Authorities Act, 2000 (No. 25 of 2000) after notifying the Minister of Regional & Local Government, Housing and Rural Development.

5.3 The Captain

5.3.1 The Captain shall be the supreme traditional leader of the Topnaar traditional community.
5.3.2 He shall be appointed or elected after nominations amongst the members of the Topnaar Traditional Authority.
5.3.3 The Captain shall serve as long as he or she is capable of serving.
5.3.4 The Chief shall be the custodian of this Customary Law and exercise his powers and perform his duties and functions in accordance with it.
5.3.5 The inauguration of the Captain shall be done only by a person equal to the Captain.
5.3.6 The inauguration of the Captain shall be done in Nama according to this customary law.
5.3.7 The inauguration procedure shall be included in the regulations of this customary law.

5.4 The Vice-Captain

5.4.1 In the absence of the Captain, the Vice Captain shall act as the Captain.
5.4.2 In all other circumstances when necessary the Vice Captain shall deputise the Captain.

5.5 Elders' Council *(Stam Oudstes)*

5.5.1 There shall be an Elders' Council for the Topnaar traditional community.
5.5.2 The eligible age for membership of the Elders' Council shall be 60 years and above.
5.5.3 The Elders' Council shall adopt its own rules for its activities within the limits of customary law.
5.5.4 The main function shall be to:
(a) advise the Captain about the customs of the Topnaar.
(b) ensure that the Topnaar "flame" does not diminish in that Topnaar culture must always be taught to the younger generation, and
(c) delegate 14 members to the Supreme Council when need be.

5.6 Topnaar Youth Group

5.6.1 There shall be a youth group for the Topnaar traditional community.
5.6.2 Membership shall be thirty-five (35) years and younger.

5.6.3 The youth group shall adopt its own rules for its activities within the limits of customary law.

5.6.4 The main functions of the youth group shall be to:

(a) organise the cultural activities of the community.

(b) keep contact with the youth and cultural groups of other traditional communities.

(c) organise income generating projects within the community, and

(d) organise sports and other activities among the youth.

5.7 Topnaar Women's Council

5.7.1 There shall be a Women's Council for the Topnaar traditional community.

5.7.2 The membership shall be open to all Topnaar women who are interested in developing and practising Topnaar Culture.

5.7.3 The Women's Council shall adopt its own rules for its activities within the limits of customary law.

5.7.4 The main functions shall be to:

(a) develop cultural projects within the community.

(b) organise and teach Topnaar culture to all women and children, and

(c) keep contact with other women's and cultural groups.

Section 6: Meetings

6.1 Traditional Assembly

6.1.1 There shall be a Traditional Assembly for the Topnaar traditional community.

6.1.2 The Topnaar Traditional Assembly shall be held annually with the traditional festival of the Topnaar.

6.1.3 The date of Traditional Assembly shall be included in the regulations. The date of the meeting of the Traditional Assembly should be as determined by the Traditional Assembly. They shall meet four times a year and convene any special meeting called by the Chief.

6.1.4 The Topnaar Traditional Assembly shall be open to all members of the Topnaar community throughout Namibia.

6.1.5 Meetings shall be advertised at least 30 (thirty) days prior to the meeting.

6.1.6 The Traditional Assembly shall have the power to amend or repeal this customary law subject to a 2/3 (two thirds) majority of members present.

6.1.7 The Traditional Assembly shall consist of 6 Senior Traditional Councillors and 6 Traditional Councillors.

6.1.8 The quorum shall consist of the Captain, at least 6 members of the Topnaar Authority and at least 100 members of the community.

6.2 Traditional Authority meetings

6.2.1 There shall be a Traditional Authority meeting once every quarter (4 times each year).

6.2.2 The meetings shall be attended by the Captain, Vice-Captain and Traditional Councillors only.

6.2.3 The meetings will discuss traditional concerns, customary conduct/laws and/or matters concerning the traditional community.

6.2.4 The Traditional Authority may invite anyone to their meetings.

6.2.5 The quorum shall be four members.

6.2.6 Every Traditional Authority member shall be obliged to attend the meeting.

6.2.7 Any Traditional Authority member who fails to attend 3 (three) consecutive meetings without a valid reason and without being excused by the Authority, will be dismissed from the Traditional Authority.

6.3 Community meetings

6.3.1 There shall be general Community Meetings for the Topnaar community.

6.3.2 Community meetings shall be open to every member of the community.

6.3.3 The meetings shall be convened by the Captain and his Councillors on a quarterly basis.

6.3.4 The purpose of the meetings will be to consult the community or to give general information on the dealings of the Traditional Council.

Section 7: Law of maintaining justice

7.1 Nobody shall take land by him- or herself without written permission from the Traditional Council.

7.2 Nobody shall settle or move into the Jurisdiction Area of the Topnaar Authority without the written permission of the Traditional Council.

7.3 Nobody shall be allowed to make uncontrolled moves from one communal farm to another without written permission from the Traditional Council.

7.4 Nobody shall be allowed to fence off communal land without written permission from the Traditional Council.

7.5 Nobody shall be allowed to hold meetings, festivals or any activities at Topnaar Cultural sites such as grave yards or any other place so declared by the Topnaar Traditional Authority without written permission of the Traditional Council.

7.6 Nobody shall be allowed to collect fire wood or any natural resources for any purpose other than household use without permission from the Traditional Council.

7.7 Nobody shall transport livestock or meat without a letter from the headman or Council of the area he or she comes from.

7.8 Nobody shall be allowed to sell livestock or meat without the written permission of the Topnaar Traditional Authority.

7.9 If a person is found guilty of having stolen someone's goat, cattle or sheep, he or she shall pay back compensation triple (3 for 1) or pay a fine determined by the Community Court.

7.10 If a person steals someone else's property other than livestock, and gets caught, he or she shall give back the person's property as it was and still be fined by the court.

7.11 If a man commits adultery with another man's wife and impregnates her, he shall pay 6 (six) head of cattle or goats. The decision to whom payment should be made will be taken in a special meeting convened. One head of cattle is equivalent to three goats.

7.12 If he does not impregnate her, he shall pay 2 (two) head of cattle or 6 (six) goats, as determined in the special meeting.

7.13 If a woman is raped, she shall be paid 4 (four) head of cattle or 12 (twelve) goats and the rapist will be fined by the court.

7.14 If a woman has sexual intercourse with another man in her house and gets caught, she shall pay 3 (three) head of cattle to the Traditional Authority.

7.15 If a man impregnates a school girl, he shall pay 2 (two) head of cattle or 6 (six) goats to the victim.

7.16 If a man impregnates a girl out of marriage, he shall pay one head of cattle.

7.17 Nobody shall be allowed to swear or fight on the streets or any other place.

7.18 If a person commits murder, he/she shall be handed over to the judicial sector of Namibia.

Section 8: Chief's house or palace

8.1 The house of the chief is traditionally and historically called the Palace according to custom. There must be a house of *Gaob*.

8.2 According to customary law, that house is the property of the whole community owned by the community through a trust, meaning that the Community Trust is the trust holder of such property.

Section 9: Regulations

9.1 The Topnaar Traditional Authority may make regulations relating to:

(a) customary marriages
(b) inheritance of land, livestock or other property
(c) grazing of livestock on commercial land
(d) traditional festivals of the Topnaar community
(e) rules of succession to the Topnaar throne
(f) a traditional anthem, and
(g) any other matter required in order to achieve the purposes of this customary law.

9.2 General points

9.2.1 The laws shall be discussed by the Traditional Council together with the Traditional Authority.

9.2.2 They shall then be approved by the Regional Council so that they may be enacted.

9.2.3 The laws shall be revised every 5 (five) years.

9.2.4 Any law not approved by the people shall be repealed.

9.2.5 Every five years the value of cattle shall be increased.

9.2.6 There are also oral laws not included here. The laws in this book are the most important ones.

9.3 These laws are not a codification of the laws of the ǂAonin and they do not substitute those laws that are orally spoken by the community members and those that were passed by the king since time immemorial. The laws that are in this book are mostly those that are significant and appropriate for today and are used by the Community Court.

9.4 These laws include natural justice, protection of widows and orphans, and the protection of natural resources like trees, grass, animals, veld and water.

9.5 Traditional leaders in the settlement and other areas are expected to be good listeners to their community's problems and needs, and they are expected to assist community members where possible. They should be exemplary leaders and are expected to be:

(a) Friendly
(b) Peaceful
(c) Patient
(d) Persistent
(e) Respectful
(f) Humble to all the people in the village and district
(g) Impartial in the administration of justice.

9.6 The traditional leaders should come to know the people under their leadership and try to establish a good relationship with them.

9.7 The traditional leaders should have good and honest advisors, as well as secretaries who can take accurate minutes of conversations, court cases and meetings.

9.8 Court presiding officers should not exercise nepotism or be biased. Justice should prevail in all their verdicts.

Section 10: Short title/commencement and amendment

10.1 This Constitution shall be called Topnaar Customary Law and shall come into force immediately after the Captain has signed it.

10.2 This Customary Law or any Section thereof may be amended or repealed by a 2/3 (two thirds) majority of members present at the Traditional Assembly.

10.3 Recommendations in connection with the Customary Law must be made at least 30 days before the commencement of the Assembly to the Secretary of the Topnaar Authority.

[Signed]
Gaob Seth Matawa Kooitjie
ǂAonin (Topnaar) Captain

Regulation 1: Court proceedings

R1.1 Any person who is owed or has been done wrong by another person and would like to open a case shall start from the settlement headman, and if they are not satisfied by the decision of the settlement head, they shall proceed to the head of the area together with the decision made by the headman.

R1.2 If the decision made by the head chief does not satisfy the complainant, he/she shall have the right to appeal against the decision to their senior headman/woman. If someone is owed something, the person owed shall not take the law into their own hands to take the other person's belongings. They shall follow the law and order.

R1.3 If the complainant is not satisfied with the decision made by the senior headman/woman he/she shall appeal to the Traditional Council.

R1.4 If the case involves stabbing or assault, a doctor's certificate shall be presented to show the extent of the injury.

R1.5 Anyone whose belongings have been confiscated in lieu of debt, or whose property has been damaged, shall not take property to make good the loss. He/she shall first ask for the goods to be returned. The parties shall first try to agree. If they cannot, the case shall be referred to the Headman's Court and thereafter may proceed to a place decided by the district, and thereafter to the Traditional Authority's High Court.

Regulation 2: Court attendance

R2.1 Any person subpoenaed to attend court shall do so. Inability to attend shall be reported to the headman. If the hearing is at the area court, inability to attend shall be reported to the head of the area where the hearing will take place. Inability to attend the Traditional Authority's High Court shall be reported to the Traditional Authority office. If the accused was in hospital at the time of the hearing, proof thereof shall be provided. If the accused is a civil servant employed elsewhere, he/she shall present the employer with the court summons so that the employer can grant him/her permission to attend.

R2.2 If the procedure stated in 1.1 is not adhered to, the accused may be fined by the court. If the accused has been subpoenaed three times and deliberately refuses to appear at any Traditional Court he/she shall be fined N$100 or more. NB: this provision includes the village headman as well as the district headman or his/her deputy.

R2.3 If the witness is in hospital, he/she shall submit proof thereof. If the witness is employed, he/she shall show the summons to the employer so that he/she can be excused.

R2.4 People employed by the Traditional Council shall not reveal council secrets or talk about issues under discussion until this has been finalised by the council. A person doing so shall be given two warnings if he/she is found guilty thereof twice. If, after two warnings, the person continues to violate this rule, he or she may be put on leave for a period of six months. If he/she continues to divulge information, the Traditional Authority shall have the right to dismiss this person.

Regulation 3: Witnesses

R3.1 Every accused person shall have the right to bring witnesses to court. A witness shall not give false testimony. A witness shall not provide evidence that would interfere with the course of justice. If the presiding officer realises the testimony given is false, the witness shall be advised to tell the truth as follows (Exodus 23:1-8):

"*Do not spread false reports. Do not help a wicked man by being a malicious witness. Do not follow the crowd in doing wrong. When you give testimony in a lawsuit, do not pervert justice by siding with the crowd, and do not show favouritism to a poor man in his lawsuit. If you come across your enemy's ox or donkey in wandering off, be sure to take it back to him. If you see a donkey of someone who hates you fallen down under its load, do not leave it there; be sure you help him with it. Do not deny justice to your poor people in their lawsuits. Have nothing to do with a false charge and do not put an innocent and honest person to death, for it will not acquit to the guilty. Do not accept a bribe, for a bribe blinds those who see and twists the words of the righteous. Do not oppress an alien; you yourselves know how it feels to be aliens, because you were aliens in Egypt.*"

Regulation 4: Murder

R4.1 If a person murders another person, he/she shall appear before the Criminal Court, while the Traditional Court shall have the responsibility to determine a fine. Traditionally a murderer shall be given a fine of 10 (ten) head of cattle.

R4.2 If someone is killed while committing a theft, the killer shall not be fined because the death will be deemed to have been to defend one's property, unless the Traditional Authority receives contrary information or a mandate from the Magistrate's Court.

R4.3 If a person is hit by a car and dies, the family of the deceased shall be paid 5 (five) head of cattle. This shall only be paid to comfort the family of the deceased as the killing was not intentional.

R4.4 If a person dies in a car accident because the car overturned or was in a collision, the Traditional Authority shall not be empowered to adjudicate the matter.

R4.5 If a person poisons another and the victim dies, a doctor's examination shall be carried out or a credible witness provided. If the doctor's examination confirms that the person was poisoned, the murderer shall be fined 10 (ten) head of cattle including the clearing of blood, meaning to wipe off the tears of the deceased's family.

R4.6 If a person is accused of aborting a baby, a doctor's examination or a credible witness shall be provided.

R4.7 If a woman gives birth and flushes the baby down the toilet or abandons it, the matter shall be reported to the nearest police station, the headman or the Chief immediately. If the baby dies the woman shall be fined for the murder.

R4.8 The Traditional Authority shall not listen to anyone claiming to be related to a family member in the absence of credible information from the magistrate or other traditional authorities in the case of a murder trial.

Regulation 5: Rape

R5.1 The older law regarding rape has not been used in the Traditional Authority since it was abolished in 1932.

R5.2 A woman who has been raped shall be taken to a doctor or the nearest police station immediately. She shall not take off the clothes she was wearing when she was raped and she shall not take a bath which may destroy evidence. If the magistrate refers a case to a Traditional Court, the rapist shall pay 6 (six) head of cattle for the rape alone.

R5.3 If a man physically assaults a woman before raping her, he shall be charged with assault and rape. The assault charge, however, shall be decided in court.

R5.4 If a man rapes and kills a woman, and if a Criminal Court provides evidence of this to the Traditional Authority, the perpetrator shall be charged with two criminal acts: rape and murder.

R5.5 If a man rapes a pregnant woman and kills her, then the perpetrator shall be guilty of three acts: rape, murder of the baby and murder of the mother and shall be punished accordingly.

Regulation 6: Adultery

R6.1 If a man sleeps with another man's wife and impregnates her, he shall pay 4 (four) head of cattle to the woman's husband. If he does not impregnate her, the payment shall be 2 (two) head of cattle. If a woman commits adultery in her husband's house and becomes pregnant, she shall pay 1 (one) head of cattle to her husband.

R6.2 If any woman is found in a couple's house, the wife of that house shall reserve the right to take the intruding woman to court on a charge of destroying her marriage. If the fault lies with the man, he shall be similarly charged.

R6.3 The court shall not involve itself in an infidelity case which lacks clear evidence.

Regulation 7: Pregnancy

R7.1 If a girl becomes pregnant, she shall have the right to open a case of compensation against the man who impregnated her.

R7.2 If the girl is over 18 and does not wish to claim compensation, than none shall be due. If the girl becomes pregnant, she shall be compensated 2 (two) head of cattle or N$1 000 per head of cattle of which N$300 shall go to the Traditional Authority's coffers. The fine shall apply to married and unmarried men.

R7.3 If a girl is engaged and becomes pregnant by another man, she shall return all that was given to her by her fiancé.

R7.4 No parent or guardian shall refuse to admit a pregnant girl if she comes to the house of the man who impregnated her to inform them of the pregnancy. If this happens the parent or guardian shall be taken to court.

R7.5 If the pregnant girl does not wish to live with the man who impregnated her, she shall have the right to live at her parents' house. If the pregnant girl wishes to leave the impregnator's house, the parents of both sides together with the headman, shall have the right to grant her permission to go back home. In other words, if the man accepts responsibility for the pregnancy, then the girl shall have the right to go back to her parents' house. If the girl is not compensated within three months, she shall open a case with the Traditional Authority, provided she is over 18. If she is under 18, her parents or guardian shall represent her.

R7.6 Traditional and national laws state that if a girl falls pregnant under the age of 16, she is too young to judge sexual relationships, and whoever made her pregnant shall be deemed to have raped her. The Council may refer this to the Criminal Court.

R7.7 Parents shall not be encouraged to allow a pregnant girl and the man who impregnated her to live together. In the case where the parents allow it, the Traditional Authority shall be immediately informed.

Regulation 8: Assault and assault by threat

R8.1 Under Traditional law no person shall be allowed to assault or victimize another person. No person shall be assaulted or threatened with a gun, knife, panga, rod, bow or any other weapon. No person shall say anything that may make the person feel victimised or in danger. If a person is threatened or assaulted, he/she shall have the right to open a court case. Witnesses, if there are any, shall be called. The warning or fine for threatening behaviour shall be determined by the court.

R8.2 The fine for physical attack shall be determined in court, according to the extent of damage suffered by the victim. If the victim goes to a hospital, evidence shall be obtained from the hospital detailing the damage caused. If the victim did not go to hospital, testimony shall be obtained from those who witnessed the incident.

R8.3 If a person damages another person's eye, he/she shall pay 6 (six) head of cattle, one of which is due to the court. If the damage was not intentional, the matter shall be decided by the court.

R8.4 If a person breaks another person's leg, he/she shall pay 5 (five) head of cattle, one of which is due to the court.

R8.5 Anyone who breaks another person's arm shall pay 4 (four) head of cattle, one of which is due to the court.

R8.6 Anyone who cuts off another person's ear shall be fined 2 (two) head of cattle.

R8.7 Anyone who cuts off another person's nose shall be fined 2 (two) head of cattle.

R8.8 Anyone who cuts off another person's lips shall be fined 2 (two) head of cattle.

R8.9 Anyone who cuts off another person's hand shall be fined 2 (two) head of cattle.

R8.10 Anyone who cuts off another person's breast shall be fined 2 (two) head of cattle.

R8.11 NOTE: All the fines above are decided by the court and can be varied according to whether the acts were committed deliberately or unintentionally.

R8.12 Guns are dangerous and shall not be carried or played with in public. Customary law shall forbid this. No one shall use guns at gatherings such as funerals or wedding ceremonies without a valid reason, unless he/she is slaughtering an animal. Anyone who does so shall appear in court and may be fined 1 (one) goat.

R8.13 All weapons shall be forbidden at the Traditional Court or in meetings. Councils and authorities shall have a person who maintains order and tells people not to come into meetings with weapons.

R8.14 Each person intending to buy a weapon which requires a license shall apply through the village headman for permission, as he knows people's behaviour in his village very well.

Regulation 9: Land distribution

R9.1 In all communal areas, all land belongs to the State (Government). No land shall belong to families. Decisions about communal land shall be made by government representatives such as the village headman, chief or Traditional Authorities.

R9.2 In communal areas, land (the field) that was used by a deceased person shall revert to the Traditional Authority, which shall decide who may use the land next. Family shall no longer decide who uses the land, as they did in the past.

R9.3 Any community member who feels unfairly treated in respect of the distribution of land previously farmed by a deceased person shall immediately report this to the Traditional Authority office.

R9.4 Past traditional laws which prohibited women from acquiring land have been abolished, as they are in conflict with human rights, as enshrined in the Namibian constitution.

R9.5 An application of land shall be lodged with the settlement headman, as he/she knows all the places in the area. Anyone who acquires land without going through the headman shall not have acquired it legally.

R9.6 No occupant of land shall have the right to extend his/her boundary without first consulting the headman. If a person does so, the headman shall open a court case with the Traditional Authority.

R9.7 In the event of a dispute about borders with neighbours, registration shall be carried out before the matter is taken to court. The Council or Traditional Authority shall send a committee to investigate the dispute.

R9.8 No person shall be allowed to take part of the common land used for herding animals or to fence it off. An exception shall be land identified by Government or Non-Governmental Organisations (NGOs) for agricultural development or other development projects.

R9.9 The guidelines on land allocation stipulate that land shall be occupied or used within three years, or the headman shall allocate it to somebody else. However, before reallocating the land, the headman shall first investigate why it was not first utilised. If there is a good reason the person shall be permitted to reapply for the land.

R9.10 If a private organisation wishes to make use of the land they shall obtain permission from the Traditional Authority. If the NGO has an agreement with the Government, it shall have proof to that effect.

R9.11 The Traditional Authority shall be entitled to put up sign boards on communal land to mark places for markets. Houses shall not be built there and nor shall fields be cultivated there. A person taking part of this reserved land shall be seen as breaking the law and the Traditional Authority shall have the right to open a case against him/her.

R9.12 Cattle posts shall be allocated to a person for the purpose of grazing his/her livestock and shall not be private property. At that place a person shall only be allowed to erect kraals to protect livestock against cold and wild animals, and to prevent livestock dispersing. When that person leaves, he should leave the place as he found it.

Regulation 10: Inheritance

R10.1 In the 1993 amendment to traditional law it was agreed that widows shall no longer be removed from their deceased husbands' land or asked to pay for the land.

R10.2 The law states that the house shall belong to the husband and wife, and if one spouse dies, than it shall belong to the other. If both of them die, then the house shall belong to one of the children.

R10.3 Traditional law shall not deal with the inheritance of crops, household utensils or other items of that nature.

R10.4 Any woman who feels mistreated regarding inheritance shall have the right to open a case with the settlement headman, area office or the Traditional Authority. The Traditional Authority expects a widow or any member of the bereaved family who experienced any mistreatment with regard to inheritance to open a court case.

R10.5 The widow or any other member of the bereaved family shall have the same access to the house that they had before the death of the deceased.

R10.6 The guidelines which regulate inheritance are as follows

R10.6.1 No one shall inherit from the estate of the deceased until the latter's body has been buried.

R10.6.2 The widow/widower together with the other members shall have the right to decide when the division of the estate shall take place, but it shall be after the burial.

R10.6.3 Traditionally, someone shall be appointed as an executor to divide the estate. This person is usually a close relative of the deceased who knows the deceased's possessions very well. The deceased may appoint this person before he/she dies. Anyone who takes anything from the deceased estate before the division of the estate shall be regarded as a thief who has contravened the law.

R10.6.4 The executor shall have the right and responsibility to make an announcement at an inheritance (also called */Umis* or *omwaale*) after the funeral so that anyone who is indebted to the deceased or is owed a debt by the deceased can declare it.

R10.6.5 After the */Umis,* no claim of the debt shall be accepted. Anyone who was not present at the */Umis* and wants to discuss debt shall talk to the executor before discussing debts with anybody else.

R10.5.6 If the deceased left a will then the widow or member of family shall follow it.

R10.5.7 Every person shall have the right to make an inventory of their possessions and record to whom they will be bequeathed after death. Land shall be excepted because land in communal areas belongs to the government and is allocated by traditional leaders.

Regulation 11: Theft

R11.1 Any victim of theft shall have a right to open a court case with the Traditional Authority or the Criminal Court.

R11.2 Stolen goods found in a person's possession shall be confiscated and returned to the owner if there is valid proof that the goods belong to him/her, regardless of whether or not the person bought the goods. A buyer of stolen goods shall be responsible for identifying the person who sold them.

R11.3 Anything lost and subsequently found shall be reported at the headman's house or at the nearest police station. Unclaimed items shall be kept safely, and the find announced over the radio, in church, or at other community gatherings.

R11.4 Any thief found guilty in the Magistrate's Court may be prosecuted in the traditional court if the owner of the stolen items wants them returned.

R11.5 A shop owner may prosecute an employee in a Magistrate's Court. If the accused is asked by the magistrate to pay the items back in the traditional way, the accused shall do this.

R11.6 A head of the household who protects a child that has been found guilty of theft shall be aware that the headman has the right to open a case against him/her.

R11.7 If stolen goods are found in the household and the head of the household has not reported these items to the headman's house or to any representative of the law in the area, the head of that household shall appear in court and be fined for keeping stolen items and not reporting them.

R11.8 If anyone sees the footprints of someone who has stolen from his/her house, this person shall inform his/her neighbours, people in the community and the headman, so that an investigation can be made and the footprints followed. A case of theft may be opened against a person whose footprints are found.

R11.9 If a person steals a cow, he/she shall return the animal and shall pay a fine of one head of cattle. If the cow is slaughtered, the thief shall pay for the animal and an additional fine of one head of cattle.

R11.10 If a person is found with goods whose owner is unknown, the headman of the area shall open a case with the traditional court.

R11.11 People in the community shall have the right to suspect strangers as criminals who have come to spy. Suspects shall immediately be reported to the village headman.

Regulation 12: Lost livestock

R12.1 The Traditional Authority shall appoint a person to be in charge of lost livestock as it is in other Traditional Authorities. This person shall be given authority, that is, the power of the Traditional Authority, to take care of lost livestock in conjunction with the village headman and district leaders.

R12.2 Any lost cattle shall be reported to the headman or to the head of Topnaar district Traditional Authority. They shall be kept in safety at the homestead where they were found for three years after which the headman shall take them to the Topnaar Traditional Authority.

R12.3 If a person loses a cow and finds it in somebody else's herd, the two cattle owners shall discuss the matter calmly. If they do not agree with each other, the person who has lost the cow shall not have the right to take the cow without informing the headman; it shall be contravention of customary law to take the cow by force.

R12.4 No person shall change the brand mark on lost cattle. Whoever does so, shall be regarded as a thief. He/she shall be taken to court and a case shall be opened against him/her.

R12.5 If a lost cow dies in somebody's homestead, the head of the house shall sell the meat but he/she shall inform the headman accordingly. The skull, chest and income from the sale shall be kept safely to be given to the original owner.

Regulation 13: Moving livestock

R13.1 Livestock in transit shall be accompanied by a permit letter from the headman of the village where they originate, including their colours and other characteristics. The village headman official stamp shall be clearly visible on the letter. Personal letters shall not be used. If the headman does not have a stamp he/she shall contact the Traditional Authority's office for permission to use their stamp or letterhead, or shall send the owner of the livestock, or the person who will travel with it, to the Traditional Authority office or anywhere where a permit can be obtained. The reason for moving livestock from one place to another, e.g. for slaughter, for grazing or for sale shall be made clear.

R13.2 Moving livestock without a permit and buying livestock from a person under the age of 16 years shall be offences punishable by a fine.

R13.3 If a person intends slaughtering a cow in the village or at a cuca shop the village headman shall be informed accordingly. No person shall slaughter a cow in a river without a valid reason. If the reason is that the cow has had an accident or could not move, the headman shall be informed accordingly.

R13.4 If a motorist runs over an animal on a tarred or gravel road he/she shall stop to make an agreement about compensation with the owner. The motorist shall not be expected to pay for hitting an animal at night.

R13.5 If livestock destroys someone's crops, the owner of the field or garden shall not detain, beat or hurt the animals, instead, he/she shall open a court case with the headman.

Regulation 14: Damage caused by domestic animals

R14.1 If a cow or goat attacks a person and the person dies, the cow or goat shall be killed. The owner of the animal shall not be prosecuted unless the owner of the animal knew about the danger, but did nothing to prevent damage occurring.

R14.2 If two oxen fight and one dies, the ox which died shall not be paid for.

R14.3 Dogs and cats shall be vaccinated regularly, either at the veterinary clinic or traditionally. Anyone who is bitten by a dog or cat shall be taken to hospital immediately.

R14.4 Pigs shall be kept in kraals and shall not be permitted to damage other people's property. A pig owner who allows a pig to roam loose and cause damage may be prosecuted.

Regulation 15: Water conservation

R15.1 Water is life. Therefore, water shall be conserved because it is important to people, animals and plants for survival.

R15.2 The Traditional Authority shall have the responsibility of protecting water, together with other Traditional Authorities. The traditional Authority shall not allow water to be misused, including through fishing with nets. Anyone found misusing water shall be prosecuted. If the headman or people from his household misuse water, the matter shall be reported to the Traditional Authority.

R15.3 Each headman shall have the responsibility of ensuring that water is not misused in the village. This can be natural water in *gorras* or tap water. Anyone found wasting water shall be taken to court by the headman and may be fined. Those who used water with fishing equipment shall be fined a goat or cow. Those who extract water lilies while they are still immature shall be fined a chicken.

R15.4 All members of the community shall have the responsibility of protecting water, regardless of whether it is river/*gorra* water or tap water. Every community member shall have the responsibility of reporting any misuse of water to the village headman, district headman or to the Ministry of Agriculture, Water and Forestry.

R15.5 Traditional law also reaffirms the custom regarding water pans, namely that fish shall only be taken from water when the water can no longer be consumed by people or livestock. This shall be announced by the village and district headmen. Fishing shall not take place before the headman has announced that it may. Anyone found fishing in the water pans before the announcement is made shall be contravening the law and should be prepared to be punished.

R15.6 No person shall take or eat fish from a water pan which is in somebody else's field or consume fish which was farmed by somebody else. Anybody reported doing this shall be fined.

R15.7 Water pipes shall not be cut to water livestock. If the water supply has been stopped, the Ministry of Agriculture, Water and Forestry shall be contacted to find out what the reason is.

R15.8 After good rains, water runs in natural courses. People wishing to build houses shall contact local leaders to gain information about areas prone to flooding from rain water. This shall be done to save work in the event of flooding.

R15.9 A person who digs a well shall control its use. Should another person wish to extract water from that well, he/she shall request permission from the owner.

Regulation 16: The environment

R16.1 Trees and shrubs

R16.1.1 Traditional authorities shall have the responsibility of conserving nature. Every member of society shall conserve nature, both for themselves and for the nation.

R16.1.2 Every person who needs to cut or collect wood shall contact the village headman for a letter to take to the Traditional Authority, which can grant authorisation to cut or collect wood.

R16.1.3 Every tree which is inside or outside the Park shall be protected. All trees shall be protected. If a tree is dry and dead, the community shall be permitted to use it for firewood. The Traditional Authority shall impose a fine of one or two goats for people who damage trees or their fruits. This includes the extraction of juice from palm trees.

R16.1.4 Permission to cut trees shall only be granted for building purposes, and not for the selling of wood. Anyone found with a vehicle containing wood to be sold shall be taken to the Community Court by the headman or any other person. Anyone carrying firewood in a vehicle shall have a letter of permission from the village headman.

R16.1.5 The Traditional Authority urges every person to handle trees like his or her own wealth, and recommends that for every tree cut, two or three should be planted in order to combat desertification.

R16.2 Animals

R16.2.1 The Traditional Authority shall have the right to prosecute anyone who destroys or harms animals.

R16.2.2 Anyone who is found mistreating animals in the following reproachable ways shall be prosecuted:
(a) Cutting its arteries or veins;
(b) Tying an animal to a car and dragging it whilst it is still alive;
(c) Keeping animals in a kraal all day without food, or
(d) Tying animals too tightly, or with wire.

R16.2.3 Wild animals like springbok, ostriches and gemsbok shall be left in peace. No harm/destruction shall be done to them so that the animals can get used to being in the rural areas and children can get to know them. Anyone who harms these animals shall be punished.

R16.2.4 No person shall collect birds' eggs or chicks, as this will reduce birdlife. Killing and shooting at birds shall also not be allowed, except in the officially announced bird hunting season.

Regulation 17: Veld

R17.1 Traditional law forbids the pulling out of grass with its roots, which degrades grazing, and the cutting of fresh grass.

R17.2 Veld fires are a danger to humans, animals and plant life. A person causing a veld fire shall be tried in the traditional court (not a village court).

R17.3 If one person sets fire to another person's home deliberately, he/she shall be sentenced according to the value of the items burnt in the house. If the person has mental problems, medical evidence shall be obtained to this effect from a doctor.

R17.4 Aloes are plants that grow in the veld and are very important in traditional medicine, healing wounds in humans and animals. Some aloe types, such as *Au-hain* also provide food and medicine for the community and livestock. Aloes shall be protected by customary law. Anyone found reducing the numbers of aloes in any way shall be fined.

R17.5 *Tsabis* (Black ebony) is another type of tree that grows in the !Kuiseb river. It is important in traditional and cultural uses. It can be used for grafting new trees. It is also used as a house building material; *Tsabis* shall be protected by the Community Court and shall not be destroyed or sold. Anyone doing so shall be fined.

R17.6 The inhabitants of the Topnaar Traditional Authority area shall be allowed to harvest the *!nara* seasonally and also after the season. Nobody is allowed to use *!nara* in any private manner without the authorisation of the Traditional Authority. Anybody found guilty of this charge shall be punished severely.

R17.7 People shall not extract, remove or damage the *!Nara-!omab* for purposes of sale. Anyone who wishes to sell without any authorisation from the Traditional Authority shall be fined. This root is also used for medicinal purposes.

Regulation 18: Herding livestock

R18.1 In summer, when the crops have grown, every cattle owner shall control his/her herd so that they do not destroy other people's crops, because communal lands are not fenced. Livestock shall be herded, and anyone who allows livestock to roam freely and destroy crops may be summoned to the Traditional Authority by the owner of the crops.

R18.2 Every crop farmer shall have the right to protect his/her crops from anything that could destroy them. If the crop owner sees that his/her crops are ripe then he/she may harvest and store them.

R18.3 It shall be the headman's responsibility to give permission to villages to let livestock out to graze on desiccated stalks after harvesting. Anyone who lets out their animals while others are still harvesting shall be fined one to three buckets of the grain that has been destroyed by the livestock.

Regulation 19: *Cuca* shops and alcohol

In the past, when people consumed traditional beer, they obeyed laws and acted sensibly. The Traditional Authority feels that, for the community to live in peace and in order to promote order and unity, the consumption of alcohol shall be limited. Alcohol leads to the following:

(a) Destruction of the economy
(b) Neglect of households
(c) Poverty and hunger in homes, and
(d) Neglect of cultivation and handicrafts.

Consumption of alcohol leads to sexual promiscuity and the spread of sexually transmitted diseases. Many rapes and murders are committed by people under the influence of alcohol. Robberies may be planned at drinking places. Poor community relations are often a result of irresponsible drinking. The abuse of alcohol may cause young people to disrespect their elders or to experiment with drugs.

R19.1 The Traditional Authority shall not accept as a defence that a person was under the influence of alcohol.

R19.2 Following the cultivation period, everyone shall be free to open their *cuca* shops for business any time they wish.

R19.3 Children under 18 (eighteen) shall not be permitted to work in *cuca* shops. Children shall receive a good education. Working in *cuca* shops keeps them from studying and exposes them to alcohol.

R19.4 Any person employing a young person in a *cuca* shop shall be summoned to appear in court.

Regulation 20: Traditional healing

Traditional healing is a skill carried over from generation to generation, traced back to ancestors who had knowledge of herbs, leaves and roots (or tubers) of plants and trees, which can treat mental illness, epilepsy, paralysis, rabies, snake bites and other conditions.

Traditionally, healing is not based on superstition. That is why there is a saying that "The healer heals to eat, the healer heals to swallow". Healing based on superstition can destroy relationships between families, friends and neighbours. Superstition in healing is often an issue in traditional law.

R20.1 Traditional healers shall be registered by the settlement headman, area headman and the Traditional Authority, who shall give their authorisation for the healer to operate. Authorisation shall only be given to those who do not heal by superstition, or those who do not practice *!Ai-aon* (witchcraft).

R20.2 Any traditional healer who causes trouble with superstitious predictions shall be summoned to the Traditional Court. Such a healer shall bring his/her alleged predictive apparatus to court.

Regulation 21: Outdated traditional practices

R21.1 In ascertaining the laws of the ǂAonin, we have noted that there are some laws that are in contravention of the Constitution and cannot be used. These laws are also in contravention of human rights. Some of the said laws include property-grabbing from widows and children after the husband dies, which mostly involves chasing the spouse from the field which they cultivated, and the practice of traditional healers who are dishonest.

Note: Article 66 of the Namibian Constitution states that all customary laws that are in contravention of the Constitution shall not be valid. Therefore, all customary laws that are in contravention of the Constitution shall not be used unless they are oral laws.

Regulation 22: Work

R22.1 The Traditional Authority emphasizes that hard work shall be respected in the community. Preparing the soil and fields shall be done in good time, e.g. clearing the fields and weeding.

R22.2 Sunday shall be respected by everyone as a rest day. Working in the fields, cutting trees, etc. shall be forbidden, and may be punished by law.

Regulation 23: Traditional child-rearing: what is expected of parents and guardians

R23.1 Children are the future of the nation. Therefore, they shall be brought up as Christians with good social behaviour. Children should be brought up to respect elders. They should be given good examples to follow. They should be brought up to love work, so they may provide for themselves. They should be brought up to be busy and not lazy.

R23.2 Parents and guardians of children shall ensure that their children go to school, because education and knowledge build the future. Parents and caregivers shall ensure that children do not drink alcohol or take drugs, and that they do not spend time at *cuca* shops. Traditionally, every parent is every child's parent, and every parent shall have the right to talk to or discipline any child who is doing wrong.

Regulation 24: Care of the elderly

R24.1 The Traditional Authority shall be responsible for taking care of senior citizens, especially because many mothers and fathers have left their place of origin to find work elsewhere. Many old people do not have enough to eat, and some spend money on alcohol instead of food.

R24.2 Pension money is often taken by young people. Senior Traditional and Traditional Councillors, and the settlement headman shall ensure that senior citizens' money is not taken from them on the day they receive their pension.

R24.3 Where the elderly have to walk long distances to receive their pension, area headmen shall contact the Traditional Authorities or Chief to arrange that the elderly receive their pension closer to where they live.

R24.4 The elderly are cheated at *cuca* shops as they cannot count their money. They need people to help them when they are making purchases. Any person robbing or cheating an old person shall be prosecuted.

R24.5 We have to take good care of the elderly because they have a lot of wisdom. They are custodians of our history and traditions. They are also good name-givers for creatures and plants. They can recall proverbs like "The world is long, the oil is short", or "A far destination is not reached in one morning". It is taboo in Namibia to insult, push, cheat or rob elderly people.

Regulation 25: Traditional prices

R25.1 The traditional livestock values are:

(a) Donkey	N$500
(b) !Nara (1kg)	N$15 – N$20
(c) Horse	N$800 – N$1 000
(d) Goat	N$450 – N$800
(e) Sheep	N$450 – N$700
(f) Chicken	N$10
(g) Cattle (*beeste*)	N$2 500 – N$6 000

THE HISTORICAL CUSTOMARY LAW OF THE ǂAONIN/TOPNAAR COMMUNITY 1893-1995[2]

1. Traditional Inauguration Ceremony

The traditional inauguration ceremony of a Traditional Council or *Kaptein*/Captain is performed by the *Kaptein* or the Deputy *Kaptein*/Senior Council member from the community according to the following format:

Kaptein: Do you acknowledge God as the Almighty King of heaven and earth?

Do you acknowledge that all the authorities were instituted by him?

Are you entirely willing to serve your nation and country with obedience, loyalty and self-sacrifice under this authority?

Will you willingly submit to the leadership of those appointed over you?

Will you lead those over whom you were appointed with love and the necessary discipline as well as good example?

Do you realise that it is necessary for the government and the church to cooperate in order to prepare people corporeally and spiritually for the blissful ultimate objective?

If all of the above are your intentions, then answer

"Yes, with the help of the Almighty".

After the taking of this oath, each one is traditionally greeted by the *Kaptein* (Deputy *Kaptein* or Senior Councillor and they are then officially introduced to the community. Congratulations take place with the "handshake".

After everybody has been congratulated in the same manner, the different offices are announced by the chairperson of the meeting.

The *Kaptein* will furthermore say the following to the community: "In my capacity as *Kaptein*, I have the privilege to present [...name of Traditional Councillor], the Traditional Council here who were elected by you as community, to serve you in obedience and loyalty based on their traditional duties".

2 The following text was submitted to the editor in addition to the preceding laws, by Chief S.M. Kooitjie.

"I, together with my Council and the other leaders, solemnly request the community to accept this Council, who declared themselves willing in all aspects to be to your service, in love, and to show them the necessary respect."

After the handshake of the *Kaptein* as well as the expression of gratitude to the official who temporarily filled the vacant post, the Supreme Council and the Private Secretary of the *Kaptein* will inform the *Kaptein* of the re-appointment.

Minutes of matters pertaining to the inauguration are taken only by the Private Secretary of the *Kaptein* and are added to the documents of importance.

2. Suspension of an official

According to the Topnaar community's traditional law, the suspension of an official occurs when he/she:

2.1 Does not perform his/her duties as council member or does not serve.
2.2 Maltreats his wife deliberately (intentionally).
2.3 Refuses to appear before the Senior Council as summoned by the Messenger of the Court.
2.4 Refuses to pay a fine imposed on him/her.
2.5 Does not attend to his/her duties or keep order.
2.6 Does not attend the meetings of the Community Council regularly (without a written apology/pardon).
2.7 Does not obey the official instructions of his/her *Kaptein* or superiors.
2.8 Divulges the secrets of the community authorities (a very serious transgression).
2.9 Negotiates or leases any community land without the knowledge of the *Kaptein* as well as of the Senior Council and the community magistrate entrusted with such matters.
2.10 Is not loyal to his/her *Kaptein*, country and the community of the Topnaar traditional area.

3. The designation (election) of a *Kaptein*

The designation (election) of a *kaptein* of the Topnaar Community happens as follows:

3.1 Traditionally and culturally the position of *Kaptein* is inherited by the son when the *Kaptein* passes away as a result of illness, or if the *Kaptein* retires because of old age.
3.2 The community also has the right to decide whether the election (designation) will be held democratically, where a certain number of people will be nominated as possible candidates at a public meeting. Such a meeting and the planning thereof is under the leadership of the Deputy *Kaptein* or Supreme Council of the community.
3.3 The election (designation) date is decided by the Council and announced within 21 (twenty-one) days before the meeting takes place.

3.4 The election (designation) may be observed by a government official in the interest (traditionally) of the Topnaar Community.

3.5 The ordaining of the *Kaptein* must be administered by a government official in order to acknowledge the dignity of the *Kaptein* legally according to the country's laws and constitution.

3.6 The cultural traditions of the community, as well as the specific law of the area, are practised on this important day, which is also a traditional festival.

3.7 This festival is historically determined on this day and held on the same date of every succeeding year, or is held as decided by the *Kaptein*'s Council.

4. Historical customary laws

4.1 Land law
4.2 Traditional land rights
4.3 Legal ownership of land
4.4 Protection of rights of ownership (tenure)
4.5 The designation of traditional leaders
4.6 Traditional criminal laws
4.7 Community Courts.

4.1 Land law

Traditional land, or communal land in the case of the Topnaar community, is land on which the community stays according to culture and tradition.

4.2 Traditional land rights

These signify the historical right of existence of such a community or birthright of the traditional residents of the area as acknowledged (recognised) by the laws of the country and the Constitution of the country (Namibia).

4.3 Legal ownership of land

4.3.1 The Government or the highest institution of the country is the trust keeper of any traditional land or state-owned land. In this case the President of Namibia is the patron (protector) of communal land.

4.3.2 The *Kaptein*, the Deputy *Kaptein* and the councils are the administrative management of such land with traditional rights.

4.4 Protection of freehold (right of ownership)

According to the traditional recognised laws of the Topnaar community, the property or possessions of each individual are protected by the *Kaptein*'s Council and members of the community.

4.4.1 Protection of property rights

The protection of property rights includes:

(a) The traditional criminal law as referred to hereunder.

(b) The protection of tradition, culture and natural resources such as the *!nara*, game, flora and fauna.

(c) The protection of water resources, etc.

4.5 The designation of traditional leaders (office)

Traditional leadership (*Kaptein* or leader) is hereditary. However, the community may also decide to elect a *Kaptein* democratically.

5. Traditional criminal laws

5.1 Any person who steals, damages or takes property without the permission of the owner, is guilty of theft and may be charged with it by the *Kaptein*'s court.

5.2 Very serious criminal cases can be referred to the Magistrate's Courts by the *Kaptein*'s court.

5.3 The following cases are heard here (by the traditional courts):

- (a) Stock theft
- (b) Illegal hunting
- (c) Illegal smuggling
- (d) Illegal use of the *!nara* fields
- (e) Damage to flora and fauna
- (f) Damage to Government property on traditional land
- (g) Conflicts (disagreements) between community members or between husband and wife, and other matters of community interest.

6. Offences, including stock theft

The traditional stock theft law and other offences of the Topnaar community.

6.1 If a person steals one head of cattle, then he/she must pay one head of cattle or 5 goats (small stock) back if he/she owns stock. If the guilty party does not own stock, then his/her family must pay the fine in another way, in relation to the fine or punishment that was inflicted on him/her. The *!nara* harvest or any other possessions to the value of the stolen goods (livestock) can also be paid.

6.2 If a person takes or steals one goat without the permission of the owner, then he/she will be fined or punished to pay back one or two goats, or as already explained in point 1.

6.3 Violations (trespassing): Violations are also traditionally heard in court and the accused is fined or punished according to the merits of the case.

6.4 In the instance where a person commits the same crime more than once, then he/she must pay double the fine.

6.5 When a minor is heard he/she must be assisted by his/her parents and the fine or punishment will depend on the finding (verdict/sentence) of the court. Corporal punishment can also be inflicted. [This is now in conflict with the current Constitution].

6.6 The alienation of land without the permission of the *Kaptein* is a serious crime. Such a person or persons will be punished severely depending on the finding and verdict of the court.

6.7 *!Nara* fields - The *Kaptein* of the area is the guardian of the *!nara* fields in the interest of the whole community. Damage, theft or any unknown trading without the permission of the *Kaptein* is punishable as it is a serious crime and can be fined or punished severely.

6.8 Any serious crime may be charged and such a person or persons can be sentenced after he/she has appeared before and is convicted by the court.

6.9 The impoverishment of community members is prevented and protected, by virtue of traditional laws, for the advantage of everybody within the area of jurisdiction of the *Kaptein*.

From the nature of laws which are linked to the Ten Commandments of God.

7. Traditional leadership structure of the ǂAonin/Topnaar Customary Court

7.1 Community (Traditional) Council – administratively 6 or more persons

Kaptein
Deputy *Kaptein* or Senior Councillor
Secretary
Members of the Council

7.2 Senior Traditional Council - Secret Council - 12 or more people

This is a traditional and cultural body consisting of:

Kaptein
Deputy *Kaptein* or Senior Council member
Magistrate
Church leader (Elder)
Secretary (of the *Kaptein*)
5 or more elders of the Community

7.3 National (Community) Council – 18 seats

The National Council is both the Community Council and the Senior Council. It is a combination of members both from the Community Council and the Senior Traditional

Council, acting according to customs, and assists the senior traditional councillor when performing functions on behalf of the *Kaptein* in his/her absence.

Other community bodies such as the Topnaar's Welfare Club or other committees exist in the interest of the community and the area for the preservation and by virtue of the stipulations of the Traditional Laws.

The designation of the *Kaptein* and the Community Council takes place traditionally and culturally by virtue of the preservation of the Constitution of Namibia.

7.3.1 Duties of the Community Council

7.3.1.1 To manage general community matters in its area.

7.3.1.2 To render the necessary help, assistance and guidance to its principal (the *Kaptein*) in executing the powers and authority vested in him (the *Kaptein*) and in executing the activities assigned to it by this law.

7.3.1.3 To further the interests, prosperity and welfare of the community and to further the development and improvement of the land in its jurisdiction.

7.3.1.4 To grant grazing rights to farmers of the communal land.

7.3.1.5 To issue written licences or legitimate permission.

7.3.1.6 To administer the land:

- (a) Hygiene, sanitation, health services in general including the establishing, management and upkeep of cemeteries.
- (b) The control over grazing, stock quotes, veld fires, the protection of trees and the co-ordination of land protection.
- (c) The conservation of flora and fauna.
- (d) The improvement of stock and stockbreeding in general, as well as the establishing of cooperative schemes (Agriculture).
- (e) The organisation of Farmers' Associations, demonstrations and competitions.
- (f) Other developments in the interests of the community.
- (g) The prevention of cruelty to animals.
- (h) The destruction of predators which harm stock.

7.3.2 Establishment of the Community (Traditional) Fund

7.3.2.1 The Community Council can establish and manage a Community Fund by virtue of the Traditional Law and may register it at the head office (Regional Office), for the use and appropriation as a development fund.
Monies for the Fund may come from the following sources:

- (a) All monies and contributions which, according to the practices of the community, are payable to the Community Council.
- (b) All contributions acquired from any property owned by the Community Council.

(c) Endowments from any person or body to the benefit of the Community Council.

(d) All monies obtained from levies as prescribed by the law.

(e) All other contributions from whatever source acquired for the benefit of the Community Council.

7.3.2.3 The estimation (budget) of income and expenses of the Community Council are annually drawn up by the Community Council and are submitted to the Regional Head Office.

8. Topnaar law on property protection

8.1 Lost goods or stolen cattle

8.1.1 Any lost goods or cattle which are found must be taken to the *Kaptein* or Deputy *Kaptein* within 1 to 3 days. The *Kaptein* may keep these goods in his care for 6 months until the rightful owner claims it with proof.

8.1.2 No such goods or cattle may be damaged, for example, the ears of cattle may not be cut and the cattle may not be branded with any other mark.

8.1.3 Unclaimed goods may be sold by the *Kaptein*'s Council, after a certain period of time, for the benefit of the community fund.

Certificate of consent to publish

Topnaar Traditional Authority
P.O. Box 2041 Walvis Bay

24 JUL 2012

The Chief

Certificate of the consent to publish

UNIVERSITY OF NAMIBIA

FACULTY OF LAW

HUMAN RIGHTS AND DOCUMENTATION CENTRE

RE: CONSENT TO PUBLICATION

I, the undersigned, Chief of the Topnaar Traditional Authority, hereby give consent to the Human Rights and Documentation Centre, to publish the following documents of the Topnaar Traditional Authority:

1. The Customary Laws
2. The Community Profile
3. Picture of the Chief
4. Logo of the Traditional Authority

I acknowledge that the Human Rights and Documentation Centre will publish the laws in our indigenous language (Khoi Khoi), as well as the English language. I am familiar with the contents of the laws that will be published and further acknowledge that they were prepared by my traditional authority.

Signed on this 24 **day of** July **2012**

At Walvisbay

Namibia

Chief

For HRDC: Mr. A. Gairiseb

Topnaar Traditional Authority
P.O. Box 2041 Walvis Bay

24 JUL 2012

The Chief

Vaalgras Traditional Authority
Orlam !Hao!nasi ǂGaeǂguis

The supreme leader of the Vaalgras Traditional Authority is Chief[1] Joel Stephanus.
Date of designation**:** 6 April 1975

Republic of Namibia

1 Traditional title in terms of section 11, Traditional Authorities Act, 2000 (No. 25 of 2000).

PROFILE[2]

The Vaalgras Traditional Authority area covers 212 296 hectares with a population of 3 540 inhabitants (1992 census figures: 3 160), under the leadership of Chief Joel Stephanus with his Traditional Councillors and Secretary.

The inhabitants of Vaalgras, descendants of the Mbanderu Herero Clan and also including many other immigrants from various areas, live on a portion of land which the Vaalgras community received as compensation for work done for the German Government in 1908 and recorded in a signed agreement. Between the early 1920s and the late 1940s in official reports and documents, the Vaalgras Herero under the leadership of the then Headman Jan Apollus, were referred to as the *Damaras* and *Klipkaffers*.

Herero communities across the country experienced a spate of land and livestock confiscations during and after the wars of the 1800s and early 1900s. In contrast, Jan Apollus, the then leader of the Vaalgras Community, signed an agreement with the German Authorities on 1st of May 1908, detailing their right to the Vaalgras area. However, despite agreements, the German authorities decided in September 1913 that the Vaalgras area should be made available as a grazing area for all Herero in the district of Keetmanshoop, and in 1914, that it should become a General Native Reserve for the district.

The First World War interrupted these plans, and the Vaalgras community successfully resisted efforts by the retreating Germans to move their community and animals northwards. Again in the early 1960s, plans were made by the South African Government to evict all those categorized as Herero from Vaalgras to their so-called homeland. Yet among the turbulent arguments that surrounded efforts to impose the Odendaal Plan, the Vaalgras community were again able to present an effective argument under the able leadership of their headman, Samuel Stephanus, for the retention of their territory. They were able to produce the documents containing details of the original agreement between Headman Jan Apollus and the German Authorities.

Furthermore, they could claim a cultural affinity with those to be settled in the new homeland (the Nama).

2 This profile was provided by the Vaalgras Traditional Authority.

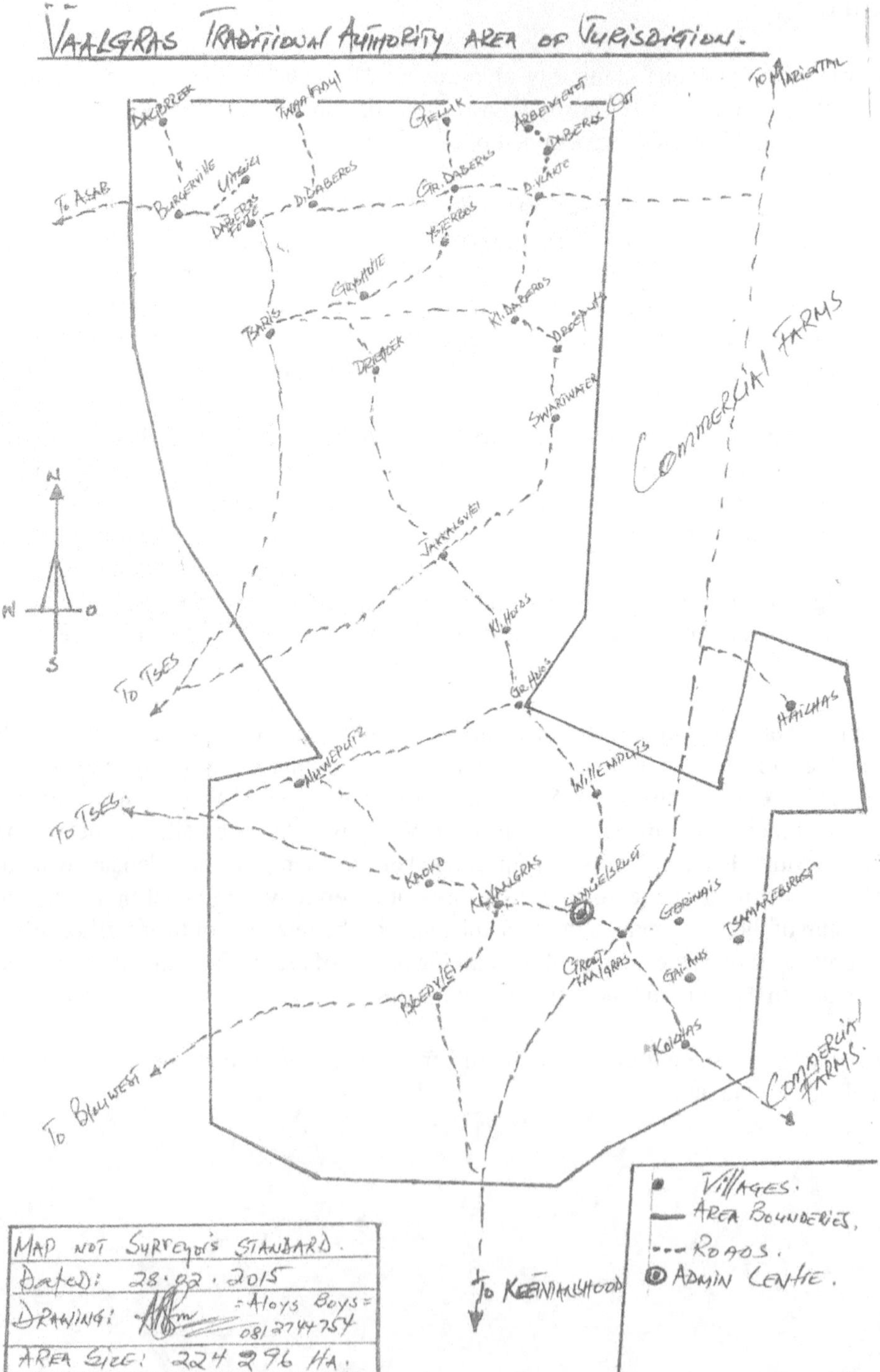

Map of the Vaalgras area, as submitted to the editor by the Vaalgras Traditional Authority.

The laws of the Orlam (Vaalgras)[1]

1 The laws were submitted in English only.

Introduction

This Constitution is regarded as the foundation upon which the traditions of the Vaalgras Community are based.

Motto

Unity – Strength – Progress

Article 1: Leadership of the Vaalgras Traditional Community

1.1 The Chief is the paramount, authoritative leader who is appointed by the community members, for the community members, from the descendants of the Chieftainship family.

1.2 The designation of the Chief by the community members from the Chieftainship family takes place in accordance with the rules of hereditary succession after the most appropriate successor has been found. All the candidates for the Chief's position must belong to the Chief's family which, in the case of the Vaalgras community, is the Stephanus family.

1.3 The Chief in his/her capacity as the leader of the Vaalgras community is responsible for announcing policies and for the execution of matters affecting the community.

1.4 New Councillors and other officials, including the Chief Councillor, will be nominated by the Chief-in-Council at a meeting held at the Chief's Court, and must be accepted by the community members. A councillor or an official need not be a member of the Chieftainship family.

1.5 The Chief Councillors will assume the same powers as the Chief in the unavoidable absence of the Chief and will be co-responsible for the functions and duties of the Chief.

1.6 When the Chief passes away, then only a rightful contender can be nominated and designated by the community members as Chief, unless the community decides otherwise as a result of cogent reasons.

Article 2: Jurisdiction of councillors and officials

2.1 Other than in the instance of the Chief and the Chief Councillor, who have jurisdiction over the Vaalgras community as a whole, the powers of the Councillors and Officials are limited to the areas in which they live.

2.2 The Councillors and Officials who are properly designated and accepted by the community members, will serve as a link between the Chief Councillor and the community.

2.3 The Councillor will from time to time report to the Chief and to the community concerning the execution of the duties assigned to him/her.

2.4 To prevent the Chief, the Chief Councillor and the Councillors from falling under corrupting influences, it is compulsory that the Traditional Council be consulted in all negotiations and consultations with other institutions. Reports regarding approved negotiations and discussions with such institutions will be introduced by the Traditional Council by way of circulars and/or community meetings.

Article 3: The Traditional Council

3.1 A Traditional Council as instituted in terms of Article 1.4 shall comprise the Chief, Chief Councillor, Secretary and twelve Councillors.

3.2 The Chief in his/her capacity as the paramount leader of the Vaalgras Community shall ex-officio be a member of the Traditional Council.

3.3 Quorum: Two-thirds of the Traditional Council members must be present at a Traditional Council meeting to constitute a quorum.

Article 4: Executive Committee

4.1 This Committee shall comprise the Chief, Chief Councillor, Secretary and two additional Councillors. They shall execute the decisions and instructions of the Traditional Council.

Article 5: Meetings

5.1 The Traditional Council shall convene a community meeting at such place and time as pleases the council or on the instructions of the Chief. The meeting of the Traditional Council shall be held as regularly as possible, depending on the circumstances from time to time.

Article 6

6.1 The Traditional Council shall at its own discretion appoint representatives from the Vaalgras community members living in urban areas of Namibia.

Article 7: Finances

7.1 The general funds of the Vaalgras Community shall be obtained from the following sources: community fund contributions by community members, income from functions, gifts, levies, donations, sales of articles etc.

7.2 All community funds shall be deposited in the bank and an application to withdraw money must be signed by the Council Treasurer and/or the Secretary and co-signed by the Chief or the Chief Councillor.

7.3 The financial year of the Vaalgras community shall start on the first day of April and end on the 31st day of March the next year.

7.4 The financial statements of the Vaalgras community must be audited by accredited auditors.

7.5 Funds which were contributed by the members for a specific reason shall not be used for another purpose, unless the Traditional Council so decides with the consent of the members.

Article 8: Locus standi

8.1 The Chief-in-Council shall have jurisdiction on behalf of the Traditional Council and the Vaalgras community as a whole.

Article 9: Dissolution or amendment of Constitution

9.1 This Constitution or any part thereof may be amended, repealed, altered or added to, by a quorum at a Traditional Council meeting in consultation with the community and Traditional Council.

9.2 Recommendations in connection with any amendments to the Constitution must be sent to the Secretary of the Traditional Council at least thirty days prior to the meeting. The proposed amendments to the constitution shall be circulated to all the localities (villages) in advance for scrutiny prior to the community meeting.

Basic customary laws of Vaalgras under a traditionally appointed chief

Trespasses and Punishments cover the following:

1. Theft

This includes the stealing of animals, both small and large stock, or personal belongings, as well as the handling of stolen items or the rendering of assistance or protection to the thief, i.e being an accomplice.

1.1 The hearing of such a case normally takes place at a traditional court headed by the Chief, in order to prove the guilt or innocence of the accused.
1.2 Punishment fines shall be double the value of the property stolen, e.g. a thief shall pay back two cattle for one stolen.

2. Robbery

2.1 Robbery is equal to theft with aggravating circumstances.
2.2 Punishment shall be referred to the Magistrate's Court.

3. Trespassing

3.1 This includes the trespassing of private property, houses and schools.
3.2 It also includes the entering of traditional areas without the necessary legal permission from the owner or authority having the capacity to grant such permission.
3.3 Procedure: The hearing of any case involving the abovementioned shall take place at a traditional court to prove the guilt or innocence of the accused.
3.4 Punishment shall correlate to the seriousness of the damage or harm caused by the act.

4. Assault

4.1 This includes all assaults which can cause bodily harm and injuries, e.g. with feet, fists, knives, sticks, stones or any sharp object.
4.2 Procedure: Hearing takes place at the traditional court.
4.3 Punishment depends on the seriousness of the action.

5. Murder

5.1 This includes any action which causes death, either intentionally or without intention to kill, e.g. by the use of firearms, knives, pangas, etc. It also includes the instruction of somebody to kill another.

5.2 Procedure: Such a case shall be dealt with by the Magistrate's Court and the High Court.

6. Illegal cohabitation

6.1 Illegal cohabitation without the contracting of a legal marriage is not contributing towards the building of a healthy nation.

6.2 Procedure: The Traditional Authority shall play its role in discouraging such behaviour and ultimately the elimination of it encouraging marriage in the community.

7. Child maintenance and education

7.1 The maintenance and education of children is the responsibility of both parents, whether married or unmarried.

7.2 Procedure: Negligence of children shall be dealt with by the Traditional Court. Ways and means shall be found to make both parents contribute fairly according to their own means to the maintenance and education of their children. Legal force shall be applied if necessary.

8. Rape

8.1 Rape is a serious and very harmful act against a human being, both physically and spiritually.

8.2 Procedure: The national police shall be informed, and the victim taken to a doctor for examination and treatment as well as a doctor's clinical report. The case shall be investigated by the police and a court case prepared for the Magistrate's Court or the High Court.

9. Teenage pregnancy

9.1 This is an issue destroying the whole of the nation. It brings about poverty and illiteracy as well an imbalanced population growth. It needs to be fought by all means and uprooted.

9.2 Procedure: Those who make themselves guilty of such an act shall be brought before the Traditional Court.

9.3 Punishment: Suitable punishment shall be considered and meted out.

10. Divorce/estrangement

10.1 This is a very unfortunate situation in any given family relationship. It is weakening the basis of the nation.

10.1 Procedure: Problems shall be discussed within the families.

10.2 Church leaders shall be involved for counseling, possible solutions and rescue of the marriages.

10.3 The case shall be tried before the Traditional Court.

10.4 The aggrieved person may appeal to the Magistrate's Court and subsequently to the High Court.

11. Inheritance

11.1 Where an estate is not governed or determined by a Will (Testament) for the estate, the government and the division of the estate shall be in the hands of the Traditional court, which shall handle the estate according to traditional laws and customs under the leadership of the Chief or his legal representative.

12. Illegal alcohol and drug dealing

12.1 This is an evil which is destroying our nation and bringing about imbalance within our communities. It needs to be fought with all means.

12.2 Procedure: The police in co-operation and collaboration with the traditional court shall carry out suppress searches to curb the illegal dealing with alcohol and drugs.

12.3 Punishment: When found guilty, transgressors shall be subjected to fines twice the value of the articles. The case shall be heard before the Traditional Courts.

13. Illegal hunting

13.1 Hunting in the area under the jurisdiction of the traditional authority shall be controlled by the Traditional Authority. Permits for hunting shall be granted by the Traditional Authority.

13.2 Procedure: Transgression of hunting arrangements shall come before the Traditional Court. The Traditional Authority shall enjoy backup from the national police.

13.3 Punishment: First transgression: if found guilty, the culprit's fine shall be equal to the value of the animals that were killed.

13.4 Second Transgression: the same as above (13.3) shall apply.

13.5 Third transgression: the firearm or any weapon or instrument being used shall be confiscated and a fine imposed equal to the value of the game killed.

14. Alcohol misuse and foul language

14.1 If somebody at any occasion misbehaves him/herself because of misuse of alcohol and uses abusive language, he or she shall be locked up until sober.

14.2 He or she will be released on payment of a fine of N$50.00 for the first offence and N$100.00 at all subsequent times.

15. Nature conservation

15.1 The whole community shall be educated to understand the need for the protection of nature under the punishment section.

15.2 Procedure: All transgressions concerning the abovementioned shall come before the Traditional Court.

15.3 Punishment: Punishment shall be determined by the court according to the extent of the transgressions and the cost of the damages.

16. Ground and land issues

16.1 The Traditional Authority responsible for the administration of the land under its jurisdiction must exercise all rights and jurisdiction concerning the ground and land under question.

16.2 Procedure: Trespasses concerning land and communal ground under the jurisdiction of the Traditional Authority shall come before the Traditional Court.

16.3 Punishment: Fines for the convicted party must correspond to the seriousness of the trespasses committed and the damages caused.

17. Lawyers in traditional court

17.1 Lawyers shall under no circumstances be allowed in Traditional Courts.

18. Land and allocation of grazing

18.1 The Traditional Authority of Vaalgras has the sole right to allocate land and grazing.

18.2 Procedure: The Traditional Council shall assist the Chief in allocating land and grazing while the Traditional Court shall hear and process land and grazing problems and disputes brought before it by the Traditional Council.

Certificate of consent to publish

Certificate of the consent to publish

UNIVERSITY OF NAMIBIA

FACULTY OF LAW

HUMAN RIGHTS AND DOCUMENTATION CENTRE

RE: CONSENT TO PUBLICATION

I, the undersigned, Chief of the VAALGRAS Traditional Authority, hereby give consent to the Human Rights and Documentation Centre, to publish the following documents of the VAALGRAS Traditional Authority:

1. The Customary Laws
2. The Community Profile
3. Picture of the Chief
4. Logo of the Traditional Authority

I acknowledge that the Human Rights and Documentation Centre will publish the laws in our indigenous language (AFRIKAANS), as well as the English language. I am familiar with the contents of the laws that will be published and further acknowledge that they were prepared by my traditional authority.

Signed on this 04 **day of** MARCH **2015**

At SAMUELRUST

Chief

VAALGRAS TRADITIONAL AUTHORITY
P.O. BOX 1615
04 MAR 2015
KEETMANSHOOP, NAMIBIA

For HRDC: Mr. A. Gairiseb

Witbooi Traditional Authority
|Khowese ǁAe ǂGaeǂguis

The supreme leader of the Witbooi Traditional Authority was
Gaob[1] Hendrik Witbooi (left)[2].
Date of designation: 01 January 1978
He passed away on 13 October 2009.
The Acting *Gaob* was Christiaan Rooi (right).
Date of designation: Vice-Captain on 28 October 1978
He became Acting *Gaob* in 1990[3, 4].
He passed away on 13 October 2015.

1 Traditional title in terms of section 11 of the Traditional Authorities Act, 2000 (No. 25 of 2000).

2 Photograph (2008) from the Khoi and San Active Awareness Group (KSAAG) website: ksaag.wordpress.com. Reproduced with permission from Bradley van Sitters who obtained the photograph from *Gaob* Witbooi's Chief Advisor Danab Steven Isaacs as an official media photograph.

3 Christiaan Rooi became Acting *Gaob* from 1990 when Hendrik Witbooi became a Member of Parliament. See the table on succession below. The successor to *Gaob* Witbooi, *Gaob* Salomon Josephat Witbooi, was installed by the community on 3 October 2015.

4 The Witbooi Traditional Authority did not submit a coat of arms.

PROFILE[5]

1. ǀKhowese ǁAes

1.1 The Nama-speaking people of Namibia are divided into eleven traditional territories. These are the Swartbooi in the north, Topnaar in the west, Rooinasie, Afrikaner, Simon Kooper, part of Bondelswarts and the ǀKhowesen in the Hardap Region and the rest in the south in the Karas Region. These Nama inhabitants have similar ways of living and traditional laws, although there are differences.

1.2 The ǀKhowese ǁAes (people) also have their own traditions and customs.

1.3 The people came from South Africa.

1.4 The ǀKhowese people are led by the *Gaob* who is called by the South Africans "*Kaptein*". The traditional title is *Gaob* which means King. The role of the *Gaob* is to take care of his people and make sure there is peace and stability among them.

2. The borders and environment of the ǀKhowese ǁAes

2.1 The northern, western and eastern borders meet with commercial farms.

2.2 The southern border is with Berseba (ǀHai-ǀKhauan).

2.3 The great Fish River and the Lewer River flow through the area of the ǀKhowesen.

2.4 Our traditional water sources are fountains in different areas such as Gaomûs area, Uibes and Gibeon, serving the people and livestock alike.

2.5 There are also different types of game which must be protected so that they do not become extinct.

3. Way of life

3.1 Men are the head of our households in our community.

3.2 The ǀKhowese people are farmers who keep household gardens and farm with goats, sheep, and cattle, and they use donkeys and horses for transport. The ǀKhowese people have also used oxen for transport in the old days.

3.3 Our manufacturing activities are sewing and leatherwork, to produce Nama dresses and Nama shoes, and constructing buildings from stone and laying flat stones, or *platklips*, for floors.

3.4 !Nanseb, the late Hendrik Witbooi, the great grandfather of the late Dr Hendrik Witbooi was one of the Kings (*Gaogu*) that fought on horseback for the liberation of Namibia with others.

5 This profile was provided by the Witbooi Traditional Authority.

4. Traditional beliefs and games

4.1 In the old days we used to practise our traditional beliefs and games, rituals and traditional skills, some listed below:

(a) *ǀǀArob* is performed during weddings.

(b) *ǀǀKhaus*, *ǀǀhus*

(c) *Kharu-ǂnûs* is performed when a girl menstruates for the first time.

5. Chronological order of succession of the traditional Witbooi kings (*gaogu*) from 1853 to the present

King	Period of rule	Traditional name
1. Cupido Witbooi	1853-1875	!Gamemab !Aǁîb
2. Moses Dawid Witbooi	1867-1888	!Aǁîmab ǀGâbeb
3. Hendrik Witbooi	1888-1905	ǀGameb !Nanseb
4. Jesaja Witbooi	1905-1922	
5. Isak Witbooi	1922-1928	!Nansmab !Nanseb
6. Dawid Witbooi	1928-1955	!Nansmab ǀHuwuöb
7. Hendrik S. Witbooi	1955-1978	!Nansmab !Gaeǀnüb
8. Hendrik Witbooi	1978-1990	ǁGawamûma ǀOnöb
9. Christiaan Rooi (Acting)	1990-2015	ǀGapomâ - !Nanseb

The laws of the |Khowese Witbooi[1]

1 The laws were submitted in English only.

1. The succession criteria for leadership

1.1 The succession of the leadership of the ǀKhowese was done through election by the people "ǁAes" when there was no one from the father's side in the royal bloodline or if the people could not find a candidate suitable to be king.

1.2 Amendment to Section 1[2]

The practice and tradition of the Traditional Leadership succession were released by the late Captain Rev. Dr Hendrik Witbooi during the 2005 Heroes Day celebrations as follows:

1.2.1 A successor is in most cases recommended by the predecessor, but is subject to the democratic modes of confirmation by both the Advisory Council and the Public Clan meeting.

1.2.2 In the event of the predecessor having passed away before a recommendation was made, the elders of the Royal House make the recommendation.

1.2.3 That a successor is strictly and preferably a next of kin to the predecessor, e.g. eldest or any of his sons or relatives in the bloodline.

1.2.4 The nomination is announced either to the Advisory Council or the Public Clan meeting before the death of the predecessor, but installment takes effect only after the death and burial or the retirement ceremony of the current chief.

1.2.5 The measuring yard of the successor is according to his or her Christian and human behaviour, his or her involvement in the affairs and interest of the Clan and the people of the country as a whole. He or she must have shown leadership abilities and passion for human dignity. He or she must have shown interest to uplift and promote the principles laid down by our heroic leader, late Captain Hendrik (!Nanseb) Witbooi in resisting colonial rule in close co-operation with the African leaders. A leader must never nominate him- or herself or lobby others to be nominated to the chieftainship.

2. Structure of the Traditional Authority

2.1 The structure of the Traditional Authority is as follows:
(a) *Gaob*
(b) Senior Councillors
(c) Traditional Councillors
(d) Secretary

2.2 The Senior Councillors and Traditional Councillors are the advisors to the *Gaob*.

---

2 This amendment was submitted on 30 June 2013 to the Customary Law Ascertainment Project by Senior Councillor of the Witbooi Traditional Authority, Mr Lukas Katuanene, who at the time was the Chairperson of the Council of the Authority and also stood in for the Acting *Kaptein* Christiaan Rooi.

2.3 The Senior Councillors (headmen) as well as the Councillors in the traditional districts are expected to be good listeners to problems and are expected to assist people where possible.

2.4 They should be exemplary leaders and must be:
(a) Friendly
(b) Peaceful
(c) Patient
(d) Persistent
(e) Respectful
(f) Humble to all
(g) Impartial in the administration of justice

3. Main seat

3.1 Main seat and office is in Gibeon.

4. Coat of arms

4.1 *Gaob* !Nanseb on horseback is the symbol of the |Khowesen.

5. Traditional flag

5.1 Two colours: white with black dots as background to the picture of !Nanseb.

6. Traditional colours

6.1 Black and white.

7. Traditional song

7.1 Anthem: *!Khu |ka re* |Khowese ǁAes (God Almighty bless the Witbooi traditional community).

8. Traditional festival

8.1 The Traditional Festival is held annually in October for the remembrance of the death of *Gaob* !Nanseb on 29 October 1905 and this is the commemoration date.

9. Meetings

9.1 The monthly meeting is for land allocation, problems in different areas, reports, sharing Government information, Land Board issues, resettlement issues and area reports.

9.2 It is according to this meeting that community members with problems are called to discuss and seek resolutions.

9.3 When a councillor absents him- or herself for three consecutive meetings without any valid reason, he/she may be put on leave with half payment.

9.4 There will be an attendance list for administrative use and verification.

9.5 The Traditional Authority shall have a secretary to run the administration of the Council together with the *Gaob* and Senior Councillor responsible for administration. The secretary is responsible for the day to day administration of the Council's office.

9.6 The Traditional Authority meeting is once a month and all Councillors, gazetted and not gazetted, must attend the meetings. Community meetings will be held from time to time for information, consultation and serious concerns.

9.7 The Management Committee (*Dagbestuur*) meets every Wednesday for day-to-day activities.

10. Court proceedings

10.1 Any person who has been done wrong by another person and would like to open a case shall do so by reporting to the Councillor responsible for that traditional area and then shall proceed to the Traditional Authority for a hearing.

10.2 No one has the right to take the law into their own hands. If the complainant is not satisfied he/she can appeal to the King who is supreme.

11. Court attendance

11.1 Any person subpoenaed to attend the court shall do so and if he/she does not adhere to this, he/she shall be fined by court. After three times he/she can be or shall be fined N$300.00 or more. It must be clear that this provision includes Senior Councillors as well as Councillors.

11.2 In the case of a witness being in hospital at the time, he/she shall submit proof thereof.

11.3 Traditional Authority employees shall not reveal Council secrets or talk about issues under discussion until these have been finalised by the Council. After two warnings a person must be put on leave and if he/she continues to divulge information, the Traditional Authority shall have the right to dismiss that person.

12. Witnesses

12.1 Every accused person shall have the right to bring a witness to court.

12.2 A witness shall not give false testimony.

13. Murder

13.1 If a person murders another person, he/she shall appear before the Magistrate's Court.

13.2 The Traditional Court shall determine a fine to comfort the family of the deceased.

14. Rape

14.1 The rapist shall appear before the Magistrate's Court.

14.2 If the girl is under the age of 16 years and falls pregnant, she is too young to judge a sexual relationship and whoever made her pregnant shall be deemed to have raped her.

14.3 The Traditional Court may refer the case to the Magistrate's Court.

15. Assault and assault by threat

15.1 No person shall be assaulted or threatened with a gun, knife, panga, or any other weapon.

15.2 If a person is assaulted or threatened, he/she has the right to open a case. The Court shall give a warning or a fine determined by the court.

15.3 If someone is stabbed or seriously injured or physically assaulted, a doctor's certificate will be necessary as proof to show the extent of injuries.

15.4 The Community Court shall determine the fine according to the extent of damage suffered by the victim. The fine shall start from N$500.00 or the equivalent in livestock.

15.5 All weapons will be forbidden at the Traditional Court or at any meetings.

16. Land allocation

16.1 No land belongs to individuals or families. All land is State-owned and governed by the Traditional Authority.

16.2 When someone is vacating land, this land shall revert to the Traditional Authority, who will allocate it accordingly. There shall be no family decision regarding re-allocation of land.

17. Water

17.1 No one has the right to refuse someone else water if someone has a water problem.

17.2 Water problems are of concern to all and a solution must be found in consultation with all those affected.

18. Grazing

18.1 No one has the right to refuse grazing for animals because no one owns land.

19. Theft

19.1 Any victim of theft shall have the right to open a court case.

19.2 For theft of household items and personal articles, the fine shall be according to the value of the stolen goods.

19.3 Stock theft

19.3.1 For the theft of one head of cattle the fine is three head of cattle. Two will go to the complainant and one to the court, or the value of the cattle.

19.3.2 For one goat or sheep the fine is three goats or sheep. Two will go to the complainant and one to the court, or the value of the goats.

19.3.3 For the theft of horses and donkeys the fine is the same as for cattle.

19.3.4 The value of an animal is not determined by market prices.

(a)	One head of cattle	N$2 000.00
(b)	One goat	N$ 500.00
(c)	One sheep	N$ 400.00
(d)	One donkey	N$ 700.00
(e)	One horse	N$ 600.00

20. Poaching

20.1 A court hearing shall take place.

20.2 If found guilty the culprit shall be fined according to the different types of game involved and the fine shall be market-related.

21. Shops

21.1 Shops on communal land shall pay a fee determined by the Traditional Authority.

22. Inheritance

22.1 The Traditional Authority shall see to it that widows and children are not mistreated when the husband dies, because in many cases the family of the husband takes all the belongings and leaves widows and children without anything.

22.2 When one of the children dies, the estate belongs to the other children.

22.3 Any widow who feels mistreated with regard to inheritance shall have the right to open a case with the Traditional Authority.

22.4 Any member of the bereaved family who has experienced any mistreatment with regard to inheritance has the right to open a case.

23. Loss of animals

23.1 Any lost animals shall be reported to the Traditional Authority.
23.2 If a person finds animal/s he/she shall keep them safe for three months.
23.3 If not claimed by the owner, the Traditional Authority shall take the animal/s and use them for the benefit of the community.

24. Confiscation

24.1 The Traditional Authority shall have the right to confiscate animals which are brought into the area of jurisdiction illegally.
24.2 The owner shall pay per head of animal to get it back. The fee will be determined by the Traditional Authority.

[Signed by the Secretary and Chairman, Witbooi Traditional Authority]

Certificate of consent to publish

Certificate of the consent to publish

UNIVERSITY OF NAMIBIA

FACULTY OF LAW

HUMAN RIGHTS AND DOCUMENTATION CENTRE

RE: CONSENT TO PUBLICATION

I, the undersigned, Chief of the Witbooi Traditional Authority, hereby give consent to the Human Rights and Documentation Centre, to publish the following documents of the Witbooi Traditional Authority:

1. The Customary Laws
2. The Community Profile
3. Picture of the Chief
4. Logo of the Traditional Authority

I acknowledge that the Human Rights and Documentation Centre will publish the laws in our indigenous language (Nama), as well as the English language. I am familiar with the contents of the laws that will be published and further acknowledge that they were prepared by my traditional authority.

Signed on this 26 **day of** June **2012.**

WITBOOIS TRADITIONAL AUTHORITY PO BOX 22 GIBEON 2012 -06- 26

At Gibeon

Khooi

Chief

For HRDC: A. Gainisel

Part III
The laws of the Ovaherero and Ovambanderu communities[1]

1 Editor's note: No submission was received from the Kambazembi and the Ovaherero Traditional Authorities.

Kakurukouje Traditional Authority
Ondjuwo Youhonapare waKakurukouje

The supreme leader of the Kakurukouje traditional community is *Ombara*[1] Vemuii Tjambiru.
Date of designation: 7 December 2004

1 Traditional title in terms of section 11, Traditional Authorities Act, 2000 (No. 25 of 2000).

PROFILE[2]

The Kakurukouje Traditional Authority is one of the oldest in Namibia. It started around 1510–1560, with Kuvare as the first leader and forefather. He was succeeded by his sons and grandsons. This family is well known as Oherero's Kingdom. The name *Oherero* means "the West", in reference to the location of the setting sun.

The Kakurukouje were among the group of Bantu peoples that moved from central Africa (formerly Tanganyika), *Kehi raruu rokombando okuvare, kotuu tu tu ha kava kozonḓonḓu zomahundju omapongo* ("...from the land of reeds, with reeds that never dry up at the rivers with angry fish[3]". They settled at Okarundu ka Mbeti (literally, "where the ancestors lived") at the border between Namibia and Angola.

Kuvare died at Otjihandjavero at an advanced age, and was buried on the Kunene River bank. He was succeeded by his son, Rupembo roNdjai, who led the clan from Otjihandjavero to Otjirambo in Angola during the estimated period of 1560–1600. He died at Otjirambo where he was then buried.

Rupembo roNdjai was succeeded by his son Njosejambangu. Njosejambangu moved from Angola back to Namibia and settled at Osiya ya Mbinge in about 1650, and lived there for a long time between 1650 and 1710. When he died, he was buried at Osiya.

Kakomba took over from his father Njosejambangu as Chief, and migrated with his people to the village of Ondao during the period of 1710–1770s, where they lived for a long time. In 1770, Kakomba died and was buried at Ondao.

From 1770 to the 1820s, Kakomba was succeeded by his son Hambuindja (also known as Hijakotuura) who settled at Omiheke and died there.

He in turn was succeeded by his son Tjikurundjimbi (also known as Tjambiru). He moved with his people to Ongoronjengua or Okauua, the same place. He became sickly and then went to the village known as Otjitjangi before moving across the Kunene River to Angola, where he stayed at a village called Otjineembo, after he was attacked by Nama troops (*Ovita vyokambari kongoro* or *ozoṱurupa zokambari kongoro*, "the war with the Nama troops"). He later died as the result of his long illness.

Tjikurundjimbi's successor was his son, Uomaoko Tjambiru. This new Chief moved from Otjineembo and went to Omitumba. It was here that he fought with the Angolan *Ovakoroka*, but he was killed by someone from the *Ovakuvare.*

---

2 The following text was submitted to the editors as part of the laws of the Kakurukouje community. As it contains information about the community expected to appear as the profile of the community, the editors moved it away from the laws and placed it under the Profile.

3 In this context, "angry fish" means big fish that eat or kill other fish, or even people.

Then his son, Kakurukouje (also known as Kasupi ka Mbepera), succeeded his father and became the Head of the Royal House. Kakurukouje moved from Omitumba back to his country of birth and then settled at the village called Omuatjivingo. Later, he moved to Omirora before returning to Omuatjivingo, where he passed away. During his migrations to and from Angola across the Kunene River, he forged strong ties with the Nama that were operating in that area.

Kakurukouje was succeeded by his son Veripaka Tjambiru. Veripaka moved from Omuatjivingo to Embuende before settling in Etanga, where he died in 1970. He was buried at Omuatjivingo.

From 1970 until 13 October 1993, his younger brother, Vetamuna Nguruua Tjambiru, took over from him after his death. Vetamuna first settled at Oozonduuombe and then returned to Etanga, where he stayed until his death.

His elder brother's son, Ukoruavi Tjambiru, son of Veripaka, succeeded him, and Ukoruavi Tjambiru died on 7 December 2004.

And he was succeeded by the current Chief, his elder brother's daughter's son, Vemuii Tjambiru. Vemuii Tjambiru led the Royal House from 2004 on, and, on 13 February 2008, was recognised by the Government as the supreme leader of the Kakurukouje.

The Oherero family is related to sister Traditional Authorities, such as the Otjikaoko Traditional Authority, with which they share similar cultural norms, traditions, beliefs and customary laws.

The Kakurukouje Traditional Authority is one of the Traditional Authorities in the Republic of Namibia gazetted in terms of the Traditional Authorities Act, 2000 (No. 25 of 2000) on 13 February 2008. The official crowning ceremonies were held on 21 March 2008 at Etanga in the Epupa Constituency of the Kunene Region.

Oveta yombazu Yondjuwo youhona waKakurukouje

ONGUNḒEVETA YOUHONAPARE WAKAKURUKOUJE

Ezeva 1: Omamemeno wondjuwo youhona

1.1 Ena rokotjiveta rotjirata tjombazu hi mari rire Kakurukouje Traditional Authority ndi mari hee kutja Otjirata tjOmbazu tja Kakurukouje poo Ondjuwo yOuhona wa Kakurukouje.

1.2 Wina ri isanewa okutja Ouhanapare wOherero, nu ihi otjirata hi tji turira motjirongo Etanga, ape nao tji tji ri omikato esere na ndano mozokirometa (105 km) koutokero wa Puwo.

1.3 Otja kombazu yetu, ouhona u memwa okuza komuze. Nu mouvara wa Kakurukouje ovandu ve pingenasana otja mozongwatero zavo. Ombara ndji ri kounane tji ya ṱu indino oyo i pingenwa i yomuangu, omuatje poo ngamwa okuza momuze na mombinḓu yondjuwo youhona wa Kakurukouje.

1.4 Eye u isanewa kutja Ombara poo Omuhona. Neye ongu ri otjiuru tjouvara mbo.

1.5 Tji mape urikwa omundu ngu ma yaruka motjihavero, eṱunḓu arihe okuza kovakwate woihe ngaa kowoina ve ya pamwe nave vareke omundu ngu mave nangarasi ongu ri ye, okuza mbo ave tjivisa kotjiwaṋa.

1.6 Otjiwaṋa tji na ousemba okuyakura poo okuhina okuyakura ndeeri matji munu nao. Nu wina tji na ousemba okuvareka omundu ngu matji munu kutja ongwa pwire po natji tjivisa kovakwate veṱunḓu.

Ezeva 2: Ohako yotjirata

2.1 Ohako mai kara nai; ma rire omake yevari womundu ngu ma zee omuriro. Mehi rokongotwe mamu kara otjivara otjihoni tji matji kara komamuho nu pokati mape ya otjivara tjoruhapo poo otjingirine, tji matji kara ovitjikasembama nu komamuho maku kara otjivara otjingara. Nu omuriro mau kondorokwa i yomawe yane. Ovivara avihe mbi mavi kuramene po otjivara tjouta wangongoro poo outa wombura.

2.2 Embo rotjikoro ma rire kutja: *Omuriro ombu twya nao.*

Ezeva 3: Eraka rokotjiveta rotjirata

3.1 Eraka rokotjiveta oro ndi rOtjihimba nOtjiherero.

3.2 Posi ya oveta ndji kai na kutjaera omaungurisiro womaraka warwe wovazorondu poo wa Afrika otja eraka rokotjiveta morupa kaaṋi ndo.

3.3 Nungwari okazeva nga 3(1) kake na okupitasana nOngunḓeveta ya Namibia, otja pu i tja eraka rokotjiveta Otjiingirisa. Mari ungurisiwa mu imbi vyokotjiveta kozomberoo na komananeno woviungura vyouhonapare.

Ezeva 4: Otjirata tjOvahona

4.1 Mape kara otjirata tjokombanda mu mamu haama ovahona avehe. Notjo matji isanewa kutja Otjirata tjOvahona tji matji kara nomasa aehe okutya nokuzeuparisa ozondyero azehe zouvara. Nu Ombara ondji mai kara otjiuru tjotjirata hi wina. Nu ngamwa zondyero nḓu tja tye maze rire zokotjiveta ku kangamwarupa rouvara wa Kakurukouje.

4.2 Ouṋepo wotjirata hi ma rire, ozorata ozohongora, na inḓa zokehi. Novo mave zikwa okuza kovirongo vyavo nu Omuhona ongu me yekuvezeuparisa/okuvetwirisa.

4.3 Oviungura vyavo mavi rire okuhongorerapo movitjitwa vyombazu motukondwa twavo nokukuramenapo ombara moviungura vyombazu mbi mavi kara movirongo vyavo.

4.4 Na wina okuhongorerapo mu ngamwa ovitjitwa mbi mavi tjitwa vyOhoromende vyomekurisiro mbi mavi kaenda movirongo vyavo.

4.5 Ovo mave rire ovahakaenise pokati kotupa twohoromende na tu tu ha wire kehi yohoromende ku na otjiwaṋa.

Ezeva 5: Omaurikiro wozorata ozohongora na inḓa zokehi

5.1 Omuhona ongu ma urike ozorata inḓa ozohongora hamboumwe (6).

5.2 Nu otjiwaṋa matji urike ovandu 6 okuza mokati kavo okurira ozorata zokehi nu omana wavo maye yandjwa kombara/omuhona kutja a zeuparise. Nu indu Omuhona tja munu kutja omundu ngwa urikwa ngo ke na kuyenenisa ovingi vyounane, ombara indino mai yenene okunakaura omuvarekwa ngo nu ai tjivisa ozorata ozohongora poo otjirata tje, nu ouṋepo wotjirata ombu mau kahakaena ku na otjiwaṋa ohunga noumune wOmuhona.

5.3 Omuhona ma ungurisa omasa we otja tji ya yandjwa ku ye moveta ndji oitja-25 yombura ndji 2000, mezeva ndi 10 (1)(a) na indi (b) roveta yovanane wombazu mOnamibia.

Ezeva 6: Ongaendero younane

6.1 Ongaendero nozondondo zounane motjirata tjondjuwo youhona wa Kakurukouje mai munika nai:

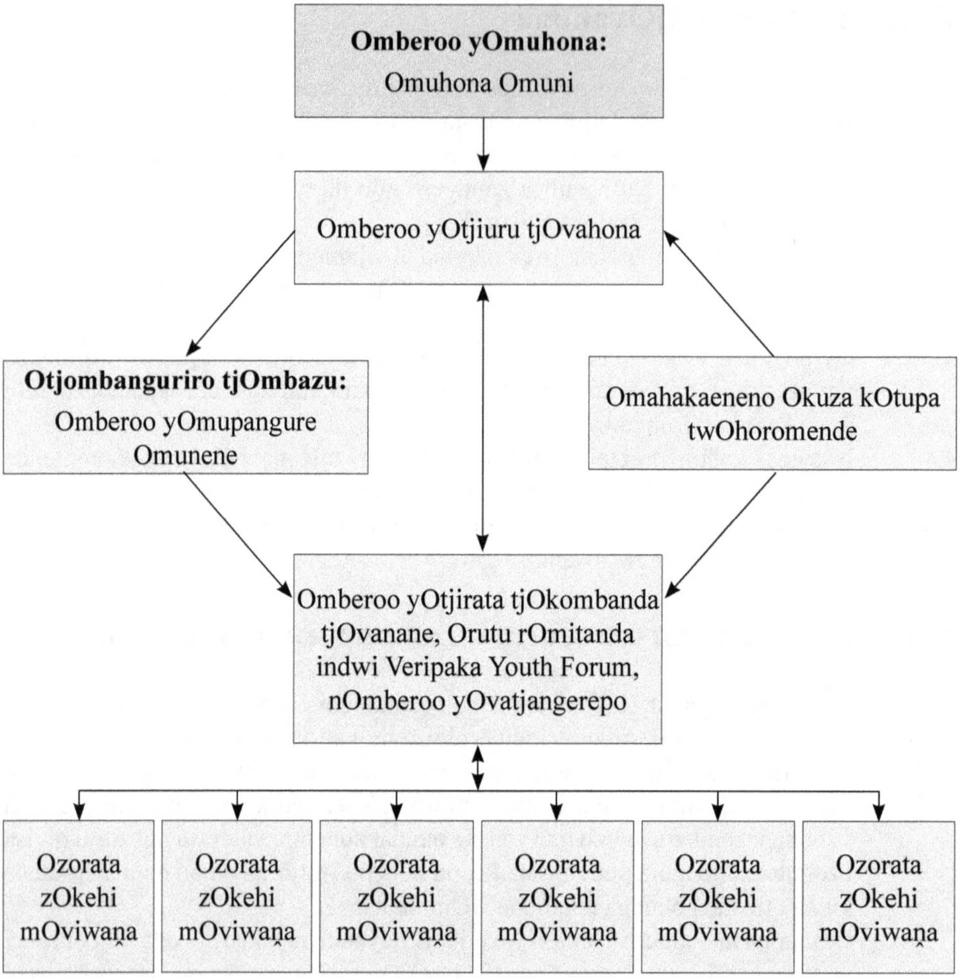

Ezeva 7: Oviungura vyOzorata Ozohongora zOmbazu

7.1 Oviungura vyOzorata Ozohongora mavi rire mbi:
- (a) Okukuramenapo Ombara.
- (b) Ngamwa ovitjitwa avihe vyokotjiveta; ovaenda, oviposa nozondjakaha zotjiwaṋa mavi sokuyetwa kOzorata rutenga nu Ozorata onḓu maze tjivisa Ombara amave tuurungire mOtjiuru tjOzorata poo Orata yokehi yOmuhona.
- (c) Nu kape na tjiṋa tji tja sere okuyatakana pu vo okukapita kOmuhona.

7.2 Otjiuru tjovahona:
- (a) Ma kuromene po ombara otjotjiuru tjokehi.
- (b) Omatjangwa ayehe maye pitire mu ye okuyenda kOmbara.
- (c) Ongu ri omundu erike ngu ma hakaene kun a Ombara movitjitwa avihe vyokotjiveta.

(d) Ongu ma tike Ombara momauyenda ayehe wokotjivefa.
(e) Ongu ma kuramene po Ombara, oyo tji i he ri po.
(f) Ongu ma hungire ku na Ombara.
(g) Ongu ma yandja ondunge nokuungurira Ombara.

7.3 Oviungura vyozorata zombazu zokehi ma rire mbi:
(a) Ovo mave rire omeho wOmbara movirongo vyavo.
(b) Ovo mave haama pozombongarero zOtjirata tjOvahona nokuyarura ondaze koviwaṋa vyavo.
(c) Okuhonaparerapo nokukaendisa ovitjitwa vyombazu movirongo vyavo.
(d) Okuzengurura omauzeu nozonddjakaha movirongo vyavo.
(e) Okuṱiza oveta noupore movirongo vyavo.
(f) Okuhongorerapo ozondando zOhoromende nḓe na otjiṋa nomekurisiro moviwaṋa vyavo.
(g) Okukuramenapo Ozorata inḓa ozonene tji ze he ri po momauyenda wokotjiveta nu tje ri ohepero.
(h) Nu ovanane mba tamunwa mbo mave sokukara notjihako otjizeuparise poo (stamp) yondjuwo youhona wa Kakurukouje, kutja ve kare noupupu okuyandja ozoparamita poo ozombapira zomausemba, nungwari mave ungurisa koviṋa vyokotjiveta porwavyo uriri.

Ezeva 8: Otjombanguriro tjOmbazu

8.1 Oviungura vyotjombanguriro tjombazu mavi rire mbi:
(a) Okuṱiza oveta nokuitwa momaungiriro.
(b) Okupangura nokuhina ongarera nu otja koveta.
(c) Okuzengurura ozonḓurumbata.
(d) Okuyapura nokuhanganisa otjiwaṋa.
(e) Okuyeta oveta momaunguriro.

8.2 Otjombanguriro matji zikama:
(a) Movapangure hambombari (7) wokombanda. Novo ma rire Omupangure Otjiuru, Ovapangure wokehi ye nOvavatere vavo.
(b) Mape kara Omutjange watjombanguriro.
(c) Nomutumwa omutware wozombuze.
(d) Ovaporise wotjiwaṋa.
(e) Novaungure varwe.

8.3 Omaandjero wozomberero

8.3.1 Onḓepero poo Otjiposa tjOkuzepa

8.3.1.1 Omundu tja zepa omundu ma sutu ozongombe omirongo vitatu na ndano (35) ndeeri kutja omuṱi omurumendu nu ongombe (1) imwe mu zo mai i koveta.

8.3.1.2 Omuṱi tje ri omukazendu, omuzepe u pewa omberero yokusuta ozongombe omirongo vine na ndano (45) mu zo imwe i yenda koveta.

8.3.2 Ombara

8.3.2.1 Omundu tja tono omukwao ombara; eye u pewa ondjo yozongombe hambondatu (8), mu zo mu mu za imwe (1) ndji yenda koveta.

8.3.2.2 Otjizi (omundu tja tono omukwao ondundura poo otjizi) u suta ozongombe mbari (2) mu zo imwe i yenda koveta.

8.3.2.3 Nu omundu tja kaṱa i yotjitoneno ho, okutja omutone ma sutu ozongombe omirongo vitatu na ndatu (33) imwe (1) i yenda koveta. Nu omuṱi tje ri omukazendu, omundu u suta ozongombe omirongo vine na ndatu (43) mu zo imwe (1) i yenda koveta.

8.3.3 Oviposa vyourunga

8.3.3.1 Ourunga wovinamuinyo: Indu omundu tja vazewa noviṋa mbi he ri motjiveta poo mbi hi na ousemba, indino eye u varwa kutja erunga. Nu eye u nondjo yokutja u na oviṋa mbi he ri motjiveta.

8.3.3.2 Indu omundu tja vaka ongombe, eye u pewa ondjo yokusuta ozongombe hamboumwe (6), nu oitjahambombari (7) oyo ndji oini, tji i na omuinyo. Nu imwe mu zo i yenda koveta.

8.3.3.3 Nu omundu tja zepa ongombe ndjo ma sutu ozongombe hambombari (7) imwe mu zo i yenda koveta.

8.3.3.4 Oviposa avihe vyovinamuinyo pozonganda namovirongo mavi ungura otja kezeva ndi.

8.3.3.5 Okuramba erya: Otja kombazu yetu pe kara otjitjitwa tjokuramba erya, indu omundu tje ya motjunda tjomuzamumwe we na toora mo otjinamuinyo, nu tja tjivisa ovaṱuta otjo ka rire ourunga. Nangarire kutja omuni worupanda ndo kepo. Nu omundu ka pewa ondjo.

8.3.3.6 Nu ndeeri pa kara kutja omuni ka vangere, indino omundu u suta otjinamuinyo tjimwe (1) tjonḓengu yaihi tja ri.

8.4 Omaerekasaneno

8.4.1 Mombazu yetu mu kara otjitjitwa tjomaerekasaneno, nu ye kaenda otja kotuzo na moviwondo notja kongwatero youramwe. Nu momuano wondengero wina.

8.4.2 Omundu umwe tja toora omapindi poo omazenge momanyando ngu maye nyandwa otja kombazu na momuano omusemba eye u pewa ondjo yokusuta ozongombe mbari (2) mu zo imwe i yenda koveta.

8.5 Omaturiro

8.5.1 Otja kombazu yetu ovandu ve tura pamwe motjirongo tjimwe nu ovinamuinyo vyavo ombi yenda mokuti okukapaha ehozu novikurya vyarwe, mbi ri omaryo.

8.5.2 Ovandu veṱunḓu rimwe ve tura pamwe ongondoroka poo moruteto.

8.5.3 Moruveze rwourumbu poo rwokuṋi ovandu ve yandjerwa okukatura kozohambo, otja pu mave zeri nokukotoka kozonganda zavo indu ombura tji ya roko.

8.5.4 Mourumbu ounene ovandu ve yandjerwa okukapaha omaryo kwarwe. Novo mave sokuningira ousemba kouhonapare mbu nanena kotukondwa ku mave zeri okuyenda novinamuinyo vyavo.

8.5.5 Ovandu mbe wa kehi youvara umwe wombazu ve haṋasana omaturiro morukondwa rwavo, nu tji mave tjindi okuza kotjirongo okuyenda kotjirongo ve tjivisasana poo ve riraera.

8.6 Omakombezumo/ovanatje wopendje norukupo

8.6.1 Mombazu yetu omuatje omukazona u raerwa kutja nga nyande kumwe novanatje wonganda handumba ndjo. Nu eye tja u pehi nu tje ya pokurira omunene poo otjikauhungu u rongerisiwa kutja tji ma vanga okukara nomurumendu nga kambure ovandu wozonganda zeṋe okuza kombazu nomuze wavo.

8.6.2 Nu tja munu omumuvareke, omukazona u tja: "Kahungire kovanene vandje." Ihi tji tjitirwa kutja pe tjiukwe kutja ouṋe ngu na omerizirira komuinyo wosukona ngo, nokutja amu ha kara ovanatje wopendje norukupo poo omakombezumo.

8.6.3 Monao Ondjuwo yOuhona wa Kakurukouje mai zeri kutja otjiwaṋa tji ṱize ombazu nu tji yaruke komuze watjo omukuru wombazu mbwi, 8.6.1 – 8.6.2.

8.7 Oukoze

8.7.1 Mombazu yetu otjitandi tjopozonganda katji yandjerwa.

8.7.2 Omurumendu otje ha yandjerwa okuyendera onganda ye uṱuku indu tja kupa. Eye u pewa omaronga okuza kovanene ve kutja a ha yendere onganda ye uṱuku.

8.7.3 Nu omukazendu wina u pewa omarongo kutja a ha katuka orukupo, nokuhina okukara norusuvero ku na ovarumendu varwe, mena rokutja ma yambururisa koyavo ka za.

8.7.4 Indu omurumendu tja vaza omurumendu warwe pu na omukazendu we ava rara poo ave ri morusuvero indino, omurunendu u varwa kutja wa katuka pomukazendu womundu warwe nu eye u pewa ondjo okusuta ozongombe zoukoze 6 (hamboumwe).

8.7.5 Mombazu yetu oukoze kau yandjewa, orondu owo u yeta otjitandi tjopozonganda motjiwaṋa.

8.7.6 Nu indu omurumendu tja kamunika a yendere onganda ye uṱuku, eye u pewa omberero yokusuta ongombe onduwombe komakura wotjiwondo ihi otje.

8.8 Omaṱa (Okurumata nokuhita eṱa)

8.8.1 Mombazu yetu omundu tja ṱu, eṱa re ri hitwa i yovangu poo ovasya ve otja koungu nourumbi wavo.

8.8.2 Nu omuangu poo omusya woina ngwa hiti meṱa u rumata mbi; ovanatje ozosewa zomunene we poo vongundwe, omuhepundu, noviṋa avihe mbya ri nomuṱi. Nu eye ouini mbo novandu u vi tjita ouini we avihe.

8.8.3 Nu ingwi omuangu poo omusya ngwa ri poo ngwa rumata omuhepundu novanatje womunene we ngo poo ongundwe ndjo, ongu rira omurumendu komuhepundu nu ongu rira ihe kozosewa nu omuvetumbe wina.

8.8.4 Ovanatje mave sokumutenga otja ihe yavo nu ingwi omukazendu ma sokumutenga otjomurumendu we.

8.8.5 Omurumendu ngwa rumata eṱunḓu ndi ma sokutoora omeriziririra omape nga otja ngwa rire omutumbe weṱunḓu nde ri weza ku indi ore nda vazewa na ro.

8.9 Onḓiro nombakero

8.9.1 Ponḓiro yomundu tja ṱu, ooihe yomuṱi ombe toora omerizirira wondyero yombakero yomuṱi ngo.

8.9.2 Ihe mukwate womuṱi u raera ihe ngwe mu kwata, onḓiro nu ihe u karaera omuhoko womuṱi mbe ri ovakwe ve.

8.9.3 Auhe ngwa tjivisiwa onḓiro poo ngwa zuu omatjivisiro wonḓiro u hepura kovakwao.

8.10 Ozongondjoza

8.10.1 Ongondjoza i yandjwa ku ihe mukururume poo ihe tjikuume womuṱi, eye ongu ze ṱiza.

8.10.2 Kombund' ombakero ozongondjoza azehe novihupe vyozombatero avihe vi yandjwa ku ihe omutupure womuṱi.

8.10.3 Nu ihe u toora oviṋa mbi a kasuta na vyo ozondjo zomuatje we ingwi omuṱi, tji ze ri po.

8.11 Orukupo poo Ozongupa

8.11.1 Mombazu yetu, omuatje omuzandu tji ma vanga okukupa, ovanene ve ombe yenda kozoukwe okukahungira orukupo.

8.11.2 Nu imba ovakwe (ovakupise/ovakupirwa) tji va itavere okutja orukupo otji maru kaendisiwa momuano wombazu. Okuza mbo ovakupasane ave utu okukara pamwe poyao.

8.11.3 Orukupo indwi orwarwe, omurumendu u yenena okukupa omukazendu auhe kangamwa ngwa toorora nu tja zu mbo e mu yeta keṱunḓu re.

8.11.4 Nu wina mombazu yetu okukupa ovakazendu kombanda yaumwe pe yandjerwa uriri.

Ezeva 9: Ovihitise vyotjimariva mombwiko yotjirata

9.1 Otjirata tja Kakurukouje (KTA) otjotjirata otjinane notjiṱize tjorukondwa ndwi tja sere okumuna omauwa notjitjamurongo mozongetjesa na avihe mbi hitisa otjimariva okuza morukondwa ndwi.

9.1.1 Onḓengu yotjimariva tji matji sokuhita motjikesa tjotjirata matji sokutuuwa po i yotjirata tjokombanda tjOmbara.

9.1.2 Inḓa ozongetjesa notutu tu matu sokuyandja ohambwarakaṋa, tumwe twazo matu ya kehi mba:

9.2 OzoConservancy nOtutu twOvaryange

9.2.1 Otutu ihwi tu ku za OzoConservancy tu tu ungura nokuungurisa ovipuka mbi ri mokuti na mozondendera zorukondwa ndwi, twa sere okuyandja otjitjamurongo kotjirata omueze auhe kombunda yaindu tji tja zu nokusuta ozondjo zatjo okumana.

9.2.2 Ozonganda azehe nḓe na otjiṋa novaryange na wina nḓe muna ehupo nomauwa varwe pekepeke za sere okuyandja ohambwarakaṋa yotjimariva kotjikesa tjombwiko tjotjirata tjombazu (KTA) omueze auhe poo ombura aihe otja kokuzuvasana.

9.3 Ozongetjesa Ozongarerere

9.3.1 Inḓa maze yenene okurira ozositora, oundingoso na zarwe tjimuna inḓa zokutjingisa keke nḓe na otjiṋa nokutjingisa okutja ze tjite otjimariva poo okuranda ovinamuinyo wina maze sokuyandja otjiṋa.

9.3.2 Omarambero wOvikariha tjiva

(a) Okandjembo (ozosipireta otjindjaindjomba),

(b) Okarahata (mbi ri mu tjo kavi iwe),

(c) Ovikariha avihe mbi he ri motjiveta otja koveta ya Namibia.

9.3.3 Ovikariha avihe mbya tamunwa kombanda mba kavi na okuyandjerwa okurandisiwa morukondwa ndwi kutja okotjimariva poo okotjinamuinyo.

9.3.4 Ngamwa ongetjesa poo omundu kourike we ngwa vazewa ama randisa ma sokusuta otjisuta tjondjo yokukatuka oveta kotjirata momuano wotjimariva poo omitwaro.

9.3.5 Otjisuta hi, matji yandjwa ku ngamwa omundu ngwa tuwa po i yotjirata tjOmbara nousemba wOmbara.

9.4 Ozomine na Vyarwe

9.4.1 Kangamwa otjiungura atjihe tji tji na otjiṋa nozomine novize vyomehi poo omapahero nomasusuriro wavyo, na wina kangamwa onganda aihe ndji na ozondando zokutjita imbi mbya tamunwa kombanda mba ya sere okusuta poo okuyandja ohambwarakaṋa kotjikesa tjomapwikiro tjotjirata momuano kangamwa auhe wonḓengu otja komazuvasaneno pokati kovira avihe mbi na orupa motjitjitwa hi.

9.4.2 Otjitjitwa tjomapahero nomaisiremo na wina omatoorero womaori nohasa (natural gas) na imbi avihe mbi za pu vyo okupitira morukondwa ndwi mavi sokuningirwa nokutjivisiwa nao kombund' omayakuriro i yotjirata.

9.4.3 Ouwa auhe mbu mau zu motjitjitwa hi mau sokuweza otjimariva poo onḓengu poo omurya kotjikesa tjombwiko tjotjirata momuano wokuyandja otjimariva poo imbi mbi na onḓengu yovimariva mbya zuvasanewa pokati kovanarupa mu imbi. Nu imbi mavi sokukayenda ngandu ovitjitwa tji vya yanda poo tji vya pu.

9.4.4 Otutu atuhe twongorongova poo ozokambani inḓa zozomine/zovize vyomehi nḓe na ozondando zokuyekusesura/kuyekususura, okupaha/okutjinga, nokutoora okutwara ovinikorwa mbi poo ngamwa ovitjitwa avihe mbi mavi ṱunu kombazu, ehupo, nongaro yomuhoko mbwi (Ovahimba), na wina kokuti nozondendera na indji ongorongova yotjiwaṋa hi nongondoroko na tjo. Ozonganda inḓa azehe maze sokukotora nokutjevera okuti nozondendera koupwe/kouwa na wina imba mbu mave ṱunwa i yovitjitwa mbi. Nu ihi otjimariva noviungura na wina ovaungure mbi mavi sokuungurisiwa ku imbi mbya tamunwa kombanda matji zu mozonganda poo mozokambani nḓa.

9.5 Ovisuta nOmberero yOkukatuka Oveta

9.5.1 Ovisuta vyondjo mavi yenene okusutwa i ngamwa omundu ngwa katuka poo ngwa teya oveta.

9.5.2 Otjisuta matji sokukara otja komazunḓiro/kongatukiro yomundu ingwi ngwa munika ondjo.

9.5.3 Ongetjesa poo ngamwa ngu randisa morukondwa ma yenene okurambwa nu ongetjesa ye ai patwa ongarerere i yotjirata.

The laws of the Kakurukouje

THE CONSTITUTION OF THE KAKURUKOUJE TRADITIONAL AUTHORITY

Article 1: Establishment of the Royal House

1.1 The official name of the Traditional Authority shall be the Kakurukouje Traditional Authority.

1.2 The Kakurukouje Traditional Authority may also be referred to as the *Kakurukouje Royal House* and the *Oherero Royal House*, whose headquarters are currently in Etanga village, 105 km west of Opuwo.

1.3 In the Kakurukouje Royal House, when the current Chief passes on, he/she can be succeeded by a suitable candidate among those in their bloodline.

1.4 His/her successor will be the Chief (*Omuhona* or *Ombara*), who shall be the supreme leader of the Traditional Authority and the community.

1.5 Family members from the patrilineal (father's) side in consultation and with consent from the matrilineal side, have the right to nominate the successor.

1.6 The family members from the patrilineal side will introduce their nominee to the entire community, which has the right and prerogative either to accept or reject the nominee with valid reasons, and to suggest to the nominating authority to bring forward another more suitable candidate of their choice from the same royal bloodline.

Article 2: The Symbols of the Traditional Authority

2.1 The symbols shall be two hands kindling the Sacred Fire (*Ondume Notjiya*) and four stones surrounding the fire. Half of the background shall be brown, separated by a thin, green diagonal stripe obliquely down the centre, and the remaining half of the background on the right shall be yellow. These three colours shall represent the colours of the rainbow.

2.2 The clan motto shall be *Omuriro ombu twya nao* ("The fire we came with").

Article 3: Official Language

3.1 The official language of the Traditional Authority shall be *Otjihimba* and *Otjiherero*.

3.2 Nothing contained in this Constitution shall prohibit the use of any other African language as a medium of communication in any sector.

3.3 Nothing contained in sub-article 3.1 shall preclude Article 3(1) of the Namibian Constitution when it is necessary to use English for official, administrative or other purposes.

Article 4: Supreme Council/Chief's Council

4.1 There shall be a Supreme Council in which supreme power shall be vested. Supreme power shall also be vested in the Chief as Head of the Council. The Council shall be the highest decision-making body, and all decisions taken and/or passed by it shall be binding on all organs of the Traditional Authority.

4.2 The members of the Council are called Senior Traditional Councillors and Junior Traditional Councillors and they are appointed by their villages and inaugurated by the Chief.

4.3 The Senior Traditional Councillors and Junior Traditional Councillors manage traditional affairs within the villages and represent the Chief in all activities taking place in their villages.

4.4 They represent the Chief in developmental activities of the government in their respective villages.

4.5 Senior Traditional Councillors and Junior Traditional Councillors serve as the liaison between the community and Government Offices, Ministries and Agencies.

Article 5: Appointment of Senior Traditional Councillors and Junior Traditional Councillors

5.1 The Chief will appoint six (6) Senior Traditional Councillors.

5.2 The community will nominate six people among themselves to serve as Traditional Councillors and submit their names to the Chief for approval. If a candidate does not meet the requirements or criteria, the Chief may disapprove the nominee and then consult on the matter with Senior Traditional Councillors, who will consult with the community.

5.3 The Chief will exercise the power vested in him/her in terms of section 10(1)(a) and (b) of the Traditional Authorities Act, 2000 (No. 25 of 2000).

Article 6: Organs and hierarchy of the Kakurukouje Traditional Authority

6.1 The organs and hierarchical leadership structure of the Kakurukouje Royal House shall be as depicted in the diagram on page 274.

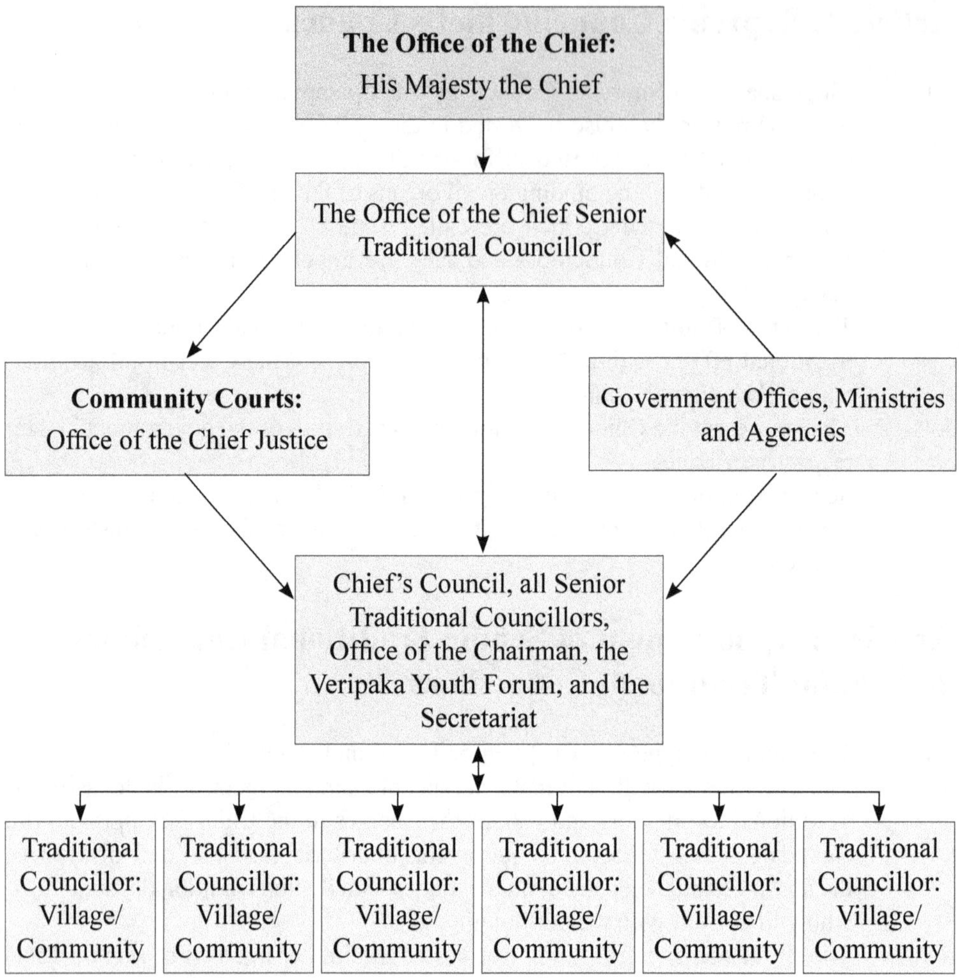

Article 7: The Duties of Traditional Councillors

7.1 The duties of all Senior Traditional Councillors shall be to:

(a) act on behalf of the Chief.

(b) ensure that all official matters, guests, court cases and any other community disputes are first addressed to a Senior Traditional Councillor, who shall forward such matters to the Chief.

(c) ensure that nothing is permitted to bypass them before being submitted to the Chief.

7.2 The Chief Senior Traditional Councillor shall:

(a) act on behalf of the Chief as the Sub-Chief.

(b) intercept all official correspondence to the Chief.

(c) be the only person authorised to address the Chief about all official matters that need to be dealt with.

(d) accompany the Chief in respect of official delegations.

(e) deputise for the Chief in his/her absence.
(f) consult with the Chief.
(g) advise and serve the Chief.

7.3 The duties of Junior Traditional Councillors shall be to:
(a) act as the eyes of the Chief in their neighbourhoods.
(b) attend the meetings of the Chief's Council and report back to their neighbourhoods or communities.
(c) spearhead traditional affairs within their neighbourhoods, villages, etc.
(d) solve conflicts and disputes within their neighbourhoods.
(e) maintain law and order in their neighbourhoods.
(f) spearhead the implementation of Government policies and projects within their neighbourhoods for the benefit and well-being of their communities.
(g) deputise for Senior Traditional Councillors on official missions if the latter are unavailable.
(h) Every leader mentioned above must be in possession of the Kakurukouje Traditional Authority's official stamp, and ensure that the official stamp is used for any and all official matters, including permits to move livestock.

Article 8: The Community Court and traditional norms and practices

8.1 The duties of the Community Court shall be to:
(a) ensure law and order prevail.
(b) ensure justice prevails.
(c) judge and litigate disputes.
(d) arbitrate or mediate in disputes.
(e) put justice into practice.

8.2 The Community Court shall consist of:
(a) at least 7 (seven) Judges, comprising the Chief Justice, incumbent Judges and Acting Judges.
(b) the Clerk of the Court.
(c) Messengers of the Court.
(d) the Community Police.
(e) other necessary personnel.

8.3 Sentences and punishments

8.3.1 Murder

8.3.1.1 Any person who commits a murder will be fined 35 (thirty-five) head of cattle plus 1 (one) of them that goes to the Traditional Authority.

8.3.1.2 If the victim is female, the perpetrator will pay 45 (forty-five) head of cattle plus 1 (one) of them that goes to the Traditional Authority.

8.3.2 Assault/wounds to the head

8.3.2.1 Serious assault to the head (*Ombara*): Anyone who seriously assaults another on the head, causing a scar will pay 8 (eight) head of cattle plus 1 (one) that goes to the Traditional Authority coffers.

8.3.2.2 Minor assault *(Ongeza poo otjizi)*: Anyone who commits a minor assault against another person will be fined 1 (one) head of cattle plus 1 (one) that goes to the Traditional Authority coffers.

8.3.2.3 If the victim dies as a result of such assault, the perpetrator will be found guilty of murder, and will be fined 33 (thirty-three) head of cattle if the victim is male and 43 (forty-three) head if the victim is female, one of which head of cattle in either case shall be for the Traditional Authority coffers.

8.3.3 Theft

8.3.3.1 If someone is found in possession of livestock without a permit or that has been stolen, he/she will be found guilty of being in possession of livestock without a permit or of possessing unlawful livestock.

8.3.3.2 If someone steals one head of cattle, the fine will be 6 (six) head of cattle, a seventh will be the stolen one if still alive and one (1) of which will be for the Traditional Authority coffers.

8.3.3.3 In the event that he/she stole one cow and killed it, he/she shall pay 7 (seven) head of cattle and 1 (one) of them to the Traditional Authority.

8.3.3.4 All domestic livestock are handled in the same way as per section 8.3.3.1 to 8.3.3.3.

8.3.3.5 "**Lawful Approach**" *(Okuramba erya)*: In our culture and in accordance with our traditional norms, there is a phenomenon known as *Okuramba erya*, which refers to taking livestock from your next-of-kin's kraal in his/her absence, but after having informed his/her herders. Such an act is not a crime in terms of our culture and beliefs and the person will not be penalised in any way for such an act.

8.3.3.6 However, if the owner of the livestock does not approve of the act, then the perpetrator or suspected perpetrator will compensate the aggrieved owner of the livestock with 1 (one) goat, sheep, cow or ox in accordance with the livestock involved in such act.

8.4 Traditional jokes (*Omaerekasaneno*)

8.4.1 In our culture and in accordance with our traditional norms, people play many jokes on each other in accordance with their paternal bloodlines and their age groups. Such joking shall always be done in a jovial, playful, lawful and respectful way.

8.4.2 If someone becomes angry or violent as a result of such jokes, that person is guilty of violating cultural norms and will be fined 2 (two) head of cattle, 1 (one) of which will go to the Traditional Authority's coffers.

8.5 Settlement

8.5.1 In our culture and in accordance with our traditional norms, it is customary for members of a community to be settled in one village, and their livestock are allowed to graze in the field.

8.5.2 Members of the same clan live on the same property and their houses are constructed close to one another.

8.5.3 During the dry season, community members can be permitted to settle at their cattle posts if they so wish, and return to their houses when the rain comes.

8.5.4 In a serious drought situation, community members are permitted to go anywhere they want to look for better grazing for their animals, provided that they gain admission from the Traditional Authority of the area concerned.

8.5.5 People who fall under the same Traditional Authority's jurisdiction share settlement areas, and can move as they wish, but need to inform each other or ask for permission from the inhabitants to settle in an inhabited area.

8.6 Children born outside marriage

8.6.1 In our culture and in accordance with our traditional norms, a girl is always advised and encouraged to play with the children of a particular house or family. As she matures, she is also advised to have a love relationship with a particular person due to family or other special bonds.

8.6.2 If a man wishes to propose to a woman, he will be advised to obtain permission from the woman's parents so that the parents will know who is responsible for the life of their daughter, to avoid illegitimate children.

8.6.3 The Kakurukouje Traditional Authority desires that the community should go back to their roots and implement sub-articles 8.6.1 and 8.6.2 in order to give our culture and traditional norms prerogative and preserve its value.

8.7 Jealousy

8.7.1 In our culture and in accordance with our traditional norms, domestic violence is forbidden.

8.7.2 When a man marries, he is given warnings from both his father and mother not to come home too late at night.

8.7.3 A married woman is also warned not to have a relationship outside the marriage.

8.7.4 If a married man finds his wife with another man, the latter shall be fined 6 (six) head of cattle, one of which shall go to the Traditional Authority.

8.7.5 Jealousy is unacceptable in our tradition because it can cause domestic violence. For this reason, it is prohibited for a man to have a sexual relationship with another man's wife.

8.7.6 If a married man arrives at his house at night, his age mates shall fine him 1 (one) young ox.

8.8 Inheritance/Estate

8.8.1 In our culture and in accordance with our traditional norms, if a man dies, his property is inherited by his younger brothers or nephews from the mother's side, in accordance with their seniority.

8.8.2 The property referred to in sub-article 8.8.1 shall include his widow and children, as well as all livestock and other valuables.

8.8.3 The young brother or nephew of the deceased who inherits his widow and children becomes the widow's husband and a father to the surviving children, and is responsible for maintenance.

8.8.4 The surviving children must respect their new father, and the widow shall respect her new husband as she did her late husband.

8.8.5 Someone who inherits the deceased's family accepts new responsibilities that are added to his own, as he must maintain the new members as well.

8.9 Death and funeral

8.9.1 After the death of someone, the deceased's father's family must be responsible for arranging the funeral and related matters.

8.9.2 The deceased's biological father must first consult with his own biological father as well as his in laws with respect to the arrangements to be made.

8.9.3 In our culture and in accordance with our traditional norms, everyone who has been notified of the deceased's death must inform others.

8.10 Funeral contributions (*Ozongondjoza*)

8.10.1 All contributions that are given as assistance towards the funeral are directed to the deceased's grandfather for safe custody.

8.10.2 After the funeral, all the contributions are given to the biological father to the deceased.

8.10.3 The deceased's biological father uses the funeral contributions to pay any debts that his deceased child may have left.

8.11 Marriage

8.11.1 In our culture and in accordance with our traditional norms, when a young man intends to marry, his parents go and propose the girl from her family and then the couple shall stay together.

8.11.2 If the parents of the proposed girl agree, then the wedding will be carried out and the couple will marry in a traditional ceremony.

8.11.3 Another type of marriage is where a man marries a woman of his choice, and then takes her to his family.

8.11.4 In our culture and in accordance with our traditional norms, polygyny is permitted, i.e. a man shall be permitted to marry more than one woman.

Article 9: Sources of revenue and income

9.1 The Traditional Authority, as the sole and legal custodian of the area inhabited by the Kakurukouje community and under the jurisdiction of the Kakurukouje Traditional Authority shall be entitled to harvest and gain benefits and revenues from all types of enterprises and ventures of an income-generating nature that are undertaken in such area.

9.1.1 Such revenue and income shall be allocated to the revenue pool and coffers of the Kakurukouje Traditional Authority as determined by the Chief's Council.

9.1.2 The types of business ventures that shall be required to contribute to the revenue pool include, but are not limited to, the following:

9.2 Conservancies and tourism

9.2.1 Conservancies, as major players in the utilisation and management of natural resources, especially wildlife, shall contribute a certain percentage of their net income/earnings to the Kakurukouje Traditional Authority revenue pool on a monthly basis.

9.2.2 All tour operators, camping site owners, lodge owners and any other entity that accrues financial benefits from tourists and tourism activities conducted within the area shall contribute an agreed percentage of their net income/earnings to the Kakurukouje Traditional Authority revenue pool on a monthly or yearly basis.

9.3. Permanent business establishments

9.3.1 Permanent business establishments may be shops, stores, shebeens, bartering businesses or others whose sole intention and inclination are to sell and exchange goods for either money or for livestock owned by inhabitants of the area, people from other parts of the country, or foreigners.

9.3.2 The following alcoholic drinks are banned:

(a) *Okandjembo* (crudely distilled spirits)

(b) *Okarahata* alcohol (constituents unknown), and

(c) All other alcoholic drinks of suspicious nature and concentrations.

9.3.3 The sale of any drinks mentioned in sub-article 9.3.2, whether for hard currency or in exchange for livestock, shall be prohibited within the Kakurukouje Traditional Authority area of jurisdiction.

9.3.4 Any business or individual involved in the sale of any drinks mentioned in sub-article 9.3.2 shall be prohibited from holding anyone liable for payment in either monetary or any other form for such goods.

9.3.5 The specific entity that attempts to contravene sub-articles 9.3.3 and 9.3.4 is liable to pay a fine as determined by the legal authority or any legal entity delegated by the Kakurukouje Traditional Authority, the Chief's Council, the Chief in person, or through a delegate, as deemed fit.

9.4 Mining, prospecting, extraction and exploration entities

9.4.1 Any type of mining, prospecting, exploration and extraction activities to be undertaken within the Kakurukouje Traditional Authority area of jurisdiction, or any entity passing through the area which intends to carry out any of the above and related activities shall be required to contribute to the Kakurukouje Traditional Authority revenue pool an agreed, fair and reasonable amount of cash or any transferable monetary items in the form of either concessions or shares or any other item of high quality valued at the agreed amount.

9.4.2 The exploration, extraction and transportation of oil or gas resources within the Kakurukouje Traditional Authority area of jurisdiction shall be subject to consultation with, approval by and the agreement of the said Traditional Authority on behalf of the affected communities.

9.4.3 Any monetary benefits to be accrued from the undertakings by any legal entity shall oblige the entity to contribute an agreed, fair and reasonable amount of money or assets or both to the Kakurukouje Traditional Authority revenue pool on a continuous and sustainable basis for the duration of the business entity's operations.

9.4.4 The entities and companies that undertake mining, exploration, expeditions, extraction, transportation or any other intensive activities that may or in fact do have a social, environmental or economic impact on the communities within and around the vicinities of such ventures shall reimburse those affected by such activities, and shall rehabilitate, protect and maintain the land involved. All costs related to such undertakings and the compensation due for their impact shall be fully and completely covered by the entity responsible.

9.5 Penalties and fines

9.5.1 Penalties and fines shall be imposed for disobedience and for breaking the laws in Article 9.

9.5.2 The severity of offences and appropriate fines shall be proportional to the offence.

9.5.3 The penalised entity shall be banned from the area, and shall be prohibited from conducting business therein.

Certificate of consent to publish

Certificate of the consent to publish

UNIVERSITY OF NAMIBIA

FACULTY OF LAW

HUMAN RIGHTS AND DOCUMENTATION CENTRE

RE: CONSENT TO PUBLICATION

I, the undersigned, Chief of the Kakuru Kouje Traditional Authority, hereby give consent to the Human Rights and Documentation Centre, to publish the following documents of the Kakuru Kouje Traditional Authority:

1. The Customary Laws
2. The Community Profile
3. Picture of the Chief
4. Logo of the Traditional Authority

I acknowledge that the Human Rights and Documentation Centre will publish the laws in our indigenous language (OTJIHERERO), as well as the English language. I am familiar with the contents of the laws that will be published and further acknowledge that they were prepared by my traditional authority.

Signed on this 08 **day of** OCTOBER **2012**

At ETANGA

V VEMUII

Chief

Kakuru Kouje Traditional Authority Okunene Region

Kakuru Kouje Traditional Authority Okunene Region

For HRDC: Mr. A. Gairiseb

Maharero Traditional Authority
Ondjuwo jouhonapare waMaharero

The supreme leader of the Maharero Traditional Authority is *Ombara*[1] Tjinaani Maharero.
Date of designation: 28 September 2012

1 Traditional title in terms of section 11, Traditional Authorities Act, 2000 (No. 25 of 2000).

PROFILE[2]

The history of the Onganda ya Mbunga Clan can be traced as far back as the 15th century, to forefathers like Kengeza, Vatje, Mbingana and Kasupi. According to elderly Ovaherero, oral narration and research concludes that the Ovaherero are descendants of the Ovambandu national group. The Ovambandu lived west of Lake Tanganyika and immigrated southwards during the 16th century. The Ovaherero came to settle in north-western Namibia in the area formerly known as Kaokoveld (*Okaoko* in Otjiherero). Tjamuaha, the son of Tjirue, erected his homestead at Okahandja in the early 1800s. When the Nama, under the leadership of Jonker Afrikaner, migrated from what was then the north-western Cape Colony to north of the Orange River in the 1830s, the peace that had prevailed among the Ovaherero people was disturbed. The Nama raided Ovaherero cattle, resulting in the loss of countless lives.

In 1842, *Ombara* Tjamuaha signed a peace pact with Jonker Afrikaner. The pact did not last, however, as the Nama continued with their transgressions – eventually reducing the Ovaherero to servitude. *Ombara* Maharero, who succeeded his father Tjamuaha in 1861, is credited with uniting the Ovaherero people under one common leader when he was appointed as the Supreme *Ombara* of the Ovaherero at Otjimbingwe in 1863. Subsequently, the Ovaherero turned the tables on the Nama through Maharero's brilliantly tactical warfare which eventually freed his people from the Nama.

Ombara Maharero is equally famous for resisting the attempted acquisition of land by European settlers by offering them sand in a basket instead. His son, Samuel Maharero, assumed the throne in 1890, and is renowned for leading his people against German colonial rule, which resulted in the Herero–German War of 1904–1907. Approximately 80% of the Ovaherero people perished in the genocide. Samuel Maharero went into exile to Botswana, where he died in March 1923. Fredrick Maharero assumed sovereignty in Botswana, while Hosea Kutako was installed as Regent in what was then South West Africa.

As a measure of protection against the Germans, who were pursuing the Maharero dynasty at the time, Traugoth Mbandaze Maharero assumed the guise of Curator of the Otjikatjamuaha Holy Fire. Traugoth Maharero was never in line for leadership. What he rather did, as a brother to Chief Samuel Maharero, was to take curatorship or rather guardianship, not of the throne – but of the Holy Fire.

Like many African peoples, the Ovaherero use the genealogical link to determine and maintain close family bonds. The matrilineage determines the social grouping of an individual and is known as *eyanda*. The patrilineal origin dictates –

- the cult of the Holy Fire, known as *Oruzo*, and
- the religious custom (*ovizerika*), which influences the pastoral livelihood and general conduct of the Ovaherero people from generation to generation.

2 This profile was provided by the Maharero Traditional Authority.

A traditional dance (known as *omuhiva* for men and *outjina* for women) and lamentation (*omutambo*) convey the religious and cultural practices of the Ovaherero people.

Traugoth Maharero died in 1947 and was succeeded by his younger brother, Edward Maripeuani Maharero, whose reign lasted to 1969. *Ombara* Alfons Kaihepovazandu Maharero – *Ombara V* – succeeded his father in 1970. *Ombara* Alfons Maharero was among the prominent Namibian leaders consulted by the then exiled SWAPO President, Sam Nujoma, in Lusaka, Zambia, in 1984, paving the way for Namibia's independence. *Ombara* Alfons Kaihepovazandu Maharero passed away on 25 April 2012, and was succeeded by his son, Tjinaani Maharero, who was designated by the community in September 2012 and was officially gazetted at the beginning of 2013.

The *Ombara* have engaged the German Government in search of dialogue for mutual respect and reparation that will finally heal the wounds of the Namibian people and lay to rest the memory that continues to haunt them. For example, in 2004, the *Ombara* conducted reconciliation talks with the descendants of General Lothar von Trotha, the German military tactician who issued the infamous Extermination Order against the Ovaherero on 2 October 1904 at Ozombuzovindimba. *Oteza uri Onduezu jaMbunga oivaza nozee po onduezu* ("If you could track down the bull, the Mbunga dynasty would reach it and convert it into a stud").

The publication of these laws seeks to promote the preservation of cultural practices, while simultaneously stimulating the dire need for research and recording of many African cultural practices and norms, particularly those of the Ovaherero. Culture should be vibrant and adaptable to social influence to secure survival in modern terms.

The history of the traditional flags

The Red Flag

The Ovaherero originally copied the use of the White Flag from the Nama people as a symbol of faith and identification. During the Herero–Nama War of 1863 at Okaokovijaja, Mainuua – Tjamuaha's son – was wounded by Nama fighters. Because he was of light complexion, the Herero fighters killed him, mistaking him for a Nama warrior. From that time on, the Ovaherero opted to use the red feathers of the crimson-breasted shrike (*Laniarius atrococcineus*) as a symbol to distinguish themselves from the Nama. *Ombara* Maharero issued a proclamation to the European traders to import red cloth and to sell it to the Ovaherero/Mbanderu as a form of identification. This practice rose to prominence in August 1923 upon the return of the remains of the late King Samuel Maharero to South West Africa (present-day Namibia) from Botswana for reburial at Okahandja, when the Ovaherero started the annual commemoration of what is known as the Samuel Maharero Red Flag Day.

The White Flag

The White Flag was resurrected by the Ovaherero of western Namibia as their symbol during the aftermath of the Herero–German War (1904–1907) when King Michael Tjiseseta of the Zeraua Royal House, with the assistance of priests, escaped capture by German troops by hiding on board ship in a cargo container covered in a white flag from Walvis Bay to South Africa. The flag has been retained as a mark of respect to the late King. Ever since 1925, the White Flag is proudly worn at the annual commemorations of King Willem Zemburuka-Zeraua at Omaruru held in October each year.

The Green Flag

The Green Flag came into existence in 1947 on the return of the remains of Chief Hijatuvao Nguvauva from Botswana to Namibia and is widely known as a symbol of the Ovambanderu community.

The White Flag

Oveta yombazu yotjiwaṋa tjaMaharero

Ezeva 1: Ouhonapare wOmbazu

1.1 Ovihavero

1.1.1 Ombara

1.1.1.1 Moure wozombura omasereondo nḓa kapita Ovaherero ve ungurisa ounane wombazu mbwa zikama movanane Ozombara mba kwatwa mozondjuwo zouhona okuisira korutanga roihe otja kondjuwo youhona woharive ndjo.

1.1.1.2 Ombara i zikwa okuza momatyasaneno nomairo wakumwe pokati kouṋepo weṱunḓu rondjuwo youhona novanene wopopezu womuhoko.

1.1.1.3 Otjihavero tjOmbara ootjihavero tjokombandambanda mounane wouhonapare wombazu. Ombara i zikwa okupingena motjihavero tjOmbara ndja ṱa, nu i zikwa moure womieze 12 kombunda yonḓiro yombara.

1.1.1.4 Omirari vyomatwirisiro wOmbara

(a) Otjiungura tjetando rombara ndja ṱa tji yetwa komaandero nu okuruwo kwe aku zemisiwa.

(b) Omahaṋeno weṱa rOmbara ndja ṱa.

(c) Omaakurisiro wokuruwo nomatwirisiro womupwee wokuruwo.

(d) Omupwe tja panḓa okukambura otjihavero tjouvara, okutja tje yandjewa ku ingwe outjavari moruteto.

(e) Ombara ombe twirisiwa motjihavero i yOmbara ongwao yotjihako tjimuna ihi otje.

1.2 Omaṱunḓu wOzondjuwo zOuhona wOvaherero

1.2.1 Ondjuwo youhona – Omunane - Otjirongo

(a) Otjikatjamuaha – Maharero – Okahandja

(b) Otjipepa – Zeraeua – Omaruru

(c) Onguatjindu – Kambazembi – Otjozondjupa

(d) Otjikaoko – Mureti – Otjipaue

(e) Vita – Vita Harunga Thom – Otjijandjasemo

1.2.2 Ozorata zOmbazu

1.2.2.1 Ombara ombe tji ya zu nokutwirisiwa otjiwaṋa tje tjombazu tji toora ondyero yokuṱiza ozorata movihavero otja tji va ri kehi yOmbara ndja ṱa nokuzika ozorata movihavero otja oruveze tji maru kawondja okuisira kozonḓiro, omaisiro woviungura motjimbe tjoukurupe nomaisiro woviungura/okurambwa poo otjiwaṋa atji yeta ondanaukiro movihavero vyozorata okutuurungira momatyasaneno mokati kotjiwaṋa tjombazu ndjo.

1.2.2.2 Otjungura otjinene tjOzorata ozonene zombazu okuvatera Ombara mokuungura oviungura vyayo mbya tjama notjiwaṋa tje tjombazu pevapayuva arihe, wina ovo mave yenene okuungura vyarwe otja komaraa wOmbara.

1.2.2.3 Otjiungura otjinene tjOzorata zombazu okuyandja ohambwarakaṋa koviungura vyOzorata ozonene zombazu mokuungura oviungura vyazo.

1.2.2.4 Ozorata zombazu maze yenene okuungura oviungura vyarwe otja komaraa wOmbara okutuurungira mozorata ozonene zombazu.

1.2.3 Omutjangerepo

1.2.3.1 Omutjangerepo u zikwa i yOmbara pamwe nomatyasaneno ku nounane wokombanda wotjiwaṋa tjombazu okurira omunyomokise/omuhakaenise pokati kotjiwaṋa tjombazu notutu twarwe motjito tjomananeno.

1.2.4 Omuhaamise wOvihavero

1.2.4.1 Omuhaamise wovihavero u urikwa i younane pamwe nomaitaverero wOmbara.

1.2.4.2 Otjiungura tje otjinene okuvatera omutjangerepo okuzikamisa omayuva wozombongarero nomakaendero omakahu wozombongarero

1.3 Otupa twOuhonapare wOmbazu

1.3.1 Eṱunḓu rOndjuwo yOuhona

1.3.1.1 Eṱunḓu rOndjuwo yOuhona ri zikama mouṋepo ovazamumwe vOmbara imbwi: ozongundwe, oohongazye, ovangu wombara, ovaramwe, Omuara novanatje vOmbara.

1.3.1.2 Otjuungura otjinene tjeṱunḓu rouṋepo wondjuwo youhona okutoora ondyero momazikiro womupingene motjihavero tjombara, ombara ndja ri po tji ya ṱu na wina okuyandja oruyameto kombara momaunguriro we movitjitwa vyohoromende novyombazu.

1.3.2 Otjirata tjombazu

1.3.2.1 Otjirata tjombazu ondu ri orutu rwokombandambanda mounane wouhonapare wombazu.

1.3.2.2 Otjirata hi tja zikama mouṋepo mbwi: Ombara, ozorata zombazu, omuhaamise wovihavero, omutjangerepo nouṋepo wetambo rotjiwaṋa.

1.3.3 Ombwiko yOtjiwaṋa

1.3.3.1 Ombwiko yotjiwaṋa orutu ru ouhonapare wombazu ndu na omerizirira momaungurisiro nomananeno omakahu yombwiko (ongorongova) yotjiwaṋa tjombazu ndjo.

1.3.3.2 Ombwiko ndji i nanwa i yOtjirata tjovanane wombwiko mbe zikwa i youhonapare wombazu.

1.3.4 Otjirata otjitjangerepo

1.3.4.1 Otjirata otjitjangerepo tji yandja ondunge nounongo momananeno na ngamwa vyarwe Otjirata tjombazu mu matji hepa ondunge otja tji tja zikama mozonongo.

1.3.5 Ozondondo zounane wErapi rOmbazu

1.3.5.1 Omarapi wombazu pekepeke yenanwa otja kovihako vyorupa rwovita ndu nOzofield Marshall otjovanane wokombanda.

1.3.5.2 Omurapi ye ungura tjinene povitjitwa vyomarangerero nge kara ko ombura aihe na pozombakero zovanane vokombanda vombazu noverapi wina.

1.3.6 Orutavi rwOmitanda

1.3.6.1 Orutavi rwomitanda ru honga omitanda kutja ve kare nondjiviro ndja yenene mongaro novitjitwa vyombazu yOvaherero na wina okuverongerisa moviṱo vyounane woruyaveze.

1.3.7 Ozombanguriro

1.3.7.1 Otja koveta yOvaherero mu zikamisiwa ozombanguriro zombazu zokehi zotjiwaṋa motukondwa atuhe okuungurisa oveta kovature pondondo yorukondwa rwoharive ndwo.

1.3.7.2 Ombara otjotjiuru tjokombanda ondji mai pangura nokuyandja ongurameno osenina moviposa mbya hindwa otjombanguriro tjomayarurakero woviposa okuza kovyombanguriro vyokehi.

1.4 Ozombongarero

1.4.1 Ozondondo pekepeke zounane maze kara nozombongarero otja moviṱo vyounane okutara moviṋenge mbi mavi hepa ondyero vyavyo.

1.5 Ousemba wokutwapo nokurundurura ozoveta

1.5.1 Ousemba wokutwapo nokurundurura ozoveta u ri momake wOtjirata tjOmbazu.

1.5.2 Otjirata tjOmbazu matji zeuparisa ozoveta ouṋepo tji u nohange kutja ozoveta nḓu maze zikamisiwa poo okurundururwa ze ri monḓero yotjiaṋa tjombazu ho nu omatyasaneno omaparanga nomairo wakumwe moumune ya tjitwa.

Ezeva 2: Otjombanguriro tjombazu

2.1 Otjombanguriro tjombazu otjiṱiṱi tja zikama mOmupangure, ovayandjandunge vevari (2), omutjangerepo wotjombanguriro, omuhindwa (omutumwa) wotjombanguriro, nozorata zombazu otjouṋepo mbu yandja oruyameto.

2.2 Otjombanguriro tjombazu tjomayarurakero woviposa matji zikama mOmbara youhonapare wombazu, ozorata mbari ozonene zombazu nouṋepo ouweziwa mbu yandja oruyameto.

2.3 Omupangure ongu ma rire omunandyero motjombanguriro tjombazu nokuungurisa omasa we ngo otja tji yandjewa ku ye.

2.4 Ovayandjandunge mave tjind omerizirira wokuyandja ondunge komupangure mokutoora ondyero yombanguriro tje ri ohepero.

2.5 Ovapangure novayandjandunge wotjombanguriro tjombazu ve zikwa, nokuungura nokurambwa otja komazeva woveta yOzombanguriro zombazu, Oveta oitja-10 yombura 2003.

Ezeva 3: Ongaendero yatjombanguriro

3.1 Omakaendisiro womarapotero wotjiposa

3.1.1 Ngamwa okaṋepo akehe kotjiwaṋa ku ke noumune wokutja ousemba we wa tombwa i yomundu woharive ke nousemba okutwa omutjemo we momatjangwa potjombanguriro tjombazu kutja otjiposa tje tji pangurwe.

3.1.2 Ngamwa okaṋepo akehe kotjiwaṋa make yenene okuhakerwa mokukatuka oveta.

3.1.3 Omerizirira womuhakerwa wondjo okuyarisa kutja eye ke nondjo.

3.1.4 Otjombanguriro tjombazu matji yenene okumuna omuhakerwa wondjo ondjo, natji yandja eraa rokutja nga sute omberero poo ovazamumwe ve ngave sute ondjo ndjo, tji pa munika kutja omupewa wondjo ke na omuano (ozomburo) okusuta omberero ndja pewa ndjo.

3.1.5 Kombund' omutjemo tji wa zu nokurapotwa ouhonapare wombazu u kaondjisa ongonḓononeno yatjimanga okutara koviṋenge avihe motjiposa nomauhatoi ayehe okuza kominda aviyevari motjiposa kutja ve yenene okuzikamisa omuzura wotjiposa.

3.1.6 Kombunda yongonḓononeno, otjiposa tji yandjewa kozorata ozonene zombazu okutoora ondyero.

3.1.7 Entja otjiposa ngatji pangurwe poo indee. Tji pa toorwa ondyero yokutja otjiposa tji nomuzura wokupangurwa, otjiposa tji yandjewa kombanguriro yombazu okuzikamisa eyuva rombanguriro.

3.2 Omapanguriro

3.2.1 Otjombanguriro tjombazu matji yenene okuyandja erakiza kotjinyo poo momatjangwa ngu maye isana omundu kutja me ye komurungu watjombanguriro.

3.2.2 Motjiṱo tjomundu ngu ma panḓa okuya komurungu watjombanguriro tjombazu, ouhonapare wombazu u ningira omupangure (magistrate) okuyandja eraa koporise okuyeta omurondorwa kotjombanguriro tjombazu. Imbwe ombu ri omuano omusemba wokuṋiṋikiza Omundu okuriwisa kehi yotjombanguriro tjombazu.

3.2.3 Ovandu avehe mbe norupe motjiposa, okuza komurapote, omurondorwa nozohatoi mave sokuya komurungu watjombanguriro.

3.2.4 Omuhakerwa womondjo auhe u nousemba okuningira ngamwa omundu auhe okumukuramenapo eye me nongamburiro yokutja me mu rwisire po ozonḓero ze nawa motjiposa motjombanguriro.

3.2.5 Otjombanguriro tjombazu katji nousemba okupangura oviposa vyotutjero.

3.2.6 Motjiṱo tjondumbiro ombi yovanatje, otjombanguriro tji yenena okuungurisa ovanene ovakwate vomuatje otjovayadjaruyameto motjiposa tjondumbiro ombi yomuatje.

3.3 Omaimbirahiro wotjiposa, omapangguriro wotjiposa nomayaruriroko wotjiposa

3.3.1 Otjiposa tji yenena okunakaurwa tji matji kaiya ouhatoi oukahu kombund' omapurateneno wombanguriro okuura.

3.3.2 Oumune wombanguriro u tjiukisiwa kotjinyo i yomupangure otjiposa tji tja pangurwa okumanuka.

3.3.3 Oumune wombanguriro u yandjewa momatjangwa moure womayuva 7 kombund' ombanguriro mu mu na omapu wokutja ongwaye otjombanguriro tji tja munu nao wina mu mu nozongunḓe ozosupi zotjiposa.

3.3.4 Ngamwa omundu auhe motjiposa ngu hi na ohange noumune wombanguriro u nousemba okuyarurako otjiposa kotjombanguriro tjomayarurakero woviposa tjombazu moure womayuva 14 okuza kombanguriro tji ya yandja oumune wayo.

3.3.5 Omurapote ma sokuyandja ondjivisiro yokuyarurako otjiposa momatjangwa komutjangerepo wotjombanguriro moure woruveze ndwa tuwa po (omayuva 14).

3.3.6 Ozondondo azehe zomapanguriro mouhonapare wombazu tji za yenenisiwa nokuhina omazenguriro motjiposa, otjiposa matji yenene okuyarurwako kohofa (Magistrate).

Ezeva 4: Ozoveta

4.1 Omahandjauriro

4.1.1 Embo ndi omuatje momatjangwa nga mari hee omundu auhe ngu hi ya tjita ozombura omurongo na hambondatu (18) mu nao ongu ri kehi yozombura nongu varwa otjomuatje.

4.1.2 Otjombanguriro tjombazu matji yenene okupangura omundu ngamwa auhe ngu ri morukondwa ndu wira kehi youhonapare wombazu mbo.
4.1.3 Orukondwa mape hewa orukondwa otja koveta ndu varwa kutja ru wira kehi youhonapare wOmbazu mbo.

4.2 Omirari mbi mavi tjaere omundu okuhina okutoorerwa omikambo vyoveta

4.2.1 Omuajte wokehi yozombura omurongo na hambondatu (18) ken a ku- yenene okuisamewa movitjitwa vyatjombanguriro motjimbe tjokutja u ri kehi yozombura.
4.2.2 Ovaungure wotjombanguriro mave yenene okuisira omundu kutja a ha toorerwa omikambo vyoveta tji va munu kutja omundu ngo otjingundi mourizemburuka.
4.2.3 Otjombanguriro tji tja munu kutja omundu woharive ngo u ri kehi yongaro yovipurukise matji yenene okutwirika otjiposa okuyandjera omundu ngo ma kotoke mongaro osemba.
4.2.4 Otjombanguriro matji yenene okuisira omundu kokurondorwa tjipa munika kutja eye wa tjita ondjito yoharive ndjo kehi yoṋiṋikizire yopendje noveta ndja tuwa ku ye, nu omundu ngo ka sokuverwa.
4.2.5 Ondjito yomakatukiro yoveta tji ya pangurwa i yotjombanguriro tjomangestrata, otjombanguriro tjombazu katji nousemba wokupangura otjiposa ho.
4.2.6 Nungwari omurondorwa tje ha munikirwe ondjo i yotjombanguriro tjomangestrata, otjombanguriro tjombazu matji yenene okupangura otjiposa ho.

4.3 Ozongatukiro zoveta

4.3.1 Omazepero womundu

4.3.1.1 Mape hee omundu okuzepa omukwao.
4.3.1.2 Otjombanguriro tjombazu katji nomasa wokupangura otjiposa tjokuzepa motjimbe tjomuzura watjo.
4.3.1.3 Oiposa vyokuzepa avihe ngavi hindwe kotjombanguriro tjomangestrata.

4.3.2 Orutjero notjitandi tjomorukatuko

4.3.2.1 Orutjero notjitandi tjomorukatuko okukara norukatuko ku nomundu nokuhina ousemba we nu kehi yoṋiṋikizire.
4.3.2.2 Otjombanguriro tjombazu katji nomasa wokupangura ondjito ndjo motjimbe tjomuzura wayo.

4.3.3 Ourunga

4.3.3.1 Ourunga ondjito yokukatuka oveta tje ri okuvaka ouini womundu warwe.
4.3.3.2 Otjombanguriro tjombazu tji yenena okupangura ondjito yourunga.

4.3.3.3 Omuhakerwa womongatukiro tja pangurwa a munika ondjo u sutisiwa tuvari onḓengu youini mbwa vaka, tje ri monḓengu yotjimariva u sutisiwa ozoperesende omirongo vitano (50%) zarwe kombanda yonḓengu youini mbwa vaka.

4.3.3.4 Omapundiro wouini maye he ondjito yourunga nu momuinyo otjingewo amape ungurisiwa omasa/otjitandi.

4.3.3.5 Otjombanguriro tjombazu katji nomasa okupangura ondjito yomapundiro youini motjimbe tjomuzura wondjito ndjo.

4.3.4 Omatoneno

4.3.4.1 Okutona omundu mongatukiro yoveta i handjaurwa otjondjito yokuhihamisa omundu korutu rwe.

4.3.4.2 Omatoneno ye varwa otjongatukiro onene.

4.3.4.3 Otjombanguriro tjombazu katji nomasa okupangura ondjito yosaneno ndjo motjimbe tjoviṋenge mbi ri motjiposa tjomatoneno.

4.3.5 Omatandero/omakunino womburuma

4.3.5.1 Omatandero poo omakunino womburuma orondu tji mo tanda omundu nomambo kotjinyo poo korutu rwe.

4.3.5.2 Omundu ngu ma tanda poo ngu ma kunu omburuma mu warwe ma sokupangurwa.

4.3.5.3 Otjombaguriro tjombazu katji nomasa wokupangura otjiposa tjomatandero poo tjomakunino womburuma motjimbe tjomuzura woviposa vyosaneno ndjo.

4.3.6 Omarandero wokeero

4.3.6.1 Ondjito yomarandero womundu keero okusuta omundu otjimariva poo okumusuta momuano warwe nombimbo ouhasemba.

4.3.6.2 Otjombanguriro tjombazu katji nomasa wokupangura otjiposa tjomarandero womundu keero.

4.3.7 Omarandisiro woviṋa momuano omuhasemba

4.3.7.1 Omahitisiro/omapitisiro/nomarandisiro woviṋa pendje yoveta.

4.3.7.2 Otjombanguriro tjombazu katji nomasa wokupangura oviposa vyosaneno ndjo.

4.3.8 Omakarero woviumbe pendje yoveta

4.3.8.1 Ondjito yokukara noviumbe pendje yoveta, ongatukiro yoveta.

4.3.8.1 Otjombanguriro tjombazu katji nomasa wokupangura oviposa vyosaneno ndjo.

4.3.9 Omananeno wonḓarata (mehi rakamwaha) nokuhina ousemba

4.3.9.1 Ondjito yomananeno wonḓarata (mehi rakamwaha) nokuhina ousemba i yomundu woharive ngo ongatukiro yoveta.
4.3.9.2 Otjombanguriro tjombazu tji nousemba wokupangura omundu kondjito yokunana onḓarata nokuhina ousemba.
4.3.9.3 Omuhakerwa womondjo tja pangurwa a munika ondjo ma verwa okusuta otjimariva kondjito ndja etisa omaisapero wonḓarata, eye tja panḓa okuisapo otja keraa rouhonapare wombazu.

4.4 Omahaṋeno weṱa

4.4.1 Otja kombazu yOvaherero omahaṋeno weṱa romurumendu noromukazendu pe nombangu nu ye haṋewa pekepeke.

4.4.2 Eṱa romurumendu

4.4.2.1 Tji pe hi nomatjangwa womahaṋeno weṱa romurumendu omuangu we ongu zikwa otjomuhaṋe weta.
4.4.2.2 Omuṱi tje hi nomuangu omusya ongu haṋa eṱa.
4.4.2.3 Omuhaṋe weṱa tjitenga u rumatisa omukazendu omuhepundu novanatje avehe womuṱi nga ku imba omakombezumo wina.
4.4.2.4 Eṱa nda hupu ri rumatwa I yovangu, ovaṱena novasya vomuṱi kutja omauini ayehe oonge nyinganyinga na nge ha nyinganyinga.
4.4.2.5 Omakareropo wovanane vombazu pomahaṋeno weṱa ye heperwa po otjovatarere wotjiungura, nokuzeuparisa komaandero womahaṋeno weṱa kutja ovimbumba avihe meṱa ndo vi nohange nomahaṋeno weṱa otja tji ra haṋika.
4.4.2.6 Omakareropo wovikutu ootjoihe notjoina vyomuṱi vi heperwa po wina pomahaṋikiro weṱa.
4.4.2.7 Omuhepundu u pewa ouyara okuriwa i yomuangu poo omusya womurumend.
4.4.2.8 Omuhepundu tja panḓa okuriwa u yarurwa kotjikutu ka ziririre nouini we auhe nga ku imbwi mbwa rumata peṱa romurumendu we.

4.4.3 Eṱa romukazendu

4.4.3.1 Kombund' ombakero yomukazendu ouini we auhe oombu nyinganyinga na mbuha nyinganyinga u yandjewa momake wovanene ve ovemukwate.
4.4.3.2 Omuhoko womuṱi nu tjinene ihe poo ongundwe, ombe haṋa eṱa.
4.4.3.3 Rutenga eṱa ri haṋewa kovanatje womuṱi avehe.
4.4.3.4 Eṱa nda hupu kovanatje ri rumatwa i yomuhoko womuṱi mbe ri ovangu, ovaṱena notjikutu tjovazamumwe.
4.4.3.4 Omuhepundu u yandja ongombe yotjize kovakwe ve momayarukiro weṱa romukazendu we otjotjiyarisiro tjokutja eye ke na ondjo monḓiro yomukazendu wenu wina ma ningire omuhitandjuwo okuza kovakwe ve.

4.5 Orukupo

4.5.1 Otja kongaro yombazu yOvaherero orukupo ru na ozondondo ine (4) zongaendero:

(a) Ondondo ondenga oyomaṱunḓu okurihangununa nokutjiwasana.

(b) Ondondo oitjavari oyomeero wotjikutu tjomukupe i yarisa onḓero yavo okukupa.

(c) Ondondo oitjatatu ndji ri omakombero worukupo okuzikamisa ovisuta.

(d) Ondondo oitjaine oyomukandi okuuta.

4.5.2 Ovisuta vyorukupo vi kara pokati koN$2 000 nga koN$10 000 nozongombe mbari (2) otja kombazu.

4.5.3 Otja kombazu, omurumendu wOmuherero u nousemba wokukupa ovakazendu ovengi pu umwe.

4.5.4 Okuza momazemburukiro womauhonapare wombazu i yOhoromende ya Namibia mo-1998, omauhonapare wombazu otji ya uta okuyandja otutuu twotukupo otja konḓero yovakupasane.

4.5.5 Ondjeverero kovahepundu

4.5.5.1 Ombazu yOvaherero ya kwizika ondjeverero yapeke komuhepundu motjimbe tjokutja eye u nousemba wokurumata eṱa romurumendu we.

4.5.5.2 Otja kongaro yomuhoko wOvaherero omuangu poo omusya womurumendu ngwa ṱu ombe nomerizirira kombwiro noruyameto komuhepundu.

4.5.6 Oukorondu

4.5.6.1 Ondjito youkorondu ongatukiro otja kongaro yombazu.

4.5.6.2 Omukatuke tja rondorwa i yomakura u pewa omberero.

4.5.7 Omahaṋikiro worukupo

4.5.7.1 Omahaṋikiro worukupo kandjito ondjandjerwa otja kombazu yOvaherero nu ngamwa ngu ma zeri orukupo okuhaṋika u suta ozongombe hamboumwe (6) ku ingwi ngwa isiwa.

4.6 Ovanatje

4.6.1 Omaṱumbaparero

4.6.1.1 Omaṱumbaparero pendje yorukupo otjiṋa otjihazerwa mombazu yOvaherero.

4.6.1.2 Omukatuke ma yenene okurondorwa nu a verwa okusuta ongombe imwe (1) poo N$2 000 nokutumba omuatje ngo.

4.6.2 Omerizirira/ondjeverero nomekurisiro wovanatje

4.6.2.1 Ovanene vomuatje pouvari wavo ve nomerizirira nge ṱeki momekurisiro womuatje nangarire kutja kave kupasanene.

4.6.2.2 Wina eṱunḓu rovazamumwe ri nohambwarakaṋa kokutumba omuatje.

4.6.2.3 Omerizirira omatenga okutumba omuatje osewa ye na omukwate ingwi ngwa sewa ko.

4.6.2.4 Ovakwate ovanene poo ovanene omuatje ke umbwa otja kondyero yovazamumwe.

4.6.2.5 Ovakwate pouvari wavo ve nomerizirira nge ṱa pamwe mokukurisa omuatje omakomezumo.

4.6.2.6 Ku ihe ku undjurwa okutumba omuatje ame kurire pu na ina.

4.6.2.7 Ihe u yenena okutoora omuatje indu eye tja yandja katjivereko (ongombe yondumbiro yomuatje) ku ina.

4.6.3 Omahongero

4.6.3.1 Omahongero womuajte ye ri momake wovanene ve aveevari pamwe nombatero yovazamumwe.

4.7 Ovakurundu

4.7.1 Omerizirira wovanatje notjikutu tjovazamumwe okutumba ovakurundu vavo, okuvepa ovikurya, ozondjuwo noviungurisiwa vyarwe.

4.8 Ouveruke

4.8.1 Ozonganga zombazu

4.8.1.1 Ozonganga zombazu novatware vovanatje ovazandu kotjivetero ve heperwa kutja ve ungure nondjeverero kouveruke noukohoke moviungura vyavo.

4.8.2 Ondwi yehinga nomutjise wehinga

4.8.2.1 Omaviururiro womahwangero wondwi nomutjise wehinga ya rira embo rovanane wombazu novanene pevapayuva arihe pomaoronganeno wotjiwaṋa okutunduuza omitanda okukara nondjeverero motukatuko.

4.8.3 Otjikariha novipurukise

4.8.3.1 Ongaro yomaungurisiro omavi wotjikariha novipurukise i pirukirwa tjinene otjomuano wokuṱiza ongaro novitjitwa vyomuhoko.

4.9 Onḓekasaneno

4.9.1 Otja kombazu yOvaherero ovarumendu novakazendu ve nomerizirira noviungura pekepeke mbya memenwa okupasana omasa nokuvaterasana.

4.9.2 Ovanene ve yandja ohambwarakaṋa onene mokutunduuza ozonḓero nombwiro yovakazendu.

4.9.3 Otjiuru (Omunnene) tjotjikutu otja kounongo nondengero ndja pewa motjiwaṋa ongu nomerizirira wokutjevera ozonḓero zorupa indwi otjingundi (omukazendu) tji kwe ya komazenguriro wombata tjimuna momaṱa notukupo.

4.10 Ehi

4.10.1 Ehi rakamwaha ouini wohoromende, ovanane vombazu ombe nomerizirira wokutjeverera po ohoromende.

4.10.2 Ovanane vombazu pamwe nomatyasaneno nozosoromana zovirongo ombe nousemba wokuyandja ehi romaturiro otja komaṱunḓu woharive mombazu.

4.10.3 Ondjito yomararakaneno wehi nokuhina ousemba ongatukiro yoveta.

4.10.4 Omundu ngwa tjiti ondjito ndjo ma yenene okurondorwa nokuverwa, tja munika ondjo.

4.10.5 Ousemba womaryo u yandjewa i osoromana yotjirongo pamwe nomatyasaneno omaparanga wovature wotjirongo tjoharive ho.

4.11 Ovinamuinyo

4.11.1 Motjiṱo tjomuṱuta tja mu nombandjarero yovinamuinyo vye u hupa kouwa noruyameto rovazamumwe novararanganda ve okuyarurako ongaro yehupo re.

4.11.2 Omatoorero wovinamuinyo moukoto nopendje yehi rakamwaha i yovaṱuta ye kaondjisiwa nousemba wozonganga zovinamuinyo okuyenenisa omazeva wouveruke wovinamuinyo.

4.11.3 Oveniovinamuinyo ombe nomerizirira okundja omeva nomaryo na wina okuyenenisa omazeva wouveruke wovinamuinyo vyavo.

4.12 Okuti (Ozondendera)

4.12.1 Ozongoporo

4.12.1.1 Omaandjero wousemba wokusa ovize vyomehi ye nohoromende okutuurungira mOministri yOzongoporo nOvikaendise.

4.12.1.2 Ozongetjefa nḓa pewa ousemba wokusa ovize vyomehi mehi rakamwaha ze nomerizirira wokuyandja otjimariva kOmbwiko yOtjiwaṋa morukondwa ndo.

4.12.2 Ondjeverero kovipuka vyokuti

4.12.2.1 Otjondjeverero kovipuka vyokuti nomaevero ye tjaerwa moruveze rowmakwatero wovipuka. Ovaeve ve rakiziwa okuhina okuzepa ovipuka ovirwite.

4.12.3 Omakururukiro wokuti

4.12.3.1 Omiti mbi ungurisiwa tjinene komaturiro wotjitamba noviunda omumbonde, omungondo, nomiseyasetu nu vi rira imbi mbya hapa okuyenena otjomuano wondjeverero kokutja okuti ku hape aku ha kururuka.

4.12.4 Oviŋenge vyomeva

4.12.4.1 Eṱunḓu arihe ri nomerizirira komasero wondjombo yomeva kokuungurisiwa i yovandu novinamuinyo vyao.

4.12.5 Ozonguŋe

4.12.5.1 Onganda aihe i nousemba okuteya omiti mbya kukuta noviungurisa otjozonguŋe.

4.12.6 Ousemba wokuyeva

4.12.6.1 Otja kombazu omundu auhe u nosemba okuyeva.

4.12.7 Omapiro wokuti

4.12.7.1 Pe tjeverwa tjinene momaakisiro womiriro kutja okuti aku ha pi.
4.12.7.2 Okuti tji maku pi ku undjirwa komundu auhe okurikwamba kozongondjero zokuzemisa omuriro.

4.13 Otjiṱo tjOvaryange

4.13.1 Omanyomokisiro wovaryange

4.13.1.1 Ovanatje ve hongwa okuza kotjiwondo tjouṱiṱi i yovanene vavo ongaro yombazu yokuyakura nokutenga omundu wosaneno ngamwa aihe.
4.13.1.2 Otjiyarisiro otjiwa ongaro ombwa yomaunguriro wakumwe ndja ri pokati kotjiwaṋa tjOvaherero nozohoze/ovarandise mba ri ovatenga okuhakaena ku na vo.
4.13.1.3 Ongaro ombwa ku novaryange nga mba opu i ri.

4.13.2 Ondjeverero yotuveze otuzere

4.13.2.1 Ondengero nomakengezero i undjirwa kovaryange (okuhina okurirunga poo okuṱuna kovizere) tji mave ryangere otuveze otuzere.

4.14 Ondjeverero komausemba wounongo

4.14.1 Ozongaro novitjitwa vyombazu vyotjiwaṋa tjOvaherero mbya hongwa kozonḓiṱona i yovanene momuano wokuserekarera pomazuko okuza kozondekurona nga kondekurona vi varwa otjuini wavo.

4.14.2 Omundu auhe u nouyara okuhandjaura ongaro ndji ma tjiwa mombazu.

4.14.3 Ouharupu womahandjauriro wounongo wombazu, ongaro, ovitjitwa vyomuhoko nomakuruhungi mondando yokuhonga nokukambura momuano wokupwika ku yandjewa.

4.14.4 Omerikutiro wakumwe pokati kovaungure woviungurisiwa vyokomake vyombazu nomauhonapare wombazu maku yandjewa oruvara kutja otupa atuyevari tu mune mo ombwiro.

4.14.5 Ondjeverero younongo, nozohako zombazu na vyarwe komarandisiro omavi

4.14.5.1 Ouhonapare wombazu u nondando okutwapo omikambo okuisira komirari vyoveta yehi okupenga omarandisiro wounongo nozohako zombazu momuano omuhasemba.

4.15 Ozongungu

4.15.1 Okuza koruveze orukuru Ovaherero aave paka ovandu vavo nokutwapo ombamba yotjiuru tjongombe otjombindi pomaendo wavo. Ongaro ndjo nga mba i ungura nga ku ndino kovandu kovanene mbe zera nao nangarire kutja ozongungu za uta okutungwa otja kouye wakandino.

The laws of the Maharero

Article 1: The Traditional Authority

1.1 Positions in the Traditional Authority

1.1.1 The King (*Ombara*)

1.1.1.1 For centuries, the Herero people have practised the dynasty model of leadership, whereby a King is appointed from the patrilinial clan (*oruzo*) in order of birth from among the direct descendants of the Royal House concerned.

1.1.1.2 The King is appointed after consultation with and consensus among the members of the Royal House and elders of the clan who are close to the Royal Family, and for the most part those who are knowledgeable on traditional leadership succession.

1.1.1.3 The King occupies the highest position in terms of the Traditional Authority leadership positions. He normally accedes to the position of Kinghood to succeed his predecessor 12 months upon the latter's death.

1.1.1.4 The coronation of the King is conducted in the following chronological sequence of events:

(a) Completion of the funeral rituals of the late King and the annulment of the holy fire.
(b) The execution of the deceased King's estate.
(c) Formal rekindling of the holy fire and coronation of its new curator.
(d) In the event that the curator of the holy fire waives his claim to the kingship, the way is cleared for another person of noble blood who is second in line to the throne.
(e) The coronation of the new king is conducted by a fellow king.

1.2 Ovaherero dynasties

1.2.1 The Royal House, the leaders, and the seat

(a) Otjikatjamuaha (the Royal House) – Maharero (the leader) – Okahandja (the seat).
(b) Otjivapa (the Royal House) – Zeraua (the leader) – Omaruru (the seat).
(c) Onguatjindu (the Royal House) – Kambazembi (the leader) – Otjozondjupa (the seat).
(d) Otjikaoko (the Royal House) – Mureti (the leader) – Otjipaue (the seat).
(e) Vita/Mbarunga (the Royal House) – Vita Thom (the leader) – Okaoko (the seat).

1.2.2 Senior Traditional Councillors and Traditional Councillors

1.2.2.1 Upon the coronation of the *Ombara*, the traditional community may decide to retain the entire leadership structure in place that served under the previous King and appoint replacements whenever vacancies occur as a result of death, retirement, resignation or dismissal, or the community may, subject to consensus among them, re-organise the leadership structure, effecting changes where necessary, or where a certain traditional leader resigns or retires for any reason, or even where such leaders are dismissed due to misconduct.

1.2.2.2 The main function of Senior Traditional Councillors is to assist the King in managing the overall affairs of the traditional community on a daily basis, although they may perform other duties as assigned by the King.

1.2.2.3 The core function of ordinary Traditional Councillors is to complement the role of Senior Traditional Councillors in the execution of their duties.

1.2.2.4 Traditional Councillors may execute any function assigned or delegated to them by the King through the Senior Traditional Councillors.

1.2.3 The Secretary

1.2.3.1 The Secretary is appointed by the King in consultation with the top leadership of the traditional community to serve as a liaison/coordinator between the community and other entities or institutions on issues pertaining to administration.

1.2.4 The Chairperson

1.2.4.1 The Chairperson is appointed by the leadership with the approval of the King.

1.2.4.2 His/her main function shall be to help the Secretary to schedule and facilitate the smooth running of meetings.

1.3 Organisations within the Traditional Authority

1.3.1 The Royal Family

1.3.1.1 The Royal Family consists of the King's uncles, aunts, brothers, sisters, cousins, nieces, nephews, wife (*Omuara*, or Queen) and children.

1.3.1.2 The principal function of the members of the Royal Family is to direct the process of determining the heir to the throne in the event of a reigning King's death, and to render moral support to the King in the performance of state matters and traditional rituals.

1.3.2 The Traditional Council

1.3.2.1 The Traditional Council is the highest administrative organ of the Traditional Authority.

1.3.2.2 The Traditional Council consists of the *Ombara*, Senior Traditional Councillors, Traditional Councillors, the Chairperson, the Secretary, and elder statesmen (who are elders in the community considered to be the spine of the community).

1.3.3 The Community Trust Fund

1.3.3.1 The Community Trust Fund, as an organ of the Traditional Authority, is tasked primarily with the key function of securing the sound management of the resources (wealth) on behalf of the community.

1.3.3.2 The Fund is administered by a Board of Trustees appointed by the Traditional Authority.

1.3.4 The Secretariat

1.3.4.1 The Secretariat renders technical advice on administrative or any other matter that might be referred to it by the Traditional Council for input.

1.3.5 The Traditional Flag structures

1.3.5.1 The various entities known as Traditional Flags consist of ranks based on military structures headed by Field Marshals.

1.3.5.2 These entities are prominent during annual traditional commemorations and at the funerals of high-ranking officials.

1.3.6 The Youth Wing

1.3.6.1 The structure of the Youth Wing offers young people a platform from which to obtain the necessary experience with regard to Ovaherero customary practices and be groomed for future leadership roles.

1.3.7 The judicial system

1.3.7.1 In terms of the Ovaherero judicial system, each district constitutes a Sub-Community Court for the administration of the rule of law in respect of the inhabitants of the district concerned.

1.3.7.2 The *Ombara* presides over the Community Court of Appeal, which is mandated to hear cases referred to it by the Sub-Community Courts for a final verdict.

1.4 Meetings

1.4.1 Meetings of the various traditional structures of leadership are held frequently, depending on the matters at hand.

1.5 The right to make and change laws

1.5.1 The right to make and change laws is vested in the Traditional Council.

1.5.2 The Traditional Council affirms a new or changed law if they are satisfied that the new law or the amendment of an existing law is required in the best interest of the traditional community concerned, and that a broad process of consultation took place and consensus was reached throughout the community.

Article 2: The Community Court

2.1 The Sub-Community Court comprises a Justice, two Assessors, the Secretary and the Messenger of the Court with Senior Traditional Councillors as supporting staff members.

2.2 The Community Court of Appeal comprises the *Ombara* of the Traditional Authority, two Senior Traditional Councillors, and additional members who act as support staff.

2.3 The Justice presides over the proceedings of the Community Court and exercises such power as accorded to him/her.

2.4 The Assessors are tasked with the responsibility of advising the Justice on the formulation of the verdict whenever such a need arises.

2.5 The Justice and Assessors of the Community Court are appointed, serve and are dismissed in terms of the Community Courts Act 2003 (No. 10 of 2003).

Article 3: Judicial Procedure

3.1 Complaint and accusation procedure

3.1.1 Any member of the community who feels his/her rights have been violated may lodge a complaint in writing with the Community Court to have his/her case heard.

3.1.2 Any member of the community may be accused of a crime.

3.1.3 The onus rests with the accused to prove his/her innocence.

3.1.4 The court may, upon finding the accused person liable to pay a fine, order the relatives of the accused to pay the fine on behalf of the accused if it has been established that the latter lacks the means to comply with the order.

3.1.5 On receiving the complaint, the Traditional Authority launches an immediate investigation into the matter to collect the necessary evidence from both parties to establish the merits of the case.

3.1.6 After the completion of the investigation the matter is referred to Senior Traditional Councillors to decide whether or not the case warrants a trial.

3.1.7 If the case is found to warrant a trial, the matter is then forwarded to the Community Court to set a trial date.

3.2 Appearing in court

3.2.1 The Community Court may issue oral or written warnings and traditional summonses that are forwarded by the Messenger of the Court to persons to appear in court. If it appears that evidence obtained from a victim or any witness is irrelevant, the court has the discretion to decide not to summons such a person.

3.2.2 In the event of the person refusing to appear in the Community Court, the Traditional Authority shall request the Magistrate to issue a warrant for the police to bring the accused to court. This is the only mechanism of submission to the jurisdiction of the court.

3.2.3 All persons related to the case, including the victim, the accused and any witnesses may appear in court.

3.2.4 The accused is entitled to request any person to represent him/her in court whom he/she feels will defend his/her best interest.

3.2.5 The Community Court does not have jurisdiction over rape cases.

3.2.6 In custody cases, the court may make use of the elders of the child's biological parents as support persons.

3.3 Dismissal, judgment and appeal

3.3.1 A case may be dismissed from the Community Court roll after a thorough trial has been conducted if there is a lack of evidence.

3.3.2 Judgment is pronounced orally by the Justice once the trial has been completed.

3.3.3 Written judgment is given within 7 (seven) days after judgment, and includes the reasons for the judgment with a summary of the facts of the case.

3.3.4 Any party to the case is entitled to the right to appeal to the Community Court of Appeal within 14 (fourteen) days of the judgment.

3.3.5 The complainant should submit written notice of appeal with the Clerk of the Community Court within the stipulated period of time (14 days).

3.3.6 When all means within the Traditional Authority have been exhausted, the complainant may lodge an appeal with the Magistrate's Court.

Article 4: Laws

4.1 Definitions

4.1.1 *Child* in this document means any person not yet 18 (eighteen) years of age and, as such, is regarded as a minor.

4.1.2 A Community Court shall have competence over all the people within the area of jurisdiction of the Maharero Traditional Authority.

4.1.3 *Area of jurisdiction* refers to the area or districts that are legally declared as areas under the jurisdiction of the Traditional Authority.

4.2 Grounds for exclusion from criminal jurisdiction

4.2.1 A person under the age of 18 (eighteen) years may be excluded from the proceedings of the Community Court on the grounds of being a minor.

4.2.2 A person may, if so concluded by Community Court officials, be excluded from prosecution on the grounds of being of poor mental health.

4.2.3 In the event of the Community Court establishing that a person is intoxicated, the said Court may postpone proceedings to allow such a person to regain his/her sobriety.

4.2.4 The Community Court may aquit an accused if the Court establishes that duress has been applied, and consequently such person will be freed from punishment.

4.2.5 If a crime has been addressed by a Magistrate's Court and it has convicted the accused, a Community Court has no right to address such a case.

4.2.6 If a crime has been addressed by a Magistrate's Court and it has acquitted the accused, a Community Court may address the case.

4.3 Criminal offences

4.3.1 Murder

4.3.1.1 *Murder* is defined as the crime of the killing of one person by another.
4.3.1.2 A Community Court is exempt from hearing murder cases due to the severity of the crime.
4.3.1.3 Cases of murder are referred to a Magistrate's Court.

4.3.2 Rape and sexual violence

4.3.2.1 *Rape and sexual violence* are defined as committing the crime of having sexual intercourse with a person without his/her consent or as forcing a person to have sexual intercourse against his/her will.
4.3.2.2 A Community Court is not qualified to prosecute cases of rape and sexual violence due to the severity of the crime.

4.3.3 Theft and robbery

4.3.3.1 *Theft* is defined as committing the crime of stealing property belonging to another.
4.3.3.2 Theft is prosecutable by the Community Court.
4.3.3.3 In the event of an accused being found guilty of theft, he/she is liable to compensate the complainant by way of double the items stolen, or in monetary terms, to pay an additional 50% (fifty percent) on top of the cash value of the stolen item.
4.3.3.4 *Robbery* is defined as committing the crime of stealing while simultaneously using force.
4.3.3.5 A Community Court is exempt from prosecuting an accused person charged with robbery due to the severity of the case.

4.3.4 Assault

4.3.4.1 *Assault* is defined as physically harming someone in such a way that the victim sustains injuries on his/her body.
4.3.4.2 Assault is regarded as a crime.
4.3.4.3 A Community Court is not qualified to preside over a case of assault due to the serious nature of the crime.

4.3.5 Harassment or intimidation

4.3.5.1 *Harassment* or *intimidation* is to threaten someone verbally or physically.
4.3.5.2 Any person who harasses or intimidates another is liable to prosecution.

4.3.5.3 A Community Court is exempt from prosecuting cases involving harassment or intimidation by alleged offenders due to the serious nature of these crimes.

4.3.6 Bribery

4.3.6.1 *Bribery* is defined as committing a crime by offering monetary value or any other form of compensation illegally to someone while expecting a favour in return.

4.3.6.2 A Community Court is not eligible to conduct hearings in bribery cases due to the serious nature of this crime.

4.3.7 Smuggling

4.3.7.1 *Smuggling* is the illegal import of banned substances or engaging in the sale of products without the authorisation of the relevant institutions.

4.3.7.2 A Community Court is not qualified to preside over persons accused of smuggling due to the serious nature of this crime.

4.3.8 Being in unauthorised possession of a weapon

4.3.8.1 It is regarded as a crime to be caught in possession of an unauthorised weapon.

4.3.8.2 A Community Court is not eligible to preside over cases of being in unauthorised possession of a weapon due to the serious nature of this crime.

4.3.9 Unlawful fencing

4.3.9.1 *Unlawful fencing* is defined as the act of engaging in the erection of a fence illegally on communal land.

4.3.9.2 A Community Court is eligible to hear cases dealing with illegal fencing.

4.3.9.3 If found guilty, the accused shall bear the financial cost incurred due to his/her non-compliance with an order of the court to remove the fence.

4.4 Inheritance

4.4.1 The estate of a deceased man is administered differently from that of a woman.

4.4.2 The estate of a deceased man

4.4.2.1 In the absence of a written will by the deceased, his younger brother is appointed executor of his estate.

4.4.2.2 If the deceased did not have a younger brother, the deceased's nephew is appointed as the executor.

4.4.2.3 The executor shall be tasked with the primary distribution of the deceased husband's estate to his widow and children, including those born outside the marriage.

4.4.2.4 The residue of the deceased husband's estate, whether it entails movable or immovable property, is distributed among his younger brothers, sisters and nephews.

4.4.2.5 The presence of traditional leaders is required throughout the proceedings as observers and to enquire as to whether or not all the beneficiaries in the estate are satisfied with the outcome.

4.4.2.6 The presence of the maternal and paternal relatives of the deceased is also required throughout the proceedings.

4.4.2.7 The widow is offered the option of being inherited by her late husband's younger brother or one of his nephews.

4.4.2.8 In the event that the widow declines the option referred to in subclause 4.4.2.7 above, she is returned home to her family of origin with all her property, including any property she may have inherited from her late husband.

4.4.3 The estate of a deceased woman

4.4.3.1 The estate of a deceased married woman, which includes her movable and immovable property, is placed under the care of her biological family immediately upon the completion of her burial.

4.4.3.2 The deceased's family, usually the father or an uncle, is appointed as the executor of her estate.

4.4.3.3 The primary beneficiaries in the estate are all the deceased's children.

4.4.3.4 The residue of the deceased woman's estate is distributed among her siblings and extended family.

4.4.3.5 The widower donates a cow to his late wife's parents to demonstrate that he had nothing to do with the death of his wife, and also to ask for a replacement wife from his bereft in laws.

4.5 Marriage

4.5.1 The process of proposing marriage is conducted over four stages:

(a) The first stage is when the families are introduced and become acquainted.

(b) The second stage is when the family of the groom-to-be visits the family of his intended bride as a token of their serious intent to complete the wedding process.

(c) The third stage is when the parties determine the bride price.

(d) The fourth stage is when the official wedding is held.

4.5.2 The bride price (*omatinjunino mozonda*) may vary from N$2 000 to N$10 000 (two thousand to ten thousand Namibia Dollars) plus 2 (two) head of cattle.

4.5.3 Ovaherero custom does not dictate the number of wives a man may have.

4.5.4 Since the official recognition of Traditional Authorities by the Namibian Government in 1998, such Authorities have been issuing customary marriage certificates at the couple's request.

4.5.5 Protection of widows

4.5.5.1 A widow is granted special protection by way of being entitled to inherit her husband's estate.
4.5.5.2 The younger brother or a nephew of the widow's late husband is accountable for the well-being and support of the widow.

4.5.6 Adultery

4.5.6.1 Adultery shall be outlawed.
4.5.6.2 Offenders may be liable to a fine.

4.5.7 Divorce

4.5.7.1 Divorce shall be outlawed, but anyone who wishes to divorce shall pay 6 (six) head of cattle to his/her spouse.

4.6 Children

4.6.1 Pregnancy

4.6.1.1 Pregnancy outside wedlock is a practice which is unacceptable in Ovaherero custom.
4.6.1.2 The offender can be charged and be fined one (1) cow or N$2 000 plus the maintenance costs of raising the child in question.

4.6.2 Custody of and responsibility for children

4.6.2.1 Both parents, regardless of their marital status, are equally responsible for their upbringing.
4.6.2.2 The child's extended family are also obliged to support him/her.
4.6.2.3 The primary responsibility for the care of an orphan lies with the surviving parent.
4.6.2.4 The secondary responsibility for an orphan lies with the child's grandparents or, in the absence of grandparents, his/her guardian, who is normally appointed from among members of the child's extended family.
4.6.2.5 Both parents are equally responsible for a child born outside marriage.
4.6.2.6 The father of a child born outside marriage is required to support him/her while the child lives with his/her mother.
4.6.2.7 The father of a child born outside marriage may obtain custody rights and adopt the child by donating 1 (one) head of cattle to the mother.

4.6.3 Schooling

4.6.3.1 The costs of a child's schooling are shared jointly by both its parents with the aid of the child's extended family.

4.7 Caring for the aged

4.7.1 The responsibility of providing food, shelter and services to an aged parent lies with his/her children and extended family.

4.8 Health

4.8.1 Traditional healers

4.8.1.1 Traditional healers and practitioners who perform circumcision on young boys are required to comply with standard basic health and hygiene practices.

4.8.2 HIV and AIDS

4.8.2.1 The prevention of HIV and AIDS has become a common daily theme at social gatherings by traditional leaders and elders alike to encourage young people to practise safe sex.

4.8.3 Alcohol and narcotics

4.8.3.1 The abuse of alcohol and narcotics is strongly discouraged as a measure to preserve acceptable traditional values and norms.

4.9 Gender matters

4.9.1 Men and women perform different roles and functions which are complementary to each other.

4.9.2 The elders in the community play an important role in promoting the interests and welfare of women.

4.9.3 When it comes to resolving disagreements in certain matters, such as inheritance and marital disputes, the patriarch, by virtue of his wisdom and the respect that he commands in the clan, naturally assumes the role of patron in respect of vulnerable parties, namely women.

4.10 Land

4.10.1 Ownership of communal land is vested in the state, with traditional leaders as custodians on behalf of the state.

4.10.2 Traditional leaders, in consultation with the village headmen, are responsible for the allocation of customary land rights to individual family households.

4.10.3 Trespassing on land is prohibited.

4.10.4 Any person who trespasses may be charged and fined accordingly.

4.10.5 Grazing rights are allocated by the village headmen after broad consultation with the inhabitants of the village concerned.

4.11 Livestock

4.11.1 Should a person lose his/her livestock, he/she depends on the goodwill and support of relatives and neighbours to establish another or alternative means of livelihood.

4.11.2 Farmers who transport livestock into or out of the communal area do so subject to veterinary authorisation in accordance with animal health regulations.

4.11.3 Owners of livestock are responsible for providing their animals with access to water and grazing and for complying with veterinary measures.

4.12 Environment

4.12.1 Mining

4.12.1.1 The allocation of mining rights in communal areas rests with the government through the Ministry of Mines and Energy.

4.12.1.2 Companies that obtain mining rights in communal areas are obliged to contribute financially to the local Community Trust Fund via donations.

4.12.2 Conservation of game

4.12.2.1 In order to conserve game, hunting is prohibited during the breeding season (spring); hunters are discouraged from hunting during the mating season.

4.12.3 Deforestation

4.12.3.1 In order to curb deforestation, only fully grown trees from the *Acacia reficiens*, *Acacia erioloba* and *Terminalia prunioides* species may be used for the construction of traditional homesteads.

4.12.4 Water issues

4.12.4.1 Every household is responsible for its own water supply for household and livestock use, such supply being derived by the digging of a waterhole.

4.12.5 Firewood

4.12.5.1 A household is limited to gathering only dry wood for firewood.

4.12.6 Hunting rights

4.12.6.1 All community members have the right to hunt.

4.12.7 Veld fires

4.12.7.1 Proper fire-lighting measures should be used when making a fire in the bush to prevent the outbreak of wildfires in the veld.

4.12.7.2 In the event of a veld fire, every member of the community is duty bound to render assistance in putting it out.

4.13 Tourism

4.13.1 Promotion of tourism

4.13.1.1 As has always been the tradition, parents should continue to teach their children to show common courtesy and respect to people from all walks of life.
4.13.1.2 The value of this is illustrated in the healthy relationships that existed between the Ovaherero and the early explorers.
4.13.1.3 A friendly atmosphere with tourists is still prevalent to date.

4.13.2 Protection of sacred places

4.13.2.1 Tourists, when visiting sacred places, are asked to pay respect and cautioned not to touch or interfere with sacred objects.

4.14 Intellectual property rights

4.14.1 The cultural practices and norms of the Ovaherero as narrated and taught around the fire to youngsters by their elders for successive generations shall be regarded as their intellectual property.
4.14.2 Every individual is freely allowed to practise any profession, thought or whatever craft in relation to his knowledge.
4.14.3 The voluntary sharing of traditional knowledge for teaching and recording purposes is highly recommended to promote and ensure the preservation of Herero history, and cultural norms and practices.
4.14.4 Economic partnerships between Traditional Authorities and community members who make traditional crafts are encouraged to the financial benefit of both parties.

4.14.5 Protection of traditional knowledge, symbols, etc. against commercial abuse

4.14.5.1 The Traditional Authority intends to introduce measures within the framework of the country's laws to curb commercial abuse of traditional knowledge and symbols.

4.15 Gravestones

4.15.1 The Ovaherero use of cattle horns as tombstones is still common among the elderly today, despite the erection of modern-day tombstones.

Certificate of consent to publish

Certificate of the consent to publish

UNIVERSITY OF NAMIBIA

FACULTY OF LAW

HUMAN RIGHTS AND DOCUMENTATION CENTRE

RE: CONSENT TO PUBLICATION

I, the undersigned, Chief of the MAHARERO Traditional Authority, hereby give consent to the Human Rights and Documentation Centre, to publish the following documents of the MAHARERO Traditional Authority:

1. The Customary Laws
2. The Community Profile
3. Picture of the Chief
4. Logo of the Traditional Authority

I acknowledge that the Human Rights and Documentation Centre will publish the laws in our indigenous language (OTJIHERERO), as well as the English language. I am familiar with the contents of the laws that will be published and further acknowledge that they were prepared by my traditional authority.

Signed on this 07 **day of** August **2012**

At Otjinene

pp [signature]

Chief

[signature]

For HRDC: Mr. A. Gairiseb

Otjikaoko Traditional Authority
Ouhonapare wOtjikaoko

The supreme leader of the Otjikaoko Traditional Authority is Chief[1] Paulus U Tjavara.
Date of designation: 30 August 1996

OTJIKAOKO TRADITIONAL AUTHORITY

KUNENE REGION

1 Traditional title in terms of section 11, Traditional Authorities Act, 2000 (No. 25 of 2000).

PROFILE[2]

Otjikaoko Royal House

The Otjikaoko Traditional Authority was established many years ago and is in line with Chapter 12, Article 102 of the Namibian Constitution. Today it is one of the recognised Traditional Authorities in an independent Namibia.

The cultural/historical background of Otjikaoko Traditional Community

Any person that is a member of the Royal Family or descendant of Otjikaoko can be crowned as Chief/King. S/he may come from the matrilineal line or the patrilineal line, as long as he/she is wanted by the Otjikaoko Traditional Community to be their chief.

Usually the traditional leaders of Otjikaoko are appointed but if there is a dispute then elections can be held to determine the successors. This is the right procedure in Otjikaoko Royal House.

The genealogy of the Otjikaoko Royal House leadership

Kaoko was the first traditional leader in Kaokoland; when he died he was succeeded by Tjavara and after Tjavara came:
Nambi
Ndjara
Kaupangua
Mureti
Rutjindo
Nguezeongo
Koujeko
Tjondjou
Mbumijazo
Muharukua and
Uziruapi Paulus Tjavara (who is the current Chief).

2 This profile was provided by the Otjikaoko Traditional Authority.

Oveta Yombazu Yotjiwaṋa tjOtjikaoko

Ozoveta zotjiwana tjombazu tjOtjikaoko

Inda onde ri ozoeta zombazu yotjiwaṋa tjOtjikaoko otja tji ze ungura moviombanguriro vyombazu mokati kotjiwaṋa, wina otja tji za ṱunwa okomiti yotjiwaṋa, aze yakurwa i youhonapare wombazu, nai kutwa i yotjiwaṋa pamwe nozondondo azehe zotjiwaṋa. Ozoveta nḓa za ungura mokati kotjiwaṋa koure wozombura ozengi, nu omatjangero wazo ya uta mo-1993 indu okomiti youṋepo 37 tji ya tjanga etjangwa ndi, noongarire kutja kombunda kwa tjitwa omaweziro ku ro. Ongwatero yomatjangero nga ya kwatwa i youyenda wOminista onguru yokehi yoveta nozombanguriro Adv. Vekuii Rukoro otjovihape vyombongarero yatji ya ri 19/09/1993 ndja ri mOpuwo pu pa ri Ominista yokehi ndji.

Ondengu yotjinamuinjo motjimariva nondando yokuzikamisa omasutiro motjimariva ku imba mbe hi na ovinamuinyo ri otja nai:

(a)	Ongombe	N$ 1 000.00
(b)	Ongombo	N$ 350.00
(c)	Onḓu	N$ 350.00
(d)	Okakambe	N$ 800.00
(e)	Okasino	N$ 600.00
(f)	Otjimori	N$ 800.00
(g)	Ohunguriva	N$ 50.00

Nu otjinamuinyo tjarwe tji tji ha tamuninwe mba otjombanguriro kehi yoveta ndji tja pewa ousemba okuyandja omberero ndji hi na okukapita ozondora esere (N$1 000.00).

1. Okuzepa

1.1 Omuṱi tje ri omukazendu poo omukazona omberero poo otjisuta ozongombe omirongo vine na ndano (45).

1.2 Nungwari omuṱi tje ri omurumendu poo omuzandu omberero poo otjisuta ozongombe omirongo vitatu na ndano (35).

1.3 Nungwari omuṱi tje ri ongwa tjiti kutja pe kare otjirwa poo ongwa tenge otjisuta – mape ya atji ṱikonaparisiwa tjandje mape tarewa nawa ongaro ndja kaenda ongondoroka nonḓiro, nu mape ya otjisuta atji ṱiṱiparisiwa. Motjiposa tjomukazendu otjisuta tji ri kombanda mena rokutja omukazendu u panduka.

2. Orutjero

Omukazendu tja tjerwa otjisuta poo omberero ozongombe omurongo (10) nga komirongo vivari (20). Omasa nomahihamisiro korutu oku maku tyerwa kutja omberero mai ṱeki pi.

2.1 Ozongombe tje ri omurongo (10) orondu orutjero tji ru ha kaendere pamwe Omasa omahihamisiro korutu.

2.2 Otjisuta poo omberero yozongombe okuza pomurongo na imwe (11) okuyenda kombanda orondu orutjero tji rwa kaenda pamwe nomahihamisiro korutu ngunda orutjero amaru kaenda poo kombunda yanao.

3. Okutona

3.1 Omatoneno tji ya tjiti kutja omundu ma kare notjito poo a twerwa, omberero poo otjisuta ozongombe hambondatu (8). Omurapotwa ingee ma sutu ozongombe hambondatu (8) noongarire kutja omihihamo ominene, wina nangarire kutja kape tikire ombin̮du nu omahihameno omamunikwa.

3.2 Omahihamisiro tji ye he ri omanene ondondo yomahihameno oku maku vihirwa kutja omunandjo ma sutu pu pe t̮a pi, kutja rumwe ongombe imwe (1) poo indano (5) poo ihambondatu (8) tjandje matji zu kongaro yomahihameno.

3.3 Wina ku tarewa nawa kutja oun̮e ngwa tenge, tje ri omuhihamwa omberero mape ya ai rire on̮dit̮i tjandje maku tarewa nawa kongaro yomatengero.

3.4 Omundu tja hihamisa omukwao warwe nu omuhihamwa a pandjara tjimwe tjovin̮epo mbi, tji pa raisiwa mape sutwa otja kehi mba:

3.4.1 Eho arihe (orumongo) = Ozongombe omurongo na ndatu (13)
3.4.2 Okurama = Ozongombe omurongo na ndatu (13)
3.4.3 Okuwoko = Ozongombe omurongo na ndatu (13).
3.4.4 Omun̮a auhe = Ozongombe omurongo na ndatu (13)
3.4.5 Eyuru arihe = Ozongombe omurongo na imwe (11)
3.4.6 Okutwi akuhe = Ozongombe omurongo na imwe (11)

Omundu tja pora omukwao okarupa kovin̮epo mbi ri kehi mba ma sutu otja tji paraisiwa kehi mba:

3.4.7 Omunwe (Katjimunene) = Ozongombe ndatu (3)
3.4.8 Omunwe (Katjiurike) = Ozongombe mbari (2)
3.4.9 Ominwe vyarwe = Ongombe imwe (1).
3.4.10 Okutembura eyuru = Ongombe imwe (1).
3.4.11 Okutembura okutwi = Ongombe imwe (1).

4. Ourunga wovinamuinyo

4.1 Tji pa vakwa ongombe imwe (1) otjisuta ozongombe hamboumwe (6), okuweza kongombe indji ndja vakwa oini et̮upa rayo, indu, tji i he ri po pe sutwa ongombe yarwe ndji yaruka pongombe ndji ndja vakwa tji ya t̮a poo tji ya randisiwa poo tji ya zenga.

4.2 Kape nakonatja kutja ongombe ndja vakwa iimwe (1) poo indatu (3) poo omurongo (10) otjisuta ozongombe hamboumwe mongombe aihe.

4.3 Oveta i isa po ongombe ndji yenda kouhonapare wombazu nu in̮da ozarwe ze enda komuvakerwa.

4.4 Otjivarero tjotjisuta tjahamboumwe tji ungura kovinamuinyo avihe kutja ongombo, okambihi, otjimori, ombinda noongarire okazera opuwo kutja ouini womuvakerwa.

4.5 Otjinamuinyo tjimwe tjinangara tja vakwa i yovandu ovengi omundu auhe ku ye omuni ma sutu ovinimuinyo hamboumwe (6). Epu oko ngwi okutja auhe wavo wa ri norupa motjitjitwa tjourunga wotjinamuinyo nu auhe wavo ma sokusuta ovinamuinyo hamboumwe (6).

5. Omanyoneno womiti otjovihenḓe vyokutunga orumbo poo oviunda na vyarwe

5.1 Omundu tja kamburwa ama randisa poo ama toora ovihenḓe okukaungurisa komakutiro wozonḓarata okuza morukondwa me tura okutwara korukondwa rwarwe otjisuta okuza pondora imwe (l) nga kundano (5)

5.2 Omundu tja twara ovihenḓe rukuru korukondwa rwarwe na kaungurisa kotjiṋa otjiwa, omberero ondora imwe (1) uriri.

5.3 Indu tja nyono, otjisuta tji ri kombanda yondora imwe (1).

5.4 Tja karandisa nondando yokuritumbisa, omberero okuza pozondora mbari (2) nga ku ndano (5).

5.5 Omundu tja zu korukondwa rwarwe na kanyona omiti korukondwa rwarwe, omberero okuza pozondora mbari (2) nga ku ine (4), indu tji vya ungurisiwa kotjiṋa otjisemba, nungwari tji vya randisiwa kokumuna mo otjiṋa, otjisuta ozondora ndano (5).

6. Omakondero poo omanyosiro womiti

6.1 Omundu tja kondo omuti okunikorako ovihape poo kehi yepu rarwe omberero ozongombe mbari (2) konyoneno yomuti.

6.2 Omundu tja nyosa omuti mena routji (wozonyutji) poo kehi yepu rarwe, omberero ozongombo poo ozonḓu ndatu (3) ozondume.

6.3 Omundu tja nyosa ehozu poo okuti omberero ongombe imwe (l) nga ku ine (4), amaku tarewa nawa kutja pa ri owina poo ya ri oumba porwawo uriri na wina kouparanga womapiro poo wonyonokero.

7. Okupora ovihape ngunda avi hi ya hora poo okukama omativa nge riwa ngunda aye hi ye kura

7.1 Okupora ovihape mbi hi ya hora omberero ongombo poo onḓu imwe (l).

7.2 Omundu worukondwa rwarwe tja pora ovihape hora morukondwa rwarwe omberero ongombe imwe (1) tje hi na ousemba wombazu worukondwa, kape nakonatja kutja vya hora poo indee.

7.3 Ihi wina matji ungura komativa nge riwa tjimuna omingu nouṱaraha nao.

8. Omurumendu tja vazewa poo tja kamburwa pomukazendu womukwao

8.1 Otjisuta ozongombe hamboumwe (6), nungwari ouhatoi u sokukoṋḓononwa nawa.

9. Okuyarurako otjiposa

9.1 Omundu tje hi na hange nOtjombanguriro tjOmbazu ho u na ousemba okuyenda ku tjarwe.

9.2 Omundu ngo wina ma yenene okuyenda kOtjombanguriro tjomagistrate nungwari ma sokupitira momirari mbi ri vyo.

10. Omukuramenepo woveta (ohahende) moviombanguriro vyombazu

10.1 Kape na ozohahende poo ovakuramenepo voveta mbu mave yandjerwa moviombanguriro vyombazu noongarire kutja kehi yonguṋḓeveta, ousemba womundu okukuramenwapo tji ma vanga nao.

10.2 Otjombanguriro tjombazu katji sasanekwa ku na ihi tjomagistrate.

11. Ovatjangerepo votjombanguriro tjombazu

11.1 Mape kara otja koveta yotjOmbanguriro tjOmbazu yombura 2003, (oveta onomora l0 yombura 2003).

12. Omasutiro wouṋepo watjOmbanguriro

12.1 Mape sutwa otja koveta yatjOmbanguriro tjOmbazu yombura 2003, (onomora, l0 yo-2003).

13. Omberero yokorutu

13.1 Omberero yokorutu morukapitaveze aai ungurisiwa moviombanguriro vyombazu yotjiwaṋa hi nu aai ungura nawa, nu nai kai ungura rukwao mena rokutja onguṋḓeveta yetu ya tjaera omberero yokorutu.

14. Omaṱa

Omundu tja ṱu omuano wombazu womahaṋeno weṱa re mau kongorerwa.

14.1 Omundu ngwa hiti eṱa poo omundu ngwa yaruka moruveze romuṱi ma rumata avihe nga kourizirira, poo nga koviungura mbyaavi sokuungurwa i yomuṱi.

14.2 Omundu ngo ma kambura ourizirira wokutumba imba mbaave u poo mbaave tumbwa i yomuṱi. Mape hee kutja ourizirira auhe mbwa ri nomuṱi mau wire momake womuhite. Avehe mbaave u kehi yomuṱi mave sokumuna omuhite momuhingo mbaave munu omuṱi.

14.3 Kohapo omuhite omunda woina erumbi povakwao moruteto rongwatero.

15. Orukupo rwombazu

Ohoromende mai ningirwa okuvara orukupo rwombazu mena rokutja:

15.1 Orukupo ndwi ru na ousemba wovanene vovakupasane.

15.2 Mombazu omurumendu u na ousema okukupa ovakazendu mbe ri kombanda yaumwe ngaa komurongo.

15.3 Kombanda yanao ohoromende komurungu mai ningirwa okuvara ovanatje mba kwaterwa pendje yorukupo otjovanatje vaihe tjingee tjimuna ovakwao imba ovaina ngwa kupwa (ve sokuvarwa pu pe ṱa). Indji ondji ri oveta yombazu yOtjiherero orondu omuatje tja kwaterwa pehi poo pendje norukupo u yandjerwa ongombe kutja ma rire owaihe kotjiveta.

15.4 Omuatje ke na ousemba okuripahera omukazendu poo omurumendu ku ye omuni. Omuatje tji ma vanga omukazendu u sokupitira movanene ve okumuningirira omukazendu nu wina ombe na ousemba okuyandjera kutja omuatje we poo wavo ma kupe poo makupwe. Kape nakonatja kutja ngu ma vanga okukupa u ṱa pi poo u na ozombura ngapi, ousemba wokuripahera omukazendu ke na wo, orondu eye tjingee u varwa otjomuatje kombazu, mu nao tji ma vanga okukupa u sokupitira movanene ve.

15.5 Otja kombazu omurumendu u yandjerwa poo u nousemba okukara nombarise poo ozombarise ngunda a kupa. Wina u na ousemba okuraera omukazendu we kutja ndino ma karara kwarwe.

16. Ousemba womukazendu otja kombazu

16.1 Oserekaze tji i tumbwa navi i yomurumendu we, i na ousemba wokurapota ongaro ndji kovanene womurumendu we poo komundu auhe omuhoko womurumendu we. Okuza mbo tji sewa ku imba ku kwa rapotwa ouzeu okuisana omuzandu wavo nokumuronga kutja a ha yaruka po rukwao.

16.2 Omukazendu wina u na ousemba pu nomurumendu we okutya avihe mbya tjama nomananeno weṱunḓu poo nonganda yavo. Omurumendu tji ma vanga okukupa omukazendu poo ovakazendu varwe u sokutjivisa omukazendu we. Ihi matji hee kutja omukazendu poo ovakazendu ve sokuṱika omurumendu we (wavo) pamwe novanene womurumendu we (wavo) indu tji ma kakupa omukazendu ingwi omuweziwa.

16.3 Tjinangara omukazendu ke na kuvanga kutja omurumendu we ma kupe u sokuyandja omapu omasemba komurumendu we. Omapu nga ye sokurira omakahu nu nga zikamena kouatjiri. Mongaro ndji omurumendu ke na okukupa poo ke na okuyandjerwa okukupa omukazendu warwe. Nu indu tji pa munika kutja kape na omapu omasemba nga ri po esupa porwaro, omurumendu ma kaenda komurungu norukupo rwe.

16.4 Ovakazendu imba ovambanda ve wa kehi ya ingwi omunene (omutenga).

16.5 Omurumendu tja tye okuyarura omukazendu kovanene ve ma tjiti nao, nu omurumendu ngwa pakura omukazendu kutja okehi yomapu nga sana pi ke na usemba wokupura poo okukotora ongombe yorutombe ndja yandjere indu tja kupa. Kape na omundu ngu na ousemba wokupakura omuatje we omukwatwa.

16.6 Ovanatje womukazendu ngwa kupwa ve ri kehi yousemba womurumendu. Okutja omurumendu ka sokuyarura ovanatje mba kovanene vomukazendu we.

16.7 Okutuka omukazendu womundu pe sutwa ozongombe omurongo (10). Okutja omukazendu ngwi nambano wa rire owe.

17. Omaturiro

17.1 Omundu ngunda e hi ya tjinda okuza poruveze rumwe okuyenda koruveze rwarwe u sokupewa ousemba i yomunane wombazu worukondwa ku ma i ngunda e hi ya tjinda.

17.2 Indu tje ha perwe ousemba kutja okehi yomapu nga sana pi ka sokutjinda.

17.3 Indu tja kamunika a tjindi nokuhina ousemba ma rambwa nokuhina maombero. Tja rambwa nu tji ma paṋda poo tji ma toora ongono okutjinda ma pewa omberero.

17.4 Omundu tji ma vanga okutjinda poruveze okuyenda koruveze morukondwa tjingero ma tjivisa ovature ovakwao ku ma i na wina imba pu ma zu.

17.5 Indu tje ha tjivisire ovakwao imba ku ma i ma rambwa okuyaruka ka za, tji ma paṋda ma pewa omberero.

17.6 Indu omuture tja turisa omundu okuza korukondwa rwarwe nokuhina ousemba womunane wombazu ma pewa omberero.

18. Ovaryange

18.1 Ovaryange mba za komahi warwe mbe yekuryanga mOkaoko tji va sutu otjitjamurongo, okutja otjimariva ho tji sokuungurisiwa poo okupwikwa mOkaoko.

19. Ondjeverero yOkuti

19.1 Ovanane vombazu novaungure vondjeverero yokuti avehe pamwe ve sokukara nomerizirira wondjeverero nomaungurisiro omazikame wozomburo zokuti nozondendera kutja vi pwire otjiwa̭na tji tja tura mbo.

19.2 Pomayuva wombazu nga zikama, povitjitwa vyombazu na pozombongarero poo pomaworonganeno wotjiwa̭na omanaṋdengu pe sokuyandjewa ombatero okuza kozondjeverero zokuti okupitira mOuhonapare wOmbazu.

19.3 Ovaungure vondjeverero kave sokuyandja ousemba womayevero kovandu nokuhina okupitira momunane wombazu worukondwa ndwo. Omunane wombazu wina ka sokuyeva nokuhina ousemba wovaungure vondjeverero yokuti.

The laws of the Otjikaoko

Customary laws of the Otjikaoko Traditional Authority

These are the customary laws as applicable in the traditional community of the Otjikaoko Traditional Authority as put forth by the community's committee, approved by the Traditional Authority and adopted by the community including all leadership structures. These laws have existed for many years, and the writing of these laws started in 1993 when the committee of 37 members wrote this document. The birth of this document was the consequence of a visit by the then deputy Minister of Justice, Advocate Vekuii Rukoro during a meeting on the 19th March 1993 at Opuwo.

Fines are usually paid in livestock. Traditional prices for paying fines for those who do not have livestock are as follows:

(a)	Cattle	N$ 1 000.00
(b)	Goat	N$ 350.00
(c)	Sheep	N$ 350.00
(d)	Horse	N$ 800.00
(e)	Donkey	N$ 600.00
(f)	Mule	N$ 800.00
(g)	Chicken	N$ 50.00

The fine for any other animal which is not mentioned here shall not exceed N$1 000.00.

1. Murder

1.1 If the victim is female the fine or compensation is 45 (forty-five) head of cattle.

1.2 If the victim is male, the fine is 35 (thirty-five) head of cattle.

1.3 If there was provocation on the part of the victim the fine will be determined in accordance with the circumstances surrounding the case and may be reduced. In the case of a female, the fine is higher because she bears children.

2. Rape

In the case where a female is raped the fine or compensation will be from 10 (ten) head of cattle to 20 (twenty). Harm caused and the extent of force used is regarded as a very important element in considering the punishment to be imposed on the perpetrator.

2.1 The fine of 10 (ten) head of cattle is imposed where the rape was not accompanied by force or infliction of any bodily harm or pain.

2.2 The fine of 11 (eleven) head of cattle is when harm was caused to the victim in the course of the act or after the act.

3. Assault

3.1 In the case where as a result of the assault the victim sustains any wound or bleeding, or is hit by any harmful object or stabbed, the fine or compensation is 8 (eight) head of cattle. The accused will still pay 8 (eight) head of cattle if harm caused is serious even if there is no bleeding, but harm is obvious.

3.2 If the assault is not serious the degree of harm done to the victim will determine whether the guilty person will pay only 1 (one) head or 5 (five) head of cattle, or even 8 (eight) head of cattle, as the case may be.

3.3 If the victim had provoked the accused, the punishment may be reduced.

3.4 If a person through assault causes harm to another person, and as a result the victim loses one of his/her body parts, the punishments will be as indicated below:

3.4.1 Whole eye: The fine shall be 13 (thirteen) head of cattle.
3.4.2 Leg: The fine shall be 13 (thirteen) head of cattle.
3.4.3 Arm: The fine shall be 13 (thirteen) head of cattle.
3.4.4 Whole lip: The fine shall be 13 (thirteen) head of cattle.
3.4.5 Whole nose: The fine shall be 11 (eleven) head of cattle.
3.4.6 Whole ear: The fine shall be 11 (eleven) head of cattle.

If a person removes any portion from the following human body parts, the fine shall be as follows:

3.4.7 Finger (thumb): The fine shall be 3 (three) head of cattle.
3.4.8 Middle finger: The fine shall be 2 (two) head of cattle.
3.4.9 Other fingers: The fine shall be 1 (one) head of cattle.
3.4.10 Nose/Part of nose: The fine shall be 1 (one) head of cattle.
3.4.11 Part of ear: The fine shall be 1 (one) head of cattle.

4. Stock theft

4.1 For stealing 1 (one) head of cattle, the fine is 6 (six) head of cattle and, in addition, to restore the stolen animal to the owner; if it is not available, another one will be required to replace it.

4.2 Whether it is 1 (one), or 3 (three) or 10 (ten), for each stolen cow, the fine is six head of cattle. In all cases the guilty person is required to restore the number of stock stolen, or alternatively, to replace them should they have already been slaughtered or disappeared.

4.3 According to the law, one of the animals fined goes to the Traditional Authority while the rest go to the owner of the stolen property.

4.4 The number of 6 (six) stock to be paid applies to all kinds of stolen stock, be it a goat, a cat, sheep, mule, pig, or even a bird; as long as it is the property of the victim of the theft.

4.5 Even if it is just 1 (one) animal stolen, by more than one person, each guilty individual shall be liable to pay the fine of 6 (six) animals. The rationale is that every one of the persons involved has committed an act of theft of the animal and thus each one must pay the fine of 6 (six) animals.

5. Destruction of trees for stakes or posts to be used, for example, as fencing and other uses

5.1 If any person is caught selling or taking stakes or posts used for fencing from the region in which that person resides to another region, the fine will be from one dollar (N$1) per stake to five dollars (N$5).

5.1 Where the person has already taken such stakes to another region and has used them for something good, the fine is one dollar (N$1).

5.2 But if it is a mere waste then the fine is above one dollar (N$1).

5.3 If the person has sold the materials to enrich himself, then the fine is from two dollars (N$2) to five dollars (N$5).

5.4 If a person from another region destroys trees in the region the fine is from two dollars (N$2) to four dollars (N$4) if the material was used for something good, but if it was sold for gain it will be five dollars (N$5).

6. Chopping or burning trees

6.1 If a person chops down a tree to pick fruit from that tree or for any other reason, the fine is 2 (two) head of cattle for the destruction of the tree.

6.2 If a person burns down a tree to collect honey (from a bees' nest) or for any other reason, the fine is three (3) goats or sheep (ram/*kapater*).

6.3 If a person causes grass to burn or sets a veld fire, the fine is from 1 (one) head of cattle to 4 (four) head of cattle, having regard to the facts such as whether it was deliberately caused or by accident, and the extent of damage or destruction.

7. Picking fruit not yet ripe and squeezing immature edible worms

7.1 For picking fruit not yet ripe the fine is 1 (one) goat, or 1 (one) sheep.

7.2 But if a person of one region picks such fruits from another region without permission from the traditional leaders of that region, the fine shall be 1 (one) head of cattle, whether such fruits are ripe or not.

7.3 The same penalties apply in the case of edible worms.

8. Sexual intercourse with another man's wife

8.1 If a man is found having sexual intercourse with another man's wife, the fine is 6 (six) head of cattle; any evidence against an accused should be closely scrutinised.

9. Appeal

9.1 If a person is not happy with a particular Community Court judgment, he/she is at liberty to go to another Community Court.

9.2 That person may even go up to a Magistrate's Court, but through appropriate channels.

10. Legal representation in Community Courts

10.1 No lawyers or legal representatives will be allowed in Community Courts, even though it is the constitutional right of a person to be represented by a lawyer if it is his/her choice.

10. 2 Traditional Courts are not comparable to Magistrate's Courts.

11. Clerks of the Community Courts

11.1 The staff of the court shall be in accordance with the Community Courts' Act, 2003 (No.10 of 2003).

12. Remuneration of members of the Community Court

12.1 The Community Courts' Act, 2003 (No. 10 of 2003) shall apply.

13. Corporal punishment

13.1 This kind of punishment was used in our courts; it worked well, but is no longer applicable in our Community Courts, due to the provisions of the Constitution of Namibia, which prohibits corporal punishment.

14. Inheritance

When a person dies, then the traditional way of distributing the estate will follow.

14.1 The person who inherits (more correctly, the successor to the estate) is expected to inherit the entire estate, including the obligations or works that should have been done by the deceased.

14.2 This person assumes responsibility for the dependants of the deceased as well. This means that all the deceased's responsibilities are in his/her hands. Dependants must see the inheritor and have regard for him in the same way they used to see and have regard for the deceased.

14.3 Usually the person who inherits will be from the maternal side of the deceased and the most senior.

15. Customary marriages

The government is being requested to recognise customary marriage because:

15.1 Such unions involve the exercise of their right by the parents of both parties.

15.2 In traditional unions, the man can take more than one wife - up to ten and even more.

15.3 The government therefore is requested further to recognise children born out of wedlock as children of that person in the same way as the children of his own legally married wife. This is the Otjiherero tradition because a child born out of wedlock is provided for by way of cattle to legally become a child of this father.

15.4 Such young person has no right to find a wife or a husband on their own. The young person must go through the parents who will go and ask on behalf of the young person. The parents are the ones with the authority to allow him or her to marry; in fact, whatever the age of the person, traditionally he/she is not allowed to go and find a wife on their own because in that respect he/she is regarded as a child and should he/she want to get married, he/she must go through his/her elders.

15.5 According to our custom, a man has the right to have girlfriends whilst married. He also has the right to tell his wife that he will spend the night elsewhere.

16. Traditional rights of a woman

16.1 If a wife is subject to ill-treatment by her husband she may report this to the parents of her husband, or to any of the husband's family. It is then left to them after receiving the complaint to call on their son (the husband) and tell him not to do that again.

16.2 The wife also has the right together with her husband to decide everything related to the management of their household. Thus, if the husband intends to marry another wife, or wives, as the case may be, he must inform his wife, since his first wife, or wives as the case may be, must accompany her/their husband to fetch the additional wife together with the parents of the husband.

16.3 If the first wife/wives is/are against it, or will not allow her/their husband to marry another woman, she/they must give convincing reasons for opposing the marriage. The reason for opposing must be based on clear facts and real grounds. In that case the man will not be able or allowed to marry another woman. But if it is found that the first wife is merely being jealous, the man can proceed and get married.

16.4 The subsequent wife/wives is/are subordinate to the first wife.

16.5 Should the husband decide to send his wife back by way of divorcing her, no matter what the reasons, then he takes back to the parents of his wife the cow or any head of cattle he gave as part of the dowry at the time of marriage.

16.6 Children of the married couple are under the authority of the husband. The father shall not hand over his own children to his parents-in-law (parents of his wife).

16.7 If a married woman is taken by another man before she is formally divorced from her husband, according to tradition that man will have to give her husband 10 (ten) head of cattle. It is only after that, that this man can keep the married woman as his wife.

17. Settlement

17.1 Before a person moves from one ward to settle in another ward, that person must obtain permission from the traditional leader of that ward.

17.2 If permission is refused for whatever reason, then that person will not be able to move.

17.3 If that person decides to settle in the other region without permission, that person shall be expelled. But if a person refuses to move or delays moving back, that person can be punished.

17.4 If a person decides to move from one area to another, within the same ward, that person must inform the neighbours.

17.5 If that person ignores the neighbours he/she can be told to move away from the area. If the person remains stubborn, appropriate punishment will be imposed.

17.6 If a person in a ward allows a person from another ward to settle in the ward without the permission of the traditional leader, that person will be punished.

18. Tourists

18.1 If tourists from other countries who visit Kaokoland happen to pay a levy during their visit, then that money should be invested in Kaokoland.

19. Nature conservation

19.1 Traditional leaders and officials from Nature Conservation should have joint responsibility for nature conservation and sustainable utilisation for the benefit of the traditional community.

19.2 Traditionally recognised days, cultural events, and any other important community meetings should get assistance from conservancies through the Traditional Authority.

19.3 Officials of Nature Conservation should not be allowed to give permits to people to hunt, even during the hunting season without the knowledge of the traditional leader of the particular region. The leader of the residents' region should also not be able to hunt without permission from Nature Conservation.

Certificate of consent to publish

Certificate of the consent to publish

UNIVERSITY OF NAMIBIA

FACULTY OF LAW

HUMAN RIGHTS AND DOCUMENTATION CENTRE

RE: CONSENT TO PUBLICATION

I, the undersigned, Chief of the OTJIKAOKO Traditional Authority, hereby give consent to the Human Rights and Documentation Centre, to publish the following documents of the OTJIKAOKO Traditional Authority:

1. The Customary Laws
2. The Community Profile
3. Picture of the Chief
4. Logo of the Traditional Authority

I acknowledge that the Human Rights and Documentation Centre will publish the laws in our indigenous language (OTJIHERERO), as well as the English language. I am familiar with the contents of the laws that will be published and further acknowledge that they were prepared by my traditional authority.

Signed on this 15th **day of** June **2011**

At Opuwo

p. Tjavara

Chief

For HRDC: Mr. A. Gainseb

OTJIKAOKO
KUNENE REGION
15 JUN 2011
P.O. Box 271, OPUWO
TEL: 065-273107
TRADITIONAL AUTHORITY

Vita Royal House
Ondjuwo Youhonapare wa Vita

The supreme leader of the Vita Traditional Authority is
Ombara[1] Tjimbuare Thom.
Date of designation: 30 July 2011

1 Traditional title in terms of section 11, Traditional Authorities Act, 2000 (No. 25 of 2000).

PROFILE[2]

1. Name of the Traditional Authority

Vita Royal House

2. Name of the Supreme Leader

Chief/*Ombara* Tjimbuare Thom

3. Names of the previous leaders

Chief Vita Harunga Oorlog Thom
Chief Kazonguiṋdi Johannes Thom
Chief Kapuka John Thom

4. Rules of Succession

Succession is determined by the patrilineal line, the blood line from the father's side.

5. Traditional Title

Ombara/King/Chief

6. Location of the Traditional Office

Opuwo

7. Composition of Chief's Council

7.1 The Chief's Council is composed of the Chief, Senior Councillors, Traditional Councillors and the Secretary.

7.2 Senior Traditional Councillors are:
- (a) Justus Mutindi Muteze
- (b) Olifant Muhata Kapi
- (c) Mika Kozondarata Muhenje
- (d) Mathew Hijazohona Tjisuta
- (e) Titus Jahena Muhenje
- (f) Vacant Post

7.3 Traditional Councillors are:
- (a) David Humu
- (b) Joseph Kangombe
- (c) Karungoojo Ruiter
- (d) Mburumba Muhenje
- (e) Tjiuenge Tjambiru
- (f) Tjombamba Tjijahura

2 This profile was provided by the Vita Thom Royal House Traditional Authority.

7.4 The Secretary is Mr. Ben Ukondjisa Kapi.

8. Language Spoken

Otjiherero

9. Districts

Division of traditional territory into 25 districts:

9.1 Kaoko-tavi - David Humu
9.2 Okorosave - Godlieb Ndjai
9.3 Otjikondavirongo - Hijazondu Kuvandara
9.4 Ongango - Sakey Musaso
9.5 Otjikukutu - Kaenda Herunga
9.6 Warmquelle - Joseph Kangombe
9.7 Otjapi-tjapi - Justus Mutindi Muteze
9.8 Oruvandjei South - Hiandekete Kandjii
9.9 Ombombo - David Kavetu
9.10 Otjokavare - Goliath Tjaveondja
9.11 Otjindjerese - Itandua Mupia
9.12 Okatutura - Jason Hipandulua
9.13 Ombazu - Mburumba Muhenje
9.14 Oruhona - Karungoojo Ruiter
9.15 Ekoto West - Mathew Tjisuta
9.16 Ehomba - Mupolise Van der Merwe
9.17 Ondoto - Mundjavara Ngombe
9.18 Otjijandjasemo - Suse Thom
9.19 Etengwa - Tjiuenge Tjambiru
9.20 Ohamaremba - Jatunja Tjiposa
9.21 Ekarandjiuo - Kandume Hevita
9.22 Omuhonga - Mbunguha Hembinda
9.23 Oukongo - Kaondeka Tjerije
9.24 Ombaka - Uaripuje Tjiumbua
9.25 Otjondeka - Tjombamba Tjijahura

10. Headed by *Otukondua* (districts/villages)

Districts/villages:		**Subordinate Courts:**
10.1	Opuwo	Opuwo
10.2	Okangwati	Okangwati
10.3	Ohandungu	Ohandungu
10.4	Kaoko-tavi	Kaoko-tavi
10.5	Ongango	Ongango
10.6	Otjapi-tjapi	Otjapi-tjapi

10.7	Warmquelle	Warmquelle
10.8	Oruvandjai	Oruvandjai
10.9	Ombombo	Ombombo
10.10	Otjokavare	Otjokavare
10.11	Otjondeka	Otjondeka
10.12	Omuhoro	Omuhoro
10.13	Ehomba	Ehomba
10.14	Okorosave	Okorosave
10.15	Oukongo	Oukongo
10.16	Etengwa	Etengwa
10.17	Oruseu	Oruseu
10.18	Otjikukutu	Otjikukutu
10.19	Oruhona	Oruhona
10.20	Ombazu	Ombazu
10.21	Otjijandjasemo	Otjijandjasemo
10.22	Okatutura	Okatutura
10.23	Ekarandjiuo	Ekarandjiuo
10.24	Okapara	Okapara
10.25	Omuangete	Omuangete
10.26	Otjindjerese	Otjindjerese
10.27	Ondoto	Ondoto
10.28	Otjivize	Otjivize
10.29	Ombaka	Ombaka
10.30	Ovijere	Ovijere

Ongundoeveta yo Ndjiwo Youhona waVita[1]

1 Omayarisiro: Omatjangwa womazeva waVita nga ya tjangwa i otjimbumba tjoun̮epo wombazu morukondwa ndaaru tjiukwa otjOkaoko, nai Okunene komanene, pamwe nombatero yOmutengwa Ben Ukondjisa Kapi, Omutengwa Hiruke Uerikambura Tjiuru Tjipepa, ovanane vombazu na wina otjiwan̮a atjihe.

OMAPU OVIURU NGERI MOVETA

EMBO EHONGONEKWA ROTJIKORO

Ekondwa 1: Ondjuwo yOuhona waVita

Orupa 1	Omazikamisiro wOndjiwo yOuhona wa Vita, no matjiukiro wayo neha rayo romerinaneno.
Orupa 2	Ozohako zOmbazu
Orupa 3	Omaraka (rokotjiveta norotjiwaṋa)

Ekondwa 2: Ouhona (omize)

Orupa 4	Ongaro yo meriyamekero (nomitjazi mbya kutwa ku yo)
Orupa 5	Ondjeverero yOndjuwo yOuhona

Ekondwa 3: Ombara yOndjuwo yOuhona

Orupa 6	Omirari vyomapingeneno mOtjirata tjOmbara
Orupa 7	Otjiuru tjOuhonapare nouṋepo wOndjuwo yOvanane vOmbazu
Orupa 8	Oruveze romakarero mounane
Orupa 9	Omayanisiro nomazeuparisiro
Orupa 10	Oviungura, omasa, omaunguriro
Orupa 11	Omeritjururiro omakwizikwa
Orupa 12	Omasutiro (Omeritjururiro omakwizikwa)
Orupa 13	Omapingeneno mounane

Ekondwa 4: Otjirata tjOmbazu

Orupa 14	Omurya wotjiṱo tjounane
Orupa 15	Oviungura, omasa, omaunguriro
Orupa 16	Omaurikiro wOzorata nOzorata Oviuru noviungura vyazo
Orupa 17	Oruyano nomayanisiro wOzorata
Orupa 18	Omaraisiro wokuhina ngamburiro
Orupa 19	Omutjangerepo wOtjirata nOmberoo

Ekondwa 5: Ondjuwo yOzorata zOmbazu

Orupa 20	Ondjuwo yOuhona, Ombara noruhindo rwayo
Orupa 21	Omasa wOmbazu
Orupa 22	Omatjaerero wouṋepo okuhina kukara norupa
Orupa 23	Omaisiremo womovihavero
Orupa 24	Omuhaamise nOmutjangerepo
Orupa 25	Omazikamisiro
Orupa 26	Otjivarero otjihepwa momahaameno

EMBO ROTJIKORO

Otja komeriyakuriro nomazikameno wOndjuwo yOuhonaOtja komayakuriro wo manyanyauriro wovirumatwa nondjuwo yOuhona i yohuurire;

Otja kombazu, ovirangera vyOmbazu, ovitjitwa vyOmbazu, ongamburiro, onḓengu nomiano vyokuhupa mbya nyanyaurwa i yomananeno womasa wohuurire;

Amape yakurwa kokutja okutungurura nokuhanganisa ozondekurona mOndjuwo yOuhona waVita otjotjiungura otjinene tji tja kuramena Ondjuwo yOuhona; Amape yakurwa onyonokero ndje ya kOndjuwo yOuhona nongamburiro yokutja oruyaveze ru ri momake wetu;

Amape yakurwa kutja otjimbi no urizemburuka wohuurire u norukoka ndu ri poruhaera;

Amape yakurwa kutja eṱe Ondjuwo yOuhona nozondekurona zEserewondo omirongo vivari na rimwe twa tya nombango ondwe okuyakura Oveta yOmbazu yOndjuwo yOuhona, eṱe oveni, ovanatje vovanatje vetu okukwizika onḓikameno yomasa wOndjuwo yOuhona;

Ombango ondwe okutwara komurungu Ondjuwo yOuhona meho rouyara nomaṱiziro wotjirumatwa tjetu; matu zeri okuwanisa ozondekurona zOndjuwo yOuhona wa Vita kombwiro yOndjuwo yOuhona ndji; orondu owo ombu ri outumbe/Ovirumatwa vyomasa vyOndjuwo yOuhona.

Mu nao eṱe ozondekurona zOndjuwo yOuhona wa Vita matu itavere natu yakura Oveta yOmbazu otjOngunḓeveta yOndjuwo yOuhona wetu.

Ekondwa 1. Ondjuwo yOuhona wa Vita

Orupa 1: Omazikamisiro wOndjuwo yOuhona wa Vita, nomatjiukiro wayo neha rayo romerinaneno

1.1 Ondjuwo yOuhona ya zikama rukuru omaserewondo ndakapita otja kEkondwa rOveta 12, Otjiartikeli 102 Onomora 5 yOngunḓ̭eveta ya Namibia nu wina iimwe yomauhonapare wombazu nga varwa otja kOveta yOndjuwo Ondye yOzoveta.

1.2 Omasa ayehe maye kara nomunane wouhona mbwi, okutja omOmbara nungwari kamOzongenerara. Ozongenerara maze u kehi yOmbara otja kozondondo nomirari.

1.3 Otutu ozongunḓ̭e mOndjuwo yOuhona otwo hwi: Ondjuwo yOuhona, Ouhonapare, noviombanguriro vyombazu.

1.4 Eha romerinaneno wouhonapare mbwi orukondwa rwa Kunene aruhe komamuho warwo nokomanene warwo ominda aviyevari vyomukoka omuserandu na apehe mOrepabirika ya Namibia pu pe na ozondekurona zOndjuwo yOuhona wa Vita.

1.5 Opuwo otji tji ri otjihuro tjOmberoo onene yOndjuwo yOuhona wa Vita posi ya Otjijandjasemo oomaturiro wOndjuwo yOuhona.

Orupa 2: Ozohako zOmbazu

2.1 Ozohako zOmbazu zOndjuwo yOuhona wa Vita ozo nḓ̭a:
- (a) Ongeyama
- (b) Outa nozoheo noviku
- (c) Eyuva
- (d) Ondjembo
- (e) Enga

Orupa 3: Omaraka

3.1 Omaraka wokOtjiveta owonga:
- (a) Otjiherero
- (b) Otjiingirisa

Ekondwa 2. Ouhona (omize)

Orupa 4: Ombepo yokurijameka

4.1 Ondjuwo yOuhona: Otjiṋ̭a otjinahepero okutjiwa kokutja ovananwa wOndjuwo yOuhona mbwi va handjauka mOnamibia aihe, posi ya Ondjuwo yOuhona wa Vita tjinene i ri mOrukondwa rwa Kunene kOmamuho nOmanene minda avijevari vyomukoka omuserandu.

Orupa 5: Ondjeverero yOndjuwo yOuhona

5.1 Ondjuwo yOuhona ya zikama koure wozombura ozengi mu nao omatjiverero wOndjuwo yOuhona omerizirira wOuhona mbo.

Ekondwa 3. Ombara yOndjuwo yOuhona

Orupa 6 Omirari vyomapingeneno mOtjirata tjOmbara

6.1 Omayarukiro womounane otjirumatwa tjOndjuwo yOuhona u kaenda otja kombiṋdu yOuhona.

Orupa 7: Otjiuru tjOuhonapare nouṋepo wOtjirata tjovanane wombazu

7.1 Ombara onguuri ohongora/otjiuru tjouhonapare wombazu, nu wina onguuri omuhaamise wOvihavero wOtjirata.

7.2 Ombara maikara no usemba wokupaṋda ondyero kombanda yovananwa ve momatyero ayehe wOveta yombazu nu tji mai ṱunu komaunguriro wOuhonapare.

Orupa 8: Oruveze romakarero mounaneno wOmbara

8.1 Ombara maikara kounane ngaa koṋdiro yayo posi ya mape ya ai rambwa mounane tji ya hipara ozondunge poo indu tjiya tjiti ondataiziro/ongatukiro onene.

Orupa 9: Omayanisiro nomazeuparisiro

9.1 Tjimanga moruvze rwomakamburiro wounane mbwa kaenda otja mongongorasaneno yongwatero poo otja komiano vyarwe mbi ri po, Ombara i sokutjita oruyano rwouṱakame kotjikorone tjOuhona na kovananwa ve.

Orupa 10: Oviungura, omasa, nomaunguriro wOmbara nOtjirata tjOmbara

10.1 Otjiuri poo Ombara yOuhonapare onguuri:

(a) Ohongora/otjiuru tjOuhonapare wOmbazu, na wina onguuri otjiuru tjOmuhoko/Otjiwana.

(b) Nu wina onguuri omuhaamise wOvihavero wOtjirata.

10.2 Otjiuri poo Ombara yOuhonapare mayingura mbi:

(a) Eye mekurisa oviungurisiwa vyomuhongo.

(b) Matumburire ovakongorere vee kOmbazu, kOveta yOmbazu, kOzongunde zOmbazu, nawina kOngaro novitjitwa vyomuhoko.

(c) Makara norupa momahaameno pamwe nOvahaame vOtjirata tjOmbazu.

(d) Maurike ovahaame mozokomiti, mozokomisara, nawina mozokomiti ozonditi ozondye zovinenge pekepeke, nuwina
(e) Mayenenisa kutja Otjirata tjOmbazu tjinane nakuhina mbangu ku kangamwa.

Orupa 11: Omeritjururiri omakwizikwa

11.1 Ombara yakwizikwa omeritjururiro nguma ye kongorere mba. Ozo kazena ku isamewa movihavero kehi:
(a) Yohani ndjima i yetwa iyovimbumba vyo polotika poo vyo tjiwana, poo
(b) Oviposa vyo polotika mbihina ndengu yokuhana poo yokutoorora ombara otjiru tjOuhonapare.

Orupa 12: Omasutiro

12.1 Ondjuwo yOuhona mai sokutjita ongwizikiro yokusuta ovaungure vayo.

Orupa 13: Omapingeneno mounane

13.1 Omapingeneno mounane otjirumatwa tjomombindu.
13.2 Tjipehina omurumate, mapeyenene okupahewa kokutja otjiwana tjiurike okanepo katjo otjOmbara.

Ekondwa 4. Otjirata tjOmbazu

Orupa 14: Omazikameno (Omurya wotjito tjounane)

14.1 Ozongunḓe zOtjirata tjOmbara ozonda:
(a) Ombara
(b) Ozorata oviuru
(c) Ozorata nOmutjangerepo
14.2 Otja kOrupa 2 (1) no (2) rOveta yOmbazu 2000 (Onomora 25 yo 2000) otjivarero otjiheperwapo tjomahaameno wombongarero yOmbara ma rire 2/3 yovahaame, tji pe hi na otjivarero ho okutja ombongarero mai yenene okuturikwa koure woviveke vivari (Omayuva omurongo na yane).
14.3 Ozongunde zarwe zOndjuwo yOuhonapare:
(a) Otjombanguriro tjOmbazu
(b) Otjombanguriro otjiyarukire tjoviposa
(c) Orutu rwOmitanda
(d) Orutu rwOzoserekaze
(e) Otukondwa twOmananeno
(f) Otjirata tjOmbara

Orupa 15: Oviungura, omasa, omaunguriro

15.1 Otja kOrupa 3 rOveta yOvirata vyOmbazu, 2000 (Onomora 25 yo 2000):
- (a) Ozorata Oviuru ombu mave rire ovayandjandunge ovanene kOmbara.
- (b) Ozorata Oviuru mave rire ovayandjamuhunga kOmbara momaunguriro wayo.
- (c) Ozorata maze rire ovanamerizirira motukondwa na momaunguriro watwo.
- (d) Ozorata maze rapota kOzorata Oviuru.

Orupa 16: Omaurikiro wOzorata nOzorata Oviuru noviungura vyazo

16.1 Omaurikiro wOzorata nOzorata oviuru maye kaendisiwa otja komazeva wOrupa 10 rOveta yOvirata vyOmbazu, 2000 (Onomora 25 yo 2000).

Orupa 17: Oruyano nomayanisiro wOzorata

17.1 Ozorata nOzorata Oviuru maze sokutjita oruyano rwouṱakame kOmbara, Otjirata tjOmbazu, na kotjiwana.

Orupa 18: Omaraisiro wokuhina ngamburiro

18.1 Ombara maiyenene okuraisa okuhina ngamburiro mOzorata zOmbazu.

18.2 Ozorata zOmbazu mazeyenene okuraisa okuhina ngamburiro mOmbara, posia maveyenene okutjita nao indu Ombara tjiyavere omutjise omuzeu nungwari ka mohani yopolitika.

Orupa 19: Omutjangerepo wOtjirata nOmberoo

19.1 Omutjangerepo wOuhonapare nowOmberoo otjihako tjimwe otja kOveta Onomora 25 yo-2000 nu omundu ngwi omuungure wOhoromende.

19.2 Oviungura nomaunguriro yeri otja kOveta Onomora 25 yo-2000.

19.3 Omaurikiro wOmutjangerepo mayekara otja korutjato rwOmbara.

Ekondwa 5. Ondjuwo yOvanane vOmbazu

Orupa 20: Ondjuwo yOuhona, Ombara noruhindo rwayo

20.1 Ombara mai sokukahaama kombongarero yozombara ombura aihe poo mai yenene okuhinda omuhindwa we otja korutjato rwe.

Orupa 21: Omasa wOmbazu

21.1 Omasa wOmbazu mayezikama mOmbara yOtjiwana tjOndjuwo yaVita otja kozOveta zOndjuwo ondye yozOveta, tjimuna:

(a) Oveta yOmauhonapare wombazu, 1995 (Onomora 17 yo 1995)
(b) Oveta yOtjirata tjOmbazu, 1997 (Onomora 13 yo 1997)
(c) Oveta yOmauhonapare wombazu, 2000 (Onomora 25 yo 2000)

Orupa 22: Omatjaerero wounepo okuhina kukara norupa

22.1 Ovinenge mbimavikongorere mba ombitjaera ounepo okuhina kukara norupa mounanane:
(a) Ounane oungundi wotjiwana
(b) Ouvere ouvi/oukendeke
(c) Etiku (ndazeuparisiwa iye raa ratjOmbanguriro)
(d) Okuhipara ozondunge

Orupa 23: Omaisiremo womovihavero

23.1 Ozorata zOmbazu mazeyenene okuisamewa movihavero vyazo kehi yovinenge mbimavi kongorere mba:
(a) Otjiwana tji tjevetoorora okuveisamo
(b) Okurambwa
(c) Ouvere oukoto
(d) Ondiro
(e) Oungundipare mokuungura oviungura vyawo

Orupa 24: Omuhaamise nOmutjangerepo

24.1 Ombara otjiuru tjOtjiwana marire omuhaamise wovihavero mozombongarero azehe zOuhonapare wOmbazu.
24.2 Ouhonapare wOmbazu maukutu omutjangerepo ngumaungura pondondo yOuhonapare wOmbazu na momberoo yOmbazu.

Orupa 25: Omazikamisiro

25.1 Otjivarero tjOzorata zOmbazu matjizikamisiwa iyo tjivarero tjOutukodwa mburi kehi yOuhonapare.
25.2 Ozorata maze urikwa iyOmbara okutuurungira mombatero yovakongorere ve.

Orupa 26: Otjivarero otjihepwa momahaameno wombongarero

26.1 Otjivarero otjihepwa momahaameno nondyero yombongarero matjirire kombanda yohinga younepo ouhaame mombongarero.

Orupa 27: Oveta yOmbazu

27.1 Ombara ongu ri omuṱize wOveta yOmbazu posi ya omaṱunino, nomawiziro poo omaisiro po ayehe maye sokutjitwa pamwe nonḓuvasaneno yotjiwaṋa.

Ekondwa 6. Otjombanguriro tjOmbazu

Orupa 28: Omazikamisiro wOtjombanguriro tjOmbazu

28.1 Ozongunḓe zOtjombanguriro tjombazu ozo nḓa:

(a) Omutjange (1)
(b) Omutumwa watjombanguriro (1)
(c) Ovapangure (5)
(d) Ovanongonone woviposa (10)

Orupa 29: Oviungura nomaunguriro wotjombanguriro tjombazu

29.1 Oviungura vyOtjombaguriro tjOmbazu okupuratena nokupangura oviposa avihe mbya yetwa ku tjo i youṋepo wotjiwaṋa nokuhina okutjita ombangu ndja memenwa kourumendu poo koukazendu, nokuhina kutara konḓengu nehupo romundu, nokuhina kutara koporotika yomundu nu tji sokuungura momuano omukohoke nu mbu he ri mekoveka.

Orupa 30: Omakutiro wovaungure

30.1 Omirari nomazeva nge ungurisiwa momakutiro wovaungure wOhoromende oku maku ungurirwa nandandire kutja mape yenene okukara nouhara tjeri ohepero.

30.2 Ovaungure wOndjuwo yOuhona mave yenene okutuurungira momaunguriro nga: Okuurikwa, okutoororua nomayarisiruo wotuveze twoviungura.

Orupa 31: Otjombanguriro tjOmbazu nondikameno yozondyero zatjo

31.1 Oviungura nomaunguriro nge ri po nai maye kaenda komurungu. Omaunguriro ngo ma ye yenenisiwa nokuzeuparisiwa i yOveta yOndjuwo Ondye yOzoveta.

Orupa 32: Omasa noviungura vyovaungure

32.1 Omasa noviungura vyovaungure votjOmbanguriro tjOmbazu vyazikama mOveta yOvyombanguriro vyOmbazu, 2003 (Onomora 10 yo 2003).

Ekondwa 7. Ozongunde zomiano vyomaunguriro wOmbazu

Orupa 33: Omekurisiruo wongaro novitjitwa vyomuhoko (Ovirangera)

33.1 Ombwiko yapeke ondji mai rire omburo yotjitjamurongo;

33.2 Omazemburukiro nomayakuriro womayuva womaamberero maye tjitwa mu Ndengani ombura aihe.

Orupa 34: Omekurisiro wokarukondwa komatoorerero kombazu pondondo yOrukondwa nopondondo yOtjiwana/kombwiro yaavehe

34.1 Ondjuwo yOuhona maikara notjiungura tjo kukurisa poo okutunga ovandu pamwe no horomende.

Orupa 35: Omaunguriro wakumwe pokati na mokati koviwana nOmauhonapare warwe wombazu

35.1 Kehi yomaunguriro wakumwe kuna omauhonapare warwe no horomende, ondjuwo yOuhona waVita ino 'merizirira wokuzikamisa nokuyenenisa ondungiro okuvaza kounepo auhe mburi keyi yomananeno wayo okuza mehi raKaoko ngandu kOutjo na kwarwe kukuna ovandu vondjuwo yaVita moukoto waNamibia.

Ekondwa 8. Ouhonapare wOmbazu

Orupa 36: Orutu orunamasa momatyero wOveta, omapitisiro, nombanguriro

36.1 Ouhonapare wOmbazu ongunde yondjuwo yOuhona nuwina omasa wehi.

36.2 Otja kOveta yOmbazu, 2000 (Onomora 25 yo 2000) Ouhonapare wOmbazu ma wuungura kumwe nauyenenisa omasa wehi, tjimuna omaunguriro wakumwe kuna ovaporise, ovyombanguriro, nozonganda zarwe zohoromende ndaungura nomekurisiro kombwiro yOtjiwana tjOmbazu poo omuture auhe wehindi.

Orupa 37: Omahaneno wOtupa twOmbazu poo Otupa twOmananeno

37.1 Orupa rwotjimariva: (Otjitjamurongo tjovirandwa noviyandjewa)
Ondjuwo yOuhona mai kurisa omaunguriro wokuwonga otjitjamurongo nokuzikamisa ombwiko yombazu.

37.2 Orupa rwomananeno wOmberoo:
Omberoo onene nozomberoo zotukondwa oku maku zikamene omananeno wotupa twombazu.

37.3 Orupa rwongaro novitjitwa vyomuhoko:
Omazemburukiro nomarangerero

37.4 Orupa rwomahongero:
Orupa ndwi maru kara nomahongero woviuṋe vyombazu, tjimuna omasukarekero na vyarwe.

37.5 Orupa rwOṱurupa yombazu, oporise yombazu nomaunguriro wayo:
Orupa ndwi rwa kara momaunguriro okuzemburuka omapiruriro wouhuura momiano avihe ngamwa.

37.6 Orupa rwotutumbo novikunwa:
Orupa ndwi ru nomerizira nourumbu, omuriro, ombepo nomipupo.

37.7 Orupa rwokuti novaryange:
Orupa ndwi maru kara nomerizirira wondjeverero yokuti novaryange

37.8 Orupa rwozondjuwo:
Orupa ndwi ru nomerizirira nomaandjero wotjimariva kondungiro yozondjuwo.

37.9 Orupa rwomananeno womaumba ngamwa nge ya po:
Orupa ndwi maru kara nomerizirira koumba mbwa etwa i yourumbu, omuriro, ombepo nomipupo.

37.10 Orupa rwOuveruke:
Orupa maru kara nomerizira wouveruke noviuṋe vyarwe ongondoroka nouveruke otja kOveta pu mai zikamisa.

37.11 Orupa rwomekurisiro wozondjira:
Orupa ndwi maru kara nomerizira wozondopa noviuṋe avihe ongondoroka nozondjira.

Ekondwa 9. Orupa rotjiomariva

Orupa 38: Omatanauriro wowini

38.1 Ehi mari ungurisiwa otja komazeva worupa rwomahi rwOhoromende nondi mari rire otjiṋa kombwiro yovananwa novature worukondwa ndo. Ehi ma ri rire tjimwe tjouini ounahepero.

Orupa 39: Ombwiko yOmbazu

39.1 Ouṋepo auhe wOndjuwo yOuhona mau sutu otjimariva tji matji zikamisiwa i yOtjirata tjOmbara okuza koruveze nga koruveze.

39.2 Ondjuwo yOuhona mai wongo otjimariva mokuyandja kotutuu twousemba mbwi:
   (a) OwovinamuinyoOwozongetjefa.
   (b) Ouhonapare wOmbazu mauzikamisa okamariva ku makesutwa i yovanazongetjefa mberi kehi yokarundwa komananeno wOmbazu. Nungwari okamariva okasutwa nga ka kozongetjefa porwe nungwari wina imba mbemuna otjitjamurongo mu kangamwa otjina, tjimuna omasekirisiro wovaryange. Okamariva okasutwa make hanika otja pounene wongetjefa kaani poo otja kotjitjamurongo tjongetjefa kaani.
   (c) Nowozonganda.

(d) Ozoprojeka zotjiwana:
Ounepo woprojeka mauyenene okuungurisa otjitjamurongo tjiwo okupwika momwiko yoyjiwana. Ouhonapare wOmbazu wina mauyenene okkuta ozoprojeka ndumaze hitisa okamariva momwiko yotjiwana.

(e) Ovapwika vopendje:
Otjiwana poo ovanane wOmbazu maveyenene oku nanga ovapwike okuza kotukondwa twarwe okuyeku pwika moyao nu mape zikamisiwa omazeva kumakupwikirwa nu wina otjihupe tjotjimarungo tjao matjipwikwa mombwiko yotjiwana.

(f) Otupa twondjeverero kovipuka:
Otja ozoprojeka azehe zotjiwana, otjimariva otjihite okuza kotupa twondjeverero kovipuka tjimuna omayevero poo ombwiko yovaryange matjiso okuhanwa pupeta. Orupa rondjeverero yovipuka maruyenene okutya kutja ekumba rotjimariva maripwikwa mombwiko yotjiwana.

(g) Otjimariva tjomaryo wovinamuinjo:
Otjiwana matjiyenene okuzikamisa okamariva okasutwa komaryo wovinamuinjo. Ovandu avehe mbena ovinamuinjo mave sutu otjimariva otja kotjivarero tjovinamuinjo mbivenavyo.

(h) Ovisuta okuza kOtjombanguriro:
Otjimariva otjisutwa otja ovisuta vatjOmbanguriro visutwa komurapote wotjiposa okupingena mbyapandjara, nungwari otjihupe matjiyenene okupwikwa mombwiko yombazu.

Orupa 40: Omakamburiro wotjimariva nomapwikiro watjo

40.1 Omambo wombaanga maye paturarwa mombaanga ndji Bank Windhoek nombaanga ndji FNB nu ovimariva avihe ovihite mavi tuwa mozombaanga nd̂a navi kurasa ombwiko ndjo.

40.2 Omatyero wotjimariva maye kaendisiwa ombura aihe. Ongwizikiro yo masutiro wotjimariva otjijazemwa maye tjitwa nozongombe nozongombo.

Orupa 41: Ovatare womambo

41.1 Omutjangerepo ma sokutjita kutja omambo wovimariva ye tarewe nokukond̂ononwa ombura aihe.

Orupa 42: Omayakuriro woviyandjewa

42.1 Ondjuwo yOuhona nOuhonopare wOmbazu mai yenene okuyakura oviyandjewa avihe ngamwa okuza kovaharupa ngamwa okukurisa Oveta yombazu nomekurisiro kombwiro yovananwa novakwatera varwe vehi.

Ekondwa 10. Otupa otutye twOmbazu nomaunguriro wakumwe kunOrutu orutye rOhoromende

Orutu orutye roviungura vyOmbazu maruzikamisiwa nu maruhakaenisa otupa tohoromende, tjimuna okomisara ondye yoviungura vyEhi, Otjirata tjOrukondwa, Otjiratwa tjOtjihuro notjOresevate, no maturiro mokarukondwa komananeno wOuhonapare wOmbazu.

Ekondwa 11. Omeero wOveta yOmbazu momaunguriro

Oveta mai ya momaunguriro kombund' omazikamisiro wayo momatjangwa.

Ekondwa 12. Omaṱunino wOveta yOmbazu

Omatanauriro wOveta yOmbazu maye yenene okuutwa tji pe notjivaro tjo-2/3 tjotjingi tjOtjirata tjOmbara.

Ekondwa 13. Ondando yomerinaneno

Ondando aihe yomerinaneno maituwa momatjangwa nai weziwa Oveta yombazu.

Ekondwa 14. Omakahururiro omasenina

"Oveta yOmbazu" mape hewa Oveta yOndjuwo yOuhona waVita.

Omarundururiro wozoveta zombazu
Omarundururiro wozoveta zombazu maye yenene okutjitwa i yOngunḓeveta ya Namibia poo Ondjuwo Ondye yOzoveta.

Omatyero wozoveta ozombe zombazu okuza kongutukiro ya Namibia 21/03/1990
(Oveta Onomora 17 yo-1995) Oveta yomauhonapare wombazu
(Oveta Onomora 8 yo-1997) Oveta yomarundururiro yOuhonapare wombazu
(Oveta Onomora 25 yo-2000) Oveta yOmauhonapare wOmbazu

Ozoveta zotjiwaṋa nḓa rundururwa
AG Onomora 8 yo-1980
Oveta Onomora 17 yo-1995
Oveta Onomora 8 yo-1997

OZOVETA ZONDJUWO YOUHONA WAVITA WOVAHERERO

Omautiro

Ovandu vOndjuwo yOuhona wa Vita va ri kehi yozOveta zOmbazu nḓa tjangerwe. Ozoveta za haṋenwe motupa noutupona otja nai.

Orupa 1: Ondikameno yousemba woundu

1.1 Omundu auhe ngu ma pura ondjo poo ouhasemba mbwa tjitwa ku ye poo ouzeu auhe mbwe nao ma yenene okutjita nao nu tji ma zeri okuyeta ouzeu we kOtjombanguriro ma yandjerwa okutjita nao.

1.2 Omaningiriro wokutara momutjemo poo otjiposa ye sokutuurungira mOmutjangerepo wOuhonapare wOmbazu pondondo ndjo.

1.3 Omutjemo mau utire po mberoo yOmuhona poo Osoromana yotjirongo ho oku maku utire otjiungura tjomaandjero wotjiposa nomakamburiro wouhatoi.

1.4 Ongaendero yotjiposa aihe ma i tjangwa nu arire tjiyapwikwa poruve orukohoke.

1.5 Tji pe ya konḓuvasaneno pondondo ndji otjiposa matji manukire mbo.

1.6 Omunda umwe motjiposa poo ominda aviyevari tji vihina hange nondyero ndja toorwa motjiposa mave yenene okukaenda komurungu notjiposa tji va zu nokuningira ombapira yombanguriro ndjo okuveyandjera okutwara otjiposa pondondo yarwe younane wokombanda.

Orupa 2: Ongaero yOtjiposa

2.1 Otjiposa tji tja etwa kOmunane wokombanda tji sokuya nouhatoi momatjangwa Okuza kondondo yokehi otjiposa ku tja pangurwa.

2.2 Otjiposa tji mwari omatirahiro wombinḓu poo omatoneno ohatoi poo ozohatoi ze sokukarapo.

2.3 Otjiposa tji tji ha pangurirwe pondondo ndjo matji sokuyetwa kondondo yokombanda ndji ri ondondo yOmbara ku maku yekutoorwa ondyero osenina. Ondyero ondenga motjiposa i yombanguriro ondenga mai sokuraisiwa ngunda ombanguriro osenina yOmbara ai hi ya uta.

Orupa 3: Onḓepero

3.1 Omuṱi tje ri omukazendu nomurondorwa tja munika ondjo omberero poo otjisuta ozongombe omirongo vine na ndano (45).

3.2 Omuṱi tjeri omurumendu nu omurondorwa tja munika ondjo omberero poo otjisuta ozongombe omirongo vitatu na ndano (35).

Orupa 4: Omatoneno

4.1 Omutonwa tja tonwa ombara poo tja ziza ombinḓu poo tja tonwa notjiṋa tji tje mu hihamisa poo tja yatwa i yomurondorwa nu tja munika ondjo kombund' ombanguriro omberero poo otjisuta ozongombe hambondatu (8).

Orupa 5: Ourunga wovinamuinyo

5.1 Omundu tja vaka otjinamuinyo tjimwe (1) tja munika ondjo ma yenene okusuta ozongombe hamboumwe (6) nu maze rire hambombari (7) kumwe na indji ndja vakwa tji i ri po, onḓu maze yandjwa komuvakerwa.

5.2 Nu tji pe ya kokutja indji ndja vakwa kai po okutja mape sokusutwa ongombe imwe kombanda yainḓa ohamboumwe; azehe kumwe kokutja ze rire hambombari (7).

5.3 Erunga tji ra vaka ozongombe ndatu (3) mari sutu ozongombe hamboumwe mongombe nu ongombe imwe mai i kotjombanguriro tjOmbazu.

Orupa 6: Omanyoneno womiti nokuti

6.1 Omundu tja kamburwa ama randisa ozopara/ouṱoroppora okuungurisiwa kozonḓarata poo kondando yarwe korukondwa rwarwe ma sutisiwa ozondora za Namibia ndano (5) mopara poo mokaṱoropora nu wina mape tarewa kutja onyonokero ndja tjitwa i nonḓengu ndji ṱa pi.

6.2 Omundu tjeye kukonda omiti nokuhina usemba okuza korukondwa rwarwe omberero poo otjisuta ozondora za Namibia Omurongo (10) mopara poo mokaṱoropora.

Orupa 7: Omakondero poo omanyosiro womiti

7.1 Omundu auhe ngwa kondo omuti nondando yokupora ovihape oupupu ma sutu ozongombe mbari (2).

7.2 Omundu tja nyosa omuti okumuna mo otjimariva poo mena repu rarwe ma sutu ozongombo poo ozonḓu ndatu (3).

7.3 Omundu auhe ngwa nyosa ehozu poo okuti ma sutu ozongombe mbari (2).

7.4. Okupora ovihape omangura poo mbi hi ya hora:

7.4.1 Omundu ngwa munika omapora ovihape omangura poo mbi hi ya hora ma sutu ongombo poo onḓu imwe (1).

7.4.2 Nungwari omukatuke motjiṋa hi tje he ri omuture worukondwa poo wotjirongo otjisuta ongombe imwe (1) tjinangara ke na usemba okuza kouhonapare wombazu wotjirongo.

7.4.3 Omberero otjingeyo mai sutwa i yomundu ngwakama omingu kutja vya hora poo kavi ya hora.

Orupa 8: Ongatukiro kunomukazendu ngwa kupwa

8.1 Omundu ngwakara norukatuko ku nomukazendu ngwa kupwa ma sutu ozongombe hamboumwe (6) kombund' konḓononeno yoviraisiro ovikahu.

8.2 Omundu tja pangurwa pondondo ndji yokehi nu indu tje hina hange neraa ratjOmbanguriro ma yenene okutwara otjiposa kondondo yorukondwa nomatjangwa wombanguriro ondenga maye sokuhondjwa ku nomaarurireko wotjiposa.

8.3 Omupangurwa wina ma yenene okuyarurisako otjiposa kOmagistrata yorukondwa mu mu notjombanguriro tjombazu.

Orupa 9: Ovakuramenepo vomOveta/Ozohahende movOviombanguriro vyOmbazu

9.1 Ozohahende kaze na kuyandjerwa moviombanguriro vyombazu na komband' okutja ongunḓeveta ya Namibia i yandjera omundu ousemba okukuramenwapo motjiposa.

9.2 Oviombanguriro vyombazu kavi ungura tjimuna ozohofa posi ya omuhoko poo omunene womundu ma yenene okukuramenapo omuhakerwa womondjo poo omurondorwa.

Orupa 10: Omutjange worukondwa nowOtjombanguriro tjOmbazu

10.1 Eye ma sokurira omuture worukondwa nu indu mOrukondwa tji mu hina ngu ma yenene, ma yenene okuningirwa okuza korukondwa rwarwe nduri kehi yOuhonapare mbwi. Wina mape yenene okupurwa ounongo komberoo yorukondwa motjiṋa hi. Omberoo yOporise wina maku yenene okukapurwa ombatero tje ri ohepero.

Orupa 11: Omasutiro wovapangure wombazu

11.1 Ovapangure wombazu ve urikwa nu ave tuwa mOngoramambo yOhoromende okupangura oviposa morukondwa.

11.2 Ovapangure worukondwa ve ungura otjovapangure worukondwa nu wina otjivarondore.

Orupa 12: Omatoneno otjomberero

12.1 Otja tji pa tjaerwa mongunḓeveta ya Namibia kape nomatoneno ngu maye yenene okuungurisiwa otjomberero komundu auhe ngwa katuka oveta nungwari omberero ma rire omasutisiro uriri.

Orupa 13: Omarumatero womaṱa

13.1 Omundu tja ṱu eṱa re mari rumatwa nokuhaṋika otja kombazu.

13.2 Omarumatero weṱa maye kaenda otja komuze woina yomuṱi.

13.3 Omukazendu novanatje tji ve ri po mave yenene okurumatisiwa i yomuhaṋe weṱa ngu ri omuyanwa womuṱi.

13.4 Ovarumate veṱa ve sokutoora omerizirira wokutumba nokutjevera ovanatje nomukazendu womuṱi tjimuna omuni paa tjiti.

13.5 Okuruwo ku rumatwa otja kongorerasaneno yovazamumwe voihe, okuza kerumbi nga komuangu, tji kwa zu mbo okuyenda komuatje otjiveri tjonganda.

Orupa 14: Orukupo rwombazu

14.1 Orukupo maru kara otja tji rwa ri mombazu yOvaherero.

14.2 Omurumendu ma yenene okukupa ovakazendu kombanda yavevari.

14.3 Omuatje/poo ovanatje mba kwatwa pendje norukupo mave rire ovanatje womurumendu ngwa kupa omukazendu ngo.

14.4 Omurumendu tji ma vanga okukupa ma sokukuramenwapo i yovanene ve, ombe sokumuhungirira orukupo. Omurumendu tji ma vanga okukupa ka sokukahungira orupo rwe omuini nandire kutja u notjiwondo tji tji ṱa pi mozombura.

14.5 Ovarumendu mba kupa mave yenene okukara novasuko, posi ya ve sokutjita nao nondengero nongengezero.

14.6 Omurumendu u nousemba okuraera omukazendu we kutja meyuva rorive ndo ma karara kwarwe.

14.7 Ozombapira zotukupo maze yenene okuyandjwa kovakupasane kombunda yokutjita omaningiriro momatjangwa.

Orupa 15: Ousemba wovakazendu morukupo

15.1 Tjimuna ovakuparumendu, ovakazendu ovakupwa ve nousemba wina okurapota ondjindiro mbi i yovarumendu vavo kovanene womurumendu, tji va katuka poo tji va zuṋda. Ovanene ve sokumuronga nokumurakiza okuhina kuyarukirapo ondjito ombi komukazendu we rukwaao.

15.2 Omukazendu u nousemba okutya pamwe nomurumendu we oviṋa poyavo. Omurumendu tji ma vanga okukupa omukazendu outjavari ma sokutjivisa omukazendu we omutenga nu wina omukazendu ngwi omutenga u sokuṱika omurumendu we korukupo ndo. Omukazendu ngwi omutenga tji ma panḓa omurumendu we okukupa omukazendu outjavari, u sokukara nomapu omazuvakwa nomakahu nungwari ka sokurira mena reruru poo resupa. Omukazendu omutenga tja kara nomapu omazuvakwa okutja omurumendu ka sokukupa omukazendu outjavari. Tji pa munika kutja omukazendu omutenga ma panḓa omurumendu okukupa omukwao mena reruru poo resupa okutja omurumendu ma yenene okukupa omukazendu ngwi nokuhina omaandjerero womukazendu ngwi omutenga.

THE LAWS OF THE VITA ROYAL HOUSE[1]

1 Acknowledgement: This edition of the laws of the Vita was prepared by a group of traditional committee members in former Kaokoland, now Kunene North, with the assistance of Mr Ben Ukondjisa Kapi, Mr Hiruke Uerikambura Tjiuru Tjipepa, traditional leaders, as well the community at large. When comparing the Otjiherero and the English versions of the laws, it was found that some parts in the English text did not appear in Otjiherero. These parts were then omitted from the English text.

Constitution of the Vita Royal House

Table of Contents

Chapter 5: The House of Traditional Leaders

Article 20. The Royal House: Chief and his/her delegation
Article 21. Traditional powers
Article 22. Disqualification of members
Article 23. Vacation of Seats
Article 24. Chairperson and Secretary
Article 25. Composition
Article 26. Quorum
Article 27. Customary law

Chapter 6: Community Courts

Article 28. Composition
Article 29. Duties and functions
Article 30. Appointment of staff
Article 31. Community Courts and the nature of their decisions
Article 32. Powers and Functions of staff

Chapter 7: Principles of traditional policy

Article 33. The development of culture and traditional rituals (rites)
Article 34. The development of the Traditional Constituency at Regional or national level for the development and benefit of all people
Article 35. Co-operation among and within traditional communities and with other Traditional Authorities

Chapter 8: Traditional Authority

Article 36. Central organ responsible for legislative, executive, and judicial functions
Article 37. Traditional Divisions or Departments

Chapter 9: Finance

Article 38. Transfer of Assets
Article 39. Traditional Revenue Fund (Traditional Tax)
Article 40. Appropriations & Savings
Article 41. The auditors
Article 42. Donations

Chapter 10: Traditional planning divisions and relations with national planning and decision making bodies

Chapter 11: Implementation of the Constitution

Chapter 12: Amendment of the Constitution

Chapter 13: Policy

Chapter 14: Final provisions

Definitions
Repeal of laws
National laws

Constitution

Preamble

Whereas recognising the inherent existence of the Royal House, and the acceptance of the harm perpetrated to our cultural heritage and to the Royal House by the colonialists or colonialism;

Whereas traditions, traditional rituals, rites, customs, beliefs, values and norms have been damaged or impaired by the colonial forces/oppressors;

Whereas admitting that the restoration of and reconciling the children within the Vita Royal House is a challenging task on the shoulders of the Royal House;

Whereas recognising the damage to the Vita Royal House and that its future is in our hands;

Whereas witnessing that the colonial hardships and recollection are clearly observable;

Whereas we, the Vita Royal House generation of the 21st century, are determined to adopt a traditional constitution for our Royal House, ourselves and our children's children to secure a firm foundation for the Vita Royal House;

Desiring to promote the Royal House within the context of our national democratic heritage; we will strive to unite the children of the Vita Royal House for the common good of our Royal House; as these are the riches and heritage of the Royal House.

Now therefore, we, the children of the Vita Royal House, accept and adopt this customary law as the supreme law of our Royal House.

Chapter 1: Royal House

Article 1: Establishment of the Vita Royal House and identification of its territorial jurisdiction

1.1 The Royal House was created centuries ago and is in line with Chapter 12, Art. 102 (5) of the Namibian Constitution, and it is one of the Traditional Authorities recognised as per Act of Parliament, the Traditional Authorities Act (No. 25 of 2000).

1.2 All power shall be vested in the leader of the Royal House, i.e. *Ombara* (King), not the Generals. The Generals are answerable to him through appropriate levels/channels.

1.3 The main organs of the Royal House are: The Royal House, the Traditional Authority and the Traditional/Community Courts.

1.4 The traditional territorial area of jurisdiction includes the whole of Kunene Region, south and northern parts of the so-called Red line, or veterinary cordon fence, and wherever you may find the generations of Vita Royal House in the Republic of Namibia.

1.5 The headquarters of the Vita Royal House are situated in Opuwo; however, the Royal Palace of the Traditional Authority is situated in Otjijandjasemo.

Article 2: Traditional symbols

2.1 The Vita Royal House's traditional symbols are:
- (a) Lion/*Ongeyama*
- (b) Bow and Arrow/*Outa uozoheo noviku*
- (c) Sun/*Ejuva*
- (d) Firearm/*Ondjembo*
- (e) Spear/*Enga*

Article 3: Languages

3.1 The official languages are:
- (a) Otjiherero and
- (b) English

Chapter 2: Royalty

Article 4: Sense of belonging

4.1 The Royal House: it is vital to know that its subjects are spread all over the Republic of Namibia, but members of the Royal House are based mainly in Kunene Region in the south and northern parts of the veterinary cordon fence.

Article 5: Defence of the Royal House

5.1 The responsibility rests upon the shoulders of the children or generations of the Vita Royal House to build up and defend the Royal House.

Chapter 3: The Chief of the Royal House

Article 6: Hereditary chieftainship

6.1 The chieftainship is hereditary and it remains so. The line of succession is with the Royalty of Vita.

Article 7: Head of the Traditional Authority and members of the Council of Traditional Leaders

7.1 The Chief/*Ombara* shall be the head of the Traditional Authority, and shall thus serve as Chairperson of the Chief's Council.

7.2 The Chief/*Ombara* shall have a right of veto over subjects and any other matters pertaining to customary laws and operation of the Traditional Authority.

Article 8: Term of office of the Chief

8.1 The Chief shall be granted life tenure of office; however, he may be removed from office for reasons of mental illness and/or for gross misconduct.

Article 9: Oath and affirmation

9.1 Immediately during the process of designation of a Chief who succeeded to the throne through hereditary means of succession or other existing ways of succession, a ceremony takes place where the designated Chief/Royal leader makes an oath or affirmation of allegiance to the throne and to his subjects.

Article 10: Functions, power and duties of the Chief and the Chief's Council

10.1 The Supreme Traditional Leader or King is:
- (a) the supreme leader of the Royal house and his designated community.
- (b) Chairperson of the Traditional Authority.

10.2 The Supreme Traditional Leader or King shall:
- (a) create traditional infrastructures.
- (b) guide [his people] with regard to the tradition, customary law, traditional values, customs and traditional rituals.
- (c) serve together with the Senior Traditional Councillors and some others on the Council of Traditional Leaders.

(d) appoint committees, or commissions or sub-committees for a variety of purposes.
(e) ensure the Traditional Authority serves all without discrimination.

Article 11: Immunity

11.1 It should be noted that the Chief enjoys the following immunities.They cannot be removed by:
(a) Socio-politically engineered divisions, or
(b) Political disputes - which are not sufficient basis to determine who should be the supreme traditional leader.

Article 12 Remuneration

12.1 The Royal House will secure remuneration for its staff.

Article 13: Succession

13.1 The line of succession is hereditary.
13.2 If there is no heir, other options are open for the community to move a member of the Royal House forward as a Chief.

Chapter 4: The Traditional Authority

Article 14: Composition of the Traditional Authority

14.1 The Traditional Authority shall comprise:
(a) the Chief/head of the community
(b) Senior Traditional Councillors
(c) Traditional Councillors and the Secretary to the Traditional Authority.
14.2 According to the provisions of section 2(1) & (2) of the Traditional Authorities Act, 2000 (No. 25 of 2000), the quorum at any Traditional Authority meeting shall be a 2/3 (two thirds) majority; if the quorum is not met the meeting shall be adjourned for 14 days.
14.3 Other Structures within the Royal House:
(a) Community Court
(b) Appeal Court
(c) Youth League
(d) Women's League
(e) Districts
(f) Chief's Council.

Article 15: Functions and duties as per relevant Act of Parliament

15.1 In accordance with the provisions of section 3 of the Traditional Authorities Act, 2000 (No. 25 of 2000):

(a) Senior Councillors of the Traditional Authority shall be the principal advisors to the Chief.

(b) Senior Councillors shall assist the Chief in the execution of his duties.

(c) Traditional Councillors shall be the Royal House representatives in specific districts.

(d) Traditional Councillors shall report to the Senior Traditional Councillors.

Article 16: The Appointment of Senior Traditional Councillors and Traditional Councillors and their functions

16.1 The appointment of the above mentioned positions shall be subject to the provisions of section 10 of the Traditional Authorities Act, 2000 (No. 25 of 2000).

Article 17: Oath of affirmation of all Traditional Councillors

17.1 The Senior Traditional and Traditional Councillors shall make an oath of allegiance to the Chief, the Traditional Authority and the community.

Article 18: Vote of no confidence

18.1 The Chief may move a vote of no confidence in the Traditional Councillors.

18.2 The Traditional Councillors may move a vote of no confidence in the Chief but can only do so on grounds of ill-health of the Chief, and not on political grounds.

Article 19: Secretary to the Royal House and the Office

19.1 The Secretary to the Traditional Authority and the office shall be just one post as per the Traditional Authorities Act, 2000 (No. 25 of 2000) and the person shall be a civil servant.

19.2 The functions and the duty of the Secretary to the Traditional Authority shall be subjected to the Traditional Authorities Act, 2000 (No. 25 of 2000).

19.3 The appointment of the Secretary to the Traditional Authority shall be left to the discretion of the Chief.

Chapter 5: The House of Traditional Leaders.

Article 20: The Royal House: Chief and his/her delegation

20.1 The Chief shall attend the annual meeting of the House of Traditional Leaders or he shall delegate a person of his choice to represent him during such meeting(s).

Article 21: Traditional powers

21.1 Traditional powers shall be vested and fully entrenched in the Chief/*Ombara* of the Vita traditional community within the legal framework enacted by parliament, e.g.

(a) Traditional Authorities Act, 1995 (No. 17 of 1995)
(b) Council of Traditional Leaders Act, 1997 (No. 13 of 1997)
(c) Traditional Authorities Act, 2000 (No. 25 of 2000, sections 3 (1 a–h) and (2 a–e).

Article 22: Disqualification of members

22.1 The following are the criteria which disqualify a Traditional Leader/Councillor:

(a) Failure to serve his/her community
(b) Ill-health
(c) Fraudulent acts (when proved by a Court of Law) and
(d) Insanity.

Article 23: Vacation of seats

23.1 The traditional Councillors may vacate their seats under the following circumstances:

(a) When voted out by the Community
(b) Dismissal
(c) Ill health
(d) Death or
(e) Failure to do their work.

Article 24: Chairperson and Secretary

24.1 The Chief/*Ombara* of the traditional community shall be the chairperson of all the meetings of the Traditional Authority.

24.2 The Traditional Authority shall employ a secretary for the purpose of its work at both Traditional Authority level and for the Traditional office.

Article 25: Composition

25.1 The total number of Traditional Councillors is determined by the number of constituencies within the Traditional community.

25.2 They are to be nominated by the Chief with the help of his subjects.

Article 26: Quorums

26.1 The quorum to guide or determine all meetings and decisions will be a 2/3 (two thirds) majority of the members.

Article 27: Customary law

27.1 The Chief is the sole custodian of the customary law. Any amendments/ alterations or repealing of provisions in customary law shall be in consultation with the community.

Chapter 6: Community Courts

Article 28: Composition of Community Courts

28.1 The Community Court shall be comprised of the following positions:
- (a) Clerk of the Community Court (1)
- (b) Messenger of the Court (1)
- (c) Justices (5)
- (d) Assessors (10)

Article 29: Duties and functions of the Community Court

29.1 The duty of the Community Court is to hear all matters brought before them by community members without any discrimination based on gender, economic status, or political affiliation, and to do so in a fair and transparent manner.

Article 30: Appointment of staff

30.1 The Procedures and Regulations guiding the employment of civil servants shall be followed in the appointment of staff, even though some flexibility might be applied.

30.2 The staff of the Royal House shall be appointed by means of selection, election and designation of duty stations.

Article 31: The traditional Courts and the nature of their decisions

31.1 The current practices and procedures in respect of the decisions of the Community Courts will continue unchanged, but the major guide will be the Community Courts Act, 2003 (No. 10 of 2003).

Article 32: Powers and functions of staff

32.1 The powers and functions of the staff of the Community Court are as provided for in the Community Courts Act 10, 2003 (No. 10 of 2003).

Chapter 7: Principles of traditional policy

Article 33: The development of culture and rituals (rites)

33.1 The Trust Fund shall be the source of income.

33.2 Traditional commemoration ceremonies and traditional days of commemoration shall be conducted (in October of each year).

Article 34: The development of the Traditional Constituency at regional or national level for the development and benefit of all people

34.1 The Traditional Royal House has sole accountability in ensuring all round development for the benefit of its subjects in collaboration with the Government.

Article 35: Co-operation among and within traditional communities and with other Traditional Authorities

35.1 In collaboration with the other Traditional Authorities and the Government, the Vita Traditional Authority has a duty to ensure and also facilitate development to reach all its members within its constituencies from Kaokoland to Outjo and everywhere where there are people from the Vita Royal House within the Republic of Namibia.

Chapter 8: Traditional Authority

Article 36: Central organ responsible for legislative, executive, and judicial functions

36.1 The Traditional Authority is an organ of both the Royal House and State powers.

36.2 According to the Traditional Authorities Act, 2000 (No. 25 of 2000) the Traditional Authority shall co-operate with and reinforce state power, for example, through the police, the courts, and all other development related agencies for the benefit of the traditional community and other citizens.

Article 37: Traditional divisions or departments

37.1 Finance: (Tax-based & Donations)
The Royal House shall develop a tax-based system and a Trust Fund.

37.2 Administration:
The Headquarters and the satellite officers will be the basis of administration of the Traditional division.

37.3 Culture: (Ceremonies, rituals, rites)
A division shall be created within the Royal House under the Traditional Authority.

37.4 Education:
A division shall be created to deal with education, especially traditional education (initiation ceremonies, etc.)

37.5 Traditional Army, Police & Service:
A division has been in existence and shall be continued in order to remember heroic resistance against colonialism in whatever form.

37.6 Agriculture: (farming, water, etc)
There shall be a division to deal with farming, water, drought, fire, flood, etc.

37.7 Environment and Tourism:
There shall be a division to deal with issues concerning the environment and tourism.

37.8 Housing:
There shall be a division to promote the financing of housing development.

37.9 Emergency Management:
There shall be a division to deal with drought, fire, wind and flood.

37.10 Health:
There shall be a division to deal with health matters and other related issues as the Act may prescribe.

37.11 Roads development:
There shall be a division to deal with bridges, roads and related issues.

Chapter 9: Finance

Article 38: Transfer of assets

38.1 The land shall be allocated in terms of the rules and regulations set by the Ministry of Lands and Resettlement and it shall be used for the benefit of the subjects of the Royal House and other citizens under the jurisdiction of the Royal House. Land is an important asset.

Article 39: Traditional Revenue Fund

39.1 All subjects of the Royal House shall pay a fee which will be determined by the Chief's Council from time to time.

39.2 The Royal House shall also generate funds through issuing permits for the following:

(a) Animals.

(b) Businesses or Cuca shops:
The Traditional Authority can decide on certain tariffs that must be paid by shops and other businesses in their areas. This does not include only cuca shops, but also, for example, tourist lodges. Different rates of levies may be charged, depending on the size or turnover of a business.

(c) Domestic.

(d) Community projects:
With community projects, the project members may decide to use part of their profit for the Community Trust Fund. The Traditional Authority may consider starting projects in order to raise money for the Trust Fund.

(e) Joint ventures:
Communities or traditional leaders might attract entrepreneurs from outside to their area and make certain conditions under which they could invest. A portion of the proceeds of their investments shall go to the Traditional Revenue Fund.

(f) Conservancies:
Similar to other community projects, the income from conservancies, like hunting concessions or joint ventures, must be distributed in a fair way. The Conservancy Committee may decide that a portion of the income shall be paid to the Community Trust Fund.

(g) Grazing fees:
A community may decide to impose a levy for grazing. In this case stockowners shall pay a certain regular fee, depending on the number of animals they have.

(h) Court fines:
Whereas part of the fines paid by persons convicted in Customary Courts is usually paid to compensate the complainant, another part may be paid to the Community Fund.

Article 40: Appropriations and savings

40.1 Accounts shall be opened with Bank Windhoek and First National Bank, and all monies are to be deposited into these accounts to develop savings.

40.2 A budget is to be drawn up annually.

40.3 Collaterals are to be donated in terms of cattle, goats etc.

Article 41: Auditors

41.1 The Secretary shall cause the Royal House financial books or its financial statements to be audited annually by hiring professional auditors.

Article 42: Donations

42.1 The Royal House and the Traditional Authority welcomes donations of all kinds from all quarters to promote traditions, customary law and development in general for the benefit of its subjects and other fellow citizens.

Chapter 10: Traditional planning divisions and relations with national planning and decision making bodies

A division will be established to deal with traditional planning and to link this with political state divisions, e.g. the National Planning Commission; the Regional Council and Town or Village Councils, and the settlements within the area of the Traditional Authority.

Chapter 11: Implementation of the Constitution

This Constitution shall also be called the *Vita Royal House Customary Law* and will come into force after it has been reduced to writing and signed/assented to by the Chief.

Chapter 12: Amendment of the Constitution/Customary law

The changes/amendments to the Constitution shall be effected only by a 2/3 (two thirds) majority of the Chief's Council.

Chapter 13: Policy

All relevant operational policy shall be reduced in writing and annexed to the Customary Law.

Chapter 14: Final Provisions

Definitions
"Customary law" refers to the law of the Vita Royal House.

Repeal of traditional laws
The customary law shall be repealed by the Namibian Constitution or by Parliament.

Newly enacted traditional laws since independence in 21/03/1990: their customary and historical significance and relevance
(Act no. 17 of 1995) Traditional Authorities Act
(Act no. 8 of 1997) Traditional Authority Amendment Act
(Act no. 25 of 2000) Traditional Authorities Act

National laws repealed
Proclamation AG 8 of 1980
Traditional Authorities Act (Act No.17 of 1995)
Traditional Authority Amendment Act (Act no. 8 of 1997)

Laws

Introduction

The people of the Vita Royal House in Kaokoland were under traditional/customary laws before these customary laws were written. The laws were divided into sections and sub-sections as follows:

Section 1: Enforcement of rights

1.1 Any person who wishes to claim debts or damage or has any other problem with somebody else, and who wishes to bring this to the Community Court is allowed to do so.

1.2 A request must be done in writing and addressed to the Traditional Authority Secretary's Office via the local authority.

1.3 The hearing will start at the headman's quarters where the parties involved and any witnesses shall start their proceedings.

1.4 Minutes must be taken and records must be kept safe.

1.5 If an agreement and a final decision is reached, the case shall be declared closed.

1.6 If one of the parties or both are not satisfied with the decision taken by the Community Court, they shall have full rights to continue with the proceeding. They shall request a letter from the local council to allow them to take the case further to the Senior Council of the Traditional Authority.

Section 2: Procedures in respect of disputes

2.1 If the case has been brought to the Senior Headman Committee, the decision taken at the initial hearing must also be submitted.

2.2 If the case involves beating or bloodshed, eyewitnesses/witnesses should be called in.

2.3 If the matter is not resolved at Headman Committee level, it shall be referred to the Chief/Chief's Council for a final resolution. The decision of the Committee dealing with the case must be included.

2.4 The first resolution of the dispute will have to be clarified before the Chief's final decision is adopted.

Section 3: Murder

3.1 If the victim is a female, the fine or compensation after the accused is found guilty is 45 (forty-five) head of cattle.

3.2 If the victim is male, the fine or compensation is 35 (thirty-five) head of cattle.

Section 4: Assault

4.1 If the victim assaulted sustains any scar/open wound, bleeding or is hit with any harmful object or kicked or stamped on by the accused, after the case has reached conclusion and the accused person is found guilty, the fine will be 8 (eight) head of cattle.

Section 5: Stock theft

5.1 If any person steals one head of livestock, the fine will be 6 (six) head of the same type of livestock, plus the animal that was stolen, if available, which will give 7 (seven) head of livestock to be handed back to the owner of the stolen livestock.

5.2. In the absence of the stolen animal, a seventh one will be required in excess of the 6 (six) livestock initially to be compensated, so that altogether 7 (seven) livestock are payable.

5.3. If a convict steals for instance 3 (three) head of livestock, he/she shall compensate 6 (six) head of livestock per head stolen (by illustration, if you steal 3 head of livestock you will be required to pay 6 (six) times 3 which will give you the number of 18 head of livestock to be paid to the complainant plus the stolen stock). One head of cattle is required for the Community Court.

Section 6: Destruction of trees/deforestation

6.1 If a person is caught selling poles or droppers to be used for fencing or any other purpose to someone in another region/constituency, the fine will be 5 (five) Namibian dollars per pole/dropper, depending on the seriousness of the impact perpetrated on the forest.

6.2 If somebody from another region comes and destroys trees in the region without authorisation, the fine will be 10 (ten) Namibian dollars per pole/dropper.

Section 7: Chopping or burning of trees

7.1 Any person chopping down a tree to pick up fruit from that tree, or for any other reason, will be charged 2 (two) head of cattle.

7.2 Any person who burns down a tree for money or for any other reason, will be fined 3 (three) goats or sheep.

7.3 Any person that causes a grass or veld fire will be fined 2 (two) head of cattle.

7.4. Picking fruit not yet ripe:

7.4.1 For any person found picking fruit that is not ripe, the fine is 1 (one) goat or a sheep.

7.4.2 If a person from another region does so, i.e picks unripened fruit, the fine is 1 (one) head of cattle, that is if he/she did not obtain permission from the Traditional Authority.

7.4.3 This applies to any fruit, whether ripe or not; the same applies to the collection of edible mopane worms.

Section 8: Adultery with another man's wife

8.1 The fine for adultery will be six (6) head of cattle; the evidence against the accused person must be closely scrutinized.

8.2 If a person in any case is aggrieved by the decision from the Senior Headman's Committee, he/she is at liberty to appeal to Regional Community Courts. He/she must appeal in writing from the area District Court and the final decision must accompany his/her appeal.

8.3 The accused may appeal up to the Magistrate's Court for the district within which the community court falls.

Section 9: Legal representatives in traditional courts

9.1 No lawyers or legal representative(s) shall be allowed in community courts, although it is the constitutional right for a person to be represented by lawyers.

9.2. Even if it is the person's wish, traditional courts are not comparable to ordinary courts; however, representation by parents or family members is allowed.

Section 10: Clerks of District and Regional Community Court

10.1 He/she must be a resident of that region. In the event that no suitable candidate may be derived from that region for that position, the Court may ask another district which falls under the jurisdiction of the Royal House to provide them with a clerk. It is also possible to seek advice from the Regional Council in respect of the appointment of the Clerk. The Offices of the Namibian Police may be approached for advice/assistance if need be.

Section 11: Appointment and function of members of the Community Court

11.1 Judges of the Community Court are appointed and gazetted in the Government Gazette to adjudicate on cases in a particular District.

11.2 The judges in a particular District shall perform both judicial and prosecutorial duties.

Section 12: Corporal punishment

12.1 In terms of the provisions of the Namibian Constitution, corporal punishment shall not be allowed as any form of punishment for a convicted person, but rather any punishment should be in the form of compensation.

Section 13 Inheritance/succession

13.1 When a person dies intestate, his/her estates shall be distributed in terms of the prevailing customary law.

13.2 Succession/inheritance shall be based on matrilineal hierarchical structures.

13.3 The wife and the children of the deceased (if any) are part of the estate of the deceased and the executor (who originates from the patrilineal line of the deceased) may also dispense them to heirs.

13.4 All persons who inherit from the deceased assume/take over the entire estate, including the obligations to look after the dependents of the deceased in exactly the same manner in which the deceased provided for them.

13.5 The inheritance of the holy fire is done in accordance with the patrilineal or father's blood line, from eldest brother to youngest brother and after that to eldest son.

Section 14 Customary marriage

14.1 Marriage exists and is practised as it was used in the tradition of the Ovaherero.

14.2 A man can marry more than one woman.

14.3 A child born out of wedlock is a child of the man who marries his/her mother.

14.4 To marry, a man must go through his parents, who will go and ask for the woman's hand on his behalf, as it is not permitted for a man to negotiate for his own marriage, whatever age the man might be. Traditionally, he is not allowed to carry out these negotiations in respect that he is still a child, so he must go through the elders.

14.5 Traditionally, men who are married are allowed to have a girlfriend as long as he behaves with respect.

14.6 A married man has the right to tell his wife that he will spend the night elsewhere.

14.7 A certificate will be given to a married couple if they have applied to have all in writing.

Section 15: The rights of women in marriage

15.1 Since the husband has the right, the wife also has the right to report ill treatment by her husband to the family or parents of the husband. The family of the husband and the parents must call him in and talk to him not to do it again.

15.2 The wife also has the right to decide together with her husband everything related to the management of their household. If the husband is willing to marry another wife, he must first inform his first wife which means that the first wife will accompany her husband and his parents to fetch the additional wife (wives). If the first wife refuses to allow her husband to marry another wife, she must give convincing reasons with clear facts. If it happens that the first wife has opposed the taking of a second wife with clear facts, the man will not be allowed to marry. But if it is found out that the first wife was only jealous, the man can proceed to marry another or that wife he intended to marry. The subsequent wife will be subordinate to the first wife.

Annexure 1
Forms

EMPLOYMENT

INQUIRIES: .... No: 0000

To whom it may concern

This is to confirm that Mr / Ms / Mrs: ....
ID no: .... is a ....
Young man/woman residing at .... village in the Opuwo, Epupa and Sesfontein Constituency in Kunene Region. He/she wants to apply for employment/ study at your institution, hence he/she has approached Vita Royal House Office for a confirmation letter to be considered for admission on affirmative action status.

Vita Royal House indigenous communities People's Organization is a newly established community organization (Date of Gazette: 1997) aimed at improving the quality of life and wellbeing of the Ovatua, Ovahimba, Ovaherero, Ovambo, Ovazemba and Ovatjimba in the south-west of Angola and north-west of Namibia. The administration is based in Opuwo, which is the capital of Kunene Region.

It is my sincere hope that his/her application for employment will be considered on the basis of his/her being a community member of the previously disadvantaged groups in former Kaokoland.

This information is provided by our recognized Traditional Authority to justify the information.

Yours in community development

Ms/Mr: .... Signature: ....

[Date]: .... Rank: ....

All official correspondence must be addressed to the Secretary of the Traditional Authority

MEMBERSHIP APPLICATION FORM

PO BOX 291, OPUWO TEL (065) 273509 FAX (065) 273510
E-MAIL ADDRESS: kapi.ben@gmail.com

SURNAME:..
FIRST NAME(S):..
PHYSICAL HOME ADDRESS: ....
....
ID NO: ....
DATE OF BIRTH: ....
MARITAL STATUS: ....

Date of employment	Permanent	Contract	Occupation	Basic Salary	Salary No

DEPARTMENT: ....
Female:..
Male: ....

STOP ORDER AUTHORIZATION FOR DEDUCTION OF MONTHLY TRADITIONAL AUTHORITY SUBSCRIPTIONS

I, the undersigned, not having authorized a stop-order for any other Traditional Authority/ having withdrawn all other such authorizations, hereby agree to the monthly deduction of one (1) percent from my basic salary, which shall be paid over to the **VITA ROYAL HOUSE** in respect of my membership of the Traditional Authority. My deduction shall be varied to meet any change in subscription rates notified to me from time to time by VRH.

EMPLOYEE'S SIGNATURE: ....
DATE: ....

SALARY DEDUCTION CODE:............................ Official stamp

....
Traditional Authority Secretary Date

(NB: COPY TO BE SENT TO THE SALARY OFFICE WITH 15 DAYS)

APPLICATION TO MOVE ANIMALS

N0: 0000

VITA ROYAL HOUSE

DOCUMENT OF IDENTIFICATION (SECTION 6 OF STOCKTHEFT ACT 12 OF 1990 OF THE REPUBLIC OF NAMIBIA REGULATION 2).

ORUTUU ROMAARISIRO (ORUPA 6 ROVETA YOURUNGA UOVINAMUINJO OVETA 12 YO REPUBLIKA YA NAMIBIA EZEVA 2).

1. NAME OF APPLICANT (Ena romuningire wousemba wokuhinga ovinamuinjo)

   ....

2. ID NUMBER OF APPLICANT (Onomora yokauru kondjiukiro)

   ....

3. NAME OF STOCK OWNER: (Ena romuni wovinamuinjo)

   ....

4. ID NO. OF STOCK OWNER (Onomora yokauru komuni wovinamuinjo)

   ....

5. LIVESTOCK (Ovinamuinjo)

Type of animal Otjikeenamuinjo	Number Otjivarero	Sex (Male/ Female) Oukaze no urume	Brand Mark Omuriro	Colour Otjivara	Carcass Onjama	Ear tag no. Onomora yokatenda

6. Name of Headman/woman: (Ena rosoromana) ....

7. ID no. of Headman/woman: (Onomora yokauru ko soromana) ....

8. Signature of Headman /woman: (Omatekeneno wosoromana) ....

9. Place to: (Otjirongo kumavii) ....

10. Place from: (Otjirongo kumavizu) ....

11. Reason/Purpose: (Epu romahingiro) ....

12. Date livestock sold: (Omayuva wovinamuinjo tjivyarandisiwa) ....

13. This document is not an animal movement permit but only authorizes the bearer to move animals to the nearest veterinary office where he/she can obtain an animal movement permit. (O mbapira ndji oyokukupa ousemba okuza kotjirongo tjoye poo pona puwatura okutwara ovinamuinjo ko Rukondwa rwarwe)

14. This document does not authorize the bearer to move animals to another Region. (Ombapira ndji kajo kuyandjera ousemba uokutuara ovinamuinjo ko Regiona yarue.)

15. Headman/woman stamp date (Ostampa yosoromana)

RECOGNITION AND REGISTRATION OF NEW OR EXISTING CUSTOMARY LAND RIGHT

No: 0000

Our Ref...
Your Ref...
Inquiries ....

The chairperson of the Communal land board...

This is to certify that Mr/Mrs/Ms ....
Identity no:... has applied for recognition/registration of customary land Right at................................. in.................................. Constituency that resorts under the Vita Royal House Traditional Authority.

He/she applied for an area of..................................ha (residential/farming unit) and for a period of ....years.

This Traditional Authority recommends the ratification or approval of his/her application by the Communal Land Board.

Traditional chief: Tjimbuare Thom of the Vita Royal House Traditional Authority.

Chief's Signature ....   Date: ..../.........../...........

Secretary's Signature ....   Office Stamp

All official correspondence must be addressed to the Secretary of the Traditional Authority

RECOGNITION AND REGISTRATION OF NEW OR EXISTING RIGHT OF LEASEHOLD:

No: 0000

Our Ref...
Your Ref..
Inquiries ....

The Chairperson of Communal Land Board..

This is to certify that Mr/Mrs/Ms...
Identity no:.. has applied for recognition/registration of a new or existing right of leasehold for..............................at.................................. in.................................. Constituency that resorts under Vita Royal House traditional community.

He/she applied for an area of.........................ha and for a period of.........................years.

This Traditional Authority recommends the ratification or approval of his or her application by the Communal Land Board.

Traditional chief: Tjimbuare Thom of the Vita Royal House traditional community.

Chief's Signature ....   Date: ..../............/............

Secretary's Signature ....   Office Stamp

All official correspondence must be addressed to Secretary of the Traditional Authority

WILL

No: 0000

DATE ....

This is the Will of:.. (full name)
Identity Number:..
Of (address)..

1. I revoke any past will made by me.
2. I nominate:..

(Full name and address of person appointed as Executor) to be Executor of my Estate).

3. I direct that my nominated Executor does not have to give security to the Master of the High Court for the proper administration of my Estate.
4. I leave my Estate to the people and in the amounts indicated here:
   ....
   ....
   ....
   ....
   .... Full names)

5. I appoint: ....
   Identity Number:..
   of (address:..
   to be the sole guardian of my minor children.

Signed at.............................. on the..................... day of..................................20.........
In the presence of the undersigned witnesses, who signed in my presence and in the presence of each other, all being present at the same time.

....
....
....
....

....
TESTATOR

As witnesses:

1................. ....

2................. ....

Date Stamp

All official correspondence must be addressed to Secretary of the Traditional Authority

MARRIAGE CERTIFICATE CONSENT LETTER

No: 0000

Inquiries: .... Date: ....

TO WHOM IT MAY CONCERN

MARRIAGE DECLARATION BY TRADITIONAL AUTHORITY MEMBERS

This serves to attest that: Mrs. .... Id no: ....

married (husband) Mr. .... Id no: ....

At .... village without ante nuptial contract.

Date: ....

Remarks: This marriage was carried out in accordance with Otjiherero tradition and is recognized by the Vita Royal HouseTraditional Authority.

The Chief, Senior Councillor and the Secretary of the Vita Royal House hereby attest that at the time of the solemnization of this marriage, I am empowered by the Traditional Council to solemnize this marriage.

Full name: .... Signature: ....

Date stamp

All official correspondence must be addressed to Secretary of the Traditional Authority

MARRIAGE CERTIFICATE

No: 0000

A. PARTICULARS OF HUSBAND

1. Surname:..Identity No:..
2. First Name in Full:..
3. Date of Birth: Date......................Month......................Year..............................
4. Country of Birth..
5. Marital Status..

B. PARTICULARS OF WIFE

6. Surname ....
7. Identity No:..
8. First Name in Full ....
9. Date of Birth: Day.....................Month.....................Year...............................
10. Country of Birth..
11. Marital Status..

C. PARTICULARS OF MARRIAGE

12. Date of Marriage: Day......................Month......................Year ....
13. Marriage Solemnized at: City/Town/Village ....
14. By/Without antenuptial contact ....
15. Remarks ....

D. (1) DECLARATION BY MARRIED COUPLE

16. This marriage between us was in the presence of the undersigned witnesses.

Signature (Husband) .... Signature (Wife) ....

17. Witnesses

(a) .... (b) ....

Signature .... Signature ....

E. (2) DECLARATION BY PARENTS OF THE MARRIED COUPLE:

18. This marriage was solemnized by us on this......................... (Day) of .... Month......................... Year.........................
19. Wife's Father: Full Name: .... Signature....................................
20. Husband's Father: Full Name: .... Signature....................................
21. Husband's Mother: Full Name: .... Signature....................................
22. Wife's Mother: Full Name: .... Signature....................................

F. DECLARATION BY TRADITIONAL COUNCIL MEMBER

I hereby declare that at the time of solemnization of this marriage, I was empowered by the Traditional Authority to solemnize this marriage.

Secretary: .... Signature ....

Date: .... At: ....

Date Stamp:

All official correspondence must be addressed to Secretary of the Traditional Authority.

CERTIFICATE OF TERMINATION OF TRADITIONAL MATRIMONY

No: 0000

INQUIRIES: .... DATE: ....

TO WHOM IT MAY CONCERN:

I, ...

The Chief of Vita Royal House Traditional Authority in Kunene region, hereby declare that the traditional matrimony between

.... ID no: ....

.... ID no: ....

which was officiated by Mr. ....

at ....

on this day .... of.............................. 20................. has been terminated.

Confirmation by VITA ROYAL HOUSE OFFICE DATE

....

(TRADITIONAL ....) STAMP

All correspondence must be addressed to the Secretary of the Traditional Authority

Certificate of consent to publish

Certificate of the consent to publish

UNIVERSITY OF NAMIBIA

FACULTY OF LAW

HUMAN RIGHTS AND DOCUMENTATION CENTRE

RE: CONSENT TO PUBLICATION

I, the undersigned, Chief of the Vita Royal House Traditional Authority, hereby give consent to the Human Rights and Documentation Centre, to publish the following documents of the Vita Royal House Traditional Authority:

1. The Customary Laws
2. The Community Profile
3. Picture of the Chief
4. Logo of the Traditional Authority

I acknowledge that the Human Rights and Documentation Centre will publish the laws in our indigenous language (Otjiherero), as well as the English language. I am familiar with the contents of the laws that will be published and further acknowledge that they were prepared by my traditional authority.

Signed on this 23 **day of** July **2012**

At Opuwo

X

Chief

For HRDC: Mr. A. Gairiseb

THE VITA THOM ROYAL HOUSE OF KAOKOLAND
(KUNENE REGION)
KUNENE REGION, OPUWO
23 JUL 2012
EMail: vitaroyalhouse@iway.na
TEL: 065-273509
Cell no:
FAX: 065-273510, BOX 291, OPUWO

Zeraua Traditional Authority
Ondjuwo Jouhonapare waZeraua

The supreme leader of the Zeraua[1] Traditional Authority was
Ombara[2] Christian Eerike Zeraua.
Date of designation: 4 October 1997
He passed away on 8 January 2012[3].

1 Also spelled 'Zeraeua'.

2 Traditional title in terms of section 11, Traditional Authorities Act, 2000 (No. 25 of 2000).

3 Editor's note: There was no information on the appointment of an acting supreme leader or a successor to the late supreme leader of the community at the time of going to press.

PROFILE[4]

1. Historical Background

1.1 Previous leaders of Otjimaruru leading Zeraua Royal House

1.1.1 *Ombara* Wilhelm Zemburuka Zeraua from 1769–1877.
1.1.2 *Ombara* Tjoheroni Mbandeuru from 1877–1884.
1.1.3 *Ombara* Manasse Tjiseseta from 1884–1898.
1.1.4 *Ombara* Michael Kajeomurungu Tjiseseta from 1898–1904.
1.1.5 *Ombara* Phillimon Kapia from 1925–1937.
1.1.6 *Ombara* Willem Kapia from 1937–1937.
1.1.7 *Ombara* Justus Kapia from 1937–1957.
1.1.8 *Ombara* Gottlieb Kapia from 1952–1979.
1.1.9 *Ombara* Christian Eerike Zeraua, born on 4 January 1934 and designated on 4 October 1977. Chief Zeraua was the supreme leader of the Zeraua Traditional Authority until his death in 2012.

Chronological order of the chieftaincies

Name of *Ombara*	**Tenure of rule**	Number of years served
1. Wilhelm Zemburuka Zeraua	1769–1877	8
2. Tjoheroni Mbandeuru	1877–1884	7
3. Manasse Tjiseseta	1884–1898	14
4. Michael Kajeomurungu Tjiseseta	1898–1904	6
5. Phillimon Kapia	1925–1937	12
6. Willem Kapia	1937–1937	1
7. Justus Kapia	1937–1957	20
8. Gottlieb Kapia	1952–1979	27
9. Christian Eerike Zeraua	1979–2011	32

2. Otjohorongo Communal Area Borders

2.1 Northern Borders: Epupa and Ugab Rivers.
2.2 Western Borders: Ugab River and Uis Communal Area.
2.3 Eastern Borders: Kalkfeld and Omaruru Commercial Farms.
2.4 Southern Borders: Okombahe Communal Area.

4 This profile was provided by the Zeraua Traditional Authority.

3. Population

3.1 The population numbers 4 300.

4. Division of traditional territory in Districts

4.1 Otjohorongo communal land is made up of six wards which include the following villages:

(a) **Omatjete:** Headed by Mr Benjamin Kariko.
Traditional Councillor: Ms Otilie Kake.

(b) **Otjohorongo:** Headed by Mr Edward Kazondandona.
Traditional Councillor: Mr David Tjiseseta.

(c) **Okongue:** Headed by Mr Edward Mate.

(d) **Okamaere:** Headed by Mr Salathiel Ngatjiheue.
Traditional Councillor: Mr Ngutjiua Tjipepa.

(e) **Ozondati:** Headed by Mr Judo Haakuria.
Traditional Councillor: Mr Fabianus Uaseuapuani.

(f) **Omihana:** Headed by Mr Fransiskus Tjiveze.
Traditional Councillor: Mr Rabbie Tjivinde.

(g) **Ohamuheke/Kaokoland:** Headed by Mr Ben Mbomboro.
Traditional councillor: Mr Japi Uaraavi.

(h) **Otjimbingue:** Headed by Mr Stephanus Hukununa.

5. Location of traditional office

5.1 The traditional office is located in Omatjete.

6. Language

6.1 The language spoken is Otjiherero.

7. Community Trust Fund

7.1 The Zeraua Royal House has opened a bank account with First National Bank in the name of Zemburuka Trust Fund, with a Committee responsible for its management.

7.2 Names of the Committee Members:

(a) **Chairperson:** Mr Edward Kazondandona

(b) **Secretary:** Ms Othilie Kake

(c) **Treasurer:** Mr Salathiel Ngatjiheue

8. Community Court

8.1 The community court consists of five (5) judges, namely:

(a) Mr Edward Kazondandona
(b) Mr Raphael Kapia
(c) Mr Manfred Kaanjosa
(d) Mr Rudolf Hongoze
(e) Mr Duludi Ndjiharine

8.2 Assessors

(a) Mr David Tjindjiumbo
(b) Ms Brigithe Kariko
(c) Mr Ben Haukambe
(d) Mr Benjamin Kariko
(e) Mr Samuel Hamburee
(f) Mr Moses Kazandu Nokanene

8.3 Clerk

Mr Benestus Rukeeveni Haakuria

THE LAWS OF THE ZERAUA[1]

1 The laws were submitted in English only.

1. Rules of Succession

1.1 The first priority is the younger brother of the *Ombara*, and if no one is available, then the community has to look to the second choice, explained below.

1.2 The firstborn of the Chief, born within wedlock, or the brother of the firstborn son, is always the one to succeed the chief.

2. Area of jurisdiction

2.1 Otjimaruru Kingdom originally covered the area of Otjimbingue, Omaruru, Otjohorongo/Omatjete and Kaokoland. The Traditional Authority has jurisdiction over the areas mentioned above.

3. Appointment of Councillors, Senior Councillors and the Acting Chief

3.1 The Chief, on the advice of the Chief Council, the Senior Traditional Councillors and Traditional Councillors shall appoint an Acting Chief.

3.2 The appointments of the Senior Councillors and Councillors are carried out by the community members of that specific ward or as per customary laws. Each person must be loyal and show clear support to the Royal House.

3.3 Traditional leaders in the villages and wards are expected to be good listeners to their community's problems and needs, and are expected to assist community members where possible.

3.4 They should be exemplary leaders and are expected to be:

(a) Friendly
(b) Peaceful
(c) Patient
(d) Persistent
(e) Respectful
(f) Humble to all people in the villages and wards and
(g) Impartial in the administration of customary law and justice.

3.5 The traditional leaders should come to know the people under their leadership and try to establish a good relationship with them. They should have good and honest advisors.

3.6 There should also be a good secretary who can take accurate minutes of conversations and meetings.

4. Community Trust Fund

4.1 Zemburuka Trust Fund is managed by a Committee composed of the following personnel:

(a) Chairperson

(b) Secretary
(c) Treasurer

5. Traditional Courts/Community Court:

The traditional court is the Zemburuka Zeraua Community Court.

5.1 Structure of the Court

The Community Court consists of:
(a) 5 (five) judges
(b) 6 (six) assessors
(c) a clerk
(d) interpreters and
(e) a representative.

5.2 Appeal Body

5.2.1 The appeal body is the second highest appeal court and it comprises the Headmen, Senior Councillors and Councillors.

5.3 Supreme Court

5.3.1 The Chief is the highest appeal authority under the customary law of the Zeraua Traditional Authority.

6. Troop (*Otrupa*)

6.1 Song of the troop *(Eimburiro ro Trupa)*

Eimburiro no: 88 Otjiherero: (*Jesus Christus eye Ombaro*).
Song no. 88 (Jesus Christ is the King).

6.2 Important activities of the troop according to the culture *(Ovitjitua ovinahepero vioTrupa otja ko Mbazu)*

(a) *Onḓerera* = traditional marching
(b) *Ombimbi* (*I tonwa i yovarumendu*) = war song (practised by men only).
(c) *Ondoro* (*I rorwa i yozoserekaze*) = ululation (practised by women only).

6.3 Leaders of the troop

(a) General leader (*Omunane otjiuru*)
(b) *General-Obest*

(c) *General-Luitnant*
(d) General-Major/*Majoor*
(e) *Obest*
(f) *Briegadier*
(g) Captain
(h) Cavalry
(i) Infantry
(j) *Soldaat*
(k) Horse-riders
(l) Cadet

6.4 Army uniform

6.4.1 Women's army wear is a white dress, a black jacket and a Herero headdress *otjikaiva* (in white), or a black and white dress.
6.4.2 Men wear khaki uniforms marked with black and white ranks on their shoulders.

6.5 Fund of the troop

6.5.1 The fund of the troop is saved according to the laws of the troop and a special committee shall keep the fund.
6.5.2 The leaders of the troop shall save and protect the funds of the troop and shall determine and allow the usage and investment of the fund

7. Zeraua Traditional Authority

The Zeraua Traditional Authority consists of the following structure:

7.1 Chief's Council

7.1.1 The Chief's Council consists of members appointed by the Chief.
7.1.2 These members form a committee within the Chief's Council.
7.1.3 The main function is to give advice to the Chief.
7.1.4 The members of the Chief's Council can be elected.
7.1.5 The Chief's Council consists of the following:
(a) Chairperson (*Ombara*)
(b) Vice-Chairperson
(c) Other Members: 8 (eight) in number.

7.2 Advisors at village level

7.2.1 Advisors at village level are appointed by the headman of that village or the councillors of that particular village. Every village under the jurisdiction of the Chief should appoint village advisor/s.

7.2.2 The advisors give advice to the Chief, represent their villages at meetings and report back to the Headman or give feedback to the Headman.

7.2.3 The advisors are responsible for reporting any problem in the village to the Headman who later will convey all issues which need to be addressed immediately to the Traditional Authority which also includes the Chief.

8. Meetings

8.1 The Traditional Authority shall hold a meeting once every month.

8.2 There shall be an Annual General Meeting held by the Traditional Authority in December of every year.

8.3 General Meetings shall be held on request.

8.4 There shall be meetings with the various departments of government, which include ministers, governors, and constituency councillors.

9. Amendment of customary law

9.1 If there is a need to amend the customary law, the authority to amend it is vested in the Community Court together with the Chief's Council, expert elders in the community and the village advisors.

9.2 In general, it is not possible to change customary law unless it is in conflict with the Supreme Law (the Constitution of the Republic of Namibia, Act 1 of 1990).

9.3 Further, if customary law or the provision of customary law is inconsistent with the supreme law it will be invalid, but a record of such customary law or provision of customary law will be kept for future reference; it shall not be destroyed.

10. Land ownership

10.1 The Chief shall own the communal land within his area of jurisdiction.

10.2 The Chief shall also allocate to his community members customary land rights.

10.3 Any person who intends to use an area or piece of land for business purposes shall make an application to the Chief for the allocation of such area or piece of land for business purposes. The applicant must pay N$200.00 upon application and once the right to carry out any business is allocated, the holder of such a right shall pay a monthly levy of N$60.00 or an annual contribution of N$720.00.

11. Trespassing

11.1 Any person who is found on the premises or area or piece of land in the jurisdiction of the Traditional Authority, or premises privately owned, without permission, shall be guilty of trespassing and liable to a fine not exceeding N$1 000.00 or one head of cattle.

11.2 If the trespasser is not from the jurisdiction of the Traditional Authority, he/she shall return to his/her area of origin.

12. Grazing rights

12.1 The Chief shall grant grazing rights with the consent of the Traditional Authority.

12.2 Grazing areas are granted under the authority or permission of the Headman at village level from August till the time the rainy season comes. Every person who applied for grazing must return to their permanent residence after the completion of the grazing cycle. Failure to return is an offence and the person is liable to a fine of N$1 000.00 or four head of small stock, or one head of cattle.

12.3 Any person who settles in the grazing areas without the necessary permission shall be guilty of an offence and is liable to a fine not exceeding N$1 000.00, or such person may be removed from the grazing area, or be liable to both fine and removal from the grazing area.

12.4 If a person is allocated a grazing area and he/she or his/her employees commit stock theft, his/her grazing rights will be terminated and the holder of the grazing right will be ordered to return to his/her permanent residence.

12.5 The offenders shall be dealt with under the stock theft laws.

13. Livestock

13.1 When livestock is lost, the owner of the livestock together with his/her family members may attempt to establish its whereabouts on others' grazing lands until they recover it or they may seek assistance from the headman and co-villagers.

13.2 If a person is found in possession of stolen livestock and he/she claims that it is his/hers, and/or brands the livestock with his/her identification mark, such person will be guilty of an offence under customary law.

13.3 Transportation of Livestock: the Headman shall issue a permit to everyone who transports or intends to transport livestock, indicating the duration of the transportation.

13.4 A person who transports livestock without a permit is guilty of an offence and liable to a fine not exceeding N$500.00, payable to the Community Court.

13.5 Transporting hours are from 7h00 to 19h00.

13.6 If a person is found transporting livestock after hours, he/she shall be fined N$500.00 and ordered to wait until the right time to transport.

14. Environment

14.1 General

14.1.1 The entire community must take care of the environment and natural resources in their area.

14.1.2 It is the responsibility of the community to conserve and manage the natural resources in a sustainable manner in order to generate income from them.

14.1.3 Mining is the main source of income and if a person conducts mining activities in an area falling within the Chief's area of jurisdiction, he/she must pay or contribute an amount not exceeding N$200.00 per annum depending on the profit made, to the Royal House/Traditional Authority.

14.1.4 No one has the right to conduct mining activities in the Chief's area of jurisdiction without informing the Chief or the Traditional Authority. If any person is found mining without informing the Chief or the Traditional Authority, he/she shall be summoned by the Community Court. The Community Court may determine the appropriate fine.

14.2 Conservancies

14.2.1 The Government of Namibia has given the right to communities to conserve and manage their resources and to derive income from them.

14.2.2 The traditional community has the right to conserve and to manage their own wildlife, to cull in a sustainable manner, and to use the money derived from wildlife to their own benefit through farming in the conservancy.

14.2.3 Conservancy Committees shall set up proper management and an equitable benefit distribution plan.

14.2.4 During their festivals, the Traditional Authority gets wildlife from the conservancies' quotas.

14.2.5 If a conservancy generates enough money, it has to contribute a certain percentage to the Traditional Authority annually.

14.2.6 The Traditional Authority has by-laws and thus can fine any person who destroys natural resources, and other resources.

14.3 Harvesting without permission

14.3.1 No person is permitted to harvest any natural resource without getting permission from the headman or, in Conservancy Areas, from conservancy committees.

14.3.2 Harvesting without permission is an offence and the offender shall be fined N$1 200.00.

14.4. Cutting trees and extracting minerals without permission

14.4.1 The following fines apply:

(a) Harvesting poles: N$10 per pole.
(b) Harvesting droppers: N$1 per dropper.
(c) Harvesting wood: N$100.00 per ton.
(d) Extracting minerals: N$2 000.00.

14.5 Genetic resources

14.5.1 Access to resources must be subject to prior informed consent which must be in writing and obtained from the Traditional Authority. Any prospective resource user/s (researchers and commercial companies) must go through the Traditional Authority (Chief or local headman/woman), or conservancy to attain access to genetic resources.

14.5.2 All benefits accruing from the commercial and/or scientific use of genetic resources must be shared equitably.

14.5.3 The holder of customary land rights on whose land or area the resource is found, should get a fair percentage of any benefit.

14.6 Traditional knowledge

14.6.1 Access to traditional knowledge must be subject to prior informed consent (PIC), which must be in writing and obtained at Zeraua Traditional Authority.

14.6.2 All traditional practitioners must register with the Zeraua Traditional Authority.

14.6.3 If traditional knowledge is registered no-one shall use it for any purpose, unless with the written consent of the knowledge holder. The holder of this traditional knowledge and the origin of knowledge should be acknowledged and registered to facilitate benefit sharing and the payment of royalties to that holder.

14.6.4 Our intellectual property rights are protected according to our traditional norms and behaviours, whether documented or not.

14.7 Poaching

14.7.1 The fine for poaching is N$1 000.00 or 4 head of small stock.

14.8 Other natural resources

14.8.1 The fine will be determined by the justices in the Community Court.

14.8.2 The community has the right to form a community forest, through the Directorate of Forestry, for the sustainable use of wood and live trees.

15. Inheritance and division of estate

15.1 Normally, among the Ovaherero, when a family member passes away, the belongings of the deceased are distributed among the family members after the funeral, and it is done by the elder father of that clan. Example: when Omukuatjivi passed away, then the Omukuejuva had to divide the Estate. These two clans are known for *ongura* (joking) with each other traditionally and thus a member from the one clan will always be expected to support the other by way of distributing his belongings after such person's demise.

15.2 In Ovaherero tradition, if a relative dies, the estate is distributed after the funeral. Customary law determines how the inheritance of property should be conducted (regardless of whether the marriage was in or out of community of property). Under customary law, the property is distributed to all the relatives, and the wish of the deceased is considered in the case where the deceased left a will.

15.3 Nobody should be discriminated against when it comes to inheritance of property, including land. The appropriate legislative provisions should be applied as required without discrimination.

15.4 Note: There is a difference in the distribution of a man's estate and a woman's estate.

16. Marriage

16.1 Procedures regarding customary law marriages

16.1.1 Customary law marriages are of equal importance, just like common law marriages. A marriage under any law in Namibia must be taken seriously, particularly under the laws of the Zeraua Royal House.

16.1.2 All customary law marriages within the Traditional Authority areas shall be reported at the office of the Royal House for registration purposes.

16.1.3 The real Ovaherero marriage starts from the parents' decision as to whether their son is responsible enough to take care of a wife, or needs a wife to help with domestic responsibilities. If they decide so, then the parents will go and look for a woman. The woman could be of their own choice or from a family they know well.

16.1.4 The family, whose son or relative wants to marry, approaches the family of the bride, for talks or negotiations. During the negotiation process they present their case that their son intends to marry the daughter of that family.

16.1.5 If both parties (parents of the groom and the parents of the bride) reach consensus on the marriage issue, the family of the bride will propose the *lobola* or bride wealth to be paid. The date for the marriage is also determined during the same round of talks, or the second, third or fourth round.

16.1.6 The family has to bring *lobola* (*ovitunya*) and this is as follows:

(a) One ox
(b) Two young cows
(c) One male sheep and
(d) One female sheep with her offspring.

Or:

(a) Today one can bring the value of an ox which can be from N$7 000.00, and
(b) Two young cows.

16.1.7 Note: A man can inherit his late elder brother's wife or his late uncle's wife after consultation with the widow.

16.1.8 If the elders of that homestead with whom the marriage was discussed, were to sicken or die before the negotiations were completed, the woman must be given to her husband to show respect to the deceased. The family of the husband has to bring two young cows and fetch their wife.

16.2 Children born within or outside marriage

16.2.1 If a child is born within or outside wedlock, he/she shall be presumed to be the legitimate child of all parents and shall enjoy equal rights to their respective parents. The law shall care for, respect and treat all children equally.

16.3 Marriage of convenience

16.3.1 The laws of the Zeraua Royal House do not allow for marriages of convenience, but might not be immune to such marriages of convenience and thus, just as in the case of common law, such marriages are fully recognized. If a dispute develops, it shall be resolved within the ambit of the laws.

16.4 Marriage not dissolved

16.4.1 Customary law shall not validate the dissolution of a marriage, if it is proved on a balance of probabilities that the correct procedures were not followed, or reasonable grounds in law or in custom prove otherwise.

16.4.2 If there is violation on the part of either parties or one party, customary law requires the violating party to pay six (6) head of cattle. In the case of the husband, he has to return the wife.

16.5 Invalid marriage

A marriage shall be declared invalid in the following circumstances:

(a) In the absence of a marriage certificate
(b) In the absence of witnesses
(c) In the absence of a ceremony
(d) In the absence of a legal process either under customary or common law
(e) In the absence of a mutual agreement
(f) If one of the parties is under 18 years
(g) If there are no legal grounds for the marriage or
(h) valid family reasons.

17. Offences and punishments under customary law

17.1 Murder

17.1.1 No one has the right to kill another person or to take the life of another person unlawfully. Therefore, customary law prohibits and outlaws any form of murder. No human being, young or old, is allowed to take the life of another with a healthy mind or even if he/she is insane. No provocative words are allowed which might lead to a situation that may result in murder and any act of that nature shall not be permitted.

17.1.2 Murder is a crime and is punishable in terms of the laws of Namibia; the perpetrator is punished by the High Court of Namibia.

17.1.3 The accused shall be fined 15 head of cattle and the family of the victim will be compensated by the accused or his/her relatives.

17.2 Rape

17.2.1 In our culture pre-independence, there was no crime of rape but now the crime of rape is prevalent in many cultures as the world develops and thus no person may have sexual intercourse with a woman or girl without her consent.

17.2.2 Any person who is found guilty of raping a woman from the age of 18 years and above and the victim wants compensation, has to pay six (6) head of cattle to the complainant and N$3 000.00 to the Community Court for the purpose of deterring the accused from committing the crime again.

17.2.3 Raping a minor: Sexual intercourse with a minor is a crime and no one is allowed to have sexual intercourse with a minor even with their consent. The case may be referred to the Magistrate's Court in the District.

17.3 Stock theft

If a person is found in possession of stolen livestock, or if he/she has been proven guilty of stealing the livestock, the following fines will be imposed:

17.3.1 Cattle:
The accused shall pay 4 (four) to 6 (six) head of cattle. One (1) head of cattle shall go to the community court and the remaining head of cattle shall go to the complainant, or the accused shall pay monetary compensation to the amount of N$24 000.

17.3.2 Goat or sheep:
The fine shall be 4 (four) to 6 (six) goats or sheep, or N$3 000.

17.3.3 Donkey:
The fine shall be 4 (four) to 6 (six) donkeys or N$3 600.

17.3.4 Chicken:
The fine shall be 4 (four) to 6 (six) chickens or N$180.

17.3.5 Dog:

The fine shall be 4 (four) to 6 (six) dogs or N$600.

17.3.6 Horse:
The fine shall be 4 (four) to 6 (six) horses or N$9 000.

17.4 Branding or earmarking livestock of another

17.4.1 No one has the right to put a brand mark on someone else's livestock.

17.4.2 If someone is found guilty of this, he/she shall be fined in terms of section 17.3.

17.5 Animals without a brand mark or earmark

17.5.1 The owner shall pay a fine not exceeding N$300 to the Community Court.

18. Bribery

18.1 Bribery is a crime that is punishable by customary law, and the penalty shall be determined according to customary law and the nature of the crime.

19. Fraud

19.1 It is a crime punishable by our customary law if the accused is found guilty of cash misuse/embezzlement.

19.2 If the accused is found guilty, the court shall order him/her to pay the amount back, and the court will fine the accused additional money depending on the nature of the crime perpetrated.

19.3 The justices shall determine the fine to be paid to the Community Court.

20. Property damage

20.1 Burning of property

20.1.1 The fine is between N$1 000–N$3 000 and the accused has to pay the value of the damaged property to the complainant.

20.2 Breaking into property

20.2.1 If an accused is found guilty of breaking in and stealing property, a fine of N$1 000 shall be paid to the community court.

20.2.2 The court shall order the accused to return the property, and to pay a fine not exceeding N$2 000 to the complainant.

20.3 Damage to property

20.3.1 A fine of N$1 000 shall be paid to the Community Court.

20.3.2 The court shall order the accused to pay the value of the damaged property to the complainant.

21. Assault

21.1 It is an offence and punishable in the Community Courts to assault another.
21.2 Nobody is permitted to assault another person and once reported, the case shall not be withdrawn.

21.1 Beating

21.1.1 A fine of N$600 shall be paid to the Community Court by the accused if he is found guilty of beating another person.

21.2 Injury

Compensation for injuring another person's body must be paid according to the following:

(a) Tooth: N$ 400
(a) Eye: N$ 3 000, or one head of cattle; specifically, a pregnant cow.
(a) Nose: N$ 1 000
(a) Ear: N$ 800
(a) Foot: N$ 4 000 or one head of cattle; specifically, a pregnant cow.
(a) Lip: N$ 3 000 or one head of cattle.
(a) Breast: N$ 800
(a) Leg: N$ 3 000 or one head of cattle.
(a) Arm: N$ 2 000 or four (4) small stock.
(a) Fingers: N$ 1 000 per finger.

22. Children and alcohol

22.1 No person under the age of 16 shall be allowed to be present where alcohol is sold, or to be with drunk or among intoxicated persons.
22.2 A fine of N$100 shall be paid by the accused.
22.3 No alcohol shall be sold to children under the age of 16. Anyone found guilty of this offence shall pay a fine of N$100.00.

23. Sending children to school

23.1 All persons must send their children to school.
23.2 If a person cannot afford to pay for school fees, he/she must apply to the government's assistance programs (Ministry of Women and Child Welfare).
23.3 A fine of N$1 000 may be imposed.

24. Respect for customary law

24.1 Everyone who lives and resides within the area of jurisdiction of the Zeraua Traditional Authority has to obey this customary law.

24.2 Any person that does not abide by the law shall be fined the amount of N$500.

25. Prognostication (foretelling the future)

25.1 Any person who disturbs the public peace by prognostication shall be fined the amount of N$3 000 or two (2) head of cattle.

26. Witchcraft

26.1 According to the culture of the Zeraua community, witchcraft activities are punishable. Therefore, three or more traditional healers have to testify that a particular person practises witchcraft before he/she can be found guilty.

26.2 If the accused is found guilty, the Community Court shall fine the accused or shall order the accused to leave the specific area in which he/she has practised witchcraft.

27. Livestock offences

27.1 Buying animals without a permit

27.1.1 Any person found guilty of buying animals without a permit, or buying animals from a minor shall be reported to the village headman.

27.1.2 He/she shall forfeit the money which he or she paid for the animal, and the animal shall be returned to its rightful owner.

27.1.3 A fine of N$300 shall be paid to the Community Court.

27.2 Confiscation of animals

27.2.1 No one has the right to confiscate an animal from another person in order to redress a dispute.

27.2.2 If such a dispute arises, it shall be reported to the village headman, and if not resolved shall be taken to the Zeraua Community Court.

27.2.3 The Court may issue punishment and if the punishment is not adhered to, a fine of N$400 shall be imposed.

28. Setting the veld on fire

28.1 No one shall start a fire in the forest/veld without a valid reason.

28.2 Any person who negligently starts a fire, shall pay a fine of N$300 to the Community Court.

28.3 If the fire was accidental, the fine shall be N$150.

29. Insults

29.1 No one has the right to insult another person's body parts.
29.2 If the accused is found guilty, the accused shall be fined N$500 or one head of small stock shall be paid to the Community Court.

30. Water wastage

30.1 The fine for wasting water shall be N$500 or one head of small stock.

31. Community Court procedures

31.1 Reporting of cases

31.1.1 The first stage is to report the case to the headmen or traditional councillors.
31.1.2 The headmen or traditional councillors will consider the case and if the case is difficult or if they cannot solve the case, then the case shall be referred to the Community Court.
31.1.3 The Clerk of the Court receives all cases.
31.1.4 The Clerk of the Court records the case and allocates a case name or number.
31.1.5 The Clerk of the Court enters the case in the case registration book.
31.1.6 The Clerk of the Court allocates the date of the hearing.
31.1.7 The Clerk of the Court announces all the cases received on the radio or informs the parties concerned telephonically or through summonses/subpoenas.

31.2 Hearing of cases and presiding officers

31.2.1 There are six judges who sit on the bench and one out of these six judges delivers the verdict after consulting with the other judges.
31.2.2 When the judges are considering the appropriate punishment to be imposed, the public is told to leave the court.
31.2.3 If a person is not satisfied with the outcome of the hearing, he/she is allowed to file the case with the Community Court again; in other words, any person dissatisfied with the judgment can appeal to the same court twice.
31.2.4 If any party to a dispute is not satisfied with the decision after appealing to the court for the second time, he/she can appeal to the Magistrate's Court.

32. *Ongura* (traditional joking relationship)

32.1 *Ongura* is traditional joking and it is practised by Ovaherero of one clan who are fit to play with the other clan because of their forefather and mother.
32.2 No one is allowed to practise this with a person if they do not have that power, dependent on their clan.

33. *Oukura* (age set of male initiates)

33.1 *Oukura* is a group of young boys who were circumcised in the same year or time, and have a ritualized joking relationship.

34. *Ovihunina* (omen)

34.1 This is something that is normally not supposed to happen, but if it does happen, it can signify bad news to someone.

35. *Oviundikwa* (confidential information)

35.1 This is a traditional secret.

36. *Okuramba erya* (permissible theft)

36.1 This is the custom whereby one may take an animal in the absence of the owner, without his/her permission but in the presence of the family or wife for consumption purposes, and let the owner be told by the family or wife; however, he must also come to report that to the owner in person.

37. *Okuyepisasana* (wife exchange)

37.1 An institution where a man gives permission to his cross cousin to enter his marriage house and sleep with his wife for love or to indicate that he has no one to show that love except his specific nephew or *Ekura.*

38. *Ovizerika* (taboos)

38.1 Something one is traditionally prohibited to do, for fear of bringing evil to that homestead.

Certificate of consent to publish

Certificate of the consent to publish

UNIVERSITY OF NAMIBIA

FACULTY OF LAW

HUMAN RIGHTS AND DOCUMENTATION CENTRE

RE: CONSENT TO PUBLICATION

I, the undersigned, Chief of the ZERAEUA Traditional Authority, hereby give consent to the Human Rights and Documentation Centre, to publish the following documents of the ZERAEUA Traditional Authority:

1. The Customary Laws
2. The Community Profile
3. Picture of the Chief
4. Logo of the Traditional Authority

I acknowledge that the Human Rights and Documentation Centre will publish the laws in our indigenous language (OTJIHERERO), as well as the English language. I am familiar with the contents of the laws that will be published and further acknowledge that they were prepared by my traditional authority.

Signed on this 21 **day of** AUGUST **2012**

At OMATJETE

Chief

For HRDC: Mr. A. Gairiseb

THE ROYAL HOUSE OF ZERAUA
ERONGO REGION
2012 -08- 21
OTJOHORONGO

Ouhonapare wOvambanderu
Ovambanderu Traditional Authority

The supreme leader of the Ovambanderu is
Ombara[1] Kilus Karaerua Nguvauva.[2]
Date of designation: 23 November 2014

OvaMbanderu Traditional Authority

1 Traditional title in terms of section 11, Traditional Authorities Act, 2000 (No. 25 of 2000).

2 This submission was prepared during the time of Ombara Munjuku Nguvauva II and submitted to the editor for publication. When Ombara Kilus Nguvava was designated, the submitted text was approved by him.

PROFILE[3]

1. Brief historical background

The name Mbanderu refers to the place of origin of the people who bear the name today. The name is composed of two words: "*Mbandu*" meaning human being and "*Oruu*" meaning reed.

The Ovambanderu people are "*Ovandu varuu*" that is, human originated from the reeds. Thus their original home was a place of reeds. One day the Mbanderu set out and left their home in Central Africa. The first to leave were the Owambo, then the Herero and finally the Mbanderu.

The Mbanderu entered Namibia from the north following the same route of the Owambo and the Herero. They stopped first at Otjitambi in Kaokoland. Then, they moved further until they reached the hill of Kahamujema in Owamboland, where the Mbanderu divided themselves into separate clans. The best known are: Katua, Kavari, Kaimu, Muundjua, Marenga. The Mbanderu moved on via Outjo, Tsumeb, and Grootfontein into the present Otjituuo reserves and eventually to Omambonde and proceeded to the southern border of the Otjozondjupa settlement (Waterberg Reserves).

The Mbanderu continued to move eastwards via Okondjatu Reserve and east down to Otjomaapu in Botswana. After a certain time they settled around the Erongo Mountains. At a place called Onguati near the Erongo Mountains, Chief Nguvauva Nguvauva I, the son of Tjozohongo, produced his first son Munjuku Nguvauva I, father of the Great Kahimemua Nguvauva of the Mbanderu who was born at Omuseraakuumba in the year 1822 and further was circumcised in 1850.

This movement of the Mbanderu people clearly shows that from their past history they had their residential area in Namibia, their own leadership or authority as well as traditional practices and customs.

When Chief Munjuku Nguvauva I was born, the Herero had not yet reached central Namibia. They entered this area later via Sesfontein, Kamanjab, Outjo and Omaruru. The Mbanderu and Herero can be distinguished from the Owambo by important cultural differences. The two groups have many customs in common; they observe the same perception in respect of the milk calabashes, the *Oruzo* (paternal line) and the *Eyanda* (maternal line). There are numerous kinship connections between the Ovaherero and the Ovambanderu, and their legal observances correspond closely.

3 This profile was provided by the Ovambanderu Traditional Authority.

2. Historic battles of the Ovambanderu: The battle of Otjunda (Stumfeld)

The Mbanderu were the first Namibian ethnic group to fight the German colonialists at Gobabis and Otjunda in 1896. Although they were defeated, this war of resistance inspired other generations of Namibians to resist German colonialism.

At the end of April and the beginning of May 1896, Samuel Maharero who earlier on had placed a mounted commando of 300 Herero at Leutwein's disposal, decided to join the German troops, similarly Hendrik Witbooi with his men also joined the German soldiers (troops). Leutwein was thus ready to continue with a war of aggression. Simon Koper also chose to fight on Leutwein's side.

3. Linguistic affiliation

The language has its roots in the Bantu language of southern Africa and is referred to as Otjimbanderu. In south-western Africa, the people who speak dialects of the Bantu language have been classified as Ovaherero, although the dialect is shared by Ovahimba, Ovambanderu and Ovaherero.

The naming of the dialect as Otjiherero was mainly due to the Ovaherero's earlier contact with missionaries and colonial authorities, but there is increasing resistance by the other two groups who call for a neutral description of the language as in the case of Khoekhoegowab.

4. Symbolism

The Green Flag represents the Ovambanderu people and appears on all official documents of the community. The coat of arms features on the flag. The Green Flag is a symbol of Ovambanderu unity and is hoisted at all public gatherings and burials in the community. It is called out frequently at public gatherings as a salute and cry of approbation. Cattle are tremendously important not just to a material economy but also to the symbolic economy of status, family and social relations in the past, and cattle remain powerfully evocative to most Ovambanderu today.

5. Food and economy

Sour milk, commonly referred to as *omaere,* and meat is the staple of most Ovambanderu to date. Maize meal is also increasingly being used as a substitute for *omaere*. People wake in the morning to a thinner version of the porridge, sometimes enriched with soured milk and/or sugar, and tea. A thicker version of the porridge, known as *otjisema,* accompanied by a stew of meat is mainly prepared for lunch. People also use rice, but it is considered more expensive and associated with Europeans. Meats include goat, sheep, cattle, and various wild game. Village evening meals may include leftovers from midday, but for many people is often just *omaere* or meat.

6. Land tenure and property

On communal land people are allocated rights to farm or build houses, and pass the rights on to descendants, but they may not transfer the rights to someone else. Grazing land is generally not allocated, but people develop claims to grazing areas through registered wells, fenced portions and water rights

7. Division of labour

There is very little specialisation in the "traditional" economy, with the exception of holy fire keepers and traditional doctors. Within the household, tasks are distributed based on age and gender.

The symbolically important area of cattle care is associated mainly with men but more and more households headed by women are appearing, owing to increased educational levels of women and girls. But women do care for and milk the cows. With the introduction of ox-drawn ploughs, and later tractors, men have become more involved in crop agriculture.

Apart from erecting the heavy wooden supports and corrugated iron sheeting, women did most of the construction and maintenance of traditional houses; today, men tend to specialise in modern construction techniques. Young boys and men, along with other dependent males, used to work at cattle posts, but now younger people attend school and Ovambanderu complain frequently about finding reliable herders. In the "modern" economy, there is no formal division of labour by gender, age or class.

The laws of the Ovambanderu[1]

1 The laws were submitted in English only.

1. Political life

Politics are centred on the Chief (*Ombara)*, Senior Traditional Councillors (*Ozorata Ozonene*), Traditional Councillors (*Ozorata*) and Advisers (*Ovayandyandunge*) from the youth, women, and elders who make up the Supreme Council (*Orutu Orunane romuhoko*). The seat of the community is at Omimbonde Vitano ("Five Camel-thorn Trees") at Omauezonjanda, Epukiro in Omaheke Region. The structures consist of an office and a Community Court (*otjOmbanguriro tjOmbazu)*, an outdoor Chief's Council Community forum.

2. Keepers of the Holy Fires (*Ozondangere*)

Another layer is the Keepers of the Holy Fires (*Ozondangere*) who perform the spiritual function of communicating with ancestors and performing healing (*okuhuhura*) and cleansing (*okukaripira*) functions in the community. This group is revered and is above criticism and serves as the spiritual advisers of the chief.

3. The traditional troop of the Green Flag (*Otruppa*)

Following on the above layer is the traditional troop led by a General Field Marshal – appointed by the Chief – who is head of the Green Flag traditional troop assisted by a well-defined structure with various ranks. All General Field Marshals are members of the Supreme Council. The traditional troop is fashioned on military discipline and ranks and performs at all official ceremonies of the Ovambanderu as well as at burials of all Ovambanderu.

4. Community General Assembly (*Ombongarero onene yomuhoko*)

Ovambanderu look upon the consensual nature of the Community Court (*otjOmbanguriro tjOmbazu)* debates, and the hearing of disparate opinions within them, as underpinning Ovambanderu's successful traditional democracy. Furthermore, the emphasis is on consensus at the end of debates and the Chief or his appointee would summarise the majority position as general agreement.

Beneath the Chief are subordinate Senior Traditional Councillors who preside over a constituency and Traditional Councillors who have authority over a group of villages. The village has often been represented as a microcosm of the tribe: composed of patrilineal linked families, headed by the senior male who negotiates disputes and guarantees well-being through ritual/religious practices.

5. Succession

Succession to the position of chief (*Ombara*) is ideally patrilineal to the first son. In cases where polygamy and practices of substituting a sister for a childless wife, and of inheriting one from a deceased uncle or brother, the first son will ascend to the throne or alternatively, the incumbent Chief would leave an oral or written testament, for it is believed that the choice is communicated to him by the ancestors.

Another practice within the Ovambanderu is the practice of legally adopting a child born out of wedlock, to become a legitimate child of his father and, if possible, to ascend to the throne.

6. Chief's Council

Cases are heard in Magistrates' Courts, based on Roman-Dutch law, and in Chiefs' Courts, based on customary law. Because the Magistrates' Courts are conducted in English and require a lawyer, most Ovambanderu prefer to bring cases to the *Otjirata* (Chief's Council), where lesser criminal cases are also heard. Here, much personal testimony is heard from all who wish to contribute, and the Chief's decisions are built upon the opinions of respected members of the community.

Theft, disputes over property, and personal relations are common cases heard in the Chief's Court. Ovambanderu deal with social problems through an extended family system, traditional healers, spiritual healers and the courts.

7. Customary laws

7.1 Murder

Murder is defined as the crime of the killing of a person by another. The Community Court is exempt from hearing murder cases due to the severity of the crime and such cases are referred to the Magistrate's Court.

7.2 Rape

Rape and sexual violence is defined as committing the crime of having sexual intercourse without the consent of that other person or forcing a person to have sexual intercourse against his/her will. The Community Court is disqualified from prosecuting rape and sexual violence cases because of the severity of these crimes.

7.3 Theft

Theft is defined as committing the crime of stealing property belonging to someone else and is prosecutable by the Community Court. In the event of the accused being found guilty of such a crime, he/she is liable to compensate the complainant in terms of items double what was stolen or, in terms of monetary value, to pay an extra 50% on top of the amount of the stolen item's value.

7.4 Stock

7.4.1 Loss of livestock

In the event of loss of livestock by an individual such a person depends on the goodwill and support of his/her relatives and neighbours to recover any means of livelihood.

7.4.2 Transport of livestock

The transportation of livestock in and out of the communal land by farmers is done with authorization by veterinary officials so as to conform to animal health regulations.

7.4.3 Access to water for livestock

The owners of livestock are responsible for providing access to both water and grazing for their livestock.

7.5 Slander

Slander is dealt with by the *Omakura* (Peer Group) and the Community Court, and punishment in the form of monetary compensation or compensation in kind is meted out to the guilty party.

7.6 Adultery

Adultery is dealt with by the community courts, after proper assessment of the evidence before court. The guilty party (normally the man) caught with the wife of another may be punished in the form of compensation (whether monetary or in kind) depending on the circumstances of each case.

7.7 Insults

Insults denote the verbal utterances of words directed to cause emotional or psychological harm to someone else. The Community Court assesses the degree of the insults and depending on the extent and motive of the insults may order the guilty party to compensate the aggrieved party. The compensation may be either in kind or monetary. However, the community court may also, if the insults are minor in nature, warn the guilty party and order him/her to refrain from conduct which may cause insult to the aggrieved party.

7.8 Assault

Assault is interpreted as to physically harm someone resulting in that person sustaining injuries on his/her body. Assault is a crime. The Community Court is disqualified from presiding over assault cases due to the serious nature of the matter.

8. Marriage

A girl's marriage would be arranged by her family, and marriages involved bride-wealth or bride-service (*Otjitunja*[2]). Mbanderu marriages in the past were best described as a process, attaining the full definition of marriage often only after many years; steps in the process included requesting marriage and preliminary exchanges, sexual relations but not cohabitation, children, a public celebration, the establishment of a household within the man's compound, and bride-wealth.

The taking of more than one wife is still practised amongst the Ovambanderu.

While most marriages are still negotiated by family members, the spouses choose each other.

Most Ovambanderu conduct marriage ceremonies according to custom at home, and thereafter register a civil marriage.

Divorce may be sought by women and men, with common reasons including adultery, failure to provide support or household labour, and abuse but it is a last resort for the Ovambanderu.

8.1 Rituals involved in marriage

In terms of the Ovambanderu customary practices the process of proposing marriage is conducted over four (4) stages:

8.1.1. The introduction phase where families get to be acquaintances.

8.1.2. The second visit by the family of the groom-to-be is a token of seriousness to complete the wedding process.

8.1. 3. The third stage is when parties determine the bride's price.

8.1. 4. The fourth stage is when the official wedding is held.

8.2 Marriage certificate

Since the official recognition of the Traditional Authorities by the Government of Namibia in 1998, Traditional Authorities have been issuing customary marriage certificates upon the request of such a couple.

2 *Otjitunja* is also known as a marriage consideration.

8.3 Brideprice

The bride price varies from N$2 000 to N$10 000 plus two (2) cows in customary practice.

8.4 Number of wives

The Ovambanderu custom does not dictate the number of wives a husband might marry.

9. Inheritance

The Ovambanderu custom with regard to inheritance dictates the following rules when it comes to the execution of the estate:

The estate of both the husband and wife are administered separately.

9.1 In the absence of a written will by the husband

9.1.1 His younger brother is appointed as the Executor of the estate.
9.1.2 In the absence of the latter, a nephew is appointed as the Executor.
9.1.3 The Executor is tasked with distributing the estate firstly to the widow and all the children of the deceased, including those born out of wedlock.
9.1.4 Secondly, the remaining portion is distributed among the younger brothers, sisters and nephews of the deceased.
9.1.5 This principle applies to all the property including immovable property alike.
9.1.6 The presence of traditional leaders is required throughout the proceedings as observers and to enquire whether all the parties to the estate are satisfied with the outcome.
9.1.7 Equally, the presence of the maternal and paternal relatives of the deceased is required.
9.1.8 The widow is offered the option of being 'inherited' by a younger brother or a nephew of her late husband; in the event that she declines, she is returned home to her family of origin, with all her property including property that she has inherited from her late husband.

9.2 The wife's estate

9.2.1 The wife's estate, including movable and immovable property, is placed under the care of her biological family immediately upon completion of her burial.
9.2.2 The deceased's family, mostly the father or an uncle, is appointed as the Executor of the estate.
9.2.3 Firstly, the estate is distributed among all the children of the deceased.
9.2.4 Secondly, the remaining portion of the estate is distributed among her family members comprising sisters, brothers and the extended family.

9.2.5 The widower donates a cow to his family-in-law upon the return of his late wife's estate as a sign of:
(a) His innocence with regard to the death of his late wife, and
(b) His request for a substitute bride from his in-laws.

10. Responsibility for children and their education

10.1 Parental responsibility

Both parents are equally responsible for the child's upbringing, regardless of the marital status of the parents, with the support of the extended family.

10.2 Custody of orphans

The primary responsibility lies with the surviving parent and secondly with the grandparents/guardian (in the absence of the grandparents) who is normally appointed from among the extended family members.

10.3 Responsibility for children born outside marriage

Both parents are equally accountable for the child's upbringing. The father is required to support the child while the child is with his/her mother. The father can obtain custody rights and adopt the child by donating a cow to the mother.

10.4 Schooling

Schooling of the child is shared jointly by both parents with the aid of the extended family.

11. Gender

11.1 Equality between men and women

In terms of Ovambanderu culture, men and women perform different roles and functions which are complimentary to each other.

11.2 Protection of women from being oppressed

Elders play an important role in promoting the interest and welfare of women.

Special areas where this is a problem are, for example, inheritance and public life. The patriarch, by virtue of wisdom and the respect that he commands in the clan, assumes naturally the paternal role for the vulnerable part (the women) when it comes to solving disagreement in, for example, inheritance and marital disputes.

12. Intellectual property rights

12.1 Ownership of traditional knowledge

Cultural practices and norms of the Ovambanderu were narrated and taught around the fire by elders to youngsters for successive generations. Individual right to knowledge is freely practised. Voluntary sharing of traditional knowledge for teaching and recording purposes is highly recommended to promote and ensure preservation of history and cultural norms and practices.

12.2 Revenue of sales of traditional crafts

Partnership between craftsmen and traditional authorities is encouraged to the financial benefit of both parties.

12.3 Protection of traditional knowledge, symbols etc. against commercial abuse

The traditional authority intends to introduce measures within the framework of the country's laws to curb commercial abuse of traditional knowledge and symbols.

13. Peer group (*Omakura*)

13.1 *Omakura* refers to a group of young boys who were circumcised in the same year, and they perform a very important social role within the community.

13.2 *Omakura* serves as a social safety net in instances of the death and/or marriage of a peer (*Ekura*), the peers' parents (father and mother) and the wife of the peers (*omukazendu womakura*). A peer cannot marry or divorce without the *Omakura* knowing, because it is an established custom that a bride is married in the peer group and they must ensure her overall wellbeing and health. Even after marriage, a newly wedded bride can only be sanctioned by the *Omakura* after *Otjikeriva tjomakura* (the removal of the wedding coat by a peer[3]) that signals she is now free to dress as she pleases.

13.3 Also, it serves as an enforcer of community guidance and discipline for all those who belong to the various peer groups. Any misconduct or ill-discipline by any member of the community is first and foremost referred to the particular

3 Ordinarily when a woman is married, she is covered with a shawl referred to as "*otjikeriva*" which covers the back of her shoulders. She remains so covered after the wedding unless and until the peer of the husband removes, through a ritual process of *omaisakero wotjikeriva tjomakura*, the wedding shawl.

peer group to which the culprit belongs. Cases would involve abuse of alcohol, vulgar language, improper conduct, physical violence, domestic violence, marriage and divorce.

14. Extended family system

14.1 Most people belong to extended families that share a compound; within the compound the domestic units are based upon a woman and her children.

14.2 The senior male is traditionally the head of the household, and is responsible for mediating internal affairs and representing the group to larger society.

15. Housing structures

15.1 Mbanderu patrilineal customs predominate through the court systems, though kin groups are organised according to patrilineal, matrilineal, double-descent, or bilateral principles, depending on the ethnic group. Some groups have named clans, others have more fluid boundaries.

15.2 Kin groups larger than the household or compound group may cooperate for healing or strengthening ritual invoking ancestors, and should participate in funerals, which are significant events for defining relationships and obligations. Ovambanderu will maintain a 'holy fire', or *okuruwo* in their compounds.

16. Greetings

16.1 Mbanderu emphasise extensive greetings and inquiries after each other. It is polite to address senior men as *Tate* (father), *Honini* (father's elder brother), *Injangu* (father's younger brother[4]) and women as *Mama* (mother), literally, father and mother.

16.2 Grown women should keep their thighs covered, but more and more women are wearing tight pants, and short skirts are seen in urban areas.

16.3 While younger people should be deferential to their elders, and women to men, these patterns are sustained more strongly in villages than in the urban areas.

17. Religious practices

17.1 The most prominent religion practised by the Ovambanderu is the traditional African Religion which communicates through ancestors to *Ndjambi*, the almighty God. A case in point is the Church of Africa – a mixture of Protestant and traditional African Religion – which was established by the Ovambanderu and is the traditional home of all Ovambanderu.

17.2 Traditional religious specialists may bring rain, diagnose misfortunes, or strengthen households against evil influences and witchcraft, using herbs, roots, and special medicines.

4 In English this may be referred to as "uncle" but differs materially from the Otjimbanderu.

17.3 Many of the local Christian churches incorporate recognition of older local religious practices and beliefs, including the influences of ancestors in people's lives, often focusing on healing and promoting well-being. Traditional beliefs among most ethnic groups focused on securing ancestral beneficence. Many people who belong to a Christian church will also conduct private family ancestor rites to protect a new compound or house, or when repeated illness and misfortune afflicts members of the family.

17.4 Most Mbanderu believe in a Christian afterlife and anticipate resurrection. People also expect the deceased to maintain interest in their descendants, as ancestral spirits.

18. Burials

18.1 People want to be buried in their home villages, even those who have not lived there for a long time.

18.2 Today most people are buried in cemeteries, but some Mbanderu are still buried inside their compounds.

18.3 Funerals are very important events, at which a wide range of relatives, neighbours, and other associates are expected to attend; the expenses are heavy for many families.

19. Commemorations

19.1 The Ovambanderu maintain ritual and holy places and the most prominent are the annual commemorations at Okahandja, Okeseta, Otjunda and Dauha in Botswana.

20. Non-governmental associations

20.1 People may also join ethnic associations, burial societies, and other self-help groups; some of these serve as rotating-credit clubs where people pool small financial contributions to give members an occasional large sum or loan.

21. Traditional health system

21.1 Some illnesses are considered "European" and some "African" and are brought to medical practitioners accordingly. Other illnesses are brought to Western medical doctors, traditional doctors, and church priests/healers, or to as many healers as people can afford for the same ailment.

21.2 Physical ailments and general misfortune are both considered treatable, and the latter is brought to the attention of traditional doctors/diviners and church healers who are likely to diagnose social causes, jealousies, malevolence, and selfish ambitions.

21.3 Women make extensive use of government clinics for prenatal and child medical care. Sexually transmitted diseases, tuberculosis, and malaria remain problems; the HIV infection rate is a serious challenge.

22. Land allocation

22.1 Traditional leaders in consultation with the village foremen are responsible for the allocation of customary land rights to individual family households.

CERTIFICATE OF CONSENT TO PUBLISH

Certificate of the consent to publish

UNIVERSITY OF NAMIBIA

FACULTY OF LAW

HUMAN RIGHTS AND DOCUMENTATION CENTRE

RE: CONSENT TO PUBLICATION

I, the undersigned, Chief of the Ovambanderu Traditional Authority, hereby give consent to the Human Rights and Documentation Centre, to publish the following documents of the Ovambanderu Traditional Authority:

1. The Customary Laws
2. The Community Profile
3. Picture of the Chief
4. Logo of the Traditional Authority

I acknowledge that the Human Rights and Documentation Centre will publish the laws in our indigenous language (Otjimbanderu), as well as the English language. I am familiar with the contents of the laws that will be published and further acknowledge that they were prepared by my traditional authority.

Signed on this 12th **day of** November **2015**

At Windhoek

OVAMBANDERU
TRADITIONAL AUTHORITY
PO Box 650, Gobabis
Tel No: 062-568761
Cell No: 081 220 2352

Kilus M. K. Nguvauva

Chief

2015/11/2

For HRDC:

Part IV
The laws of the San communities[1]

1 Editor's note: No submission was received from the ǂKaoǁeasi Traditional Authority.

!Kung Traditional Authority
!Kung !hao Gaoxahn

The supreme leader of the !Kung Traditional Authority was
Gaoxa[1] John Arnold
Date of designation: 28 February 1990
He passed away on 13 July 2013.

The supreme leader is now
Gaoxa Glony Arnold (above)
Date of designation: 28 March 2015

1 Traditional title in terms of section 11, Traditional Authorities Act, 2000 (No. 25 of 2000).

Profile[1]

The !Kung live in the Kalahari Desert of north-western Botswana, the Cuando–Cubanga Province in south-east Angola, and in north-eastern Namibia. According to history, the !Kung San were the first people we know of in Africa. There are about 50,000 San in southern Africa today, only about one third of whom continue their traditional nomadic lifestyles. Many of them were made to work in other people's homes and on their farms.

Families are traditionally extended. Although women may be in the position of head of household, usually men hold this status. The !Kung do not deem it necessary to reflect on such issues as almost no problems arise in respect of sharing tasks and responsibilities. Men do not oppose women's employment, e.g. as teachers or as cleaners.

1 This profile was provided by the !Kung Traditional Authority.

The laws of the !Kung[1, 2]

1 The laws of the !Kung were submitted in English only.

2 During the process of editing the texts for this publication, the Human Rights and Documentation Centre learned that there was a discussion about the rules on succession to the position of the supreme leader of the !Kung community. The concern of the discussions was that the said rules did not reflect the tradition of the !Kung. As stated in the Introductory remarks to this Volume, it was not the task of the editorial team of this publication to verify the internal process that led to the self-stating of customary law by the various communities. For the editorial team, it was important to be given the duly stamped certificate of consent for publication by the Traditional Authority. It was not shown to the HRDC and the editorial team that the consent received from the !Kung Traditional Authority under the late supreme leader of the !Kung community was not valid. This leaves it to the community, as the case may be, to enter into a process of amending or changing the laws as they are stated in this publication, in accordance with the rules of the respective communities and the provisions of the Traditional Authorities Act.

PART I: ADMINISTRATIVE MATTERS

1. The Traditional Authority

1.1 The !Kung have established their own traditional authority, namely the !Kung Traditional Authority, which is the highest Traditional Authority of the !Kung community, with full powers vested in it by the community, and officially recognised by the Government of the Republic of Namibia.

2. The Chief

2.1 The Chief is the supreme head of the !Kung community and the custodian of all the communal land within his jurisdiction.

3. The Supreme leader

3.1 The supreme leader of the !Kung is a Chief, and not a *Kaptein* or Chairperson, as is the practice among some other communities in Namibia.

4. Functions of the chief

4.1 As the supreme head of the !Kung, the Chief shall have the following obligatory duties to his subjects:
4.1.1 He shall protect the community from dangerous activities.
4.1.2 He shall advise the community to refrain from traditional politics.
4.1.3 He shall be the spokesman of the community.
4.1.4 He shall be the link between the government and his people, using the established channels of communication from the Traditional Authority to Village Councillors and the community.
4.2 The Chief shall also have the responsibility to protect and conserve natural resources.

5. Rights and privileges of the chief

5.1 Being the head of the !Kung community, the Chief shall have the following rights and privileges:
5.1.1 He shall have rights over all communal land in his area of jurisdiction.
5.1.2 He shall have rights over the natural resources in his area of jurisdiction.
5.1.3 He must not be approached by anyone unless she or he is escorted and introduced by his Councillors.
5.1.4 The Chief shall have the right to hire or fire an employee within 24 (twenty-four) hours if such employee does not understand what the Chief has said to him/her.
5.2 The community shall cultivate the Chief's land.

6. Functions of the Senior Traditional Councillors

6.1 A Senior Traditional Councillor shall:
(a) represent the districts of villages.
(b) act as a messenger between the Traditional Authority and the village.
(c) deal with community members' court cases by passing judgments and levying fines.

7. Functions of the Secretary

7.1 The Secretary of the Traditional Authority shall:
(a) keep the minutes of meetings of the Traditional Authority.
(b) write letters to the districts of villages and to institutions.
(c) reply to requests from the people.
(d) be one of the signatories on all Traditional Authority correspondence.

8. The leadership of the !Kung Traditional Authority

8.1 The Chief shall lead the Traditional Authority in Tsumkwe West.
8.2 The Chief shall be from and be approved by the Royal Family.
8.3 The Royal Family shall choose the successor to the Chief or the current chief may appoint his successor before he dies; in the event that the Royal Family cannot provide the successor to the Chief, an election shall be held in which the eligible community members of !Kung in Tsumkwe West may vote in order to appoint the successor to the Chief from the Royal Family.

Part II: General rules

The customary laws of the !Kung Traditional Authority exist in order to maintain the values and norms of the traditional community and to ensure that they are known and maintained by the Traditional Authority.

9. Murder

9.1 A person who kills another intentionally shall be guilty of a crime in customary and Namibian criminal law.
9.2 The guilty party shall wipe away the tears of the deceased's family. According to customary law, the family of the guilty party shall bear responsibility for paying for the crime as soon as possible in order for peace to be restored between the two families.
9.3 The fine shall be either 10 (ten) head of cattle, 1 (one) of which shall be for the Traditional Authority, or N$45 000 (forty-five thousand Namibia Dollars), of

which N$10 000 (ten thousand Namibia Dollars) shall be for the Traditional Authority.

9.4 If the killing was committed unintentionally, for example, if a person was hit by a motor vehicle on the road and died, the accused shall pay half of the fine referred to in subclause 9.3, i.e. 5 (five) head of cattle, plus half a cow for the Traditional Authority.

9.5 If one person kills another by administering poison, and if a doctor provides clear evidence of such poisoning, and if the victim wants to have the offender tried, further investigation shall be conducted and then the offender shall be tried.

9.6 If the person who administered the poison is found guilty, he or she shall pay a fine of 10 (ten) head of cattle, 1 (one) of which shall be given to the Traditional Authority and the money generated by the sale of the animal shall be held in the Traditional Authority's safe.

9.7 A woman who aborts her foetus shall pay a fine of 5 (five) head of cattle, 4 (four) of which shall be paid to the man who impregnated the woman, and 1 (one) of which shall go to the Traditional Authority. In the past, all the cattle were paid to the Traditional Authority.

10. Rape

10.1 Any woman who has been raped, i.e forced to have sexual intercourse against her will, shall be taken to the police as soon as possible, after which she shall be taken to a hospital for medical examination by a doctor.

10.2 Medication may be required if the assailant had an infectious disease.

10.3 If the complainant wishes to open a case against the assailant at the Community Court, evidence may be required from the doctor.

10.4 Any person found guilty of rape shall pay 6 (six) head of cattle to the victim, and 1 (one) head of the cattle shall be paid to the Traditional Authority.

10.5 If the perpetrator rapes the victim and kills her, then the perpetrator shall pay two fines, namely 6 (six) head of cattle for rape, and 6 (six) head of cattle for murder, 1 (one) of which head of cattle in each case shall be given to the Traditional Authority.

11. Loss of body parts

11.1 If a person causes another to lose an eye or any other body part, the accused shall be tried and punished if found guilty.

11.2 The fine shall be 7 (seven) head of cattle, 1 (one) of which shall go to the Traditional Authority.

12. Insults and assaults

12.1 No one shall insult or assault another person.

12.2 Transgressors shall be tried and punished if found guilty.
12.3 Such persons shall be punished because they have violated the rights of another person.
12.4 The fines payable for an insult or incident of assault shall be N$500 (five hundred Namibia Dollars), N$100 (one hundred Namibia Dollars) of which shall go to the Traditional Authority.

13. Adultery

13.1 Adultery shall be a serious offence, and under !Kung customary law, no woman shall be permitted to sleep with more than one man.
13.2 If there is clear evidence that a man slept with another man's wife and impregnated her, he shall pay 4 (four) head of cattle to the woman's husband.
13.3 If there is no pregnancy, but the adulterous couple were caught in the act together, the man shall pay 2 (two) head of cattle to the woman's husband.
13.4 The adulterous woman shall also pay a fine to the Traditional Authority equal to half of the cattle paid by the man to her husband.

14. Pregnancy outside marriage

14.1 Traditionally, !Kung girls who were made pregnant were not compensated, but since the 1940s, a girl under 18 years of age who has been impregnated shall be compensated by the man by way of 2 (two) eland.
14.2 However, according to !Kung customary law today, the person who impregnated the girl shall pay 5 (five) head of cattle, 1 (one) of which shall go to the Traditional Authority.

15. !Kung traditional weddings

15.1 Long ago, traditional marriages were called *!ghom*. A woman was obliged to marry, and the traditional wedding ceremony took place at *!ghom |khea*.
15.2 If a woman fell pregnant before she was married, she was regarded as pregnant outside marriage, meaning that she became pregnant outside of the law that forbade a girl to have sex before marriage.

16. Inheritance

16.1 The laws concerning women and children shall be obeyed because they should no longer suffer injustice.
16.2 Widows shall be taken care of by all members of the community.
16.3 Widows shall not be driven off from their late husband's fields.
16.4 Assets shall be regarded as collectively owned by a husband and wife.
16.5 Traditionally, men and women can inherit the deceased's possessions. In general, men could inherit other men's hunting tools and the widow, but this

should be done with the consent of the widow and family members of the deceased husband and the widow to support the children.

17. Divorce

17.1 In the case of divorce, the husband and wife shall share their assets equally.

17.2 The husband shall transfer his former wife's livestock to his former wife's family.

Certificate of consent to publish

UNIVERSITY OF NAMIBIA

FACULTY OF LAW

HUMAN RIGHTS AND DOCUMENTATION CENTRE

RE: CONSENT TO PUBLICATION

I, the undersigned, Chief of the !Kung Traditional Authority, hereby give consent to the Human Rights and Documentation Centre, to publish the following documents of the !Kung Traditional Authority:

1. The Customary Laws
2. The Community Profile
3. Picture of the Chief
4. Logo of the Traditional Authority

I acknowledge that the Human Rights and Documentation Centre will publish the laws in our indigenous language (________________), as well as the English language. I am familiar with the contents of the laws that will be published and further acknowledge that they were prepared by my traditional authority.

Signed on this 16 day of March 2012

At Grootfontein

Chief

John Arnold

For HRDC: A. Graindel

!Kung Traditional Authority
!Aiha - Chief
John Arnold
P.O. Box 1391 GROOTFONTEIN Namibia
Date 16/03/2012

!Xoo Traditional Authority
!Xoo Gixamte

The supreme leader of the !Xoo Traditional Authority was
Gaoxa ǁagi[1] Sofia Jacobs.
Date of designation: 18 July 2009
She passed away on 23 October 2014[2].

1 Traditional title in terms of section 11, Traditional Authorities Act, 2000 (No. 25 of 2000).

2 Editor's note: Hendrik Martin was installed by the community as the successor to the late supreme leader but had not yet been gazetted at the time of going to press.

PROFILE[3]

1. The previous supreme leader of the !Xoo was Chief Willem Leubert.

2. The traditional office is located in Corridor 17 in the Aminuis District.

3. The languages spoken by the !Xoo community are !Xoo and Naro.

4. The traditional territory is divided into the:
   (a) Aminuis District, headed by Theresia Tanitue;
   (b) Leonard Wert District, headed by Frits Namseb, and
   (c) Corridor 13 District, headed by Piet Skeppers.

3 This profile was provided by the !Xoo Traditional Authority.

THE LAWS OF THE !XOO[1]

1 The laws of the !Xoo were submitted in English only.

Regulations and fines

1. Murder

1.1 In the past, the traditional law of the !Xoo dictated that a murderer would be killed in punishment for his/her crime. Because capital punishment is outlawed in Namibia today, a murderer shall be punished by way of a fine.

1.2 If a person is killed unintentionally, the murderer shall be let off with a warning.

1.3 If one person bewitches or poisons another without killing them, his/her family shall obtain medicine to bewitch the perpetrator in turn.

1.4 If a woman tries to abort her pregnancy, she shall be guilty of a crime and shall be tried by the Community Court.

1.5 If a woman gives birth but abandons her baby, she shall be guilty of a crime and shall be tried by the Community Court.

2. Rape

2.1 A person found guilty of rape or attempted rape shall be fined N$500 (five hundred Namibia Dollars).

2.2 A person found guilty of sexual harassment shall be fined N$250 (two hundred and fifty Namibia Dollars).

2.3 An adult found guilty of having sexual relations with a child shall be fined 3 (three) head of cattle.

3. Adultery

3.1 A man who sleeps with another man's wife and impregnates her shall be fined 2 (two) head of cattle.

3.2 A woman who sleeps with another man in her husband's house shall be fined 2 (two) head of cattle.

4. Pregnancy outside marriage

4.1 Historically, a man who impregnated a woman to whom he was not married was urged to bring 2 (two) gemsbok and remain with the woman forever; nowadays the man's parents shall inform the woman's parents about the pregnancy, and the two families shall negotiate on the possible compensation.

4.2 The standard practice is that the man or his parents shall bring one cow and a calf as compensation for impregnating the woman outside marriage.

5. Assault and physical injury

5.1 Assault has always been rare among the !Xoo community.

5.2 A person who is found guilty of assaulting another shall be fined N$ 600 (six hundred Namibia Dollars) or 1 (one) goat, either of which shall be payable to the Traditional Authority.

5.3 If one person physically injures another person's ear, eye, nose, arm or leg, or beats up another person, the perpetrator of the injury shall be fined as follows:

(a) Ear: N$1 500 (one thousand five hundred Namibia Dollars) or equivalent, e.g. 2 (two) goats and 1 (one) sheep; see traditional prices in section 27.

(b) Eye: N$4 000 (four thousand Namibia Dollars) or equivalent, e.g. 1 (one) head of cattle; see traditional prices in section 27.

(c) Nose: N$3 000 (three thousand Namibia Dollars) or equivalent e.g. 4 (four) goats and two sheep; see traditional prices in section 27.

(d) Arm: N$10 000 (ten thousand Namibia Dollars) or equivalent; see traditional prices in Section 27.

(e) Leg: N$10 000 (ten thousand Namibia Dollars) or equivalent; see traditional prices in Section 27.

6. Land allocation

6.1 The village headman/-woman, together with government representatives, shall have the power to allocate land.

7. Weapons

7.1 Weapons shall not be carried in public, but shall remain in the veld.

8. Alcohol

8.1 Alcohol brings hunger in the home as well as misunderstanding and conflict, and makes you vulnerable to losing your property.

8.2 Alcohol consumption shall be limited.

9. Shebeens

9.1 All shebeens shall be closed at all times during week days (from Monday to Friday).

9.2 A child under the age of 18 shall not be permitted to enter a shebeen. The !Xoo Traditional Authority wants children to take their education seriously and become social assets to the community in future.

9.3 If a shebeen owner does not comply with these rules, he/she shall be punished.

10. Inheritance

10.1 An estate for inheritance comprises both interior and exterior goods.

10.2 When a married man dies, all his property shall be inherited by his surviving spouse and children.

10.3 When a married woman dies, all her property shall go to her surviving spouse and children. If the man remarries or engages in a live relationship with another woman, all her property shall go to her children.

11. Theft

11.1 Theft was always rare among the !Xoo.

11.2 Any person who steals shall be fined twice the value of the stolen goods; e.g. any person who steals a blanket shall pay back 2 (two) blankets.

12. Looking after livestock

12.1 Every person shall take care of his/her grazing land and animals.

12.2 No person shall have the right to destroy another person's field (or allocated land) for any reason.

12.3 The owner of the field onto which another person's animals have strayed shall go to the village headman/-woman to solve the problem.

13. Loss of livestock

13.1 Any person who finds a lost animal shall take it to the village headman/-woman, who will take care of the animal until it is claimed by its owner.

13.2 Lost livestock shall be kept by the village headman/-woman for 5 (five) years, after which period it shall become the property of the Traditional Authority.

14. Branding irons and cattle registers

14.1 Every person shall have his/her own branding iron and cattle register.

14.2 The Traditional Authority shall have the right to take to court any person who uses a branding iron unlawfully.

15. Transportation and slaughtering of livestock

15.1 The headman/-woman shall supply each community member with a Traditional Authority stamp for the transport or slaughter of livestock.

15.2 If a person does not abide by the rules, he/she shall be fined N$150.00 per head of cattle or N$50.00 per head of small stock.

16. Protection of water

16.1 Water is life.

16.2 Both the Traditional Authority and the community shall be responsible for looking after water in the communal area.

16.3 The Traditional Authority shall punish any person who wastes water.

17. Trees

17.1 The Traditional Authority urges and encourages the community to conserve trees in the communal area.

17.2 Any person found cutting down a protected tree shall be fined N$200 (two hundred Namibia Dollars).

18. Animals

18.1 Before the !Xoo went hunting, they decided beforehand which type of antelope to kill.

18.2 The !Xoo also hunted according to the seasons.

18.3 The Traditional Authority shall have the right to take to court any person found hunting game without permission.

19. Veld and grass

19.1 There is special grass for building houses or huts.

19.2 Grass is a useful food for the community's animals.

20. Fire

20.1 If the grass has grown too long and impedes walking, the community shall have the right to set fire to the grass in a controlled manner so that new grass can grow.

20.2 Fire in the veld kills animals; someone found guilty of killing animals during a veld fire shall be taken to court.

21. Traditional healers

21.1 Traditional healers shall be accorded respect because they heal people with herbs and tree roots, etc.

21.2 All traditional healers shall have a licence before they will be allowed to practise in the community.

21.3 The Traditional Authority shall prohibit witchdoctors from practising in the !Xoo community.

22. Immorality

22.1 It is immoral for a man to have sexual relations with another man.

22.2 A person shall be fined a minimum of N$400 (four hundred Namibia Dollars) for engaging in homosexual activity.

22.3 If a blood test is taken and the result is positive, the man will be fined N$4 000 to N$5 000 (four thousand to five thousand Namibia dollars).

23. Lobola (bride price)

23.1 When a man wishes to marry a woman, he shall pay lobola. If the woman should later decide not to marry the man who paid lobola, she shall pay the man back.

23.2 Traditionally, if a future bride is chosen when she is a young girl, her husband-to-be was obliged to bring her parents wild animals like *gemsbok* until she was mature enough to marry. The man's parents would then ask the woman's parents for their permission for the marriage. If their blessing was given, the bride would then go and live with her husband.

23.3 The man paying lobola should bring his intended future wife's parents the following: a blanket (*gemsbok* skin); ring; traditional dress; shawl; earrings; necklaces; headdress made of beads; a sheep (ram); 12.5 to 10 kg sugar; 250 kg tea; bread flour; baking powder; cooking oil; tobacco; milk; smoking pipe; matches and candles.

23.4 If the woman opts for another man, she brings all these things back.

23.4 Lobola paid in cash should be N$10 000 (ten thousand Namibia Dollars).

24. Divorce

24.1 A married couple shall have the right to appeal to the Traditional Authority to declare a divorce.

24.2 If either member of the couple is found guilty of having caused the problem leading to the divorce, he/she shall be fined 1 (one) head of cattle or 3 (three) sheep.

25. Raising children

25.1 Parents should set a good example for their children.

25.2 Children should be raised with respect.

25.3 Children should be brought up to respect their elders in society.

25.4 Children must not be sent to buy alcohol or tobacco.

25.5 Parents/caregivers must ensure that their children are healthy.

26. Care of the elderly

26.1 The Traditional Authority shall take care of the elderly.

26.2 The Traditional Authority shall make sure that the elderly receive their pensions and that the money is used to buy food and clothing and not alcoholic beverages.

26.3 The children and grandchildren of an elderly person shall be responsible for washing their elderly parent's or grandparent's clothes.

27. Traditional prices

27.1 Donkey: N$ 600 (six hundred Namibia Dollars)
27.2 Horse: N$ 1 000 (one thousand Namibia Dollars)
27.3 Goat: N$ 600 (six hundred Namibia Dollars)
27.4 Sheep: N$ 300 (three hundred Namibia Dollars)
27.5 Chicken: N$ 100 (one hundred Namibia Dollars)
27.6 Dog: N$ 250 (two hundred and fifty Namibia Dollars)
27.7 Cow: N$ 4 000 (four thousand Namibia Dollars)
27.8 Pig: N$ 800 (eight hundred Namibia Dollars)
27.9 Mule: N$ 1 500 (one thousand five hundred Namibia Dollars)

28. Chieftainship

28.1 Chieftainship shall follow through the bloodline, and thus the Chief's descendants shall succeed him/her.

28.2 The chief is appointed from the Royal Family; the successor to the chief shall be the Chief's sisters, brothers, or the Chief's children, or her father's brother's daughter or son, cousins or the children of the cousin.

29. Chief's Council

29.1 The Chief's Council consists of the Chief, Senior Traditional Councillors, Junior Traditional Councillors, and a Secretary.

30. Community Court

30.1 The Community Court structure is as follows:
(a) Chief
(b) Magistrates

30.2. The Chief presides over the highest Community Court, which sits according to the number of cases reported.

30.3. All Community Court cases, together with all the evidence presented, are recorded.

Certificate of consent to publish

Certificate of the consent to publish

UNIVERSITY OF NAMIBIA

FACULTY OF LAW

HUMAN RIGHTS AND DOCUMENTATION CENTRE

RE: CONSENT TO PUBLICATION

I, the undersigned, Chief of the !Xoo Traditional Authority, hereby give consent to the Human Rights and Documentation Centre, to publish the following documents of the !Xoo Traditional Authority:

1. The Customary Laws
2. The Community Profile
3. Picture of the Chief
4. Logo of the Traditional Authority

I acknowledge that the Human Rights and Documentation Centre will publish the laws in our indigenous language (!Xoo), as well as the English language. I am familiar with the contents of the laws that will be published and further acknowledge that they were prepared by my traditional authority.

Signed on this 15 **day of** November **2012**

At Windhoek

Sofia Jakob

Chief

!XOO TRADITIONAL AUTHORITY
P.O.BOX 1017
GOBABIS
CELL 0813332896

For HRDC: Mr. A. Gairiseb

Hai||om Traditional Authority
Hai||om !hao!nâbe

The supreme leader of the Hai‖om Traditional Authority is
Gaob[1] Dawid ǁKhamuxab.
Date of designation: 17 December 2000

1 Traditional title in terms of section 11, Traditional Authorities Act, 2000 (No. 25 of 2000).

PROFILE[2]

The Hai||om have always lived in and around the Etosha Pan and Outjo.

We call our leader ***Gaob*** (chief). The *Gao-i* always serves as the Chairperson at community activities and offers guidance and direction whenever the community needs it.

2 This profile was provided by the Hai||om Traditional Authority.

Hai||om !hao!nâsi ||Kharab

ǂGae‡Gui‡Gās

Hai‖om !haos ge Elob hoa|gaixaba ra gangan nē !hūb di !noras !aroma, tsî ǂguro presidena nē !hūb diba ra gangan |gapi ‖garagoab ge a ǂnûiǂgās !aroma, i ge sida di khoen di !goâsiba oahā-ūba, tsî ra ganga bi ‖aeb ai, tsî gā-ai mî‖guis !hao!nâsi |hûhâsib tsî ‖îdi di ǂgaeǂgui-oagu tsîna. !Khūba abi |khae re ǂHanub tsî sida îxa !hūba.

1. ‖Î Artikels: ǂGuro !âros

1.1 Nē !hao!nâsi ǂūsigu di ‖garab !nâ, hana di ga xoa!gā!gāde |kharati mî!gā!gā tama hâs kōse i ge:

(a) *Hā|aro ra ‖anib*: Nēs ge nî ǂâibason, mâ kara hâse ī khoe-i hoa-i Hai‖om !haosa xun hâse ī-i ge mā-ams !nâga nî huisîsen, !gâi!gâibasensa i Hai‖om ‖aesa Namibiab hoab !nâ ǂnû‖khaebas |kha.

(b) *Gaob/-i*: Nēs ge nî ǂâibasen *Kai danab Hoan di |Gapib ase* nî mî!gā!gāhe, Xoamâihe hâ khami !hao!nâsi ǂgaeǂguidi di ǂhanumās !nâ, 2000‖î kurib disa. Hai‖om |hûhâsib ge nî ‖nae‖gau Gao-i **â**sa.

(c) *|Haoh***âse** ǂgari-ais *di !hūb*: Nēs ge nî ǂâibason mî!gā!gāhes karao, |haosase, |haohâbi xa ra ǂgari-aihe !hūb ase, Xoamâihe hâ khami !hao!nâsi ǂgaeǂguidi di ǂhanumās !nâ. 2000‖î kurib disa. Tsî noxopa nî !khōǂgā hâ nîse ī !hū-i Hai‖om an dise ī-i hoa-e.

(d) *!Hao!nâsi ǂhanub*: !hao!nâsi ǂhanub ge nî ǂâibason !ōhâ ǂūsib ai !gā!gāsa ǂhânugu ai tsî Xoamâihe hâ khami !hao!nâsi ǂgaeǂguidi di ǂhanumās !nâ. 2000‖î kurib disa.

(e) *|Gapi Gowaǂûira |abemâ!nâns:* Nēs ge nî ǂanhe |Guriga mâbason hâ !nans Hai‖om !hao!nâsi |haohapia ǂgom!gâhe hâs tsî |gaiba mâhe hâs, ‖hûiǂui, ‖hûi-‖nâs tsî ‖gau mâis di ‖khasigoa mâhe hâ Gao-i ai.

(f) !Hao!nâsi |hûhâsib: Nēs ge nî ǂâibason Hai‖om |hûhâsib ti, di xoa!gā!gāhe-i hâ khami hao!nâsi ǂgaeǂguidi di ǂhanumās !nâ.2000‖î kurib disa, |gamdisi koro|a‖î !gaos(25) !nâ.

(g) !Hao!nâsi ǂgaeǂgui ao-i: Nēs ge nî ǂâibason tsî nî !khōǂgāhe xoa!gā!gāhe khami !hao!nâsi ǂgaeǂguidi di ǂhanumās !nâ, 2000‖î kurib disa. |gamdisi koro|a‖î !gaos(25) !nâ.

(h) !Haosi Aixan di !hūb: Nēs ge nî ǂâibasen hâse Aixan gere ‖ânai !hūb |oro ‖aeba xu, Etoshas !nâ tsî Etoshas !auga.

(i) !N**â**ga ǂnôa Dana khoe-i: Nēs ge nî ǂâibasen ǂguro dana khoe-i !haosi |hûhâbi xa ‖hûi-mâihe tsî Gao-i !nāga ǂnôab ase nî ǂanhe, tsî Gao-i nî !khō!gâhe Gao-i ga kara i khamasi xa nî ǂnû‖khaebase.

2. ‖Î Artikels: |gam‖î !âros

2.1 |Gaigu

2.1.1 |Gaiba ūhâ mâ-khoe-i hoa-e u‖nâsa !hao!nâsis |kha hâ ǂnûkhaidi hoade xu, ‖ao-amgu di hoadi kara hîtsâhes khao!gâ.

(a) Hana i ga ‖î-e ‖î-*i* di *sîsen*-e *sîsen* tama kara io.
(b) Hana i ga ‖î-e, |hûhâsiba !kharagagu !ai!ā kaio tamas kara io ǂgaeǂguis !nâ |homaxa kais karao.
(c) Hana i ga ‖î-e tsūse !khari-i tsî Xûi-i tsîna *sîsen* ‖aeb ai nî ās kara io.
(d) Hanab ga |hûhâsiba !gâibahe tama kara io ‖nā ǂgaeǂgui-ao-i |kha.

2.1.2 Didi a, b, c, d, kose mîdi khami nî hîhe, tsî !gâi |gaub !nâ !haosi ǂhanumādi 2000‖î kurib |kha !khō‖ôagu hâse. ǂGaiǂguis !nâ nî hâse in saogudi ge !nan!ârodi.

2.1.3 Gao-i ge !gâise nî !khōǂhomihe !gâi *sîsen-es* ‖aesa nî hîbahes !aroma.

2.1.4 Gao-i ge ‖î-*i* di autos tsî oms tsîna māhesa a mā-amsa.

2.1.5 Mâ !khai-i hoa-I, ǂnûs nî īs hoas, ‖khā‖khākhâis nî īs hoasa i ge sarihe hâ !ās di Dana khoe-e nî ǂhomi î i Goa-e !gâi ‖goe!khais ai ‖goe, tsî nî ǂhomi ǂnûdi tsî ‖Khā‖khādi !gâi !khaidi ai nî hâsa.

2.2 Gao-i di ‖Gaumais tsî Ū!khunis

2.2.1 Gao-i ge !hoa!nâsi ‖Garagu ra mî khami nî ‖gaumâihe.

2.2.2 Gao-i ge ‖î-*i* di om-arisa xu tsubu nî ū!khunihe: gao-i di |gôan !gammeb !nâ hōhe hâna xu. O tamas kara-i Goa-i di ǂhunuma !gâsana xu.

2.2.3 Gao-i ge ‖î-*i* di omarisa xu tsubu nî ‖gaumâihe, Omaris kara hōgu toas khao!gâb ge |hûhâsiba nî !khō!gâ. Aisa !oas ge !hao!nâsi ǂhanumas 2000‖î kurib disa nî dao‖gau.

2.2.4 ‖Aebi nî |oas kao, Gao-i nî kaira|oas karao, o di ge !nan!ârodi (2.2.1, 2.2.2, tsî 2.2.3 tsîna nî dao‖gau).

2.2.5 Gao-i ge |gaiba ūhâ omarisa xu ū!khuni-ao-e ‖gaumâisa.

3. ‖Î Artikels: !nona‖î dana!âros: ǂam kurin di |gam|khāb

3.1 Mâ Aoro-khoeb hoab îa ǂam kurina ūhâ skola ra ǂgâ |gôasa nî |gam|khā kaib hoab ge !nona gomade nî kha-am (3 Gomadi) o tamas kara io marisa nî kha-am N$6 000 (!nâni |oadisi Namibiab di dollaga). |gam|khā kaihe go |gôas di ‖gûna.

4. ‖Î Artikels: Haka‖î dana!âros: |gai!khōs

4.1 Hana i kara |gai!khōguhe-o. O i ge |gai!khō-ao-e !nani (6) gomade nî kha-am – N$12 000, o tamas kara io disi|gam|a |oadisi Namibiab Dollaga nî kha-am. |gai!khōhe go khoe-i di ‖gû hâna

5. ‖Î Artikels: Koro‖î dana!âros: !gams

5.1 !Gamsi xa, !gams !nâ ga |hapixase kara hōhe khoe-i !gams !nâ-i ge disi (10) gomadi, o tamas ka io – N$20 000. Nēs ge nîra māhe tsâ|khāsa |aokhoen !oa.

6. ||Î Artikels: !nâni||î dana!âros: ǂnûdi

6.1 Khoe-i ge mā-amhe tide ǂnûs, Gaob ||âudīb tamas ka io o nî hâ ǂgamǂgamsen |huruna dīsa Gaob di mā-ams ose. ||Nāti ī !ûǂamao-i ge !nani gomadi (6) = N$10 000.

7. ||Î Artikels: Hû||î dana!âros: Aitsama !khū!khūsens

7.1 Khoe-i hîa ga projekdi, ǂharugub tamas io ǂhanub !auga mâbasen !nân-e Hai||om |haunasib |ons !nâ kara dīhe Gaob mā-ams ose, ||nāti i !ûǂamao-i ge nîra ||kharahe = N$150 000 tsî ||nātimîsi i ge |honkhoesisa nîra ū!khunihe.

8. ||Î Artikels: ||khaisa||î dana!âros: ǂgaeǂgui!nâ ǂharis

8.1 Khoen hîna Lodgedi, !haokhoe faramdi, hoteldi tamas ka io ǂharugu!khaina |honkhoe-ai hân Gaob ta ǂgaeǂgui!nâ ǂharis !nâ ||an ge |nî khamakō persensa nîra matare !hoaǂharugudi !nâ-ū ||în di hōǂgāde xu.

8.2 Tsî nēs ge ||khāti Sa khoen di ||gau||gaun |kha ra ǂharugun tsîna !khōǂgā hâ.

9. ||Î Artikels: Khoese||î dana!âros: !narib

9.1 Khoe-i kara nau khoe-i di ûitsama |guruna !nario, ai||gause gomas, piris, gūs, donkib, hāb, ||nāti ī khoe-i ge !honarisase nîra mâdare.

10. ||Î Artikels: Disi||î dana!âros: Hai||om khoen di hî|nuruhes

10.1 !garo!ādi |honkhoen hîa !kharaga !nâgu !ādi ai sida khoena ra ǂhabasa tama |gaub ai sîsenūn tsî ||khāti ||în di mâsib hîan tsûtsû!nâhe hâgu ge nîra !hoaǂamhe !garo!ā |honkhoen tsî sida khoen ||aegu. Kaise tsûgase ǂnautsûtsûhe hâ khoen xa i ge matib tsû hâ !khaisa nîra kōhe.

11. ||Î Artikels: Disi|gui|a||î dana!âros: !Hao|goras tsî !gôa||nâs

11.1 Khoen hîa ra !hao|gora tsî sida di !haosi ǂūsi ga mî||gai||gain tsî sida !gôa||nân, ||nati ī khoe-i ge nîra ||kharahe |gam (2) gomadi tamas ka io marisi ||khāsiba.

12. ||Î Artikels: Disi|gam|a||î dana!âros: |Omidi tsî !Gamegu

12.1 !Gameb

12.1.1 Gaob ge |gui taras |guisa nîra ūhâ, !aromas ge:

(a) nētsēs ûib !nâ i ge ǂgui !garaga!nâgu |aena hâ ai||gause, HIV/AIDS khama īna,

(b) tsî |guis xa !nāsa tarasa ūhâs ge toa tama ||gâu!nâbe ǂkhawaba ūhâ. |Omidi ge Testamens ǂhaweb !nâ i a xaomâisa khami nîra |goraǂuihe.

12.2 |Omidi

12.2.1 |Omis ge ||ō go khoe-i di ǂhanusi |omis di Xoa||guib ta mî khami nî hîhe. !Aromas ge !gaidī-aon ge khoena ra !gai!an tsîn ge ǂhunuma khoena |omi !âde hō tama ra i. !Hoaǂharogu di ge nîra dīhe nēti ī xūna mâ!oas !aroma.

12.2.2 |Gaub ge nî ǂâiǂuihe |khugus tsî xomagus tsina ||khaes !aroma.

12.2.3 |Gôan hîa !gameb !auga tamas ga io !hao!nâbe !gameb !auga ra !naen !nāsase ||khaubahe tama hâ. !hao!nâbe ||kharab ge nîra mûǂam î in ||nāti ī |gôana ||khaubahe.

12.2.4 Taradi, |gôan tsî aogu ||îgu tsîn ka tsā|khāheo |omis a ||khaubahe ||khā, ǂnoagudixa, on ge ||gâi |ā he xawe.

12.2.5 Nē ǂhanub ge nîra mûǂam hoaraga khoen nîra |guitkōse domdore !khaisa.

12.2.6 !Ûǂamao-i ge nîra ||kharahe ôa!nâdi khao!gâ.

12.2.7 ***!Gamekhôas***: Khoe-i ga !gameba xu |gora o, o i ge ||nāti i khoe-e hoa xūna oms ai xū tsî nî !gû.

!Aromas ge !gaidī-aon ge khoena ra !gai!an tsîn ge ǂhunuma khoena |omi !âde hō tama ra i. !Hoaǂharogu di ge nîra dīhe nēti ī xūna mâ!oas !aroma.

13. ||Î Artikels: Disi!nona|a||î dana!âros: Tare khoedi ||khaubas

13.1 Mâ khoe-i hoa-i hîa ga tare khoes tamas ka io |gôasa kara |gai!khō tamas ka io |gôasa kara |gai!khō tamas ka io ||gâu!nâbe ||ore-i ge sao rase nî ||kharahe |gai!khōb tsî ||gâu!nabe ǂkhawab – !nani (6) gomadi = N$12 000.

13.2 Mâ khoe-i hoa-i hîa ga khoes, axab tamas ka io |gôasa kara, mâ-amsa tamase |nara|khā-i ge ||khaisa (8) gomadi tamas kai o N$16 000. !Aromas ge nē-amme |nara|khāes ge |gai!khōs xa gaxu ||aeba ra ū tsî ||nā khoero-i di tsâsiba ra !gam.

13.3 Taradi ge nîra ||khaubahe hana i di ga ||îdi ge ai!â ūhâ i aoga kara ||ō-o, ||aupexa hoaraga xun ge ra ūhe.

13.4 ǂHanu-o!nâ i ge a mâ aore khoeb hoab ga tarare khoes ||îb di tamasa kara |nāra|khāo, sîsen-i !nâ. ||Nāti ī khoe-i ge ||î-i di sîsengu tamas ka io||î i di !harosa a ǂoa!nâ ||khā.

13.5 Mâ khoeb tamas ka io khoes hoas ge |gui khoe-I |kha |gui !gamesa a mā-amsa.

14. ||Î Artikels: Disihaka|a||î dana!âros: ǂUrusib

14.1 !Gaid ī aob (!hao!nâbe ǂgauǂgau-aob)

14.1.1 ||îgu ge hâ sida |hao!nâsib !nâ tsî a mā-amsa. ||Îgu ge mā-amsas tsîna i |hûhâsib !nâ sîsensa kai !gôahesa |gaub !nâ xawe gu ge !âisa nîra !kharu!nâ ǂan!gâhes !aroma.

15. ||Î Artikels: Disikoro|a||î dana!âros: !Nomades (HIV/ AIDS)

15.1 Mî!khā!khās – koro (5) piridi – N$2 500

15.1.1 |Khaubasen tamase ga ||goe||ae kondoma sîsenū tamase ǂans a hîa sats tamas ka io sas ge a ǂhīsa nē |aeb |kha – disi (10) piridi – N$5 000.

16. ||Î Artikels: Disi!nâni|a||î dana!âros: !khari!khōs tsî |hubu|hubusen xūn

16.1 !Khari||gâudi tsî |hubu|hubusen xūna ||amax ūs ge mā-amhe tama hâ Hai||oman di !hao!nâsi !hūs ai.

16.1.1 !Ûǂamaon tsîn ge mā-amhe tide tsî |hawixasets ga hōheo, ots ge ||kharab – N$2000||î kurib tsî !nona ||nâu!gâs khao!gâ i ge ||nāti ī khoe-e ||nā ||an!nâ ǂharisa xu nîra !haeǂûihe.

17. ||Î Artikels: Disihû|a||î dana!âros: !hūb

17.1 |Honkhoesis

17.2 !hū!âde |goraǂuis

17.3 Ûitsama |gurun

17.4 !Û-aib

17.5 !Ûǂam-aon (mā-ams ose ra ǂgâ nâ) - koro(5) piridi

17.6 Hai||om !hao!nâbe ǂgaeǂguis ge nîra ||goeha ||garagu(Landboards), ai||gause ||garagu tsî sîsenxasigu tsîna nîra sao.

18. ||Î Artikels: Disi||khaisa|a||î dana!âros: ||Ama!gûnis

18.1 Mā-amhe tama ǂhanu-o !nâ a tsî |hawixasets ga hōheo – N$1 000

19. ||Î Artikels: Disikhoese|a||î dana!âros: |Howa|uigu

19.1 ||nāti ī aiǂhanu-i ge nîra ǂnûiǂgāhe aixan di |howade !gâi!gâi !nâ tsî |asa|asa!nâsa.

20. ||Î Artikels: |Gamdisi||î dana!âros: !Hao!nâsi !hūb

20.1 !Hao!nâsi !hūb ge nî ||nâ !hū-i Hai||om |hûhâsib xa ||an!nâhe hâba tsî ||khāti Hai||oman xa nî ǂansa iba ||nā !garo!ādi ǂhanub ta ||amadi Hai||om |hûhâsib !aroma |ō-aisase hâ!khaiba mās di ǂhanumādi cabinets ge !khō!gâdi !nâ-ū.

20.2 Dana ǂnû!khais

20.2.1 Dana ǂnû!khais ge !garo!ās Seringkops ai nî hâ ||îs a ǂguro !garo!ā Hai||om |hûhâsiba ||amahe tsî gere ||khae||nâhesa |guikaidisi (100) kurin !hū-osis khao!gâ.

21. ||Î Artikels: |Gamdisi |gui|a||î dana!âros: |Ûb

21.1 ǂHoa|ûb: nē |ûb ge |aude ra ǂâibasen

21.2 !Am|ûb: nē |ûb ge ûiba ra ǂâibasen

21.3 |Hai|ûb: nē |ûb ge !hūba ra ǂâibasen

21.4 ǂHoa|ûb,!am|ûb tsî |hai|ûb tsîn ge dana |ûga sida !khaub ai hâga tsî Daub tsî Aukoreb tsîna.

21.5 !hao!nâbe Ams

21.6 !hao!nâbe ams ge nîra hâ Hai||om |hûhâsib !aroma. nē ams ge !hao!nâsi ǂgaeǂuis xa mâi-ai!âhe.

22. ||Î Artikels: |Gamdisi|gam|a||î dana!âros: ||Nâugu Hai||om !hao!nâbe |hûhâsib tsî Hai||om !hao!nâbe ǂgaeǂguis digu

22.1 !Hao!nâsi ǂgaeǂguis ge nî hâ Hai||om !hao!nâsi |hûhâsib !aroma. /gaigu tsî sîsenxasigu tsî hoan ge //nâi xoamâihe ha !hao!nâsi ǂhanumās, 2000||î kurib dis !nâ tsî sao rana xu nî hâ:

22.1.1 |Gapi gowaǂuira |awemā!nans

22.1.1.1 |Gapi gowaǂuira |awemā!nans ge nî hâ, Hai||om !haos !aroma

22.1.1.2 Sao rases ge |Gapi Gowaǂuira |awemā ra !nansa nî !am|haohe:

(a) Hoaraga (disihaka|a(14) Dana Khoen ge nî hâ tsî,

(b) |Gamdisi ||Khara khaikhoen di |awemā ra !nansa xu.

22.1.1.3 Dana sîsenǂuigu |Gapi gowaǂuira |awemā!nans digu ge

(a) ||Gaumâi dî !nâs khao!gâ ||Khamuxan di omarisa tsî |hûhâsib di !khō!gâde xu. !Hao!nâsi ǂūgu tsî ǂgom|gauga, tsî ||Kharakhoen di |apemāsa xu.

(b) Gaoba ū||nâsa, ǂhabasa tsî |oasa !gao!gaoba ūhâ !aromadi kara hāo. Tsî nēs ge hîhe ||khaisa||î xoa|goraros ǂhanumās, 2000||î kurib disa !oa.

(c) Mâiǂgās ||hui toahe hâ Gao-i dis tsî mûǂamsa ǂhanumas 2000||î kurib dis ǂhanuse nî hîhese. Tsî di Ministrisa nî ǂanǂanhe sa.

22.1.2 Gao-i

22.1.2.1 Gaob ge hao Hai||om !haosi ǂgaeǂguisi xa |gapi nî ī, tsî aiǂnû-ao nî ī !hao!nâsi ǂgaeǂguis diba.

22.1.2.2 Gao-i ge nî ||Khamuxan |aokhoen om-arisa xu /gui nî ||gaumâihe.

22.1.2.3 Gao-i ge nî !nonadisi koro|a (35) kurixa nî ī tsî |gawiga.

22.1.2.4 Gao-i ge nî a !ûi!gâ-ao !hao!nâsi ||kharab Hai||om !haos diba, tsî nî sîsen |îb di sîsenga !hao!nâsi ||kharagu tsî !hao!nâsi ǂgaeǂguidi di ǂhanumās ta mîsa !oa.
22.1.2.5 |Nauǂgās Gao-i dis ge kai omeb gao-i dibia nî hîhe (||Khamuxan Gaosi||gâus diba).
22.1.2.6 |Nauǂgās ge Hai||om |hûhâsib !nâ nî hîhe.
22.1.2.7 |Nauǂgās ge nî hîhe Hai||om !hao!nâsi ||garagu |kha |hao hâse.

22.1.3 ||Kharakhoen di |awemā!nâns

22.1.3.1 ||Kharakhoen di |awemā!nans ge nî hâ Hai||om !hao!nâsi |hûhâsib !aroma.
22.1.3.2 ||Anisis ||Kharakhoen dis |apemā ra !nans dis ge !nânidisi (60) kurin |khā a ||anihe ||khā o tamas kara io |gapi kurin ||khāsia.
22.1.3.3 ||Kharakhoen di |apemā!nans ge ||îsdi ||garaga kuru tsî nî !khō!gâ xawe gu ge tā Hai||om !hao!nâsi ||garagu |kha nî ǂîgu, ||îs di *Sîsen*xasib !aroma.
22.1.3.4 Dana sîsen ǂuigu ge:
(a) |Apemā Gao-e !haosi ǂūsigu Hai||om ||aes diga.
(b) !Ereamsa ūs !haosi ||naetigu tsî ǂūsigu ai, îs ta !haosi |aesa |ari, ûisase !haosi ||naetigu tsî ǂūsiga ūhâ.
(c) ǂhamasasib nî hâs kara-io. |gamdisi 20 ||kharakhoe nî sî |Gapi gopaǂûira |apemâra !nansa !oa.

22.1.4 ǂKhamkhoen di |hûs

22.1.4.1 ǂKhamkhoen di |hûs ge nî hâ Hai||om !hao!nâsi |hûhâsib !nâ.
22.1.4.2 ||Anisis nē |hûs dis ge !nonadisi koro|a(35) kurin !nâga nîra hâ.
22.1.4.3 ǂKhamkhoen di |hûs ge nîra ||îs di ǂhunuma ||garagu tsî sîsenxasigu tsîna ūhâ !hao!nâbe ||kharab !nâga.
22.1.4.4 Dana sîsenxasigu:
(a) !hao!nâsi ǂnāga aiǂhomis.
(b) Sîsenxasiba ūhâs ǂkhamkhoen |kha tsî !hao!nâbe |hûdi |kha.
(c) Hōǂgāde |awe||guis tsî projectde ǂnubis |hûhâsib !nâ.
(d) ǂgamǂgamsen |huruna |awe||guis ǂkhamkhoesib |kha.
22.1.4.5 Nēdi i |awe||guigu hoagu ge Gaob di ǂans |kha nîra dīhe.

22.1.5 Tara di |hûs

22.1.5.1 Tara di |hûs ge nîra hâ Hai||om |hûhâsib !nâ.
22.1.5.2 ||Anisis ge hoa tare khoesib !oa nî ||khowa-amsa i ||nāti i mâsenxasiba ūhâ-e omkhâis !nâ tsî !hao!nâbe ǂūsiba |hurus !nâ.
22.1.5.3 Nē |hûs ge ||îs di ǂhunuma ||garaga nîra ūhâ !hao!nâbe ||kharab !nâga.
22.1.5.4 Dana sîsenxasib:
(a) !hao!nâsi projectde ǂnuwi khâis |hûhâsib !nâ.
(b) Aiǂhomi tsî ||khā||khā Hai||om ǂūsiba taradi tsî |gôan !oa.
(c) Sîsenxasiba ūhâs |nî taradi tsî !hao!nâbe |hûdi |kha.
22.1.5.5 Nē sîsenxasigu ge Gaob di ǂans |kha nîra dīhe.

23. ‖Î Artikels: ǀGamdisi !nonaǀa‖î dana!âros: ǂnûdi tsî !hao!nâsi ǀhûdi

23.1 !hao!nâbe ǀhûdi ge nîra hâ Hai‖om !hao!nâsi ǀhûhâsib !nâ.

23.2 Hai‖om !hao!nâbe ǀhûdi ge nîra hâ kurib !nâ ǀgui !nâsa Gaob di !hao!nâbe ‖âudib ǀkha.

23.3 !hao!nâbe ǀhûs di tsēs ge nîra !khōǂgāhe nē ‖garagu !nâ.

23.4 Namibiab ǂhaba khama is ge Hai‖omandi !hao!nâbe ǀhûsa hoa ‖anin !oa a ‖khowa-amsa.

23.5 ǂNûdi ge nîra ǂanǂanhe !nonadisi tsēdi aisi !gaūhâ hîa.

23.6 Hai‖om !hao!nâsi ǀhûs ge ‖nadi-i ǀgaiba ūhâ ǀaros tamas ka io uǂuis diba !hao!nâbe ‖kharab !nâ 2/3 !âb di ‖anin ga hâo.

24. ‖Î Artikels: ǀGamdisihagaǀa‖î dana!âros: !hao!nâbe ǂgaeǂhuis di ǂnûdi

24.1 !hao!nâsi ǂgaeǂguidi di ǂnûs ge nîra hâ haka !nâde kurib !nâ.

24.2 nē ǂnûdi ge nîra Gaob, danaǀawemā-oan tsî ǀawemā aon tsîn ǀhuin xa nîra hâ !nâhe.

24.3 nē ǂnûs ge nîra !hoaǂam; !hao!nâbe ǂâiǂhansendi, !hao!nâbe ‖kharagu tsî ‖hōgu ǀhûhâsiba ra tsâǀkhāgu tsîna.

24.4 !hao!nâbe ǂgaeǂguis ge ǂhawas ta khoena nē ǂnûsa !oa a ‖khau ‖khā.

24.5 ǂNûs ge hû ǂgaeǂgui-aon ga hâ o a ǂnûdīhe ‖khā.

24.6 Mâ !hao!nâbe ǂgaeǂgui aob ge nē ǂnûsa ‖khaosa a ‖gui-aisa.

24.7 Mâ !hao!nâbe ǂgaeǂgui ao-i hoa-i hîa ga !nona !nâde saogu sase ǂnûdi !nâ hâ tama-i i ge aitsama ra !haesen !hao!nâbe ǂgaeǂguisa xu.

24.8 !hao!nâbe ǂgaeǂgui ao i hîa ‖nāti ī sîsengu !hao!nâbe ǂgaeǂguis diga dī ǀoaǀoa tama kara i-e ‖îb tamas ka io ‖îs ge !haehesa anu hâ.

24.9 ‖nāti i ǂgaeǂgui ao-i !kho!oaran tsî !kho!oa tama hâ i hîa ǂgomaxa sîsen ga !hao!nâbe ǂgaeǂguis ǀons !nâ ǀhûhâsiba !hao!nâbe ǂgaeǂguis ‖gui ai tama khama kara di-i ge !haehesa anūhâ.

24.10 Gaosisats kara ǀhaoǀhaobasen tsî ama tama ǂhoan ǀkha ǀhûhâsiba kara gāxa!nâ-o, ǀhûhâsib di ǂnûde !hao!nâbe ǂgaeǂguis ǀon !nâ ra ǂgaikhaise ‖nāti i khoe-i ge !haehesa anu hâ.

24.11 ǂGaeǂgui ao-i hîa ga ‖îb tamas ka io ‖îs sîsenga dī ǀoaǀoa tama kara i-e ‖nāti i khoe i ge Gaob ǀguse hâsa ǂkhāhe tama hana i ga ǀgaisa !ûǂam-e Gaob !oa-i di tama i-o.

24.12 mâ ǂgaeǂgûi-ao i hoa-i, ǂhanub di autosa !gâi tamase *sîsen* u i ge nî ‖garas !nâ mi !garu.

24.13 mâ ǂgaeǂgûi-ao i hoa-i /aî 3 !nâdi /garahe hâ-i i ǂhanub di autosa !gâi tamase *sîsen* us!nâ. ‖kha-i ge ‖îdi *sîsen*a xu nî hâ khaihe.

24.14 mâ #gae#gui-ao-i hao-i /apixase /gaisa !gu#amdi aini hōhese i,i ge ‖îdi *sîsen*a xu nî ha khaihe.

24.15 mâ ‖haoha ‖ani-i hoa-i #hanumxa ma-amhe tama xūna ‖ama tsî ‖amxu i hoa-i ge ‖hau!nâsis di goba di !nâ nî #gai#gahe tsî /apixase i nî hōhes kara io #hamasa mi‖uiga nē uhe.

25. ‖Î Artikels: |Gamdisikoro|a‖î dana!âros: |hûhâsib ǂNûdi

25.1 Hoa!nâ-aixa |hûhâsib ǂnûdi ge nîra hâ Hai‖om |hûhâsib !aroma.
25.2 Nēdi i ǂnûdi ge nîra ‖khowa-amsa i hoa Hai‖oman !oa.
25.3 ǂNûdi ge nîra dīhe Gaob tsî ǂgaeǂguis tsîn kara mûǂui o.
25.4 !aromadi nēti i ǂnûdi di ge |haonaba ǂanǂans, !nuriba mâs tsî hoa!nâ aixa ǂanǂande mâsa.

26. ‖Î Artikels: |Gamdisi!nâni|a‖î dana!âros: ǂNamipeb !ûi!gâs

26.1 ǂNamipeb Hai‖oman ‖an!nâ hâb ge nîra !ûihe!garaga!nâgu haindi hî |nuruhes !hao!nâbae.
26.2 ǂgaeǂguis mā-ams ose tsî ǂhunumâ ministris tsîn xa. !Gûǂam ao-i ge nîra ‖kharahe.
26.3 Conservancy di (!garob !ûi!gâs).
26.4 Hoaraga conservancy di (!garob!ûi!gadi), lodge di hîa !hao!nâbe |hûhâsib ǂharis !nâ ‖goedi ge 10% ga |hûhâsib trust !nâ nî mâtare ‖khagorobe.
26.5 |Gurun ta ǂnoa aihe !garo!âdi ge 5% ga nî mâtare.

27. ‖Î Artikels: |Gamdisihû|a‖î dana!âros: |Omidi tsî ‖gau‖gaudi

27.1 Hoaraga !khaidi tamas ga io khoen hîa Hai‖om Sa-khoen ‖gau‖gaute ūhân ge 25% ga trust ǂgaes Hai‖om |hûhâsib dis !nâ nîra mâtare.

28. ‖Î Artikels: |Gamdisi‖khaisa|a‖î dana!âros: ǂhanumādi

28.1 Hai‖om !hao!nâbe ǂgaeǂguis ge ǂhanumāde nîra kuru saorase:
(a) !hao!nâbe !gamegu
(b) !Hūde |omis, ûitsama |gurun, tamas ka io |nî xū-i hoa-i
(c) !ûre-aib ûitsama |gurun dib !garo!âdi ai
(d) !hao!nâbe ‖âudib Hai‖oman dib (ǂguro wekheb Tara‖khumu ‖khâb dib)
(e) ‖Garagu sao!gonao-i digu
(f) !Haos ams
(g) !aru|î a ǂhawasa !aromadi nē ǂhanuba sī!nâs !aroma.

29. ‖Î Artikels: |Gamdisikhoese |a‖î dana!âros: !Nubu xoa!as,tsoatsoas tsî |arodi

29.1 Nē ǂhanub ge nî ǂanhe Hai‖oman di !hao!nâsi ‖kharab ase tsîb ge nî *sîsen* tsoa-tsao Gaob kara xoa!gao bio.

29.2 Nē !hao!nâsi ‖kharab !nâ mâse i xun haon ge a /khara/kharahe ‖kha, hanan ga ‖kha 2/3 di ǂaûsa khoen kara ha-o, ‖kha |haos !nâ.

29.3 ǂGan-amsendi tamas ga io |arohe nî xūn nē !hao!nâbe ‖kharab !nân ge 30 tsedi !gau hâ hîa !hao!nâbe ǂgaeǂguis xoa-aob !oa nîra sîhe.

The laws of the Hai||om

Preamble

The Hai||om traditional community thank God the Almighty for the independence of this country; further, we thank the Founding Father of our Republic for the Supreme Law that brought back the dignity of our people, and we thank the Head of State for the wise and timely decision to recognise the traditional community and their leaders.

God bless our Government and our beautiful Republic.

Article 1: Definitions

1.1 In this Customary Law, unless the context indicates otherwise:

(a) A*dditional member* shall mean any member from the Hai||om traditional community assigned by the Hai||om Traditional Authority to assist the leadership, or who has the interest in representing the Hai||om Traditional Authority anywhere in Namibia.

(b) *Gao-i* shall mean *Chief* as defined in the Traditional Authorities Act, 2000 (No. 25 of 2000) and named *Gao-i* by the Hai||om traditional community.

(c) *Communal land* shall mean communal land as defined in the Traditional Authorities Act and shall include any other land belonging to the Hai||om.

(d) *Customary law* shall mean distinctive cultural and traditional laws as defined in the Traditional Authorities Act.

(e) *Supreme Council* shall mean the sole organ of the Hai||om traditional community entrusted with the power to select, remove or designate *Gao-i*.

(f) *Traditional community* shall mean the Hai||om community as defined in the Traditional Authorities Act.

(g) *Traditional leader* shall mean and shall include the traditional leader as defined in the Traditional Authorities Act.

(h) *Traditional ancient territories of the Hai||om* shall mean the geographic area habitually inhabited by Hai||om ancestors earlier in and around Etosha Pan.

(i) *!nâga‡gûa Dana Khoe-i* shall mean a senior councillor nominated by the traditional community and endorsed by the *Goa-i* to deputise him/her or serve as acting *Gao-i* in the absence of *Gao-i.*

Article 2: The Chief is the supreme leader (*Gao-i*)

2.1 Powers and privileges

2.1.1 The *Gao-i* shall have the power to remove any person from a position in the Traditional Authority on the following grounds after all punitive measures are exhausted:

(a) If he/she does not perform his/her duties.
(b) If he/she disrupts the Traditional Authority's duties or causes conflict resulting in disunity within the leadership or community.
(c) If he/she abuses alcohol when on duty.
(d) If the community is not satisfied with the performance of his/her duties.

2.1.2 If any leadership position becomes vacant due to subarticle 2.1.1, subsections a, b, c or d, the traditional community, in harmony with the Traditional Authorities Act of 2000, will nominate candidates on democratic principles to fill the position in the best interest of the affected community.

2.1.3 The *Gao-i* must be treated well for the great work he/she does for the traditional community.

2.1.4 The *Gao-i* shall be entitled to his/her own house as well as a car to enable him/her to drive to wherever duty calls.

2.1.5 Wherever the *Gao-i* attends a meeting or workshop, the Traditional Councillors at the location concerned shall ensure that the *Gao-i* sleeps in a comfortable place and that the meeting or workshop is held in an enclosure or hall.

2.2 Appointment and succession of *Gao-i*

2.2.1 The *Gao-i* shall be appointed according to customary law.

2.2.2 The *Gao-i* shall be succeeded only by direct family bloodline: The biological children of the *Gao-i* with his/her wife/husband and/or biological brothers and sisters of the *Gao-i* are legitimate members of the *Gao-i* family.

2.2.3 The *Gao-i* shall be nominated within the *Gao-i* family; after consent is reached internally in the family then the traditional community will endorse the candidate for further procedures to be taken in accordance with the Traditional Authorities Act of 2000.

2.2.4 When the time comes for the *Gao-i* to retire, his/her successor will be considered according to Article 2: 2.2.3.

2.2.5 The *Gao-i* shall have the power to appoint the successor from within his/her bloodline.

Article 3: Impregnating a girl who is under age

3.1 Any man who has impregnated an under-age school-going girl shall be fined 3 (three) head of cattle or money to the value of N$6 000 (six thousand Namibia Dollars) which will be paid to the victim's family.

Article 4: Rape

4.1 In the case of an incidence of rape 6 (six) head of cattle or money to the value of N$12 000 (twelve thousand Namibia Dollars) shall be given to the victim's family.

Article 5: Murder

5.1 In the case where a murder is committed and the accused is found guilty, the culprit will be charged a total of 10 (ten) head of cattle or will be fined money to the value of N$20 000 (twenty thousand Namibia Dollars) which shall be given to the victim's family.

Article 6: Public meetings

6.1 No person shall be allowed to hold a meeting, festival or other activity without the written permission of the *Gao-i*. If found guilty of this the person shall be fined 6 head of cattle or money to the value of N$12 000 (twelve thousand Namibia dollars) which shall be given to the Community Trust Fund.

Article 7: Self-enrichment

7.1 Any private individuals, groups or non-governmental organisations who undertake projects or do business in the name of the Hai||om community without the permission of the *Gao-i* shall pay an immediate fine of N$150 000 (one hundred and fifty thousand Namibia Dollars).

Article 8: Area of jurisdiction

8.1 Any private individuals, groups or non-governmental organisations who have a lodge, guest farm or hotel and who operate in business in the Hai||om area of jurisdiction shall contribute a percentage of their income to the traditional community as negotiated between the parties.

8.2 This also includes those business partners who attract business with iconic San images or with the names "Hai||om" or "Bushman".

Article 9: Theft of livestock

9.1 If anyone steals another person's livestock, namely cattle, goats, sheep, donkeys or horses, he/she shall pay triple the market value of that animal.

Article 10: Exploitation of Hai||om community members

10.1 Any farm owners who exploit Hai||om community members on their farms to the extent that such members are prejudiced financially shall be prohibited from unlawful and physical harassment, and mediation shall be held between the farm owner and the aggrieved person in order to redress such exploitation.

Article 11: Discrimination and underestimation

11.1 Anyone who discriminates based on the culture and diversity of the Hai||om or belittles the cultural values of the traditional community shall be fined 2 (two) head of cattle or the equivalent in money.

Article 12: Marriage and inheritance

12.1 Marriage

12.1.1 The *Gao-i* shall have only 1 (one) wife because:
(a) the HIV and AIDS pandemic today is a danger, and
(b) having more than one wife brings conflict between families.

12.2 Inheritance

12.2.1 Inheritance shall be administered according to the deceased's last will and testament as in some cases witchcraft deprives people of their right to inherit.

12.2.2 There must be a way to counter witchcraft.

12.2.3 Children born outside marriage shall be protected under the laws of the Hai||om in respect of their inheritance from a deceased parent.

12.2.4 Women, men and children, if affected negatively by family inheritance issues, will be protected against any unlawful forms of exploitation.

12.2.5 This customary law shall ensure each heir receives equal benefit from a deceased person's estate.

12.2.6 Any person dishonest with inheritance distributions or handling, or intentionally exploiting a rightful beneficiary, after being found guilty of this criminal offence will be fined accordingly.

12.2.7 Divorce: if someone divorces and leaves, he/she must leave everything behind. The reason is that witchdoctors also bewitch people and so they do not inherit their rightful share. There must be negotiations to prevent such activities.

Article 13: Protection of women

13.1 Any person found guilty of raping a woman or a girl child, or of domestic violence against her or a girl child, shall be fined 6 (six) head of cattle or N$12 000 (twelve thousand Namibia Dollars).

13.2 Any person found guilty of sexually molesting a woman or a boy/girl child shall be fined 8 (eight) head of cattle or N$16 000 (sixteen thousand Namibia Dollars) because this abuse usually occurs over a longer period of time than rape and it destroys the victim emotionally.

13.3 A widow shall be protected from oppression by her late husband's family with regard to property to which she is legally entitled.

13.4 No man shall be permitted to sexually harass a woman at the workplace. All serious attempts of sexual harassment towards a member of the opposite sex may lead to the guilty person losing his/her job or position.

13.5 One man and one woman will be allowed to be married to only one person.

Article 14: Health

14.1 Witchdoctors or traditional healers shall be allowed to perform their rituals in their respective communities provided they are registered.

Article 15: HIV and AIDS

15.1 Any person who discriminates against someone living with HIV or AIDS shall be fined 5 (five) goats or N$2 500 (two thousand five hundred Namibia Dollars).

15.2 Any person who has unprotected sex by not using a condom while knowing he/she is infected with HIV shall be fined 10 (ten) goats or N$5 000 (five thousand Namibia Dollars).

Article 16: Alcohol and drug abuse

16.1 Inhabitants and visitors selling or dealing in liquor or drugs shall be prohibited in the Hai||om communal or resettlement areas or farms.

16.2 Trespassers shall also be prohibited from dealing in alcohol and drugs in the Hai||om communal or resettlement areas or farms.

16.3 Any person found guilty of selling or dealing in alcohol or drugs as referred to in subarticles 16.1 or 16.2 shall be fined N$2 000 (two thousand Namibia Dollars) and shall be ordered to leave the settlement or communal area after 3 (three) hearings and having been found guilty of such offence 3 (three) times.

Article 17: Land

17.1 Ownership: All the lands or farms bought entirely within the jurisdiction.

17.2 Land allocation: Entrust community members with internal distribution of land.

17.3 Livestock (controls/responsibility).

17.4 Able to put up grazing control measures.

17.5 Any person who trespasses on communal land by entering without a permit shall be fined 5 (five) goats or money to the value of N$2 500 (two thousand five hundred Namibia Dollars).

17.6 The Hai||om Traditional Authority shall follow the rules, regulations and structures of the Land Board in dealing with communal land matters in regards to land ownership and land allocation.

Article 18: Bribery

18.1 Bribery shall be prohibited.
18.2 Any person found guilty of any form of bribery shall be fined N$1 000 (one thousand Namibia Dollars).

Article 19: Gravestones and their maintenance

19.1 A platform shall be set up to protect, upgrade and maintain the graves of our ancestors.

Article 20: Traditional land

20.1 The traditional land of the Hai||om community shall be the geographical area habitually inhabited by the Hai||om people and known to have been bought by the Government of the Republic of Namibia for the Hai||om people under the special resettlement programme as approved by the Cabinet decision 36th/07.12.04/900.
20.2 The main seat of the Hai||om traditional community shall be Farm Seringkop, being the very first farm bought by the Government of Namibia for the Hai||om community after a century of landlessness.

Article 21: Traditional colours, flag and anthem

21.1 Blue shall symbolise springs.
21.2 Green shall symbolise life.
21.3 Grey shall symbolise land.
21.4 Blue, green and grey shall be the principal colours of the Hai||om traditional community.
21.5 The flag of the Hai||om traditional community shall bear a kudu which symbolises the importance of its materials and use of its skin for clothing, and an aloe plant which symbolises the importance of medical plants and healing knowledge used for keeping the whole society healthy.
21.6 There shall be a traditional anthem (*!Haos-Ams*) for the Hai||om community.
21.7 The Hai||om anthem shall be decided on by the Hai||om Traditional Authority.

Article 22: Organs of the Hai||om Traditional Authority

22.1 There shall be a Traditional Authority for the Hai||om traditional community. Its establishment, powers and duties are defined in the Traditional Authorities Act, 2000 (No. 25 of 2000), and shall consist of the following:

22.1.1 The Supreme Council

22.1.1.1 There shall be a Supreme Council for the Hai||om traditional community.

22.1.1.2 The Supreme Council shall comprise:

(a) at least fourteen (14) paid-up members of the Hai||om Traditional Authority, and

(b) a total of 20 (twenty) members of the Council of Elders (*Stam Oudstes*).

22.1.1.3 The main functions of the Supreme Council shall be to:

(a) appoint, after consultation with family members of the ||Khamuxab Royal House and the community, and accept the succeeding *Gao-i* in accordance with the traditional customs and guidance of the Hai||om elderly.

(b) remove the *Gao-i* from office provided that there is sufficient reason to warrant the removal of *Gao-i*, and it is in line with section 8 of the Traditional Authorities Act (No. 25 of 2000) and customary law.

(c) designate the selected candidate as the *Gao-i* in accordance with the Traditional Authorities Act, which stipulates procedure on how notification must be done with the relevant ministry.

22.1.2 The Gao-i

22.1.2.1 The *Gao-i* shall be the supreme traditional leader of the Hai||om traditional community and shall be Chairperson of the Hai||om Traditional Authority.

22.1.2.2 The *Gao-i* shall be appointed from the ||Khamuxab bloodline.

22.1.2.3 The *Gao-i* shall be 35 (thirty-five) years of age or above.

22.1.2.4 The *Gao-i* shall be the custodian of the Hai||om traditional community's customary law and shall perform his/her duties and functions in accordance with customary law and the Traditional Authorities Act.

22.1.2.5 The inauguration of the *Gao-i* shall be done only by the oldest uncle of the royal family of the ||Khamuxab bloodline.

22.1.2.6 The inauguration of the *Gao-i* shall be done in the Hai||om community.

22.1.2.7 The inauguration procedure shall be executed in keeping with Hai||om customary law.

22.1.3 The Council of Elders

22.1.3.1 There shall be a Council of Elders for the Hai||om traditional community.

22.1.3.2 Elder persons from 60 (sixty) shall be eligible for membership of the Council of Elders.

22.1.3.3 The Council of Elders shall develop and adopt its own rules for its activities in line with Hai||om customary law.

22.1.3.4 The main function shall be to:

(a) advise the *Gao-i* on customs and cultural aspects of the Hai||om traditional community.

(b) ensure that the Hai||om customs and aspirations can shine and shall not diminish, but shall be relevant for generations to come.
(c) delegate 20 (twenty) members to the Supreme Council when needed.

22.1.4 Youth Cultural Group

22.1.4.1 There shall be a Youth Cultural Group for the Hai||om traditional community.
22.1.4.2 Membership shall be for persons under 35 (thirty-five) years.
22.1.4.3 The Youth Cultural Group shall develop and adopt its own rules for its activities provided that they are not in conflict with the customary law.
22.1.4.4 The main function shall be to:
(a) organise the community's cultural dances.
(b) keep contact with youth and cultural groups with different traditional communities in the country.
(c) organise income-generating projects within the community.
(d) organise sports and other activities of the youth.
22.1.4.5 The activities must not be in conflict with the customary laws of the Hai||om traditional community.

22.1.5 Women's Cultural Group

22.1.5.1 There shall be a Women's Cultural Group for the Hai||om traditional community.
22.1.5.2 All Hai||om women who are interested in developing and practising Hai||om culture shall be eligible for membership of the Women's Cultural Group.
22.1.5.3 The Women's Cultural Group shall adopt its own rules for its activities provided that they are not in conflict with the customary law.
22.1.5.4 The main function shall be to:
(a) develop cultural projects for women in the community.
(b) organise gatherings aimed to teach and promote Hai||om culture to all the women and children in the community.
(c) keep in contact with external women's networks and cultural groups.
22.1.5.5 The activities must not be in conflict with the customary laws of the Hai||om traditional community.

Article 23: The Traditional Assembly

23.1 There shall be a Traditional Assembly for the Hai||om traditional community.
23.2 The Traditional Assembly shall be held annually with the traditional festival of the Hai||om.
23.3 The dates of the Traditional Assembly sessions shall be stipulated in separate or additional documents.
23.4 The Traditional Assembly shall be open to all members of the Hai||om community throughout Namibia.
23.5 Meetings shall be advertised at least 30 (thirty) days in advance.

23.6 The Traditional Assembly shall have the power to amend or repeal rules, laws and regulations stated in Hai||om customary law, if a two-thirds majority of the members present voted for the amendment.

Article 24: Traditional Authority meetings

24.1 There shall be Traditional Authority meetings once every quarter, that is, 4 (four) times each year.

24.2 Attendance of Traditional Authority meetings shall be restricted to the *Gao-i*, Senior Traditional Councillors and Traditional Councillors.

24.3 The meeting shall discuss traditional concerns, customary conduct or laws, and matters concerning the traditional community different from traditional concerns.

24.4 The Traditional Authority may invite anyone to their meetings.

24.5 The quorum shall be formed by 7 (seven) members from Senior Traditional Councillors and Traditional Councillors.

24.6 Every Traditional Authority member shall be obliged to attend the meetings.

24.7 Any Traditional Authority member who fails to attend 3 (three) consecutive meetings without a valid reason and without being duly excused automatically discharges him-/herself from the Traditional Authority.

24.8 The Traditional Authority shall fire any traditional leader who fails to fulfill his/her obligations and duties.

24.9 Any leader, regardless of gender who is gazetted and has received a subsidy, but carries out in the name of the Traditional Authority illegal activities which have a negative impact in the community shall be discharged from duty if found guilty.

24.10 Any person who, when campaigning for chieftainship, spreads misinformation at a community meeting in the name of the Traditional Authority in order to confuse them, shall be discharged if found guilty.

24.11 Any leader who has failed to fulfil his/her duties and has committed a serious offence to the *Gao-i* by virtue of such failure shall be prohibited from having access to the *Gao-i.*

24.12 Any leader who misuses the Government vehicle assigned to the *Gao-i* shall receive a warning.

24.13 Any leader who has been warned 3 (three) times for having misused the Government vehicle assigned to the *Gao-i* shall be discharged.

24.14 Any leader who commits a serious crime shall be discharged.

24.15 Any community member who practises or sells anything illegal, such as alcohol or drugs on a resettlement farm, shall undergo disciplinary hearings and be judged accordingly.

Article 25: Community meetings

25.1 There shall be general community meetings for the Hai||om community.

25.2 Meetings shall be open to every member of the Hai||om community.

25.3 Meetings shall be convened by the *Gao-i* and his/her Councillors whenever necessary.

25.4 The purpose of such meetings shall be either to consult the community or to give reports and general information.

Article 26: Environmental protection and hunting

26.1 The environment where the Hai||om community resides shall be protected from exploitation.

26.2 The cutting down of trees shall be illegal in resettlement farms of the Hai||om community unless the Traditional Authority and the relevant Ministry permits it.

26.3 Anyone found guilty of sub-articles 26.1 and 26.2 shall be fined in Namibia Dollars or the equivalent in the value of labour.

26.4 All conservancies, lodges and game farms under the jurisdiction of the Hai||om Traditional Authority shall contribute to the community trust funds by donating 10% (ten per cent) of the net profit of their yearly income generated.

26.5 Hunting farms shall contribute 5% (five per cent) of net profits per year.

Article 27: Heritage and rock art

27.1 All areas with Hai||om (Bushman) art and artefacts shall contribute to the welfare of the community by donating 25% (twenty-five per cent) of the net profit yearly to the Community Trust Fund.

Article 28: Regulations

28.1 The Hai||om Traditional Authority may make regulations relating to:

(a) customary marriages

(b) land use rights for livestock, or any other property rights

(c) the grazing of livestock on communal or resettlement farms

(d) the Hai||om traditional festival in the first week of September each year

(e) the rules of succession to the Hai||om throne

(f) the traditional anthem (*!Haos-Ams*), and

(g) any other matter required in order to achieve the purpose of this customary law.

Article 29: Commencement and amendment

29.1 This constitution shall be called the Hai||om Customary Law and shall come into force immediately after the *Gao-i* has signed it.

29.2 This customary law or any section thereof may be amended or replaced if a two-thirds majority of members present at a Traditional Assembly voted for the amendments thereof.

29.3 Recommendations in connection with the customary law shall be sent to the secretary of the Hai||om Traditional Authority at least 30 (thirty) days before the commencement of the Traditional Assembly.

CERTIFICATE OF CONSENT TO PUBLISH

UNIVERSITY OF NAMIBIA

FACULTY OF LAW

HUMAN RIGHTS AND DOCUMENTATION CENTRE

RE: CONSENT TO PUBLICATION

I, the undersigned, Chief of the Hai-//om Traditional Authority, hereby give consent to the Human Rights and Documentation Centre, to publish the following documents of the Hai-//om Traditional Authority:

1. The Customary Laws
2. The Community Profile
3. Picture of the Chief
4. Logo of the Traditional Authority

I acknowledge that the Human Rights and Documentation Centre will publish the laws in our indigenous language (KHOEKHOE), as well as the English language. I am familiar with the contents of the laws that will be published and further acknowledge that they were prepared by my traditional authority.

Signed on this 2 day of August 2012

At Outjo

D.Khomuxab

Chief

For HRDC: Mr. A. Gairiseb

HAI-//OM TRADITIONAL AUTHORITY
0 3 AUG 2012
P.O. BOX 86, OUTJO
TEL: 067-313790

Ju|'hoan Traditional Authority
Ju|'hoan !'Haoh Juasi

The supreme leader of the Ju|’hoan Traditional Authority is
ǁ’Aiha[1] Tsamkxao ǂOma.
Date of designation: 5 July 1990

1 Traditional title in terms of section 11, Traditional Authorities Act, 2000 (No. 25 of 2000).

Profile[2]

1. Ju|'hoan is made up of 4 districts

Districts		Heads of districts
(a)	North	ǁUce ǁxari
(b)	Central	Cwi H Gheuu
(c)	South	Diǁxao ǁao
(d)	West	Erastus ǂOma

2. Elections

2.1 The headmen/-women are nominated by the chief and placed in position according to the law.

2.2 Each headman leads a district, which is made up of villages. The villages are grouped into clusters called *N!oresi*. Each cluster comprises *N!oresi* villages.

3. Borders

Tsumkwe is an area with geographic contiguity with

(a) to the east – Botswana.
(b) to the west – !Kung Traditional Authority Boundary.
(c) to the north – Sikeretti
(d) to the south – Gam

4. Population

4.1 There are many people in Tsumkwe because members of other tribes from other regions also live in Tsumkwe settlement.

5. Important places

The important places in Tsumkwe are as follows:

(a) |Nyae Nyae pan
(b) Gura pan
(c) ǁXa|oba hunting living museum
(d) Djokhoe *holboom*/hollow tree
(e) Dorsland *boom*/Dorsland Trekker tree
(f) Khebi pan
(g) Aha mountains
(h) Tsumkwe East, where the Ju|'hoan Traditional Authority is based.

2 This profile was provided by the Ju|'hoan Traditional Authority.

6. Traditional attire

6.1 Ju|'hoan women wear different traditional skins, beads, such as ostrich eggshell beads, copper wire rings and necklaces made from the seeds of traditional plants.

6.2 Men wear aprons or loincloths made from the skins of small antelope, eland hide shoes and carry traditional weapons such as bows and arrows, spears, knives, knobkerries and long sticks with hooks.

7. Important trees

The most important are baobab, marula, tamboti, mangetti and fruit trees such as berry trees and palm trees.

8. Previous headmen of Ju|'hoan

(a) Kaptein Kxao Kxami
(b) Kaq'ece Jo|'o Geelbooi

9. The chief of Ju|'hoan

(a) Title: ||'Aiha (Chief)
(b) Full names: Tsamkxao Bobo ǂOma
(c) Date of birth: 20 December 1941
(d) Place of birth: Maxamis |Nyae Nyae.
(e) Parents: !Uu Dabe and ǂOma Tsamkxao.

Ju|'hoan Vetasi

1. Ka n‡ai !'hansi

Tci gesin sa g||a ka |'aesi he se ||xama ka |'aesi kana du ||xama ka |'aesi ko vetasi ko Ju|'hoansi khoea ||'a ka sa o:

(a) Kxoe n|ang ju waqnhe koqea.
(b) G!a'ama ||'ae sa g||a ka |'aesi, ||ama tsa'a khoe
(c) N‡ai n‡om |'haibi n|ang ce n‡ai n|a'nga |'an si sa ||ae !ka ta'm|kau.

!'Hao-n!ang tci-ooa ku n‡ai |xao-a ju ko gumi, ko ||ama ‡oa ju koh du, te ka o |xao si n!anga ||xoa gea n!ore-n!ang ko Afrika.

Te ||xoasi kuria ke he o (2011) gumi n|e'e ||'a ha maria cansi o (N$ 2 500.00) te kahin ‡'hanu kana veta ku n‡ai |xao-a ||xama ju ko gumi n|e'e kana ||'a mari tcia.

‡Xanua he ||ae veta-si, te ||'a veta sa !xoekxam ||xama ju ko Hofa ko ||ama ||'a |xoa tcia ke he koh n||a ka |'ae ko ||ama tca veta zaiahn, !'hao-n!ang ||'aihasi, tju|ho-kxaosi, ||'aiha sa g||ao tca hi !ae!ae, n!ore-!an jua !ae!ae ko !'hao-n!angsi wece zaihan ||'a veta sa.

Ju !hun ||ama ko tca porotakxao koh oo sea ka he ||ama ||'a !aia ||'a ka g|aohsi ku ||ama tsa'a-a khoe ko !an waqn tsan kota !'Haohn!ang G||a-|'ankxaosi.

1.1 N‡ai tsa'a khui

(a)	Ka a n‡a'm |xoa ha ko g!au.	N$ 100.00
(b)	Ka a n‡a'm |xoa ha ko g||om.	N$ 200.00
(c)	Ka a n‡aq'au |xoa ha ko ko n||aq'ari.	N$ 150.00
(d)	Ka a ||'am ha.	N$ 60.00
(e)	Ka a !aih ha.	N$ 250.00

‡Xanu-|'huia ||ama doko ko n|om-tjua hin o n‡ai sea kahin !'ang-g!a'in |'an a ko tca a koh du.

1.2 G!aun!ang sa |xao ka |'aesi ko n‡ai tsa'a khui sa ke

G!aun!ang sa ke ku |xao ka |'aesi ko ka ju nai tsa'a ju tcisa he ko khui:

(a)	Da'ama-|haia-si	N$ 350.00
(b)	Jua o n!au. (ju n!a'an)	N$ 250.00
(c)	Da'ama ha kuria-si o 18	N$ 150.00
(d)	Dshau-ma kana dshaua ha kurisi o 18	N$ 200.00
(e)	Dshau n!a'an	N$ 250.00
(f)	Dshau kana !'hoan ka ha gu ha |'ae	N$ 300.00

Jua n|ui n‡ai tsa'a khui ku porota ha |'ae ko parisi kana !'hao-n!ang ||'aihasi. Khama n|a |oa o tca veta ku kare, te jua ||xoasi ku ‡'aun !'o-|'u ha |'ae ko barasi.

2. N‡ai ‡Xam

2.1 Ka g!aun!anga ku o N$ 500.00, ko tca ka koh oo n!anga ka |'ae ko veta khoea.

3. Gua g|aoh

3.1 Gua g|aoh o tca n‡ai tsa'a khui he jua du ka ku ||xara ha |'ae ko tunukhoe, te ka tci n|uia |oa jan koh !an ||'akoa ka ‡'aun tani ua ka |'ae ko parisi.

4. Ka dshau tih (G!ko, ||ae ha gu)

4.1 Ka dshauma kana ju n|ui n‡ai tiha ha |'ae, ha kxae tosia o porota jua n‡ai tiha ha.
4.2 Te ||'a !airikxao- ma kana ||'a !'hoan koh n‡ai tiha ||'a dshauama ku ‡'aun |xao g!aun!anga ||ama N$13000.00 ka ua N$15 000,00. Te ||'a oosi n!anga, !an-n|ui ka tani ua a ko tca ku khoe N$ 4 500.00. Ko ||'aea ha ku g|aea !'haohn!ang ||'aihasi.Te |xao ‡'asarasisi ka g|ae ||am jua koh gu dshau kota ha |oa gu dshau.
4.3 Ka !'hoan n‡ai tiha dshauma ciniha |oa g!aáma tju ha ‡'aun |xao gumi-di sa ku o 6.

5. |'Ang tcaq

5.1 Ka |'ang tcaq ka |'ae ||xoasi ju |xao N$300.00 kana ||'aba, ka cete ||ama tca ka oo n!a'an.

6. Za

6.1 Za ku n‡ai |xaoa ka |'ae ko N$ 80.00.

7. !Aing|aoh

7.1 Ku ju ku du !aing|aoh okaa ||xoasi ju ku ho ||xara he o |xao g!aun!anga o N$300.00 kana ||koa |'an ha ko beke n!ani.

8. Ju ama n!ang khoesi

8.1 Ka a n‡ai n!oma ju n|ui, n!ana ka ha ‡'han !ooa kana ha n|ai n‡a'm !hara ka |'ae, tci n|ui waqn kxuia ha ama-n!ang ka |xao-si o:

(a)	|'Habi sa sin g||a	N$ 2 000.00
(b)	Kaa du ||aqian ha |'hui	N$ 5 500.00
(c)	Ka a du !hara ha g|a'a	N$ 8 000.00
(d)	Ka a du ||aqian ha tzi|'o	N$ 6 000.00
(e)	Ka a n‡a'm xai ha tzausi	N$ 900.00

(f)	Ka a du !o'a ha ǂ'han	N$ 6 000.00
(g)	Ka ha g!au g|ai	N$ 4 000.00
(h)	Ha g!au!aqmisi	N$ 2 000.00
(i)	Ka ha ku tsa'a khui	N$ 6 000.00
(j)	Ka ha dhari tsa'a khui	N$ 6 000.00
(k)	Ka ha |ho !hara	N$ 12 000.00
(l)	Ka hatzun ‖aqin	N$ 7 000.00
(m)	Ka ha |kai !o'a	N$ 6 000.00
(n)	|Kai!aqmisi	N$ 2 000.00
(o)	!Om	N$ 10 000.00

9. !Hamh ǂanisisi

(a)	Gumi-di	N$ 3 000.00
(b)	|oeh	N$ 2 000.00
(c)	Dongi	N$ 500.00
(d)	Pari	N$ 500.00
(e)	Guu	N$ 600.00
(f)	Gǂhuin	N$ 200.00
(g)	Khukhu-g!oq kana ha di	N$ 50.00

10. Nǂai ‖koa ko !auhn tci-ooa-si

10.1 Kxoe n|ang !auhn tci-ooa n‖ah n!a'an sin koara.

11. Da'abi-!oa kota !auhn tci-ooasi

11.1 Da'abi !oa sa hi kuria-si gea 18 koa ts-ǂaehke koara tosia o ku ua kana ku gea !xari nǂai ‖'ama-sisi.

11.2 Jua ju ho,he ha nǂai ‖'ama !xari koda'abi-!oa sa hi kuria-si gea 18 koa tsi-ǂaehke, ku nǂai |xaoa ha |'ae ko N$ 200.00.

11.3 Te ju ho ha |'ae, he hahin ku ‖koa ha da'ama kana da'ama n|ui ka ha ku ‖'ama |'an ha ko!xari, ku |xao N$ 100.00.

12. ‖Xara tci-ooa

12.1 Te veta o Ju|'hoansi ma ku se |'an ‖koa |ho sa du ‖'aba ǂ'hanu ko tcisi, te nǂai |xao-a ku o N$ 300.00.

(a) Ko ka a ku ‖koa Sonda.
(b) Ko ku |'ua da'abi kana da'ama ha kuria-si gea 18 ko ‖koasi.
(c) Ko ku kxuia g!u.
(d) Ko ku nǂai dua hofa tci-ooa ko tca ka te o ji.
(e) Koku |'ua itsa n|ui !u ko |kuri.
(f) Ko ku koara |xoa !'hao-n!ang ‖'aiha ko ko ǂom.

13. N!ausi kota !kom |kain|kainsi

13.1 Jua ku |'ua jusa n|hui-a khoe ‖'a si ‖'ami-n!ang ko n‡oq'obi, ‖'a kxoe ju |oa jan ‖'a jua ku ho ha ‖xara.

13.2 Te ka ku o gumi-di sa o 5, he hi n!ani ku ua !'hoan hahin to'a he ka !kom koh !aia, ka ha n|ui ua ha ‖koa kxaosi.

13.3 Ka !kom !an jut san sa sa n|ui gua ha |'ae he sa n|ui |oa gu ha |'ae, ha dshau|!'hoan to'a he |oa gu ha |'ae ku |xao gumisa o g!au ko tci n|e'e. ‖'A gumisa ‖'a hisa o bine ku ua haa to'a koh dua ha |'ae ko !kom ‖'a ha dshau|!'hoan; ha n|e'e ko ‖'aiha, ka ha n|e'e ua !'Haohn!ang G‖a-|'an kxaosi ‡aeh.

14. Tihsi ‡'asara

14.1 ‡'asara ku du ‖xama ka |'ae ko osi !xare gesin sa ge.

14.2 N!ana ‖'ae n|ui ju n|ui ku kxae tca ka khoara kahin ha kare ka sa n|ui sa ha dshau kana ha !'hoan ‡'asara, ten!ang n|ui ka sin n!anka koara tca n‖ae he ka n!an.

14.3 |Xoa sin khuian khoe ko xabe dshau n‡hao ha !'hoan kana !'hoan n‡hao ha dshau.Ka kxae tci gesin sa dua ka |'aesi ko ‖'akoa. ‡'asara koara tca ka n‖ae ka n!an.

15. !Kom !aia

Hahin to'a he n‡hao sa n|ui ‖'a hahin ku |xao sa n|uiko gumi-di sa6. Hi sa o 4 ku ua ha to'a he n‡hao ha |'ae. Ka ha n|e'e ua !'hao-n!ang ‖'aiha ka han|ui ua !'hao-n!ng‖koa kxaosi.

15.1 ‡'Asara kxae tca ka n‖ae ka n!an. He ka ‖'aike ku g|ae o ha dshau kana ha 'hoan. Ku |xao gumi-di sa o 7.

15.2 Kahi sa o 5 ua ha to'a he n‡hao ha |'ae. Ka ha n|ui ua !'hao-n!ang ‖'aiha ka ha n|ui ua !'hao-n!ang ‖koa kxaosi.

15.3 Ka ju n|huia khoe kxae si ‖'ami-n!ang ko ‖oa tsa'a khoe. Okaa si ‡'aun n‖a n!anga ka ua !'hao-n!ang ‖koa kxaosi, ka si ‡'asara ‖'a tiha. Te sa |oa n‡ai !'han ju he sin kxaea sa ‖'ami-n!ang ko ka. Okaa sa ku ho ‖xara tcia ku n!ana, sa n|ui waqnhe ku coe gumi-di tsan ka |'an !'hao-n!ang ‖koa kxaosi.

15.4 Gua ju n|ui ko dshau|!'hoan: jua gua sa n|ui ko dshau|!'hoan he g|ae kxaea ha ko !kom ku |xao gumisa o g!au-ko-tsan. Hisa o g!au ku ua jua hin ha dshau|!'hoan gu ha |'ae; ha n|e'e ku ua ‖'aiha, te ha n|e'e ku ua !'Haohn!ang G‖a-|'ankxao ‡aeh.

15.5 Jusa n|huia khoe he kxaea sa !kom n!ang ko tih ku kxae tosi ko ka sa ua !'Haohn!ang G‖a|'ankxaosi ka ua ‡'asara !kom tiha. Ka se ce he g|ae n|hui cea khoe he |oa n‡ai !'han !'Hoan!ang G‖a-|'ankxaosi ka o veta !o'a. ‖'A jut san sa ku ‖xara sa |'aesi te sa g!aun!ang |xaoa o gumi tsan sa ku ua !'Haohn!ang G‖a-|'ankxaosi.

16. Dcaa

16.1 Dcaa kxao ku ||xara ||xama ha |'ae ko ||ama tci-tcia kahin to'a he ha koh dcaa, ko ||ama ka ju ho g!xa ha.Te tcin to'a he ha koh dcaa ka |'ae okaa ǂ'aun |'an ce |'ae ko ka jua.

17. N!aih tcia-si:

(a) N!aohsi
(b) Koahnsi
(c) !u!usi (||xaisi)
(d) Pangasi
(e) |'aisi
(f) !uru kota n!aohsi (n!aoh kota tchisi)
(g) boro

17.1 N!aih tciasi ju |oa sin ||ae |xoa ju |'ae ka nǂhao n||hoo, ko ||'aea ju koara tca kahin n||ae he ju ||ae ka.
17.2 Ka ju sin ||aea n||hoo ju g!au-n!angsi ko ko n!aih tciasi, he he !xau |xoa, parisi ku !'au |'an he |'aesi ko a.
17.3 Te veta he o ha gea kana g!a'ama ju n|ui waqnhe te ha ǂ'aun !'han.

18. !Xau ka |oa kare tsa'a

18.1 G!aun!anga o N$ 200 ku |xao ka |'ae ko khoesa ke:

(a) Ka ju kare nǂai |xao-a a he a !xau.
(b) Ka a !xau tca ju ku !oa a ǂaeǂae.
(c) Ka ju ko a teken |'an tca a koh du, he a ku !xau.
(d) Ka a |oa kare ǂaeǂae ||'ae hofa |'an a.
(e) Ka a ku ji |'an ju.

19. ||'Ama nǂai-||'ama !'hamh

19.1 Ka a sin koara ǂxanu |'huia o ||'ama ga, he sin ||'ama ju n|ui ko !ha-ma.!ha-ma to'a ku gu g!xa ka |'ae ko a, ka ua ka kxao.

20. Ju-wece Projekasi

20.1 Ju n|ui waqnhe ku kare ka ha coacoa ju-wece projeka ku ǂ'aun kxaice tsa'a tju|hokxao, he hahin ku ceka g|ae nǂai !'han ||'Aiha ko ||'a projeka he ku gǂara ka |'ae.
20.2 ||'Aiha n|e'esi hin ku |'an ||'a projeka tcia ko tosi. Ju n|ui waqnhe |oa ||xam ka !uh ku ||xara ha |'ae te ku kxoa ka ha |xao |xaokxama o gumi n|e'e kana N$2 000,00

21. N!ore-jua

21.1 Koara ju n|uia ku ho n!ore kana kurua tju ko Ju|'hoansi kxa|ho ko ka ha koara N!ore !xoana ǂxanua kana ha o jua ǁxoasi koh ku !xoana Namibia.

21.2 N!ore-jua waqnsa ǁama n!ore !'on!ang he ku kare tsi !xoana Ju|'hoansi kxa|ho ku ǂ'aun kxae nǂai !'han ǂxanu-!ae waqnsi.

21.3 Ka n!ore juasi gesin sa ǁama !'on!ang ku kare !xoana Ju|'hoansi kxa|ho, ha tju|hokxao ku ǂ'aun nǂai !h'an kxa|ho ǁ'aiha ka ha hin kota !'Haohn!ang Gǁa-|'ankxaosi ǁ'aiha, he hahin ku ǁau-se nǂai !'hansi sa o ǁ'a n!ore-juasa.

The laws of the Ju|'hoan

INTRODUCTION

The objectives of the customary law of the Ju|'hoansi are to:

(a) maintain peace
(b) effect reconciliation, and
(c) heal the wounds and anguish of those that are aggrieved.

Traditional fines are paid with cattle, which are the symbols of wealth in Africa.

The 2011 value of one (1) head of cattle was two thousand five hundred Namibian Dollars (N$2 500.00). Payment of a fine or compensation will restore peace as soon as possible in accordance with customary law.

This book of laws will assist presiding officers at court hearings, Traditional Authority headmen, community members, senior headmen, district heads, and the nation.

A murder committed will be fined as determined per the complaint, depending on the extent of the incident (murder) and by agreement between the complainant, the accused and the Traditional Authority.

1. Assault

1.1 The following fines apply:

(a)	With the fist	N$ 100.00
(b)	With a knobkerrie	N$ 200.00
(c)	With a sjambok	N$ 150.00
(d)	With an open hand	N$ 60.00
(e)	With the feet	N$ 250.00

A doctor's letter detailing the injury or the report from the clinic shall determine the method of injury.

1.2 Fines for the assault of the following:
The following fines apply for the assault of different victims:

(a)	A baby	N$ 350.00
(b)	An elderly person	N$ 250.00
(c)	A child under the age of 18 years	N$ 150.00
(d)	A girl or woman over the age of 18	N$ 200.00
(e)	A woman	N$ 250.00
(f)	A married person	N$ 300.00

An assault shall be reported to the police or Traditional Authority because this is a criminal offence and could lead to imprisonment for many years.

2. Abortion

2.1 The fine shall be N$ 500.00, in accordance with the customary law.

3. Rape

3.1 Rape is an offence for which a perpetrator can be sentenced to a term of imprisonment. Any incident shall be reported to the police.

4. Pregnancy

4.1 If a girl becomes pregnant, she shall have the right to open a case for compensation against the man who impregnated her.

4.2 If a boy or a man impregnated a girl or a woman, then he shall pay a fine of N$13 000.00 to N$15 000.00, depending on the circumstances, of which N$4 500.00 shall go to the Traditional Authority coffers. The fine shall apply equally to a married or unmarried man.

4.3 If a man impregnated a virgin, he shall pay a fine of six head of cattle.

5. Spillage of blood

5.1 Spillage of blood shall incur a fine of N$300.00 or more, depending on circumstances.

6. Insults

6.1 Insults shall be fined N$80.00.

7. Stubbornness

7.1 Stubborn behaviour shall be subject to a fine of N$300.00 or about three (3) weeks' work.

8. Injury to body parts

8.1 If one person causes harm to another, a full investigation shall be launched into the matter. If the accused is found guilty, the fines shall be as follows:

(a)	Open wound	N$ 2 000.00
(b)	Piece of the ear	N$ 5 500.00
(c)	Partial damage of eye	N$ 8 000.00
(d)	Partial damage to the lips	N$ 6 000.00

(e)	Tooth	N$ 900.00
(f)	Arm	N$ 6 000.00
(g)	Hand	N$ 4 000.00
(h)	Finger	N$ 2 000.00
(i)	Breast	N$ 6 000.00
(j)	Tongue	N$ 6 000.00
(k)	Face	N$12 000.00
(l)	Nose	N$ 7 000.00
(m)	Foot	N$ 6 000.00
(n)	Toe	N$ 2 000.00
(o)	Leg	N$10 000.00

9. Cash value of animals

(a)	Cow	N$ 3 000.00
(b)	Horse	N$ 2 000.00
(c)	Donkey	N$ 500.00
(d)	Goat	N$ 500.00
(e)	Sheep	N$ 600.00
(f)	Dog	N$ 200.00
(g)	Hen/cock	N$ 50.00

10. Alcohol and substance abuse

10.1 Alcohol and drugs shall be avoided as much as possible.

11. Children and alcohol

11.1 No person under the age of 18 shall be allowed where alcohol is sold.

11.2 Any person found guilty of selling alcohol to persons under the age of 18 shall pay a fine of N$200.00.

11.3 Any parent found guilty of sending his children to buy alcohol shall be fined N$100.00.

12. Punishment

12.1 The law of Ju|'hoan stipulates a fine of N$300.00 or more for the following offences:

(a) Working on a Sunday
(b) Employing a child under 18 years of age
(c) Misusing or wasting water
(d) Contempt of court
(e) Abusing the rights of another person
(f) Disrespect for the Ju|'hoan Traditional Authority.

13. Adultery and other sexual crimes

13.1 Any person who has an affair with a married man or woman and causes problems which lead to the break-up of the marriage shall be punished.

13.2 The fine shall be five head of cattle, of which three go to the husband or wife whose marriage has been broken; one to the chief, and one to the Traditional Authority coffers.

13.3 If sexual intercourse occurs between a married and an unmarried person, the unmarried woman/man shall pay six head of cattle. Four of these go to the wife/husband of the person with whom he/she had sexual intercourse; one to the chief, and one to the Traditional Authority coffers.

14. Lobola

14.1 In the olden days, the Ju|'hoansi people were married according to the choice of the parents.

14.2 Both parents were paid lobola, which is to exchange handmade crafts as well as traditional food.

14.3 The man shall kill an eland for the wedding celebrations.

15. Divorce

Divorce occurs in the following circumstances:

15.1 One partner (spouse) may have a reason to seek a divorce, or may seek a divorce without a reason. Payment (or the fine) shall be the same, whether the husband divorces the wife or vice versa, and shall be as follows:

15.2 Divorce without a reason: the partner who divorces the other shall pay a fine of six head of cattle. Four of these shall go to the one who is being divorced; one goes to the chief, and one to the Traditional Authority coffers.

15.3 Divorce with a reason: the partner who is divorcing the other shall pay a fine of five head of cattle. Three of these shall go to the one who is being divorced; one goes to the chief, and one to the Traditional Authority coffers.

15.4 Taking somebody's wife/husband: a person who takes somebody's wife/husband and then gets married to him/her shall pay a fine of seven head of cattle. Five of these shall go to the person whose wife/husband has been taken away; one goes to the chief, and one to the Traditional Authority coffers.

15.5 Married people who have problems in their marriage shall be entitled to go to the Traditional Authority to dissolve the marriage. If they reconcile and continue with their marriage without informing the Traditional Authority, it shall be an offence. Such a couple shall be punished and each person shall be fined two head of cattle which go to the Traditional Authority.

16. Theft

16.1 The fine for theft shall be determined according to the value of the stolen item. The stolen item should be returned to the owner.

17. Weapons

(a) Guns
(b) Knives
(c) Spears
(d) Pangas
(e) Axes
(f) Bow and arrow
(g) Knobkerrie

17.1 Weapons shall not be carried in public without a valid reason.
17.2 The police shall be called if a person refuses to comply with this law.
17.3 This law shall also apply to weddings and funerals.

18. Refusal

18.1 A fine of N$ 200.00 shall be payable for the following:
(a) Refusal to pay a fine
(b) Refusal to attend a hearing
(c) Refusal to give evidence
(d) Refusal to adhere to a court decision
(e) Giving false testimony

19. Buying trading animals

19.1 Any person found guilty of buying an animal without a permit, or buying an animal from an unassisted minor, shall forfeit the money which he or she paid for the animal, and the animal shall be returned to its rightful owner.

20. Community projects

20.1 Any person wishing to start a community project shall first consult the village headman, who shall consult the district headman, who in turn shall inform the Chief about the proposed project.
20.2 Only the Chief shall authorize such a project. Any person who does not follow this procedure shall be punished and required to pay a fine of one head of cattle or N$ 2 000.00.

21. Citizenship

21.1 No person shall receive land or build a homestead in the district of Ju|'hoansi unless that person has Namibian citizenship or is a permanent resident of Namibia.

21.2 All foreign citizens that would like to settle in Ju|'hoansi shall be in possession of all relevant documents.

21.3 Before foreign citizens settle in Ju|'hoansi, the village head shall inform the district head and the head of the Traditional Authority, who shall verify the credentials of such citizens.

Certificate of consent to publish

UNIVERSITY OF NAMIBIA

FACULTY OF LAW

HUMAN RIGHTS AND DOCUMENTATION CENTRE

RE: CONSENT TO PUBLICATION

I, the undersigned, Chief of the Ju/'hoansi Traditional Authority, hereby give consent to the Human Rights and Documentation Centre, to publish the following documents of the Ju/'hoansi Traditional Authority:

1. The Customary Laws
2. The Community Profile
3. Picture of the Chief
4. Logo of the Traditional Authority

I acknowledge that the Human Rights and Documentation Centre will publish the laws in our indigenous language (Ju/'hoansi), as well as the English language. I am familiar with the contents of the laws that will be published and further acknowledge that they were prepared by my traditional authority.

Signed on this 09 **day of** December **2011.**

At Tsumkwe.

Constituency

Chief

ǂTSAM K×AO ǂOMA

For HRDC: A. Gairiseb

JUTA
Office of the Ju/'hoan Traditional Authority
Tjam!kui Kxa/he
Private Bag 2071
GROOTFONTEIN - Namibia
Date: 29/02/2012

JUTA
Office of the Ju/'hoan Traditional Authority
Tjam!kui Kxa/he
Private Bag 2071
GROOTFONTEIN - Namibia
Date: 29/02/2012

1

Annexures

Annexure 1
Statutes

ANNEXURE 1A

EXCERPTS FROM THE NAMIBIAN CONSTITUTION

Article 19 Culture

Every person shall be entitled to enjoy, practice, profess, maintain and promote any culture, language, tradition or religion subject to the terms of this Constitution and further subject to the condition that the rights protected by this article do not impinge upon the rights of others or the national interest.

Article 66 Customary and Common Law

(1) Both the customary law and the common law of Namibia in force on the date of Independence shall remain valid to the extent to which such customary or common law does not conflict with this Constitution or any other statutory law.

(2) Subject to the terms of this Constitution, any part of such common law or customary law may be repealed or modified by Act of Parliament, and the application thereof may be confined to particular parts of Namibia or to particular periods.

Article 102 Structures of Regional and Local Government

(1) For purpose of regional and local government, Namibia shall be divided into regional and local units, which shall consist of such region and Local Authorities as may be determined and defined by Act of Parliament.

(2) The delineation of the boundaries of the regions and Local Authorities referred to in Paragraph (1) shall be geographical only, without any reference to the race, colour or ethnic origin of the inhabitants of such areas.

(3) Every organ of regional and local government shall have a Council as the principal governing body, freely elected in accordance with this Constitution and the Act of Parliament referred to in Paragraph (1), with an executive and administration which shall carry out all lawful resolutions and policies of such Council, subject to this Constitution and any other relevant laws.

(4) For the purposes of this chapter, a Local Authority shall include all municipalities, communities, village councils and other organs of local government defined and constituted by Act of Parliament.

(5) There shall be a Council of Traditional Leaders to be established in terms of an Act of Parliament in order to advise the President on the control and utilisation of communal land and on all such other matters as may be referred to it by the President for advice.

Article 140 The Law in Force at the Date of Independence

(1) Subject to the provisions of this Constitution, all laws which were in force immediately before the date of Independence shall remain in force until repealed or amended by Act of Parliament or until they are declared unconstitutional by a competent Court.

(2) Any powers vested by such laws in the Government, or in a Minister or other official of the Republic of South Africa shall be deemed to vest in the Government of the Republic of Namibia or in a corresponding Minister or official of the Government of the Republic of Namibia, and all powers, duties and functions which so vested in the Government Service Commission, shall vest in the Public Service Commission referred to in Article 112.

(3) Anything done under such laws prior to the date of Independence by the Government, or by a Minister or other official of the Republic of South Africa shall be deemed to have been done by the Government of the Republic of Namibia or by a corresponding Minister or official of the Government of the Republic of Namibia, unless such action is subsequently repudiated by an Act of Parliament, and anything so done by the Government Service Commission shall be deemed to have been done by the Public Service Commission referred to in Article 112, unless it is determined otherwise by an Act of Parliament.

(4) Any reference in such laws to the President, the Government, a Minister or other official or institution in the Republic of South Africa shall be deemed to be a reference to the President of Namibia or to a corresponding Minister, official or institution in the Republic of Namibia and any reference to the Government Service Commission or the government service, shall be construed as a reference to the Public Service Commission referred to in Article 112 or the public service of Namibia.

(5) For the purpose of this article the Government of the Republic of South Africa shall be deemed to include the Administration of the Administrator-General appointed by the Government of South Africa to administer Namibia, and any reference to the Administrator-General in legislation enacted by such Administration shall be deemed to be a reference to the President of Namibia, and any reference to a Minister or official of such Administration shall be deemed to be a reference to a corresponding Minister or official of the Government of the Republic of Namibia.

ANNEXURE 1B

TRADITIONAL AUTHORITIES ACT 25 OF 2000

[ASSENTED TO 21 DECEMBER 2000]
[DATE OF COMMENCEMENT: 17 MAY 2001]
(Signed by the President)

ACT

To provide for the establishment of traditional authorities and the designation, election, appointment and recognition of traditional leaders; to define the powers, duties and functions of traditional authorities and traditional leaders; and to provide for matters incidental thereto.

ARRANGEMENT OF SECTIONS

1 Definitions

In this Act, unless the context indicates otherwise –

"chief" means the supreme traditional leader of a traditional community designated in accordance with section 4(1) *(a)* and recognised as such under section 6;

"Chief's Council" means a Chief's Council established by section 9;

"communal area" means the geographic area habitually inhabited by a specific traditional community, excluding any local authority area as defined in section 1 of the Local Authorities Act, 1992 (Act 23 of 1992);

"Community Trust Fund" means a Community Trust Fund contemplated in section 18(3);

"Council of Traditional Leaders" means the Council of Traditional Leaders established by section 2 of the Council of Traditional Leaders Act, 1997 (Act 13 of 1997);

"customary law" means the customary law, norms, rules of procedure, traditions and usages of a traditional community in so far as they do not conflict with the Namibian Constitution or with any other written law applicable in Namibia;

"designation", in relation to the institution of a chief or head of a traditional community, includes the election or hereditary succession to the office of a chief or head of a traditional community, and any other method of instituting a chief or head of a traditional community recognised under customary law;

"head", in relation to a traditional community, means the supreme traditional leader of that traditional community designated in accordance with section 4(1) *(a)* or *(b)*, as the case may be, and recognised as such under section 6;

"investigation committee" means the investigation committee appointed in terms of section 12(2);

"member", in relation to –

(a) a traditional community, means a person either or both of whose parents belong to that traditional community, and includes any other person who by marriage to or adoption by a member of that traditional community or by any other circumstance has assimilated the culture and traditions of that traditional community and has been accepted by the traditional community as a member thereof;

(b) a traditional authority, means a chief, a head of a traditional community, a senior traditional councillor, or a traditional councillor;

"Minister" means the Minister responsible for Regional and Local Government;

"prescribed" means prescribed by regulation made under section 19;

"repealed Act" means the Traditional Authorities Act, 1995 (Act 17 of 1995);

"senior traditional councillor" means a senior councillor of a traditional community appointed or elected in accordance with section 10;

"this Act" includes any regulation prescribed thereunder;

"traditional authority" means a traditional authority of a traditional community established in terms of section 2(1);

"traditional community" means an indigenous homogeneous, endogamous social grouping of persons comprising of families deriving from exogamous clans which share a common ancestry, language, cultural heritage, customs and traditions, who recognises a common traditional authority and inhabits a common communal area, and may include the members of that traditional community residing outside the common communal area;

"Traditional Council" means a Traditional Council established by section 9;

"traditional councillor" means a councillor of a traditional community appointed or elected in accordance with section 10; and

"traditional leader" means a chief, a head of a traditional community, a senior traditional councillor, or a traditional councillor designated and recognized or appointed or elected, as the case may be, in accordance with this Act, and by whatever traditional title named.

2 Establishment of traditional authorities

(1) Subject to this Act, every traditional community may establish for such community a traditional authority consisting of –
   (a) the chief or head of that traditional community, designated and recognized in accordance with this Act; and
   (b) senior traditional councillors and traditional councillors appointed or elected in accordance with this Act.

(2) A traditional authority shall in the exercise of its powers and the execution of its duties and functions have jurisdiction over the members of the traditional community in respect of which it has been established.

3 Powers, duties and functions of traditional authorities and members thereof

(1) Subject to section 16, the functions of a traditional authority, in relation to the traditional community which it leads, shall be to promote peace and welfare amongst the members of that community, supervise and ensure the observance of the customary law of that community by its members, and in particular to –
   (a) ascertain the customary law applicable in that traditional community after consultation with the members of that community, and assist in its codification;
   (b) administer and execute the customary law of that traditional community;
   (c) uphold, promote, protect and preserve the culture, language, tradition and traditional values of that traditional community;

(d) preserve and maintain the cultural sites, works of art and literary works of that traditional community;

(e) perform traditional ceremonies and functions held within that traditional community;

(f) advise the Council of Traditional Leaders in the performance of its functions as provided under Article 102(5) of the Namibian Constitution, the Council of Traditional Leaders Act, 1997 (Act 13 of 1997), or under any other law;

(g) promote affirmative action amongst the members of that traditional community as contemplated in Article 23 of the Namibian Constitution, in particular by promoting gender equality with regard to positions of leadership; and

(h) perform any other function as may be conferred upon it by law or custom.

(2) A member of a traditional authority shall in addition to the functions referred to in subsection (1) have the following duties, namely –

(a) to assist the Namibian police and other law enforcement agencies in the prevention and investigation of crime and, subject to the provisions of the Criminal Procedure Act, 1977 (Act 51 of 1977), the apprehension of offenders within their jurisdiction;

(b) to assist and co-operate with the Government, regional councils and local authority councils in the execution of their policies and keep the members of the traditional community informed of developmental projects in their area;

(c) to ensure that the members of his or her traditional community use the natural resources at their disposal on a sustainable basis and in a manner that conserves the environment and maintains the ecosystems for the benefit of all persons in Namibia;

(d) to be ordinarily resident in the communal area of the traditional community which he or she leads, failing which such traditional leader may be removed from office, if he or she is a chief or a head of a traditional community, under section 8(1) or, if he or she is a senior traditional councillor or traditional councillor, in accordance with the applicable customary law, but a person who is not so resident at his or her designation and recognition or appointment or election as a traditional leader in terms of this Act shall not be disqualified to be so designated and recognized or appointed or elected; and

(e) to respect the culture, customs and language of any person who resides within the communal area of that traditional authority, but who is not a member of the traditional community which such member leads.

(3) In the performance of its duties and functions under this Act, a traditional authority may –

(a) in addition to any contributions contemplated in section 18(3), raise funds on behalf of its traditional community, which funds shall be paid into the Community Trust Fund of that community;

(b) hear and settle disputes between the members of the traditional community in accordance with the customary law of that community;
(c) make customary laws; and
(d) use on all its correspondence an office stamp of its own design.

(4) Where a traditional authority referred to in section 2(1) has been established for a traditional community, and a group of members of that traditional community establishes in conflict with the provisions of this Act another authority purporting to be a traditional authority for such group, and any member of such last-mentioned authority exercises or performs any of the functions contemplated in paragraphs *(b)* and *(h)* of subsection (1) and paragraphs *(a)* and *(b)* of subsection (3) of this section –
(a) any such act shall be null and void; and
(b) such member shall be guilty of an offence, and upon conviction be liable to a fine of N$4 000 or to imprisonment for a period of twelve months or to both such fine and imprisonment.

4 Designation of chief or head of traditional community

(1) Subject to sections 5 and 6, members of a traditional community who are authorised thereto by the customary law of that community, may designate in accordance with that law –
(a) one person from the royal family of that traditional community, who shall be instituted as the chief or head, as the case may be, of that traditional community; or
(b) if such community has no royal family, any member of that traditional community, who shall be instituted as head of that traditional community.

(2) The qualifications for designation and the tenure of, removal from and succession to the office of chief or head of a traditional community shall be regulated by the customary law of the traditional community in respect of which such chief or head of a traditional community is designated.

5 Prior notification of designation of chief or head of traditional community

(1) If a traditional community intends to designate a chief or head of a traditional community in terms of this Act –
(a) the Chief's Council or the Traditional Council of that community, as the case may be; or
(b) if no Chief's Council or Traditional Council for that community exists, the members of that community who are authorised thereto by the customary law of that community,

shall apply on the prescribed form to the Minister for approval to make such designation, and the application shall state the following particulars:

(i) The name of the traditional community in question;
(ii) the communal area inhabited by that community;
(iii) the estimated number of members comprising such community;
(iv) the reasons for the proposed designation;
(v) the name, office and traditional title, if any, of the candidate to be designated as chief or head of the traditional community;
(vi) the customary law applicable in that community in respect of such designation; and
(vii) such other information as may be prescribed or the Minister may require.

(2) On receipt of an application complying with subsection (1), the Minister shall, subject to subsection (3), in writing approve the proposed designation set out in such application.

(3) Notwithstanding subsection (2), if in respect of an application referred to in subsection (1) the Minister is of the opinion that –

(a) (i) the person sought to be designated as a chief or head of a traditional community represents a group of persons who are members of a traditional community in respect of which a chief or head of a traditional community has been designated and recognised under this Act; or

(ii) such group of persons do not constitute an independent traditional community inhabiting a common communal area detached from another traditional community; or

(iii) such group of persons do not comprise a sufficient number of members to warrant a traditional authority to be established in respect thereof; and

(b) that there are no reasonable grounds for recognizing such group of persons as a separate traditional community, the Minister shall advise the President accordingly.

(4) The President shall on receipt of the Minister's advice under subsection (3) refer the matter to the Council of Traditional Leaders for its consideration and recommendation.

(5) The Council of Traditional Leaders shall submit to the President any recommendation it may wish to make in respect of any matter referred to it in terms of subsection (4) not later than 12 months after the date of referral of that matter to it.

(6) On –

(a) receipt of a recommendation referred to in subsection (5); or

(b) failure of the Council of Traditional Leaders to make such recommendation within the time frame prescribed by that subsection,

the President shall in his or her discretion and in writing, either reject the proposed designation on any of the grounds mentioned in subsection (3) *(a)* or *(b)* , or grant approval for such designation to the members of the traditional community in question.

(7) On receipt of any written approval granted under subsection (2) or (6), the Chief's Council or Traditional Council or, in a situation contemplated in subsection (1) *(b)* , the members of the traditional community, as the case may be, shall in writing give the Minister prior notification of the date, time and place of the designation in question, whereupon the Minister or his or her representative shall attend that designation, and shall –

(a) witness the designation of the chief or head of the traditional community in question; and

(b) satisfy himself or herself that such designation is in accordance with the customary law referred to in paragraph (vi) of subsection (1).

(8) The chief or head of the traditional community shall at his or her designation under subsection (7), make or subscribe to such oath or solemn affirmation with regard to his or her office as chief or head as the relevant customary law may require.

(9) If –

(a) the provisions of subsection (1) or (7) have not been complied with; or

(b) the designation of a chief or head of a traditional community has not been conducted in accordance with the customary law referred to in paragraph (vi) of subsection (1),

the designation of the chief or head of the traditional community concerned shall be invalid.

(10) If, in respect of a traditional community –

(a) no customary law regarding the designation of a chief or head of a traditional community exists; or

(b) there is uncertainty or disagreement amongst the members of that community regarding the applicable customary law,

the members of that community may elect, subject to the approval of the Minister, a chief or head of the traditional community by a majority vote in a general meeting of the members of that community who have attained the age of 18 years and who are present at that meeting.

6 Recognition of chief or head of traditional community

(1) If the Minister is satisfied that a chief or head of a traditional community has been designated in accordance with the requirements of this Act, he or she shall notify the President of such designation in writing, specifying the name, office, traditional title, if any, date of designation of such chief or head, and the name

of the traditional community in respect of which such chief or head has been designated.

(2) The President shall on receipt of a notice referred to in subsection (1) recognise the designation of the chief or head of the traditional community concerned by proclamation in the *Gazette* , setting out in such notice the particulars referred to in subsection (1) with regard to such chief or head.

(3) Notwithstanding any other provision to the contrary in this Act contained, a chief or head of a traditional community shall be deemed not to have been designated under this Act, unless such designation has been recognized under this section.

(4) Any application in terms of section 5 of the repealed Act for the designation of a chief or a supreme traditional leader of a traditional community which does not have a chief, which has not been finalized prior to the repeal of that Act by this Act shall be dealt with and finalized in terms of the corresponding provisions of this Act.

7 Powers, duties and functions of chief or head of traditional community

A chief or head of a traditional community –

(a) shall be the custodian of the customary law of the traditional community which he or she leads;

(b) shall exercise his or her powers and perform his or her duties and functions and in accordance with that customary law;

(c) may, subject to sections 8(2) and 15(5), appoint any other member of his or her traditional community to act in his or her place, when he or she is for any reason unable to act as chief or head of that traditional community;

(d) shall perform such other powers and exercise such other duties or functions as may be conferred upon him or her by statutory law or the applicable customary law;

(e) shall assign one or two senior traditional councillors to assist him or her in the administering of the affairs of the Chief's Council or the Traditional Council, as the case may be.

8 Removal and succession of chief or head of traditional community

(1) If there is sufficient reason to warrant the removal of a chief or head of a traditional community from office, such chief or head may be removed from office by the members of his or her traditional community in accordance with the customary law of that community.

(2) If, by reason of removal from office as contemplated in subsection (1) or death, a chief or head of a traditional community ceases to perform the functions of his or her office, the members of that traditional community, who are authorized thereto

by customary law, may designate in accordance with this Act a member of that traditional community to replace such chief or head.

(3) If a chief or head of a traditional community has been removed from office as contemplated in subsection (1), the Minister shall notify the President of such removal in writing, specifying the name, office, traditional title, if any, date of removal of the chief or head concerned, and the name of the traditional community in respect of which such chief or head has been removed from office.

(4) The President shall on receipt of a notice referred to in subsection (3) recognize the removal from office of the chief or head of the traditional community concerned by proclamation in the *Gazette,* setting out in such notice the particulars referred to in that subsection with regard to such chief or head of the traditional community.

9 Establishment of Chief's Council and Traditional Council, and powers, duties and functions thereof

(1) There is hereby established –
- *(a)* for every traditional community which has a chief, a Chief's Council;
- *(b)* for every traditional community which has a head of a traditional community, a Traditional Council.

(2) A Chief's Council or Traditional Council shall comprise –
- *(a)* such number of members of the traditional authority of the traditional community in question as the chief or head of that traditional community, as the case may be, may appoint to serve as members of the Council in question; and
- *(b)* in addition to the members referred to in paragraph *(a)* , such number of members of the traditional community in question as the chief or head of that traditional community, as the case may be, may co-opt to serve as members of the Council in question.

(3) The chief or the head of a traditional community shall be the chairperson of the Chief's Council or Traditional Council which has been established for his or her traditional community, as the case may be, and such chairperson may appoint such other office-bearers of the Council in question as he or she may deem necessary.

(4) The Chief's Council or Traditional Council shall be responsible for the day- to-day administration of the affairs of the traditional authority of the traditional community in respect of which it has been established.

(5) The chairperson of the Chief's Council or Traditional Council, as the case may be, shall cause a written record to be kept of the proceedings of the meetings of that Chief's Council or Traditional Council, as the case may be.

10 Appointment of senior traditional councillors, traditional councillors and secretary, and their powers, duties, and functions

(1) A chief or head of a traditional community shall appoint from amongst the members of his or her traditional community or cause to be elected by such members from amongst their number –

(a) senior traditional councillors, who shall assist such chief or head in the performance of his or her functions, and exercise or perform such other powers, duties or functions as may be delegated or assigned to any of them by such chief or head; and

(b) traditional councillors, who shall advise such chief or head and the senior traditional councillors of that community with regard to the performance of their functions, and exercise or perform such other powers, duties or functions as may be delegated or assigned to any of them by such chief or head.

(2) The qualifications for appointment or election and the tenure of, and removal from, office of a senior traditional councillor or traditional councillor shall be regulated by the customary law of the traditional community in respect of which such councillor is appointed or elected.

(3) A chief or head of a traditional community shall from time to time appoint from amongst the members of his or her traditional community one person as secretary, and such secretary shall perform such duties and functions as may be assigned to him or her by that chief or head.

(4) Any chief or head of a traditional community who has in accordance with this section appointed a senior traditional councillor or traditional councillor or caused any such councillor to be elected shall notify the Minister of such appointment or election in writing, specifying the name, office, traditional title, if any, date of appointment or election of the senior traditional councillor or traditional councillor concerned, and the name of the traditional community in respect of which such senior traditional councillor or traditional councillor has been appointed or elected.

(5) The Minister shall on receipt of a notice referred to in subsection (4) make the appointment or election of a senior traditional councillor or traditional councillor known by notice in the *Gazette,* setting out in such notice the particulars referred to in that subsection with regard to such senior traditional councillor or traditional councillor.

11 Use of traditional titles

Nothing in this Act contained shall be construed as precluding the members of a traditional community from addressing a traditional leader by the traditional title accorded to that office, but such traditional title shall not derogate from, or add to, the status, powers, duties and functions associated with the office of a traditional leader as provided for in this Act.

12 Settlement of disputes

(1) If a dispute arises amongst the members of a traditional community as to whether or not a person to be designated as –

(a) chief or head of the traditional community in terms of section 4 is the rightful or a fit and proper person under the customary law of that community to be so designated; or

(b) successor in terms of section 8 is the rightful or a fit and proper successor to the office of chief or head of the traditional community under the customary law of that community,

and the members of that traditional community fail to resolve that dispute in accordance with such customary law, they may submit to the Minister a written petition, signed by the parties to the dispute, stating the nature of the dispute.

(2) On receipt of a petition referred to in subsection (1), the Minister may appoint an investigation committee consisting of such number of persons as he or she may determine, to investigate the dispute in question and to report to the Minister concerning its findings and recommendations.

(3) The Minister shall on receipt of the report referred to in subsection (2) take such decision as he or she may deem expedient for the resolutions of the dispute in question.

(4) In the investigation or resolution of a dispute under this section regard shall be had to the relevant customary law and traditional practices of the traditional community within which the dispute has arisen.

13 Powers of investigation committee

(1) An investigation committee, or any member thereof authorized by such committee for the purpose, may, in the investigation of a dispute contemplated in section 12(2) –

(a) in its or his or her discretion determine the nature and extent of the investigation in question;

(b) have access to all books, minutes of meetings, or other documents which the investigation committee or the member concerned deems necessary to investigate in connection with that investigation;

(c) request particulars and information from any person which the investigation committee or the member concerned deems necessary in connection with the investigation in question;

(d) without payment of any fees, make enquiries into and extracts from, or copies of, any such books, minutes or other documents which the

investigation committee or the member concerned deems necessary in connection with that investigation;

(e) by notice in writing request any person to appear before it or him or her in relation to that investigation at a date, time and place specified in such notice and to submit all such books, minutes or other documents or things in the possession or under the control of that person which the investigation committee or the member concerned deems necessary in connection with that investigation.

(2) Any person appearing under subsection (1), before an investigation committee or any member thereof, may be requested –

(a) to co-operate with the investigation committee or the member concerned and to disclose truthfully and frankly any information within his or her knowledge relevant to the investigation in question;

(b) to produce any book, minutes, other documents or thing to the investigation committee or the member concerned which the investigation committee or that member deems necessary in connection with that investigation.

(3) The provisions of subsection (1) and (2), in so far as they provide for a limitation on the fundamental right to privacy contemplated in Article 13 of the Namibian Constitution by authorizing interference with such privacy, are enacted upon the authority conferred by the said Article.

14 Limitation of powers of traditional authorities

In the exercise of the powers or the performance of the duties and functions referred to in section 3 by a traditional authority or a member thereof –

(a) any custom, tradition, practice, or usage which is discriminatory or which detracts from or violates the rights of any person as guaranteed by the Namibian Constitution or any other statutory law, or which prejudices the national interest, shall cease to apply;

(b) the customary law of a traditional community shall only apply to the members of that traditional community and to any person who is not a member of that traditional community, but who by his or her conduct or consent submits himself or herself to the customary law of that traditional community; and

(c) a traditional leader shall not permit his or her political opinions or allegiance to influence –

(i) the functions of his or her office as traditional leader; or

(ii) the members of the traditional community in respect of which he or she was designated and recognized, or appointed or elected, as the case may be.

15 Holding of political office by chief or head of traditional community

(1) Every chief or head of a traditional community elected or appointed to a political office shall –

(a) upon such election or acceptance of such appointment be considered to have taken leave of absence from the office of chief or head of a traditional community for the duration that he or she holds such political office; and

(b) forthwith notify the Minister in writing of the date with effect from which he or she holds such political office.

(2) The Minister shall cause notice to be given in the *Gazette* of the election or appointment of any chief or head of a traditional community to a political office and of the date from which such election or appointment is of force.

(3) Any person holding a political office who becomes a chief or head of a traditional community shall with effect from the date that he or she is recognised as such under section 6, be considered to have taken leave of absence from the office of chief or head of the traditional community for the duration of the period that he or she holds such political office.

(4) A chief or head of a traditional community who by virtue of subsection (1) *(a)* or (3) is considered to have taken leave of absence from the office of chief or head of a traditional community shall, during that period of leave of absence, not be entitled to be accorded the status of chief or head of a traditional community and to receive the allowance payable to a chief or head of a traditional community under this Act.

(5) Where a chief or head of a traditional community is considered to have taken leave of absence under subsection (1) *(a)* or (3), the members of that traditional community who are authorized thereto by customary law may designate, in accordance with section 4 and subject to sections 5 and 6, a member of that traditional community to act as chief or head of the traditional community for the duration of that period of leave of absence.

(6) A person duly designated and recognized to act as chief or head of a traditional community as contemplated in this section shall during the period that he or she acts as chief or head of the traditional community exercise the powers and perform the duties and functions of chief or head of that traditional community and receive allowances payable to a chief or head of a traditional community under this Act.

(7) For purposes of this section "political office" means the President of the Republic of Namibia, a member of the National Assembly, National Council or a Regional Council, and includes a leader of a political party registered under section 39 of the Electoral Act, 1992 (Act 24 of 1992).

(8) To the extent that this section authorises a limitation upon the right of a chief or head of a traditional community to hold a political office or the holder of a political office to hold the office of chief or head of a traditional community, such

limitation is authorised on grounds of public interest as contemplated in Article 17(3) of the Namibian Constitution.

(9) Nothing in this section contained shall be construed as derogating from section 8.

16 Relationship of traditional authorities with government organs

A traditional authority shall in the exercise of its powers and the performance of its duties and functions under customary law or as specified in this Act give support to the policies of the Government, regional councils and local authority councils and refrain from any act which undermines the authority of those institutions.

17 Payment of allowances to traditional leaders

(1) Subject to subsection (2), there shall be paid from moneys appropriated by Parliament for such purpose allowances –

(a) to the following traditional leaders of a traditional community, namely:

(i) One chief or head of a traditional community, as the case may be;

(ii) not more than six senior traditional councillors; and

(iii) not more than six traditional councillors,

designated and recognised, or appointed or elected, as the case may be, in accordance with this Act, notwithstanding the fact that more than six senior traditional councillors and more than six traditional councillors may have been appointed or elected in respect of a particular traditional community under this Act; and

(b) to the secretary of a traditional community appointed under section 10(3).

(2) *(a)* The Minister, in consultation with the Minister responsible for Finance, may prescribe allowances payable in respect of the traditional leaders, and the secretary, referred to in subsection (1).

(b) Different allowances may be prescribed under paragraph *(a)* , regard being had to the status, duties and responsibilities of each office referred to in that paragraph.

(3) Every traditional community in respect of whom more than six persons have been appointed or elected as senior traditional councillors and more than six persons have been appointed or elected as traditional councillors, shall notify the Minister in writing of the names of those senior traditional councillors and traditional councillors who shall be entitled to receive allowances under this Act.

(4) Subsections (1) and (3) shall not be construed as preventing a traditional community from paying allowances to senior traditional councillors and traditional councillors who are not under those subsections entitled to allowances.

18 Assets and Trust Fund of traditional community

(1) A traditional authority may with the consent of the members of its traditional community acquire, purchase, lease, sell, or otherwise hold or dispose of movable and immovable property in trust for that traditional community, and shall have such rights in respect of the acquisition and disposal of such property as may reasonably be necessary or expedient for the carrying out of its functions under this Act.

(2) Any immovable property acquired as contemplated in subsection (1) shall be registered in the name of the traditional authority concerned in accordance with the provisions of the Deeds Registries Act, 1937 (Act 47 of 1937) or the Registration of Deeds in Rehoboth Act, 1976 (Act 93 of 1976).

(3) A traditional authority may with the consent of the members of its traditional community establish a Community Trust Fund, to be held in trust for the members of that traditional community, and towards which such members may contribute for the purposes of –

(a) financing projects in that community which promote and uplift the culture, preserve cultural sites, works of art and literary works of that community;

(b) meeting the administrative costs of running the office of the traditional authority;

(c) meeting the costs of performing any of the functions and duties of a traditional authority under this Act; and

(d) meeting any other costs that the traditional community may agree upon.

(4) A traditional authority shall with the consent of the members of its traditional community determine the manner in which and the persons by whom the contribution contemplated in subsection (3) shall be made, as well as the amount of that contribution.

19 Regulations

The Minister may make regulations relating to –

(a) the establishment and composition of a Board of Trustees to manage and control a Community Trust Fund;

(b) the duties, functions, and powers of a Board of Trustees;

(c) the tenure and vacation of office of members of a Board of Trustees;

(d) the meetings of a Board of Trustees and the election of office-bearers of such a Board;

(e) the establishment of committees for a Community Trust Fund by a Board of Trustees, and the composition of a committee;

(f) the duties, functions and powers of a committee referred to in paragraph *(e)*;

(g) the keeping of accounting records of a Community Trust Fund and the auditing of that records;

(*h*) the financial year of a Community Trust Fund;

(*i*) the method by which the number of persons comprising a traditional community may be determined; and

(*j*) generally all other matters which are by this Act required or permitted to be prescribed, or which are necessary or expedient to be prescribed in order to achieve the purposes of this Act.

20 Repeal of laws and savings

(1) Subject to subsection (2), the Traditional Authorities Act, 1995 (Act 17 of 1995), and the Traditional Authorities Amendment Act, 1997 (Act 8 of 1997), are hereby repealed.

(2) A traditional authority which was established under any law repealed by subsection (1) and which existed immediately before the commencement of this Act shall from such commencement continue to function as such and the provisions of this Act shall apply to such traditional authority as if it were a traditional authority established under this Act, and any person who immediately before such commencement was a member or office-bearer of such traditional authority by virtue of his or her designation and recognition or appointment under any such repealed law –

(*a*) as a chief or supreme traditional leader shall from such commencement be a chief or, in the case of the supreme traditional leader, be a head of a traditional community as if he or she were designated and recognized under this Act; and

(*b*) as a senior traditional councillor, traditional councillor or secretary shall from such commencement respectively be a senior traditional councillor, traditional councillor or secretary as if he or she were appointed or elected under this Act.

(3) Anything done under a provision of a law repealed by subsection (1) shall, in so far as it is not inconsistent with any provision of this Act, be deemed to have been done under the corresponding or related provision, if any, of this Act.

21 Construction of a certain expression

Any reference to the chief of a traditional community in any other law shall be construed as to include a reference to the head of a traditional community.

22 Short title and commencement

(1) This Act shall be called the Traditional Authorities Act, 2001, and shall come into operation on a date to be determined by the Minister by notice in the *Gazette* .

(2) Different dates may be determined under subsection (1) in respect of different provisions of this Act.

ANNEXURE 1C

COMMUNITY COURTS ACT 10 OF 2003

[ASSENTED TO 31 JULY 2003]
[DATE OF COMMENCEMENT: 17 NOVEMBER 2003]
(Signed by the President)

ACT

To provide for the recognition and establishment of community courts; to provide for the appointment of Justices and for clerks and messengers of court; to provide for the application of customary law by community courts; to provide for the jurisdiction of and procedure to be adopted by community courts; to provide for appeals from community courts to other courts; and to provide for connected and incidental matters.

ARRANGEMENT OF SECTIONS

1 Definitions

In this Act, unless the context indicates otherwise –

"area" , in relation to a traditional community, means the geographic area habitually and predominantly inhabited by that traditional community;

"area of jurisdiction" , in relation to a court recognized or established under this Act, means the area for which that court has been so recognized or established;

"assessor" means an assessor who has been appointed as such under this Act;

"community court" means a community court recognized under section 2 or established under section 4;

"customary law" means the customary law, norms, rules of procedure, traditions and usages of a traditional community in so far as they do not conflict with the provisions of the Namibian Constitution or any other statutory law applicable in Namibia;

"financial institution" means a financial institution authorised to conduct banking business under the Banking Institutions Act, 1998 (Act 2 of 1998), or a building society finally registered as such under the Building Societies Act, 1986 (Act 2 of 1986);

"Justice" means a Justice appointed in terms of section 8;

"magistrate" means the magistrate of a district and includes an additional magistrate of that district;

"magistrate's court" means the magistrate's court of a district in which the community court concerned is situated;

"Minister" means the Minister responsible for Justice;

"prescribe" means prescribe by regulation under this Act;

"this Act" includes any regulation made under section 32;

"traditional authority" means the traditional authority referred to in section 2 of the Traditional Authorities Act, 2000 (Act 25 of 2000);

"traditional community" means an indigenous, homogenous, endogamous social grouping of persons comprising of families deriving from exogamous clans which share a common ancestry, language, cultural heritage, customs and traditions, recognises a common traditional authority and inhabits a common communal area; and includes the members of that community residing outside the common communal area;

"traditional leader" means a traditional leader as defined in section 1 of the Traditional Authorities Act, 2000 (Act 25 of 2000).

2 Application for recognition of courts

(1) Where immediately before the commencement of this Act –

(a) any person or body had pursuant to any law repealed by section 33 jurisdiction to hear and determine any civil or criminal matter in the area of a traditional community or in any part of such area;

(b) any person or body (hereinafter in this Act referred to as a body of appeal) had pursuant to any law repealed by section 33 jurisdiction to hear and determine any appeal against an order or decision made or given by a person or body referred to in paragraph *(a)* ,

and one or more traditional authorities have been established and recognized in accordance with the Traditional Authorities Act, 2000 (Act 25 of 2000) for that traditional community, such authority or authorities may apply in writing to the Minister for recognition in respect of the area of the traditional community of a court (hereinafter referred to as a community court).

(2) An application referred to in subsection (1) shall be made within such period as may be determined by the Minister by notice in the *Gazette* and shall contain the following particulars:

(a) The name of the traditional community in respect of which a court is to be recognized;

(b) the area of such traditional community in respect of which jurisdiction is to be exercised by such court;

(c) whether a body of appeal contemplated in subsection (1) *(b)* existed in such area before the commencement of this Act;

(d) the names of the persons who in terms of this Act are qualified to be appointed as Justices or assessors;

(e) such further information as the Minister may require.

(3) If on receipt of an application referred to in subsection (1) the Minister is satisfied that the requirements referred to in that subsection have been met and that the application contains all the particulars required by subsection (2), the Minister shall in respect of the area to which the application relates recognize by notice in the *Gazette* a community court for that area.

(4) A notice under subsection (3) shall state the traditional community in respect of which the community court is recognized; whether the court so recognized comprises a body of appeal; and the area in respect of which such court shall exercise jurisdiction.

(5) A community court recognized under subsection (3) shall upon recognition have the jurisdiction contemplated in section 12: Provided that where it is evident from a notice issued under subsection (4) that the court so recognized comprises a body of appeal, such court shall in addition have jurisdiction to hear and determine any appeal relating to a matter referred to in paragraph *(a)* of that section.

(6) The provisions of this Act shall, except to the extent otherwise provided, apply to a community court recognized under subsection (3) as if it were a community court established under section 4.

3 Application for establishment of community courts

(1) A traditional authority of a traditional community may apply in writing to the Minister for the establishment of a community court in respect of the area of that traditional community, but only if no court has been recognized or established under this Act for that area.

(2) An application referred to in subsection (1) shall contain the following particulars:
- *(a)* The area to which the application relates;
- *(b)* the reasons for applying for the establishment of a court;
- *(c)* the names of the persons who in terms of this Act are qualified to be appointed as Justices or assessors for that area;
- *(d)* such further information as the Minister may require.

4 Establishment of community courts

(1) If on receipt of an application referred to in section 3 the Minister is satisfied that such application contains the required particulars and that no court has been recognized or established under this Act in respect of the area to which the application relates he or she shall by notice in the *Gazette* establish a community court for the area mentioned in the notice, and such community court shall within that area exercise the jurisdiction conferred on it by or under this Act.

(2) A community court may, by the notice mentioned in subsection (1), be allowed to carry such name as may be appropriate for the area in question.

(3) The Minister may, by notice in the *Gazette* , amend or revoke any notice referred to in this section.

5 Financial assistance

The Minister with the concurrence of the Minister of Finance shall, subject to such conditions as the Minister acting with such concurrence may determine or prescribe, at any time grant to a community court out of moneys appropriated by Parliament such financial assistance as may be necessary for defraying expenses in connection with the administration of such community court.

6 Revenue account of community court

(1) A traditional authority shall on behalf of the community court in its area open and operate a revenue account with any financial institution into which shall be paid all moneys accruing to such court in terms of this Act.

(2) The moneys in the revenue account of a community court shall be utilized to defray all expenses incurred in connection with the administration of such court, but moneys received by virtue of any grant under section 5 shall be utilized in accordance with the conditions determined or prescribed under that section.

(3) Notwithstanding the State Finance Act, 1991 (Act 31 of 1991), any fines and fees received by a community court in terms of this Act shall be paid into the revenue account of such community court.

(4) A traditional authority may realize any payment in kind received by a community court and shall, if such payment is so realized and is due to the community court, pay the money so obtained into the court's revenue account.

(5) The secretary of the traditional authority concerned shall, subject to the directions and control of such traditional authority, and in accordance with generally accepted accounting principles, keep such accounting and related records as are necessary to fairly represent the financial affairs of the community court.

(6) The accounting and related records referred to in subsection (4) shall be examined and audited annually by the Auditor-General.

7 Composition of community courts

(1) A community court shall be presided over by one or more Justices appointed by the Minister in accordance with the provisions of section 8 for such community court.

(2) A community court may appoint one or more assessors, each of whom shall be selected from amongst persons mentioned in the list approved in terms of subsection (3), to advise the community court on any matter to be adjudicated upon by the community court in the proceedings in question.

(3) For the purposes of the appointment of assessors, the Minister shall by notice in the *Gazette* , out of a list of names referred to in section 3(2) *(c)* , approve not less than five and not more than ten assessors-designate.

(4) The grounds for disqualification and removal referred to in section 8(2) and (3), respectively, shall apply with the necessary changes to assessors.

(5) An assessor appointed in terms of subsection (2) shall be paid from moneys appropriated by Parliament such allowances as the Minister, with the concurrence of the Minister of Finance, may prescribe.

(6) A community court shall give due consideration to, but shall not be bound by, the opinion of any assessor.

(7) If during any proceedings before a community court, an assessor dies or he or she for any reason becomes incapable of taking his or her seat, the Justice or Justices presiding may either adjourn the proceedings in order to invoke the assistance of another person as assessor or proceed with the hearing with the remaining assessor.

(8) No person shall sit as a Justice or an assessor in any proceedings before a community court if he or she has any interest direct or indirect or personal or pecuniary in any matter before such court.

8 Appointment of Justices

(1) Subject to subsection (2), the Minister shall for each community court in writing appoint as Justices the persons who in are in terms of section 3(2) *(c)* named for appointment as Justices, and shall cause any such appointment to be made known by notice in the *Gazette* .

(2) No person shall be eligible for appointment as a Justice of a community court unless –

(a) he or she is conversant with the customary law of the area in question;

(b) by virtue of his or her integrity he or she is a fit and proper person to be entrusted with the responsibility of the office of Justice;

(c) he or she is not a member of –

(i) Parliament;

(ii) a regional council; or

(iii) a local authority council; or

(d) he or she is not a leader of a political party, whether or not that political party is registered under section 39 of the Electoral Act, 1992 (Act 24 of 1992).

(3) The Minister may, after consultation with the traditional authority concerned, by notice in the *Gazette* remove from office any Justice if he or she becomes subject to any disqualification contemplated in subsection (2), but only after the Minister afforded such Justice an opportunity to be heard.

(4) If a community court is unable to sit by reason of the absence of a Justice, the traditional authority concerned may, subject to subsection (6), request the Minister to appoint as an acting Justice the person designated by it.

(5) The Minister shall on receipt of a request referred to in subsection (4) in writing appoint the person designated by the traditional authority as an acting Justice to act during the absence of the Justice in whose place he or she has been so appointed.

(6) The provisions of subsection (2) shall apply in relation to the appointment of an acting Justice.

9 Appointment of clerks and messengers of court

A community court shall appoint a clerk of the court and a messenger of the court to exercise such functions as may be conferred or imposed upon such clerk or messenger by the community court or in terms of this Act.

10 Allowances of Justices and remuneration of clerks and messengers of court

(1) Subject to subsection (3), there shall be paid from moneys appropriated by Parliament such allowances to Justices and such remuneration to clerks and messengers of court appointed under this Act as may be prescribed under subsection (2).

(2) The Minister, with the concurrence of the Minister of Finance, shall prescribe the allowances payable to Justices for attending court sittings and the remuneration payable to clerks and messengers of court for duties performed under this Act.

(3) A Justice or a clerk or messenger of the court who receives remuneration as a traditional leader or a secretary under the Traditional Authorities Act, 2000 (Act 25 of 2000), shall not be entitled to allowances or remuneration under this Act.

(4) Any person who acts as a Justice under section 8(5) shall be entitled to be paid the allowances that would have been payable to the Justice in whose place he or she acts.

11 Oath of office

(1) A Justice shall not perform any function as judicial officer of a community court unless he or she has taken an oath or made an affirmation, which shall be subscribed by him or her, in the form set out below, namely:

"I, ... (full name), do hereby swear/solemnly and sincerely affirm and declare that I will in my capacity as a judicial officer of a community court administer justice to all persons alike, without fear, favour or prejudice, and as the circumstances in any particular case may require, in accordance with the laws and customs of the Republic of Namibia.".

(2) Any such oath or affirmation shall be taken or made in the official language or in any other language before the magistrate of a district in which the community court in question is situated, who shall at the foot thereof in writing make a statement to the effect that it was taken or made before him or her and of the date on which it was so taken or made and append his or her signature thereto.

12 Jurisdiction in respect of cases and persons

A community court shall have jurisdiction to hear and determine any matter relating to a claim for compensation, restitution or any other claim recognized by the customary law, but only if –

(a) the cause of action of such matter or any element thereof arose within the area of jurisdiction of that community court; or

(b) the person or persons to whom the matter relates are in the opinion of that community court closely connected with the customary law.

13 Application of customary law

In any proceedings before it a community court shall apply the customary law of the traditional community residing in its area of jurisdiction: Provided that if the parties are connected with different systems of customary law, the community court shall apply the system of customary law which the court considers just and fair to apply in the determination of the matter.

14 Ascertainment of customary law

If a community court entertains any doubt as to the existence or content of a rule of customary law relevant to any proceedings, after having considered such submissions thereon as may be made and such evidence thereon as may be tendered by or on behalf of the parties concerned, it may, without derogation from any other lawful source to which it may have recourse, consult decided cases, text books and other sources, and may receive opinions, either orally or in writing to enable it to arrive at a decision in the matter: Provided that –

(a) any cases, text books, sources and opinions consulted by the court shall be made available to the parties; or

(b) any oral opinion shall be given to the court in the same manner as oral evidence.

15 Language to be used in community courts

(1) The official language or any other language including the sign language which a community court may decide upon may be used during any proceedings before that community court.

(2) If the proceedings are conducted in a language with which any party to the proceedings before the community court –

(a) professes not to be conversant; or

(b) in the opinion of such community court, appears not to be sufficiently conversant,

a competent interpreter shall be called by the community court in order to translate such evidence into a language with which such party professes or appears to the community court to be sufficiently conversant.

16 Representation

A party to any proceedings before a community court shall appear in person and may represent himself or herself or be represented by any person of his or her choice.

17 Service of process

(1) Every process of a community court shall be of force throughout the Republic of Namibia.

(2) A messenger of the court appointed under section 9 shall serve any process of the community court for which he or she was appointed.

(3) Notwithstanding subsection (2), a member of the Namibian Police Force shall be competent to serve any process in connection with a matter in a community court as if he or she were a duly appointed messenger of that community court.

(4) For the purposes of this section "process" means any order, notice, summons or other writing issued under this Act by a community court.

18 Court records and attendance registers

(1) Every community court shall be a court of record.

(2) The proceedings in a community court shall be recorded in writing by the clerk of the court.

(3) Copies of the records of the court referred to in subsection (2), shall within such period and in such manner as may be prescribed be furnished to the magistrate's court and the Permanent Secretary: Justice.

(4) Any person may –

(a) under the supervision of the clerk of a community court and at all reasonable times, peruse a copy of any of the records of the court compiled in accordance with subsection (2); and

(b) on payment of such fee as may be prescribed obtain a copy of such records.

(5) For the purposes of determining the allowance payable under section 7 or 10 to an assessor or a Justice of a community court, as the case may be, the clerk of that court shall keep proper record of all sittings attended by any such assessor or Justice.

19 Proceedings in community courts

(1) Subject to this Act, the practice and procedure in accordance with which the proceedings of a community court shall be conducted, including procedures and rules relating to evidence, the manner of execution of any order or decision and the appropriation of fines shall be in accordance with the applicable customary law, but all proceedings shall be in accordance with the principles of fairness and natural justice.

(2) No person shall give evidence or be examined as a witness in a community court unless he or she –

(a) takes an oath, which shall be administered by such court in the following form:

"I swear that the evidence that I shall give, shall be the truth, the whole truth and nothing but the truth, so help me God."; or

(b) makes an affirmation, which shall be accepted by such court in the following form:

"I solemnly affirm that the evidence that I shall give, shall be the truth, the whole truth and nothing but the truth.".

20 Summoning of persons

(1) A community court may issue a summons requiring any person to appear at the time and place mentioned therein to testify to a subject matter before the community court.

(2) A community court may order the arrest of any person who, without reasonable excuse, fails to obey any summons issued under subsection (1) and served on him or her personally, or to remain in attendance throughout the proceedings.

(3) Where an order is made by a community court under subsection (2), the person whose arrest has been ordered shall be arrested and brought before the community court concerned –

(a) by the messenger of the community court; or

(b) if the messenger of the community court is for any reason unable to arrest that person and the requirements of subsection (4) have been met, by a messenger of a magistrate's court or by a member of the Namibian Police Force to whom the order is transmitted.

(4) If an order is to be executed as contemplated in subsection (3) by a messenger of a magistrate's court or by a member of the Namibian Police Force, that order shall be lodged with the magistrate's court for endorsement by a magistrate, and the magistrate shall, if he or she is satisfied that such order was lawfully issued, endorse it for execution.

(5) The community court may impose a fine not exceeding N$100 or payment of an equivalent amount in kind as determined by that community court after hearing the person who has been brought before it in terms of subsection (3).

21 Transfer of cases

(1) In any proceedings before a community court, the community court may –

(a) if it is of the opinion that such community court does not have jurisdiction to hear the matter; or

(b) for any other good cause,

at any stage before an order is made, either of its own accord or on application by any interested party, refer the matter to the magistrate's court for directions as to the transfer of that matter to any other court.

(2) The magistrate's court to whom a matter has been referred in terms of subsection (1) may –

(a) annul the proceedings and transfer the case to be heard *de novo* by any other community court or by a magistrate's court of competent jurisdiction; or

(b) direct that the proceedings be continued in the community court which referred the matter to it.

22 Orders of community courts

(1) Subject to this Act, a community court may in proceedings before it make any or all of the following orders –

(a) an order for compensation, damages, restitution or specific performance according to customary law;

(b) any order as to costs, fees or other charges,

payable in money or an equivalent amount in kind.

(2) Any order made under subsection (1) –

(a) shall be fair and reasonable and not be in conflict with the Namibian Constitution or any other statutory law;

(b) may provide that the amount payable thereunder (whether in money or in kind) be paid over a period not exceeding one year in such instalments and intervals as may be determined by the community court concerned.

23 Enforcement of orders of community courts

(1) If an order of a community court is not satisfied within the period specified by that community court, the person in whose favour it was given may register the order at the magistrate's court by lodging with the clerk of such magistrate's court a copy of the order of the community court duly certified as such by the clerk of the community court.

(2) The clerk of the magistrate's court shall, at the request of a person who has registered an order of a community court as contemplated in subsection (1), issue to such person a writ of execution in respect of the order and such writ shall be executed by a messenger of the magistrate's court in all respects as if the order were that of the magistrate's court.

24 Limitation of liability for compensation

(1) Where compensation was awarded by a court other than a community court to an injured person under any law for any damage or loss suffered by such person and the compensation was accepted by him or her, the person against whom such award was made shall not be liable at the suit of the first-mentioned person to any proceedings in a community court in respect of the injury for which the award was made.

(2) Where compensation was in accordance with the customary law awarded by a community court under this Act to an injured person for any damage or loss suffered by him or her, the person against whom the award was made shall not be liable at the suit of the first-mentioned person in any other court (including a community court) for the payment of compensation in respect of the injury for which the award was made.

25 Matters being dealt with in other courts

If during proceedings before a community court it comes to the attention of such court that there is already an action pending in another court (including a community court) between the same parties based on the same cause of action, and in respect of the same subject matter, such court shall stay those proceedings until –

(a) the proceedings in such other court, including proceedings on appeal, have been disposed of; or

(b) the proceedings in such other court have been withdrawn.

26 Appeals against orders or decisions of community courts

(1) A party to any proceedings in a community court who is aggrieved by any order or decision of that community court may appeal to the magistrate's court: Provided that where the appeal is lodged against an order or decision of a community court recognized under section 2, and such court is vested with the jurisdiction contemplated in the proviso to subsection (5) of that section, an aggrieved party shall first exhaust his or her rights of appeal existing within such community court: Provided further that if such party is dissatisfied with the decision of such last-mentioned court he or she may appeal against such decision to the magistrate's court.

(2) An appeal under subsection (1) to a magistrate's court shall be lodged with the clerk of that magistrate's court within 30 days from the date of the order or decision appealed against or within such extended period as the magistrate's court hearing the appeal may allow, but where such party is in terms of the first proviso to that subsection required to exhaust his or her rights of appeal as contemplated in that proviso, such appeal shall be lodged and further dealt with in accordance with the applicable customary law or be lodged within such period and in such manner as may be prescribed.

(3) The execution of any order or decision of a community court shall be suspended until the appeal (if any) relating to such order or decision has been decided or withdrawn or in the opinion of the magistrate of the magistrate's court been abandoned.

(4) In hearing an appeal under subsection (1) a community court may confirm, set aside, amend or vary any order or decision or give or make any order which, in accordance with the applicable customary law, the circumstances may require.

27 Hearing of appeals by magistrates' courts

(1) Notwithstanding the provisions of the Magistrates' Courts Act, 1944 (Act 32 of 1944), a magistrate's court shall have jurisdiction to hear and determine any appeal against any order or decision of a community court, and for the purposes of such appeal the magistrate presiding –

(a) shall appoint two assessors, each of whom shall be selected from amongst persons mentioned in the list approved in terms of section 7(3), to advise him or her with regard to the appeal;

(b) may, where the records submitted to him or her do not furnish sufficient evidence or information for the determination of the appeal, hear such further evidence as he or she thinks necessary.

(2) If during any such proceedings before the magistrate's court an assessor dies or he or she for any other reason becomes incapable of taking his or her seat, the presiding magistrate may either adjourn the proceedings in order to invoke the assistance of another person as assessor or proceed with the hearing with the remaining assessor.

(4) No person shall sit as an assessor during the hearing of an appeal in a case in which he or she has a personal or pecuniary interest or which was dealt with at any stage by a court of which he or she was then a member or an assessor.

(5) An assessor appointed under subsection (1) shall be entitled to be paid from moneys appropriated by Parliament such allowances as the Minister, with the concurrence of the Minister of Finance, may prescribe.

(6) The magistrate hearing the appeal shall give due consideration to, but shall not be bound by, the opinion of any assessor.

28 Decision of magistrate's court on appeal

(1) Subject to subsection (2), a magistrate may in determining an appeal against an order or decision of a community court (hereinafter in this section referred to as the court of first instance) –

(a) confirm such order or decision;
(b) amend or set aside such order or decision;
(c) remit the case to the court of first instance for further hearing with such instructions as to how any defect in the earlier proceedings might be overcome;
(d) give or make any order which, in accordance with the applicable customary law, the circumstances may require.

(2) A magistrate shall not on appeal give or make any order that exceeds the jurisdiction of the court of first instance.

29 Further appeals

(1) An appeal against an order or decision made or given by a magistrate's court under section 28 shall lie to the High Court.

(2) An appeal referred to in subsection (1) shall be noted and dealt with in the same manner as if it were an appeal in civil proceedings referred to in Chapter XI of the Magistrates' Courts Act, 1944 (Act 32 of 1944).

30 Contempt of community court and other related offences

(1) Any person who wilfully –

(a) obstructs or in any way interferes with, or knowingly prevents, the service of any summons issued by a community court; or

(b) dissuades, hinders or prevents or attempts to dissuade, hinder or prevent any person lawfully summoned to appear as a party or witness before a community court, from so appearing,

shall be guilty of an offence and upon conviction by the community court be liable to a fine not exceeding N$1 000 or to the payment of an equivalent amount in kind as determined by that community court.

(2) Any person who wilfully –

(a) insults any member of a community court during any sitting of the community court; or

(b) interrupts the proceedings of a community court; or

(c) otherwise wilfully disturbs the peace or order of such proceedings,

shall be guilty of an offence and may forthwith be removed and detained in custody, as if he or she were a prisoner awaiting trial, until the rising of the community court and shall in addition to such removal and detention be liable to a fine not exceeding N$1 000 or the payment of an equivalent amount in kind as determined by that community court.

31 Other offences

No person shall act as a member of a community court unless such person has been appointed as a Justice of a community court recognized or established under this Act, and where such person purports to act as a duly appointed Justice without having been so appointed –

(a) any order or decision made or given by such person shall be null and void; and

(b) such person shall be guilty of an offence and upon conviction be liable to a fine not exceeding N$4 000 or to imprisonment for a period not exceeding twelve months or to both such fine and such imprisonment.

32 Regulations

(1) The Minister may make regulations in relation to –

(a) the instituting of proceedings in community courts;

(b) the procedure to be observed in community courts;

(c) the times and places of holding court sittings;

(d) the manner in which records shall be kept of evidence and of proceedings in the court and the custody and disposal of such records, and the duties of the clerk of the court in respect thereof;

(e) the manner of procuring the attendance of witnesses;

(f) the appointment of interpreters and the allowances payable to them;

(g) the service or execution of any process of a community court and the fees payable in respect thereof;

(h) the hours during which the office of the clerk of a community court shall be open for the transaction of business;

(i) the translation of court records by a sworn translator;

(j) any matter required or permitted to be prescribed by regulation under this Act or which the Minister may consider necessary or expedient to prescribe in order to ensure the proper dispatch and conduct of the proceedings of a community court.

(2) Different regulations may be made under subsection (1) in respect of different community courts and any regulation made under that subsection may in respect of any contravention thereof or a failure to comply therewith prescribe a penalty not exceeding a fine of N$2 000 or imprisonment for a period not exceeding six months.

(3) No regulation made under subsection (1) shall be of any force unless published in the *Gazette* .

33 Repeal of laws, and savings

(1) Subject to subsections (3) and (4), the laws specified in the Schedule are hereby repealed to the extent indicated in the third column of that Schedule.

(2) Anything done under a law repealed by subsection (1) and which could have been done under a corresponding provision of this Act shall be deemed to have been done under that corresponding provision.

(3) Where immediately before the commencement of this Act any person or body had jurisdiction as contemplated in section 2(1) *(a)* or *(b)* , such person or body shall from such commencement continue to have such jurisdiction as if this Act had not been passed, but only until a date determined by the Minister by notice in the *Gazette* or, if a community court is under this Act recognized in the area in which such person or body had exercised jurisdiction, until the recognition of such court.

(4) Any case pending before any person or body referred to in subsection (3) immediately before the date determined by the Minister under that subsection, shall from such date stand removed to the court which in terms of this Act has jurisdiction to hear and determine the same: Provided that any case partly heard at that date may be further heard and determined as if such person or body had not, by virtue of a notice issued under that subsection, ceased to have such jurisdiction.

34 Short title and commencement

This Act shall be called the Community Courts Act, 2003, and shall come into operation on a date to be determined by the Minister by notice in the *Gazette*.

Schedule
LAWS REPEALED
(Section 33)

No. and year of law	Title of law	Extent of repeal
Proclamation 28 of 1923	Rehoboth Community: Confirmation of Agreement Proclamation, 1923	The whole
Proclamation R348 of 1967	Civil and Criminal Jurisdiction: Chiefs, Headmen, Chiefs' Deputies and Headmen's Deputies, Territory of South West Africa Proclamation, 1967	The whole
Proclamation R222 of 1969	Civil and Criminal Jurisdiction: Chiefs, Headmen, Chiefs' Deputies and Headmen's Deputies, Territory of South West Africa Amendment Proclamation, 1969	The whole
Proclamation R320 of 1970	Jurisdiction of Chiefs, Chief Tribal Councillors (*Ngambela*s), Tribal Councillors (*Khuta* Members), Tribal Councils (*Khuta*s), Headmen of Wards (*Silalo Induna*s) and Representatives of Chiefs. – Eastern Caprivi Zipfel Proclamation, 1970	The whole
Proclamation R304 of 1972	Civil and Criminal Jurisdiction: Chiefs, Headmen, Chiefs' Deputies and Headmen's Deputies, Territory of South-West Africa Amendment Proclamation, 1972	The whole
Proclamation R241 of 1973	Civil and Criminal Jurisdiction: Chiefs, Headmen, Chiefs' Deputies and Headmen's Deputies, Territory of South-West Africa Amendment Proclamation, 1973	The whole
Proclamation 160 of 1975	Proclamation to provide for the establishment of a Nama Council, Tribal Authorities and Village Management Boards in Namaland, 1975	The whole
Proclamation AG 70 of 1980	Jurisdiction of Traditional Authorities in Hereroland in respect of Civil and Criminal Amendment Proclamation, 1980	The whole
Act 27 of 1985	Native Administration Proclamation Amendment Act, 1985	The whole
Ordinance 2 of 1986	Damara Community and Regional Authorities and Paramount Chief and Headmen Ordinance, 1986	The whole
Ordinance 3 of 1986	Tswana Chief and Headmen Ordinance, 1986	The whole

ANNEXURE 1D

REGULATIONS TO THE COMMUNITY COURTS ACT, 2003 (NO. 10 OF 2003)

GOVERNMENT GAZETTE

OF THE

REPUBLIC OF NAMIBIA

N$2.00 WINDHOEK - 17 November 2003 No.3095

CONTENTS

Page

GOVERNMENT NOTICES

Government Notices

MINISTRY OF JUSTICE

No. 236 2003

COMMENCEMENT OF THE COMMUNITY COURTS ACT, 2003

Under the powers vested in me by section 34 of the Community Courts Act, 2003 (Act No. 10 of 2003) I determine that the Act comes into operation on 17 November 2003.

A. KAWANA
MINISTER OF JUSTICE Windhoek, 12 November 2003

MINISTRY OF JUSTICE

No. 237 2003

REGULATIONS OF COMMUNITY COURTS:
COMMUNITY COURTS ACT, 2003

The Minister of Justice, under section 32 of the Community Courts Act, 2003 (Act No. 10 of 2003), has made the regulations set out in the Schedule.

SCHEDULE

Definitions

1. In these regulations a word or expression that is defined in the Act has the same meaning, and -

"the Act" means the Community Courts Act, 2003 (Act No. 10 of 2003); and

"Traditional Authorities Act" means the Traditional Authorities Act, 2000 (Act No. 25 of 2000).

Instituting of proceedings in community court

2. (1) The process of the community court for commencing an action shall be by summons –

(a) served in accordance with the applicable customary law practice and procedure; and

(b) calling upon the defendant to appear before the community court to answer to a claim of the plaintiff.

(2) Unless the applicable customary law practice and procedure otherwise requires, the summons shall -

(a) be issued by the clerk of the court and shall bear his or her signature, the subject matter, date of issue, place, date and time of hearing;

(b) show the surname of the defendant by which he or she is known to the plaintiff, the defendant's gender and residence or place of business, and, where known, his or her first name or initials and his or her occupation, and if defendant is sued in his or her representative capacity, the capacity in which he or she is so sued;

(c) show a full address where the plaintiff will accept service of process, notices or documents and also the postal address;

(d) show the first name, surname, gender, occupation and the residence or place of business of the plaintiff;

(e) where the plaintiff sues as cessionary, show the name, address and description of the cedent at the date of the cession, and the date of the cession; and

(f) where the plaintiff sues in a representative capacity, state the capacity in which he or she sues.

Procedure to be observed in community courts

3. A community court when conducting its proceedings shall observe its customary law practice and procedure which had been observed for years, but only to an extent it considers fair and just in accordance with the principles of fairness and natural justice contemplated in section 19.

Times and places of holding court sittings

4. Sittings of a community court shall be held at the time and place decided upon by the traditional community concerned.

Keeping of records of evidence and of proceedings in court and custody and disposal of such records and duties of clerk of court in respect of such records

5. (1) The record of proceedings to be recorded in writing by the clerk of the community court in terms of section 18(2) of the Act shall include -

(a) any oral evidence given in court;

(b) any objection made to any evidence received or tendered;

(c) any judgment given by the court; and

(d) any record of any inspection *in loco*.

(2) The clerk of the community court shall also mark each document put in evidence and note such mark on the record.

(3) The clerk of the community court shall furnish copies of the records of the proceedings of the court referred to in subregulation (1) to the magistrate's court and the Permanent Secretary: Justice within a period of 60 days from the date a record was made.

(4) Any person, upon request made to the Permanent Secretary: Justice, or the clerk of the community court concerned, may obtain a copy of the record of the proceedings of the court referred to in subregulation (1) on payment of a fee of N$1,50 per folio.

Manner of procuring attendance of witnesses

6. (1) The process of community court for procuring the attendance of any person to give evidence on a subject matter or on any aspect thereof or to produce any book, paper or document shall be in accordance with the applicable customary law practice and procedure, otherwise, it shall be by subpoena issued by the clerk of the court and sued out by the party desiring the attendance of such person.

(2) Service of a subpoena on a witness may be effected -

(a) in accordance with the applicable customary law practice and procedure; or

(b) through the messenger of the court, if the party suing out the subpoena so desires at his or her own expense.

(3) There shall be handed to the messenger of the court (if the party suing out the subpoena desires it to be served through the messenger) together with the subpoena so many copies of the subpoena as there are witnesses to be summoned.

Appointment of interpreters and their allowances

7. An interpreter referred to in section 15 of the Act shall -

(a) be a competent person who is sufficiently conversant in the language that a community court has decided to use during its proceedings and also in the language he or she is called upon to translate into and from;

(b) be appointed by the clerk of the court;

(c) be paid the allowance set out in Table D; and

(d) take an oath or make an affirmation before the Justice presiding over the matter in the form set out below -

"I, ...(full name), do swear/solemnly and sincerely affirm and declare that I shall truly and correctly to the best of my ability interpret into and from the language I am called upon to interpret and from and into the language being used in this proceedings. So help me God.".

Service or execution of process of community court

8. (1) Service or execution of process of a community court referred to in section 17 of the Act shall be effected in accordance with the applicable customary law practice and procedure, otherwise it shall be effected in accordance with this regulation.

(2) A party requiring service or execution of process of community court by the messenger of the community court shall deliver to the messenger the original of such process together with as many copies thereof as there are persons to be served.

(3) The messenger of the community court to whom a process is entrusted for service or execution shall in writing notify -

(a) the clerk of the community court and the party who sued out the process that service or execution has been duly effected, stating the date and manner of service or the result of execution and return that process to the clerk; or

(b) the party who sued out the process that he or she has been unable to effect service or execution, and of the reason for such inability, and return the said process to such party, but the messenger shall keep a record of any process so returned.

(4) The messenger of the community court -

(a) shall effect the service or execution of the process of the community court without any avoidable delay;

(b) has power to call upon any member of the Namibian Police Force to render him or her aid, in any case where resistance to the due service or execution of the process of the community court has been met with or reasonably anticipated.

Business hours for office of clerk of community court

9. Unless the customary law practice and procedure provides otherwise –

(a) the business hours for the office of the clerk of the community court start at 8h00 and end at 17h00;

(b) the office of the clerk of the community court shall be closed on every Saturday, Sunday and public holiday.

Translation of community court records

10. (1) A community court shall cause its records which are a subject of appeal to the magistrate's court to be translated into the official language.

(2) A party to the matter on appeal to the magistrate's court may cause the records referred to in subsection (1) to be translated into the official language by a sworn translator at his or her own expense.

Appeal against order or decision of community court

11. (1) A party to any proceedings in a community court who is aggrieved by any order or decision of that community court may appeal to -

(a) the same community court, if that community court in terms of section 2(5) of the Act comprises a body of appeal and is vested with the jurisdiction to hear and determine any appeal relating to a matter referred to in section 12(a) of the Act; or

(b) the magistrate's court, if -

(i) the community court does not comprise a body of appeal vested with the jurisdiction to hear and determine any appeal; or

(ii) it is a further appeal against any appeal judgment made by the court referred to in paragraph (a).

(2) Upon request in writing by any party within 14 days from the date of the judgment of the community court, or within such extended period as the court may allow, the clerk of the community court shall -

(a) within 21 days of the request, supply the party with a copy of the record of proceedings, including a written judgment showing -

(i) the facts the Justice found to be proved; and

(ii) the Justice's reasons for the order or decision.

(b) after supplying the party with a copy of the record of proceedings referred to in paragraph (a), forthwith endorse on the original minutes of record the date on which the copy was so supplied.

(3) An appeal under subsection (1)(b) shall be noted by the delivery of notice to the clerk of the magistrate's court within 30 days from the date of the order or decision appealed against or within such extended period as the magistrate's court may allow.

(4) A notice of appeal shall state -

(a) whether the whole or a part of the judgment is appealed against, and if it is a part, then what part;

(b) the grounds of appeal, specifying the findings of fact or rulings of law appealed against, and whether it is a further appeal; and

(c) the name of -

(i) the magistrate's court to which the appeal is noted;

(ii) the community court whose order or decision is appealed against; and

(iii) the parties to the appeal.

Remunerations and allowances

12. Remunerations and allowances payable under the Act are set out in Tables A, B, C and D.

Take note that in terms of section 10(3) of the Act, a Justice or clerk or messenger of the court who receives remuneration as a traditional leader or a secretary under the Traditional Authorities Act shall not be entitled to allowances or remuneration under the Act.

TABLE A

SITTING ALLOWANCES PAYABLE

TO JUSTICES

(Section 10(2), regulation 12)

1. For every attendance:

(a) Per hour or part thereof.................. an amount equal to the allowances payable to a traditional leader under section 17(1)(a)(ii) of the Traditional Authorities Act per hour;

(b) Per day... an amount equal to the allowances payable to a traditional leader under section 17(1)(a)(ii) of the Traditional Authorities Act per day.

2. Attendance to be reckoned from the hour for which the Justice is summoned to the hour at which judgment is given or reserved, or to the hour at which the Justice is expressly released by the court from further attendance, whichever is the earlier.

3. When the case is adjourned, postponed or settled, attendances to be reckoned from the hour for which the Justice is summoned to the hour at which the case is adjourned, postponed or settled, or to the hour at which the Justice is expressly released by the court from further attendance, whichever is the earlier.

4. A Justice who has neither a residence nor a place of business within five kilometres of the court-house is also entitled to a travel allowance at the rate of 60 cents per kilometre for each journey actually and necessarily taken between the court-house and his or her residence or place of business.

TABLE B

ALLOWANCES PAYABLE TO ASSESSORS

(Sections 7(5) and 27(5), regulation 12)

1. Assessor in the community court, for every attendance:

(a) Per hour or part thereof .... N$4,00;

(b) Per day.. N$32,00;

2. Assessor in the magistrate's court, for every attendance:

(a) Per hour or part thereof.................. an amount equal to a fee payable to state witness in magistrate's court per hour;

(b) Per day... an amount equal to a fee payable to state witness in magistrate's court per day.

3. Attendance to be reckoned from the hour for which the assessor is summoned to the hour at which judgment is given or reserved, or to the hour at which the assessor is expressly released by the court from further attendance, whichever is the earlier.

4. When the case is adjourned, postponed or settled, attendances to be reckoned from the hour for which the assessor is summoned to the hour at which the case is adjourned, postponed or settled, or to the hour at which the assessor is expressly released by the court from further attendance, whichever is the earlier.

5. An assessor who has neither a residence nor a place of business within five kilometres of the court-house is also entitled -

   (a) to a travel allowance at the rate of 60 cents per kilometer for each journey actually and necessarily taken between the court-house and his or her residence or place of business, in the case of an assessor in the community court; or

   (b) to travel and accommodation allowances applicable to state witnesses in the magistrate's court, in the case of an assessor in the magistrate's court.

TABLE C

REMUNERATIONS PAYABLE TO CLERKS AND

MESSENGERS OF COMMUNITY COURT

(Section 10(2), regulation 12)

1. Clerk of community court:

A remuneration... equal to the allowances payable to a secretary under section 17(1)(b) of the Traditional Authorities Act.

2. Messenger of community court:

A remuneration .... equal to the allowances payable to a secretary under section 17(1)(b) of the Traditional Authorities Act, minus 20%.

TABLE D

ALLOWANCES PAYABLE TO

INTERPRETERS

(Section 32(1)(f), regulation 12)

1. For every attendance:

   (a) Per hour or part thereof .... N$2,00;

   (b) Per day... N$16,00.

2. Attendance to be reckoned from the hour for which the interpreter is summoned to the hour at which judgment is given or reserved, or to the hour at which the interpreter is expressly released by the court from further attendance, whichever is the earlier.

3. When the case is adjourned, postponed or settled, attendances to be reckoned from the hour for which the interpreter is summoned to the hour at which the case is adjourned, postponed or settled, or to the hour at which the interpreter is expressly released by the court from further attendance, whichever is the earlier.

4. An interpreter who has neither a residence nor a place of business within five kilometres of the court-house is also entitled to a travel allowance at the rate of 30 cents per kilometre for each journey actually and necessarily taken between the court-house and his or her residence or place of business.

MINISTRY OF JUSTICE

No. 238 2003

DETERMINATION OF PERIOD FOR APPLICATION FOR RECOGNITION AS COMMUNITY COURT: COMMUNITY COURTS ACT, 2003

Under the powers vested in me by section 2(2) of the Community Courts Act, 2003 (Act No. 10 of 2003), I determine the period 17 November 2003 to 31 March 2004 as the period within which an application under subsection (1) of that section for recognition as community court in respect of the area of a traditional community shall be made.

A. KAWANA
MINISTER OF JUSTICE Windhoek, 12 November 2003

Annexure 2

List of officially recognised Community Courts of the Nama, Ovaherero, Ovambanderu, and San Communities

GOVERNMENT NOTICES RECOGNISING/ESTABLISHING THE CUSTOMARY COURTS OF THE NAMA, OVAHERERO, OVAMBANDERU AND SAN COMMUNITIES[1] IN TERMS OF THE COMMUNITY COURTS ACT, 2003 (NO. 10 OF 2003)

The Nama communities

Establishment of ǀAman[2] Community Court and appointment of assessors and justices:
Community Courts Act, 2003
GN No. 102 of 2011

Blouwes Traditional Authority[3]

Establishment of Bondelswartz Community Court and appointment of assessors and justices:
Community Courts Act, 2003
GN No. 86 of 2009

Recognition of Fransfontein[4] Community Court as community court and appointment of assessors and justices:
Community Courts Act, 2003
GN No. 106 of 2009

Recognition of ǀHaramūb[5] Community Court as community court and appointment of assessors and justices:
Community Courts Act, 2003
GN No. 59 of 2011

Recognition of Kai-/Khauben[6] Community Court as community court and appointment of assessors and justices:
Community Courts Act, 2003
GN No. 92 of 2009

---

1 The spelling of the names of the community courts listed here follows the spelling used in the government notices.

2 The ǀAman [correct spelling: !Aman] Community Court is the community court of the Soromas traditional community.

3 According to information from the Ministry of Justice, there is no community court of the Blouwes Traditional Authority.

4 The Fransfontein Community Court is the community court of the Swartbooi traditional community.

5 The ǀHaramūb Community Court is the community court of the Afrikaner traditional community.

6 Correct spelling: Kaiǁkhaun.

Recognition of !Khobesen[7] Community Court as community court and appointment of assessors and justices:
Community Courts Act, 2003
GN No. 104 of 2009

Simon Kooper Traditional Authority[8]

Topnaar Traditional Authority[9]

Vaalgras Traditional Authority[10]

The Ovaherero communities

Application[11] of Kakuru-Kouye[12] Customary Court as community court and appointment of assessors and justices:
Community Courts Act, 2003
GN No. 76 of 2013

Recognition of Kambazembi Community Court as community court and appointment of assessors and justices:
Community Courts Act, 2003
GN No. 93 of 2009

Recognition of Maharero Community Court as community court and appointment of assessors and justices:
Community Courts Act, 2003
GN No. 96 of 2009

Recognition of Otjikaoko Community Court as community court and appointment of assessors and justices:
Community Courts Act, 2003
GN No. 111 of 2009

---

7 Witbooi or [correct spelling] !Khowesen Traditional Authority.

8 According to information from the Ministry of Justice, there is no community court of the Simon Kooper Traditional Authority.

9 According to information from the Ministry of Justice, there is no community court of the Topnaar Traditional Authority.

10 According to information from the Ministry of Justice, there is no community court of the Vaalgras Traditional Authority.

11 It is assumed that the title of GN 76 of 2013 should correctly read Recognition and not Application of Kakuru-Kouye Customary Court.

12 Kakurukouje Traditional Authority.

Establishment of Vita Thom Royal House Community Court and appointment of assessors and justices:
Community Courts Act, 2003
GN No. 88 of 2009, amended by GN No.

Recognition of Zeraua[13] Community Court as community court and appointment of assessors and justices:
Community Courts Act, 2003
GN No. 61 of 2010

The Ovambanderu community

Ovambanderu Traditional Authority[14]

The San communities

Establishment of Hai-||om Community Court and appointment of assessors and justices:
Community Courts Act, 2003
GN No. 87 of 2009

Ju/'hoan[15]

Establishment of !Kung Community Court and appointment of assessors and justices:
Community Courts Act, 2003
GN No. 173 of 2015

Establishment of !Xoo Community Court and appointment of assessors and justices:
Community Courts Act, 2003
GN No. 145 of 2013

ǂKau-||'easi

13 Also spelled Zeraeua.

14 According to information from the Ministry of Justice, the Ovambanderu Traditional Authority applied for recognition of the Ovambanderu Community Court, but this has not been decided yet.

15 According to information from the Ministry of Justice, the Ju/'hoan Tradtional Authority applied for recognition of the Ju/'hoan Community Court but this has not been decided yet.

Annexure 3
Contact details for the Nama, Ovaherero, Ovambanderu, and San Traditional Authorities

TRADITIONAL AUTHORITY	ACTING/ SUPREME LEADER	POSTAL ADDRESS	TEL/CELL PHONE	FAX
ǀHoaǀaranǁaixaǁaes (Afrikaner)		P.O. Box 857 Mariental	081-691 3787	063-251 406
Blouwes	J. Barman (Acting)	P/Bag 2185 Keetmanshoop		063-257 022
!Gamiǂnun (Bondelswartz)		P.O. Box 212 Karasburg	081-667 3459 063-270 193	063-270 393
Kaiǁkhaun	P.S.M. Kooper	P.O. Box 209 Kalkrand	081-616 2522 (Chief's wife)	
ǁKhara-Khoen (Simon Kooper)	D. Hanse	P.O. Box 580 Mariental	081-414 8212 (Chief) 081-619 4230 (Secretary)	063-683 837
!Aman (Soromas)	D. Frederick	P.O. Box 135 Bethanie	063-283 059 081-259 1162 (Secretary Lucy Bok)	
ǁKhau-ǀgoan (Swartbooi)	D.S. Luipert	P.O. Box 416 Khorixas	081-203 2107 (Secretary Ingrid Nerongo) 067-331 194	067-331 692
ǂAonin (Topnaar)	S.M. Kooitjie	P.O. Box 2041 Walvis Bay	064-207 103	064-207 103
Orlam (Vaalgras)	J. Stephanus	P.O. Box 1615 or P/Bag 2066 Keetmanshoop	081-124 9974 081-274 4754 (Cllr Aloys Boys)	
ǀKhowese (Witbooi)	S.J. Witbooi	P.O. Box 27 Gibeon	081-825 6751 (Cllr Jacobs) 063-245 800	063-251 404
Kakurukouje	V. Tjambiru	P.O. Box 301 or P/Bag 3003 Opuwo	081-606 9763 (Secretary) 065-274 406	
Maharero	T. Maharero	P.O. Box 45 Otjinene	081-259 6216 (Chief) 081-836 0505 (Secretary)	
Otjikaoko	P.U. Tjavara	P.O. Box 271 Opuwo	065-273 107 081-290 9197 (Secretary)	

Ovambanderu	K.K. Nguvauva	P O Box 650 Gobabis	081-220 2352 (Spokesperson)	
Vita	T. Thom	P.O. Box 291 Opuwo	081-263 2528 (Secretary) 065-273 509 (Royal House)	065-273 510
Zeraua		P.O. Box 178 Omaruru	081-467 3243 (Clerk of Court) 064-570 716	064-570 716
!Kung	G. Arnold	P.O. Box 41600 Ausspanplatz	081-698 7074 (Authorised Representative)	
!Xoo	H. Martin	P.O. Box 1017 Gobabis	081-333 2896 (Chief)	
Hai‖om	D. ‖Khamuxab	P.O. Box 86 Outjo	081-348 6924 (Secretary) 067-313 756	067-313 756
Ju|'hoan	T. ǂOma	P/Bag 2070 Grootfontein	067-244 030	067-244 031

The following titles are also available in this series:

Hinz, Manfred O, assisted by Ndateelela Emilia Namwoonde (Eds). 2010. *Customary law ascertained, Volume 1. The customary law of the Owambo, Kavango and Caprivi communities of Namibia.* Windhoek: Kuiseb Publishers/Namibia Scientific Society.

Hinz, Manfred O., assisted by Alexander Gairiseb. (Eds) 2013. *Customary law ascertained, Volume 2. The customary law of the Bakgalagari, Batswana and Damara Communities of Namibia.* Windhoek: University of Namibia Press.

www.ingramcontent.com/pod-product-compliance
Lightning Source LLC
LaVergne TN
LVHW060012210926
848481LV00013B/3696
* 9 7 8 9 9 9 1 6 4 2 1 2 3 *